NAVWEPS 01-40AVC-1

NATOPS
Flight Manual

NAVY MODEL

A-4E

AIRCRAFT

THIS PUBLICATION IS INCOMPLETE WITHOUT
CONFIDENTIAL SUPPLEMENT NAVWEPS 01-40AVC-1A

ISSUED BY AUTHORITY OF
THE CHIEF OF NAVAL OPERATIONS

CHANGE NOTICE

NAVAIR 01-40AVC-1

NATOPS
Flight Manual

NAVY MODEL

A-4E

AIRCRAFT

THIS PUBLICATION IS INCOMPLETE WITHOUT
CONFIDENTIAL SUPPLEMENT NAVAIR 01-40AVC-1A

AVC-1A P-29996-1

ISSUED BY AUTHORITY OF THE CHIEF OF NAVAL OPERATIONS
AND UNDER THE DIRECTION OF THE COMMANDER,
NAVAL AIR SYSTEMS COMMAND

1 February 1964
Changed 15 November 1966

Reproduction for non-military use of the information or illustrations contained in this publication is not permitted without specific approval of the issuing service (NASC or AFLC). The policy for use of Classified Publications is established for the Air Force in AFR 205-1 and for the Navy in Navy Regulations, Article 1509.

LIST OF CHANGED PAGES ISSUED

INSERT LATEST CHANGED PAGES. DESTROY SUPERSEDED PAGES.

NOTE: The portion of the text affected by the current change is indicated by a vertical line in the outer margins of the page.

Page No.	Date of Latest Change	Page No.	Date of Latest Change	Page No.	Date of Latest Change
*A	15 November 1966	1-56	1 November 1965	*1-116H	15 November 1966
*B	15 November 1966	1-56A Deleted	1 November 1965	*1-116J	15 November 1966
*C	15 November 1966	1-56B Deleted	1 November 1965	*1-116K	15 November 1966
*Flyleaf	15 November 1966	1-58	15 March 1965	*1-116L	15 November 1966
i	15 May 1966	1-59	15 March 1965	*1-116M	15 November 1966
iii	15 May 1966	1-62	15 March 1965	*1-116N	15 November 1966
iv	15 May 1966	1-63	15 March 1965	*1-116P	15 November 1966
v	15 March 1965	1-64A	15 May 1966	*1-117	15 November 1966
1-1	1 November 1965	1-66A	15 May 1966	1-118	15 March 1965
1-2 Blank	15 March 1965	*1-66B	15 November 1966	1-119	15 March 1965
1-3	1 November 1965	1-66C	15 May 1966	1-120	15 May 1966
1-4	15 March 1965	1-66D	15 May 1966	1-122	15 March 1965
1-9	15 March 1965	1-66E	15 May 1966	1-123	15 May 1966
1-10	15 March 1965	1-66F	15 May 1966	1-124	1 November 1965
1-11	15 March 1965	1-66G	15 May 1966	1-125	15 May 1966
1-12	1 November 1965	1-66H Blank	15 May 1966	1-128	15 May 1966
1-12A	15 March 1965	1-67	15 May 1966	1-129	1 November 1965
1-13	15 May 1966	1-72	15 March 1965	1-131	15 May 1966
1-14	15 May 1966	1-73	15 March 1965	1-135	15 March 1965
1-15	15 March 1965	1-76	15 March 1965	1-138A	1 November 1965
*1-16	15 November 1966	1-79	15 March 1965	1-139	1 November 1965
*1-16A	15 November 1966	1-80	15 March 1965	1-140	1 November 1965
1-17	15 May 1966	1-82	15 May 1966	1-140A	1 November 1965
1-18	15 May 1966	1-86	15 March 1965	1-141	15 March 1965
1-19	15 May 1966	1-87	15 May 1966	1-142	1 November 1965
1-20	15 May 1966	1-89	15 May 1966	1-147	15 March 1965
1-21	15 May 1966	1-93	15 March 1965	1-148	15 March 1965
1-22	15 May 1966	1-94	15 March 1965	1-149	15 March 1965
1-22A	15 May 1966	1-95	15 March 1965	1-150	15 March 1965
1-23	15 May 1966	1-96	15 May 1966	1-151	15 May 1966
1-24	15 March 1965	1-97	15 May 1966	1-152	15 March 1965
1-25	15 May 1966	1-99	1 November 1965	1-153	15 March 1965
1-26	15 May 1966	1-100	15 March 1965	*1-154	15 November 1966
1-27	15 May 1966	1-101	15 March 1965	1-155	15 March 1965
1-30	15 March 1965	1-102	15 March 1965	1-156	1 November 1965
1-31	1 November 1965	1-102A	15 May 1966	1-157	15 March 1965
1-32	1 November 1965	1-102B	15 December 1965	1-158	1 November 1965
1-33	1 November 1965	1-102C	15 December 1965	*1-159	15 November 1966
1-37	15 March 1965	1-102D	15 December 1965	1-160	15 March 1965
1-38	15 May 1966	1-102E	15 May 1966	1-161	15 March 1965
1-39	1 November 1965	*1-103	15 November 1966	1-162	15 March 1965
1-40	15 March 1965	1-104	15 March 1965	*1-163	1 November 1965
1-41	15 March 1965	1-106	15 May 1966	*1-164	15 March 1965
1-43	15 May 1966	1-107	15 March 1965	*1-165	15 November 1966
1-44	15 May 1966	1-108	15 March 1965	2-1	15 May 1966
1-45	1 November 1965	1-110	15 March 1965	2-2	15 March 1965
1-46	1 November 1965	1-110A	15 March 1965	2-3	15 March 1965
1-48	1 November 1965	1-114	15 March 1965	2-4	15 May 1966
1-49	1 November 1965	1-115	15 May 1966	2-5	1 November 1965
1-50	15 March 1965	1-116	15 March 1965	2-6	15 March 1965
1-51	15 March 1965	*1-116A	15 November 1966	3-1	15 May 1966
1-52	1 November 1965	*1-116B	15 November 1966	3-4	15 May 1966
1-53	15 May 1966	*1-116C	15 November 1966	3-7	1 November 1965
1-54	15 May 1966	*1-116D	15 November 1966	3-8 Blank	15 March 1965
1-54A	1 November 1965	*1-116E	15 November 1966	3-9 Deleted	15 March 1965
1-55	15 May 1966	*1-116F	15 November 1966	3-10 Deleted	15 March 1965
		*1-116G	15 November 1966	3-11	15 May 1966

*The asterisk indicates pages changed, added, or deleted by the current change.

ADDITIONAL COPIES OF THIS PUBLICATION MAY BE OBTAINED AS FOLLOWS:

NASC

USAF ACTIVITIES.—In accordance with Technical Order No. 00-5-2.
NAVY ACTIVITIES.—Use DD FORM 1348 and submit in accordance with the instructions contained in NAVSUP PUBLICATION 437—Navy Standard Requisitioning and Issue Procedure.
For information on other available material and details of distribution refer to NAVSUP PUBLICATION 2002, SECTION VIII and NAVAIR 00-500A.

Changed 15 November 1966

LIST OF CHANGED PAGES ISSUED

INSERT LATEST CHANGED PAGES. DESTROY SUPERSEDED PAGES.

NOTE: The portion of the text affected by the current change is indicated by a vertical line in the outer margins of the page.

*The asterisk indicates pages changed, added, or deleted by the current change.

LIST OF CHANGED PAGES ISSUED

INSERT LATEST CHANGED PAGES. DESTROY SUPERSEDED PAGES.

NOTE: The portion of the text affected by the current change is indicated by a vertical line in the outer margins of the page.

*The asterisk indicates pages changed, added, or deleted by the current change.

DEPARTMENT OF THE NAVY
OFFICE OF THE CHIEF OF NAVAL OPERATIONS
WASHINGTON, D.C. -20350

LETTER OF PROMULGATION

1.   The Naval Air Training and Operating Procedures Standardization Program (NATOPS) is a positive approach towards improving combat readiness and achieving a substantial reduction in the aircraft accident rate. Standardization, based on professional knowledge and experience provides the basis for development of an efficient and sound operational procedure. The standardization program is not planned to stifle individual initiative but rather, it will aid the Commanding Officer in increasing his unit's combat potential without reducing his command prestige or responsibility.

2.   This Manual is published for the purpose of standardizing ground and flight procedures, and does not include tactical doctrine. Compliance with the stipulated manual procedure is mandatory. However, to remain effective this manual must be dynamic. It must stimulate rather than stifle individual thinking. Since aviation is a continuing progressive profession, it is both desirable and necessary that new ideas and new techniques be expeditiously formulated and incorporated. It is a user's publication, prepared by and for users, and kept current by the users in order to achieve maximum readiness and safety in the most efficient and economical manner. Should conflict exist between the training and operating procedures found in this manual and those found in other publications, this manual will govern.

3.   Check lists and other pertinent extracts from this publication necessary to normal operations and training should be made and may be carried in Naval aircraft for use therein. It is forbidden to make copies of this entire publication or major portions thereof without specific authority of the Chief of Naval Operations.

4.   This change to the NATOPS Flight Manual is effective upon receipt. These pages supersede like pages in NAVWEPS 01-40AVC-1 dated 1 February 1964, changed 15 May 1966.

PAUL H. RAMSEY
Vice Admiral, USN
Deputy Chief of Naval Operations (Air)

Changed 15 November 1966

INTERIM CHANGE SUMMARY

CHANGE NUMBER	CHANGE DATE	PAGES AFFECTED	PURPOSE
1 thru 20			Canceled or previously incorporated
21	18 July 1966	1-159	Asymmetric load limitations
22	10 Aug 1966	1-103	Fuze function control system warning
23	28 Sept 1966	4-39	Refueling operations warning

TABLE OF CONTENTS

NOW HEAR THIS!

The Letter of Promulgation from the Chief of Naval Operations outlines the reasons for combining the Naval Air Training and Operating Procedures Standardization Manual with the present A-4E Flight Manual. The combined NATOPS Flight Manual, and Confidential Supplement along with the Pocket Check List present up-to-date, readily-available flight information that will enable the pilot to realize the full potential of the A-4E airplane. Opera-tional procedures in the combined flight manuals have been developed from Navy training and operating experiences, while the presentation of the systems operational procedures and engineering changes reflect continuing study and development by the engineering groups at Douglas Aircraft Co. Careful study and application of the information contained in these manu-als will pay dividends to the pilot who under-stands and uses this information correctly.

SCOPE

The combined manual contains a general discussion of the aircraft systems, flight characteristics, and specific normal and emergency operating procedures. The manual is designed to perfect the techniques of the experienced pilot as well as teach new procedures to the inexperienced pilot. Thorough knowledge of these procedures will be of great benefit to the pilot in time of need. This is especially true in the case of multiple emergencies, adverse weather, or terrain problems that could require a change from the printed procedures. Know your aircraft well enough to handle it in any emergency and you will react correctly when necessary.

ARRANGEMENT

The flight manual is divided into 11 sections. This arrangement facilitates ease of study and ready reference. Section I is subdivided into four parts; Part 1 is a general description of the aircraft and its use; Part 2 describes the aircraft systems, controls, and normal and emergency systems operation; Part 3 discusses aircraft servicing, starting requirements, danger areas, and power requirements; Part 4 discusses the airplane operating limitations.

Section II has to do with the training requirements, operating criteria, personal flying equipment, etc.

Section III is subdivided into five parts and deals with normal procedures; Part 1 discusses briefing and debriefing; Part 2 shows how to plan missions; Part 3 discusses shore-based procedures; Part 4 discusses carrier-based procedures; Part 5 discusses hot refueling procedures.

Section IV is subdivided into two parts and covers all flight characteristics and procedures from familiarization and transition to flight test. Part 1 discusses flight characteristics and Part 2 discusses flight procedures.

Section V discusses emergency procedures.

Section VI describes all weather operation from simulated to actual weather conditions.

Section VII deals with communication procedures.

Section VIII covers the weapon systems from station loading to flight procedures for weapons delivery.

Section IX Flight crew coordination (not applicable).

Section X sets forth NATOPS evaluation procedures.

Section XI contains performance data.

The Confidential Supplement incorporates all material classified as confidential in a separate binder.

NATOPS FLIGHT MANUAL CHANGES

WHO MAY SUBMIT CHANGE RECOMMENDATIONS

Anyone in the Naval Establishment may submit recommendations for changes to this NATOPS Flight Manual.

TYPES OF CHANGES

Change recommendations initiated in the field shall be designated URGENT or ROUTINE. URGENT changes are those which involve safety of flight and require immediate promulgation. ROUTINE changes are issued to promulgate new information or to modify or correct existing material.

PROCEDURES FOR SUBMITTING CHANGE RECOMMENDATIONS

URGENT change recommendations are submitted by priority message to the NATOPS Advisory Group Member in the chain of command. (Advisory Group Members are: CNO, COMNAVAIRPAC, COMNAVAIRLANT, C. G. FMFPAC, C. G. 2nd Marine Air Wing, CMC, CNATRA, NAVAVNSAFECEN, and BUWEPS.) ROUTINE change recommendations are submitted to the aircraft Model Manager (Commanding Officer, VA44, NAS Cecil Field, Florida), with a copy to Navy Tactical Doctrine Development and Production Activity, Washington Navy Yard, Washington, D.C. using OPNAV Form 3500-22 (10-63).

PROCEDURES FOR PROCESSING CHANGE RECOMMENDATIONS

Advisory Group Members and Model Managers shall process recommendations for changes to this manual in accordance with OPNAV 3510.9 series.

WARNINGS, CAUTIONS, AND NOTES

From time to time the pilot will see "Warnings", "Cautions", or "Notes" inserted in the running text. The reason for this is to call to the attention of the pilot some phase of aircraft operation that is especially important as follows:

WARNING

Operating procedures, practices, etc., which will result in personnel injury or loss of life if not carefully followed.

CAUTION

Operating procedures, practices, etc., which if not strictly observed will result in damage to equipment.

Note

An operating procedure, condition etc., which it is essential to emphasize.

CHANGE SYMBOLS

Changed text is indicated by a black vertical line in either margin of the page, like the one shown next to this paragraph. This indicates where the change was made. It may indicate new text added, text deleted or text restated. Read the paragraph and compare with the old page to determine what has been done.

OPNAVINST 3510.9B

1 January 1964

NATOPS MANUAL/NATOPS FLIGHT MANUAL/FLIGHT MANUAL CHANGE RECOMMENDATION FORM

OPNAV FORM 3500-22 (10-63)   Reference OPNAVINST 3510.9 (Current revision)

RECOMMENDED CHANGE TO MANUAL (Check one)   AIRCRAFT (Specify)

[X] NATOPS MANUAL   [ ] NATOPS FLIGHT MANUAL   [ ] FLIGHT MANUAL   E-1B

REVISION/CHANGE DATE

SECTION	PAGE	PARAGRAPH	PARAGRAPH TITLE	
4	4-6	407	FCLP AND CQ	

RECOMMENDATION (Be Specific)

Change paragraph 407.2 to read as shown in enclosure (1).

SAMPLE

REASON

Revise to conform to COMNAVAIRLANT/COMNAVAIRPAC CATC procedures.

NAME	DATE
LCDR U. B. STANDARD, USN	10/5/63

ADDRESS

VAW-12 c/o FPO, N.Y., N.Y.

OP-561

Enclosure (2)

Figure 1-1. Model A-4E Aircraft

SECTION I
THE AIRCRAFT

TABLE OF CONTENTS

PART 1

GENERAL DESCRIPTION

TABLE OF CONTENTS

TEXT

ILLUSTRATIONS

DESCRIPTION

The Navy Model A-4E Skyhawk (figure 1-1) is a single-place monoplane with a modified delta-planform wing manufactured by the Douglas Aircraft Company, Aircraft Division, Long Beach, California. It is powered by a P&W-AJ52-P-6/6A gas turbine engine producing a sea-level static thrust rating of 8500 pounds.

Designed as a high performance, lightweight attack aircraft, it mounts two 20-mm guns internally, carries a variety of external stores, and is capable of operating either from a carrier or from a shore base. The basic weight of the A-4E is 11,156 pounds which includes a 180-pound pilot, parakit, guns, oil, two 300 gallon drop tanks, and a parachute.

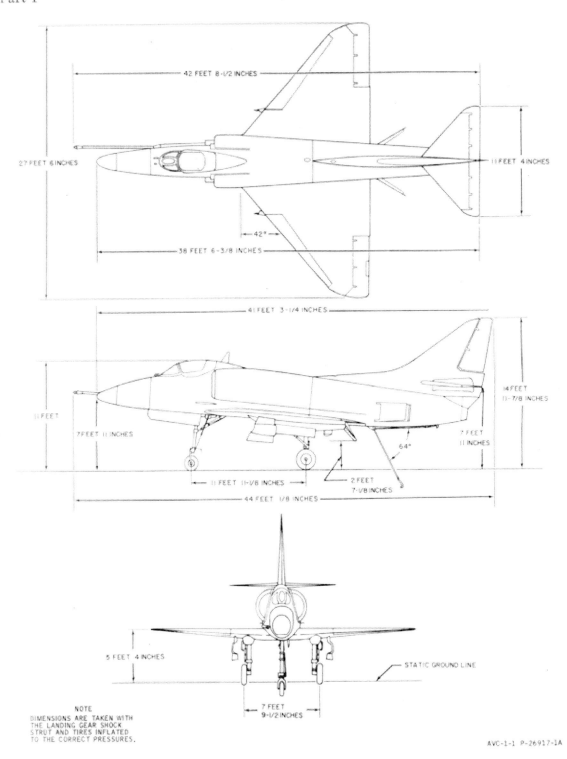

42 FEET 8-1/2 INCHES

27 FEET 6 INCHES

11 FEET 4 INCHES

42°

38 FEET 6-3/8 INCHES

41 FEET 3-1/4 INCHES

11 FEET

14 FEET 11-7/8 INCHES

7 FEET 11 INCHES

7 FEET 11 INCHES

64°

11 FEET 11-1/8 INCHES

2 FEET 7-1/8 INCHES

44 FEET 1/8 INCHES

5 FEET 4 INCHES

STATIC GROUND LINE

7 FEET 9-1/2 INCHES

NOTE
DIMENSIONS ARE TAKEN WITH
THE LANDING GEAR SHOCK
STRUT AND TIRES INFLATED
TO THE CORRECT PRESSURES.

AVC-1-1 P-26917-1A

Figure 1-2. Principal Dimensions

Changed 15 March 1965

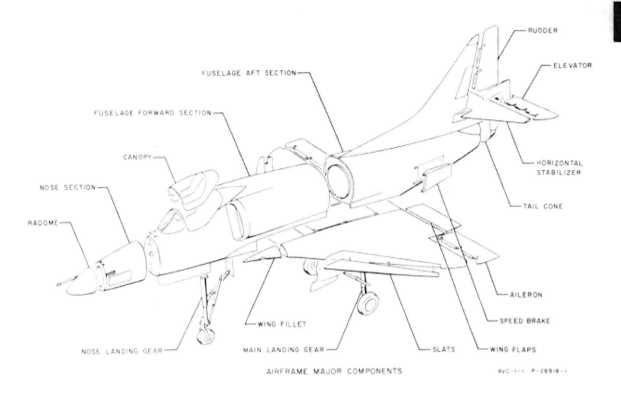

Figure 1-3.   Airframe Major Components

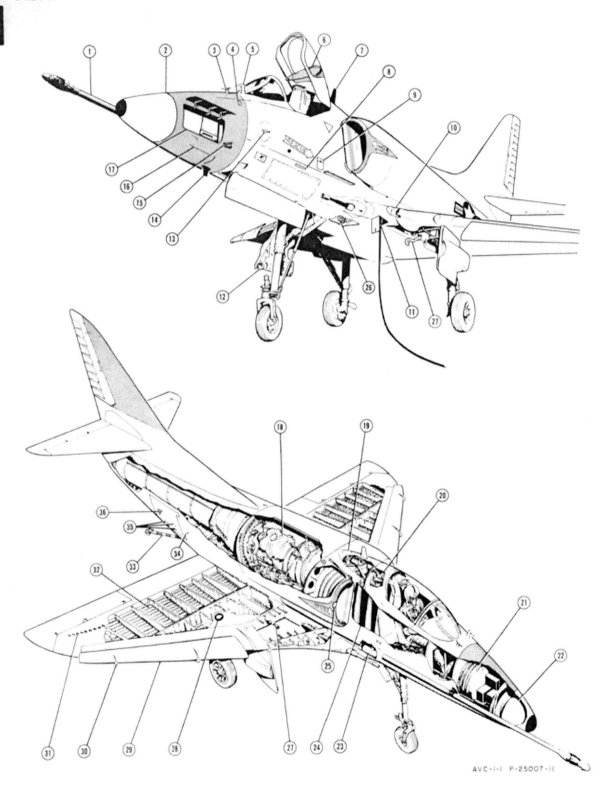

Figure 1-4. General Arrangements

Key to figure 1-4

1. Air refueling probe

2. Radome

3. Total temperature sensor

4. Brake fluid level window

5. Pitot tube

6. Thermal radiation closure

7. AN/ARC-27A (UHF) radio antenna

8. Normal cockpit entry handle

9. External canopy-jettison handle

10. Approach lights

11. External power receptacle and access door

12. Taxi light

13. Angle-of-attack vane and transducer

14. TACAN (V) antenna

15. Static orifice

16. AN/ARA-25 (UHF-ADF) antenna cover

17. Nose compartment access door

18. Oil tank

19. Fuselage fuel tank fillercap

20. Cockpit canopy air bungee cylinder

21. AN/ASQ-17B integrated electronic central

22. AN/APG-53A radar transmitter and receiver group

23. Emergency generator

24. Fuselage fuel tank

25. Air refueling probe light

26. Oil tank pressure fillercap

27. Catapult hook

28. Wing tank fillercap

29. Slat

30. Barricade engagement detent

31. Vortex generators

32. Integral wing fuel tank

33. Arresting hook

34. JATO igniter terminal

35. JATO mounting hooks

36. Speedbrake

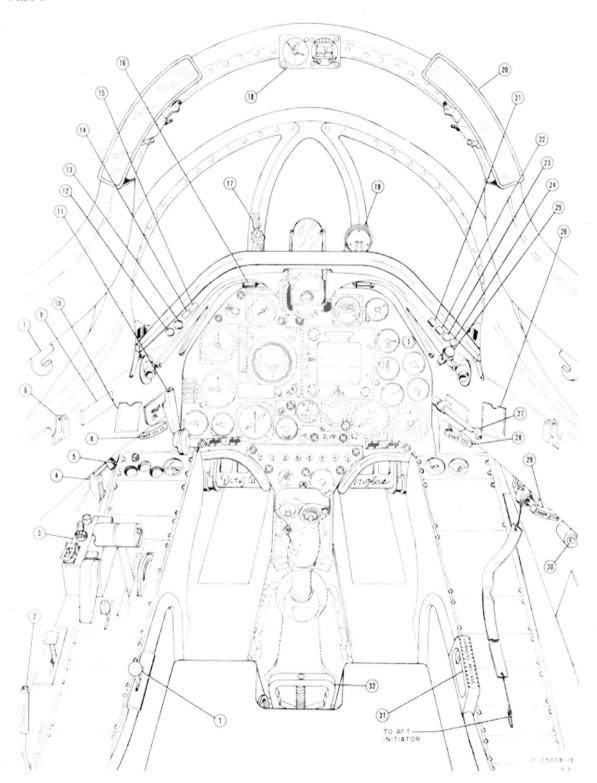

Figure 1-5. General Arrangement — Cockpit

Key to figure 1-5

1. Shoulder harness control handle
2. Manual canopy control handle
3. JATO control panel
4. Catapult handgrip
5. JATO firing button
6. Canopy latch rollers
7. Canopy latch hooks
8. Emergency landing gear release handle
9. Compass deviation card
10. Compass correction card
11. Landing gear control handle
12. Left turn light
13. Marker beacon light
14. LABS light
15. WHEELS warning light
16. Cockpit floodlights

17. Angle-of-attack index light
18. Standby compass and elapsed time clock
19. Remote channel indicator
20. Rear view mirror
21. FIRE warning light
22. OBST warning light
23. Right turn light
24. ARM/ORD light
25. Utility floodlight
26. Standby compass deviation card
27. Arresting hook handle
28. Emergency generator release handle
29. Canopy jettison handle
30. White floodlights control
31. Harness release handle
32. Secondary ejection handle

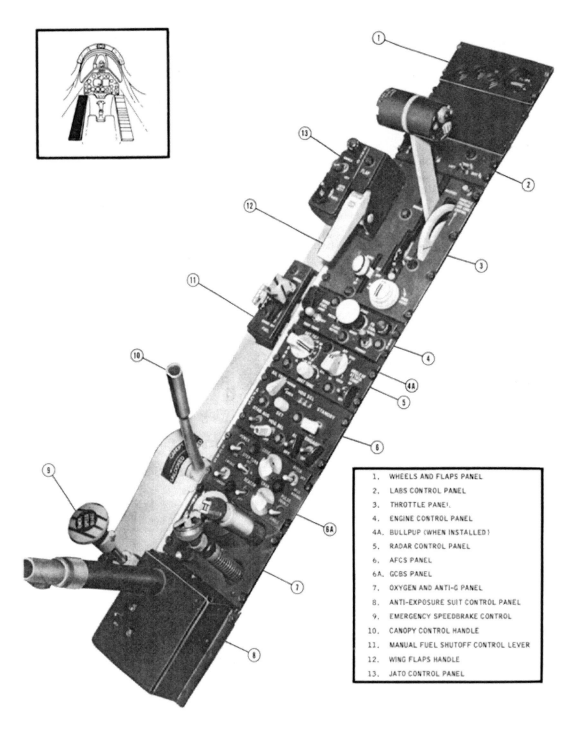

1.   WHEELS AND FLAPS PANEL

2.   LABS CONTROL PANEL

3.   THROTTLE PANEL

4.   ENGINE CONTROL PANEL

4A. BULLPUP (WHEN INSTALLED)

5.   RADAR CONTROL PANEL

6.   AFCS PANEL

6A. GCBS PANEL

7.   OXYGEN AND ANTI-G PANEL

8.   ANTI-EXPOSURE SUIT CONTROL PANEL

9.   EMERGENCY SPEEDBRAKE CONTROL

10. CANOPY CONTROL HANDLE

11. MANUAL FUEL SHUTOFF CONTROL LEVER

12. WING FLAPS HANDLE

13. JATO CONTROL PANEL

P-25009-1D

Figure 1-6.   Cockpit-Typical Left Console

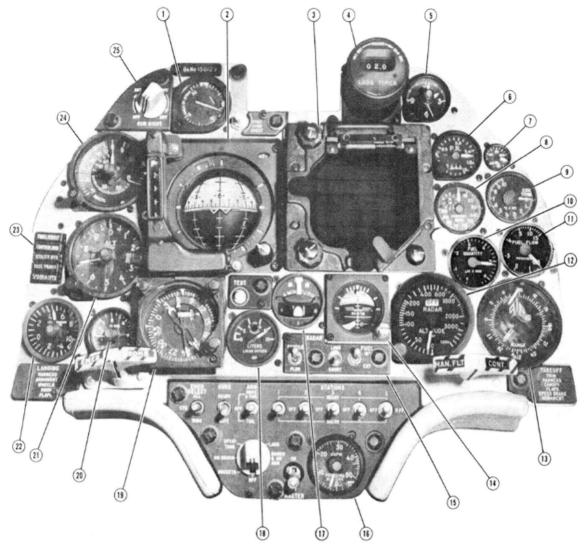

1. ANGLE OF ATTACK INDICATOR	14. STANDBY ATTITUDE INDICATOR
2. ALL ATTITUDE INDICATOR	15. MISCELLANEOUS SWITCHES PANEL
3. RADAR SCOPE	16. ARMAMENT PANEL
4. LABS TIMER	17. TURN AND BANK INDICATOR
5. 8-DAY CLOCK	18. OXYGEN QUANTITY INDICATOR
6. PRESSURE RATIO INDICATOR	19. BEARING-DISTANCE-HEADING INDICATOR
7. OIL PRESSURE INDICATOR	20. RATE OF CLIMB INDICATOR
8. TACHOMETER	21. ALTIMETER
9. EXHAUST GAS TEMPERATURE INDICATOR	22. ACCELEROMETER
10. FUEL FLOWMETER INDICATOR	23. CAUTION PANEL (LADDER LIGHTS)
11. FUEL FLOW INDICATOR	24. AIRSPEED INDICATOR
12. RADAR ALTIMETER	25. GUNSIGHT PANEL
13. DEAD RECKONING INDICATOR	

AVC-1-1   P-25010-1C

Figure 1-7.   Cockpit -- Typical Instrument Panel (Early Configuration)   (Sheet 1)

Changed 15 March 1965

1. ANGLE OF ATTACK INDICATOR
2. ATTITUDE DIRECTOR INDICATOR
3. RADAR SCOPE
4. LABS TIMER
5. 8-DAY CLOCK
6. PRESSURE RATIO INDICATOR
7. OIL PRESSURE INDICATOR
8. TACHOMETER
9. EXHAUST TEMPERATURE INDICATOR
10. FUEL QUANTITY INDICATOR
11. FUEL FLOW INDICATOR
12. RADAR ALTIMETER

13. STANDBY ATTITUDE INDICATOR
14. MISCELLANEOUS SWITCHES PANEL
15. ARMAMENT PANEL
16. AIRCRAFT WEAPONS RELEASE SYSTEM PANEL
17. OXYGEN QUANTITY INDICATOR
18. BEARING-DISTANCE-HEADING INDICATOR
19. RATE OF CLIMB INDICATOR
20. ALTIMETER
21. ACCELEROMETER
22. CAUTION PANEL (LADDER LIGHTS)
23. AIRSPEED INDICATOR
24. GUNSIGHT PANEL

AVC-1-1　P-29458-1A

Figure 1-7. Cockpit-Typical Instrument Panel (Late Configuration) (Sheet 2)

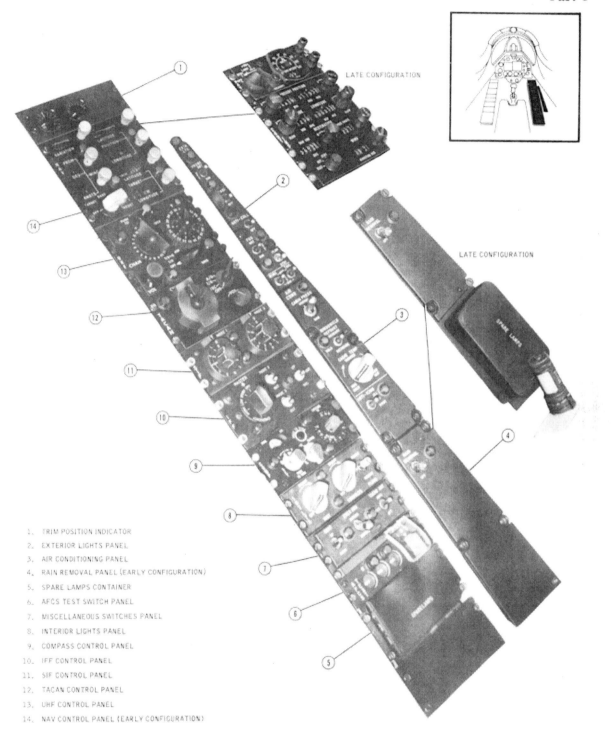

LATE CONFIGURATION

LATE CONFIGURATION

1. TRIM POSITION INDICATOR
2. EXTERIOR LIGHTS PANEL
3. AIR CONDITIONING PANEL
4. RAIN REMOVAL PANEL (EARLY CONFIGURATION)
5. SPARE LAMPS CONTAINER
6. AFCS TEST SWITCH PANEL
7. MISCELLANEOUS SWITCHES PANEL
8. INTERIOR LIGHTS PANEL
9. COMPASS CONTROL PANEL
10. IFF CONTROL PANEL
11. SIF CONTROL PANEL
12. TACAN CONTROL PANEL
13. UHF CONTROL PANEL
14. NAV CONTROL PANEL (EARLY CONFIGURATION)

AVC-1-1   P-25011-1C

Figure 1-8.   Cockpit — Typical Right Console

PART 2

SYSTEMS

TABLE OF CONTENTS

TEXT

Changed 15 March 1965

ILLUSTRATIONS

TABLES

ENGINE

The P&WA J52-P-6/6A turbojet is a continuous flow gas turbine engine utilizing a split 12-stage axial compressor. The 5-stage low-pressure unit is connected by a through shaft to the second-stage turbine rotor. The 7-stage high-pressure unit is connected independently by a hollow shaft to the first-stage turbine rotor. The rpm of the high-pressure rotor (N_2) is governed by the engine fuel control, whereas the low-pressure rotor rpm (N_1) is completely independent and is entirely a function of the pressure drop across the turbines. There are nine combustion chambers (No. 1 at the top). Numbers four and seven have spark igniters.

The J52-P-6/6A engine, in a static condition, standard atmospheric day at sea level, develops 8500 pounds thrust.

Also included as part of the engine is the anti-icing air system, compressor airbleed system, cooling air system, internal airbleed system, lubrication system, pressure oil system, scavenge oil system, oil breather system, fuel system, and ignition system. The J52-P-6A engine incorporates a fuel heater.

IGNITION

The engine ignition system consists of two spark igniters, an ignition timer, and dual (20-joule and 4-joule) ignition units. The spark igniters are located in the two combustion chambers at the 4 and 8 o'clock positions. For engine starting, the timer energizes the high-power ignition unit supplying 20 joules to both igniters for a 30- to 45-second firing cycle. Whenever the engine-driven or emergency generator is operating, the 4-joule ignition system operates continuously, firing only the igniter that is located at the 4 o'clock position. The ignition switch, which energizes the ignition timer, is a momentary-contact limit switch that is actuated by movement of the throttle outboard from the OFF position.

STARTER

The engine is started on the ground by a pneumatic starter driven by compressed air from a mobile gas turbine compressor (GTC). The compressor can be carried externally on the centerline or inboard store racks. (When the GTC unit is carried on the centerline store rack, a carrier landing is permitted. With the GTC unit installed on either inboard store rack, carrier landing is not permitted and the flight limitations as set forth in Section I, Part 4 must be complied with.)

ENGINE FUEL SYSTEM

The function of the engine fuel system is to supply and regulate the fuel to the combustion chambers at pressures and flows required by engine air flow at all operating altitudes and temperatures. The system has two major components: the engine fuel pump and the fuel control.

ENGINE FUEL PUMP

The engine pump consists of a centrifugal booster stage and a high-pressure single gear stage with a 40-micron filter between the two. A filter bypass, a pressure relief valve, and a vapor return to the fuselage fuel cell are also incorporated.

FUEL CONTROL

The engine fuel control is a hydromechanical control that senses inlet air temperature, burner pressure, high-pressure compressor speed (N_2), and throttle position. When the throttle setting is changed and while accommodating to a new steady-state fuel rate, the fuel control varies the fuel flow between the limiting values established by safe tailpipe temperature and mixture combustibility. The control permits the fuel flow to reach these limits during acceleration and deceleration but does not permit transgression in either direction, thus preventing compressor stalls, overtemperaturing, or flameouts. The fuel control has a manual system that bypasses the automatic features noted above and is only pressure altitude compensated.

The engine fuel control operation may be changed from PRIMARY to MANUAL at all altitudes during flight. If airspeed at the time of switchover is above 225 KIAS, selection of MANUAL may be made at any throttle setting from IDLE to MILITARY. If airspeed is below 225 KIAS, select a minimum throttle setting of 65% RPM prior to switchover.

Note

During flight testing it has been demonstrated that the manual fuel control position can be safely selected while at MILITARY up to 30,000 feet.

The switchover to the manual fuel system may be accompanied by a minor surge in engine speed and EGT.

After a switchover, the throttle should be moved slowly and smoothly to the desired power setting. Observe the engine operating limitations given in section I, part 4. It must be remembered that when operating on the manual fuel control system, all fuel metering to the engine is accomplished by direct movement of the throttle; therefore, all power changes must be made with care, not only to prevent overspeeding and extreme temperatures, but also to avoid a flameout from the possible inability of the engine to parallel in speed the rapidly changing fuel flow during quick accelerations and decelerations.

ENGINE CONTROLS

THROTTLE

The throttle (see figure 1-6) located on the left console is mechanically linked to the engine fuel control unit and is the means of selecting engine thrust. Marked positions of the throttle are OFF, IGN (ignition), IDLE, NORMAL and MILITARY. The OFF position closes a fuel cutoff valve in the fuel control unit stopping all fuel flow to the engine. The IGN position actuates the ignition timer when

the throttle is moved outboard from the OFF position. The IDLE position has a detent to prevent inadvertent movement of the throttle to the OFF position. The NORMAL position indicates the operating range of the engine. At MILITARY the engine should develop maximum thrust and rpm, which will vary with atmospheric conditions. Switches for the radio microphone and speedbrakes are located on the inboard side of the throttle grip, with the exterior lights master switch on the outboard side. Inboard of the throttle, on the console, is the throttle friction wheel, which is rotated forward to increase friction on the throttle. To prevent retarding the throttle during catapulting, a catapult handgrip (4, figure 1-5), which extends from its spring-loaded position against the cockpit rail, is grasped in conjunction with the throttle. The JATO firing button is incorporated in the catapult handgrip.

ENGINE CONTROL PANEL

The engine control panel, just aft of the throttle, contains all other controls for the operation of the engine. On the panel are the manual fuel warning light, the drop tanks pressurization and flight refuel switch, the emergency transfer and wing fuel dump switch (airplanes with ASC 209 incorporated), the engine starter switch, and the fuel control switch.

FUEL CONTROL SWITCH. A two-position fuel control switch on the engine control panel (figure 1-6) is used to select the mode of operation of the engine fuel control unit. With the switch at PRIMARY, the automatic metering devices in the fuel control unit regulate the flow of fuel to the engine as described above. With the switch at MANUAL, the control compensates automatically only for variations in altitude.

MANUAL FUEL CONTROL WARNING LIGHT. The manual fuel control warning light located on the engine control panel comes on when the fuel control has shifted to the manual mode of operation. The light indicates the position of the emergency transfer valve which directs the fuel to either the primary of manual fuel control system. The emergency transfer valve is kept in the manual fuel control position by spring load until overcome by engine-driven fuel pump pressure, regardless of the position of the fuel control switch. Consequently, the light will be on during normal engine starts until fuel pressure within the control shifts the transfer valve to the PRIMARY position at approximately 5-10 percent rpm. The light will also come on shortly after engine shutdown indicating a shift to the MANUAL mode upon loss of fuel pressure. With normal fuel pressure, the position of the emergency transfer valve and the mode of fuel control will always correspond to the position of the fuel control switch.

ENGINE STARTER SWITCH. Actuation of the starter is controlled by the engine starter switch on the engine control panel (figure 1-6), and is labeled START-ABORT. When the switch is depressed to START, the starter air supply solenoid valve opens, allowing compressed air from the gas turbine compressor to rotate the starter. A holding relay retains the switch in the START position. When the engine speed reaches approximately 50 percent rpm, a centrifugal switch opens, allowing the engine starter switch to pop up, thus stopping the air supply to the starter. Manually pulling out the engine starter switch will also stop the starter air supply.

ENGINE INSTRUMENTS

EXHAUST GAS TEMPERATURE (EGT) INDICATOR

The exhaust gas temperature indicator (figure 1-7), located on the instrument panel, indicates the temperature of the exhaust gases immediately downstream of the turbine assembly in degrees centigrade. The range of indications is from 0 to 1000 degrees centigrade.

Note

High rates of roll or positive and negative accelerations may cause the EGT indicator to give erroneous indications. However, upon return to stabilized flight, readings return to normal.

TACHOMETER

A tachometer (figure 1-7), located on the instrument panel, indicates the speed of the high pressure compressor rotor (N_2) as a percentage of 11,600 rpm. Both EGT indicator and tachometer operate independently of aircraft electrical power and function whenever the engine is running.

PRESSURE RATIO INDICATOR

A pressure ratio indicator (figure 1-7), located on the instrument panel, is provided to indicate the ratio of tailpipe pressure to pressure at the pitot tube as a means of checking takeoff thrust at military power. The instrument is calibrated from 1.2 to 3.4. A knob on the lower left-hand side of the instrument operates a counter dial and simultaneously moves an index pointer that travels along the perimeter of the index face. The knob is turned until the minimum acceptable takeoff pressure ratio is displayed on the counter dial. (See figure 3-3, Takeoff Pressure Ratio chart, to determine the minimum acceptable takeoff pressure ratio.) When the throttle is advanced to military power, a needle on the dial should coincide with, or exceed, the setting of the index pointer to indicate that minimum acceptable takeoff thrust is available. The pressure ratio indicator reflects a direct measurement of the engine thrust output and is recommended as the primary cruise control variable when selecting engine thrust output to establish cruise schedules.

FUEL FLOWMETER

A fuel flowmeter indicator (figure 1-7), located on the instrument panel, shows engine fuel consumption in pounds per hour. The portion of the dial between 300 and 5000 pounds per hour is divided into 100-pound increments. Above 5000 pounds per hour, the dial is marked into 1000-pound increments. Flow rates between 0 and 300 pounds per hour will be indicated as 300 pounds per hour. The fuel flowmeter indicator, because of engine tolerances and overhaul life, does not accurately measure engine thrust output. It should be used only as a secondary indication when establishing cruise schedules.

ENGINE OPERATION

The control of the engine consists essentially of selecting throttle positions. If the engine is in trim, the pressure ratio indicator will reflect any thrust setting (operating condition) that the pilot selects with the throttle. Exhaust gas temperature (EGT) indicates how much "effort" the engine is making, rather than how much work the engine should be, or is, doing. EGT must never be used, therefore, as a basis for setting thrust except when it becomes necessary to reduce a throttle setting to avoid exceeding a temperature limit, or to cope with unstable operation.

The pilot must not only know and observe the engine operating limitations specified in figure 1-62, he must also recognize relationships like those between operating temperatures and temperature limits. For example, although it is permissible for an engine to operate at the actual temperature limit corresponding to a selected thrust setting (operating condition), an engine that does so may have something wrong that causes it to run abnormally hot. Also, it is the thrust setting, not the EGT indication, that determines the allowable time limit specified in Section I, Part 4. That is, the time limit is 30 minutes because the thrust setting is Military Rated—not because the EGT indication happens to be 610°C. In fact, if the EGT indication is 610°C at Military Rated, the pilot should be concerned about a possible malfunction. Report as an engine discrepancy every instance of overtemperature, noting not only the peak temperature reached, but also the length of time that the EGT exceeded limits.

WARNING

Under conditions of severe rainfall intensity, maintain a minimum engine power setting of 70 percent rpm. This will assure adequate acceleration margin and prevent possible speed hangups.

STARTING

Engine exhaust gas temperature will not normally rise above 300°C on ground start. Conditions may exist however, which will give rise to EGTs, which may approach the maximum permissible of 455°C. Under these conditions, the EGT tendency will be a better indication of proper engine operation than will the actual value attained. Thus, a ground starting EGT of 400°C and rising rapidly should concern a pilot more than a start where the EGT slowly peaks out at 450°C. The cause of the start above 300°C (extremely high ambient temperatures, starting a hot engine, high wind up the tail pipe, etc.) should always be determined as start EGT may be indicative of some engine malfunction. Refer to Section V for abnormal starts.

ACCELERATION

The acceleration temperature limit and corresponding time limit apply to engine rpm. Although the EGT limit specified in Section I, Part 4, applies to both cold and hot engines, its relatively high value was set to take care of cold engines. A cold engine is defined as one that has just been started or has been permitted to cool at IDLE for at least 5 minutes before an acceleration. The limits for acceleration and maximum temperature should be interpreted to mean that EGT may go to 650°C during acceleration but must decrease to 610°C or less within 2 minutes after acceleration.

The acceleration performance of an engine is not acceptable if it exceeds either the EGT or time limit. The acceleration temperature limit applies only when an acceleration is made over the full thrust range of the engine, as from IDLE to MILITARY. For an acceleration from IDLE to Normal Rated, the EGT limit for Normal Rated, instead of for acceleration, applies.

STEADY STATE OPERATION

Exhaust gas temperatures for Normal Rated (figure 1-62) should be thought of as the temperature which, if exceeded at approximately 3 percent less than MILITARY rpm, warns of a possible engine malfunction. The temperatures shown for Military Rated and Normal Rated are positive limits that can not be exceeded without compromising the engine's service life. A normally functioning engine should operate somewhat below the EGT limits published for the several operating conditions. The IDLE EGT limit is intended only as a guide, and is not a firm operating limit.

Specified temperature limits serve two purposes: they assure that an engine will always be operated at internal temperatures that will not shorten the service life expectancy of engine components; they enable the pilot to detect an engine fuel control system or instrumentation malfunction in time to take proper corrective action.

The length of time that an engine may be operated at each of the thrust settings (operating conditions) was established to conserve the life of the engine and to make the time between overhauls predictable.

An engine's service life "budget" has just so many hours of operation at high thrust. Whether these hours are used up quickly or are distributed throughout a normal, calculated period depends on how conscientiously the EGT and time limits are observed by the pilot.

The time limit for operation at Military Rated is specified not so much to permit a cooling period between intervals of operation at high thrust as it is to distribute the rate of blade creep throughout the engine's normal life. Nothing is gained, therefore, by reducing a high thrust setting only momentarily before repeating it — just to be able to report that time limits were not violated.

In the high thrust range, an increase of only 5 °C may double the rate of turbine blade creep. Just so much creep can be tolerated by each

blade. The rate at which blade life is depleted depends on proper pilot technique. Unfortunately, no operational technique can reverse the effect of blade creep.

OIL SYSTEM

The engine lubrication system is a self-contained, high pressure system which supplies lubrication to the main engine bearings and to the accessory drives. Oil delivered by the engine-driven oil pump is cooled by means of an oil cooler prior to entering the bearing compartments. The oil cooler is a heat exchanger, employing the fuel flowing to the engine as a coolant. A scavenge system returns oil withdrawn from the bearing compartments and the accessory drive gearbox to the oil tank. A breather system connects the individual bearing compartments and oil tank with the breather pressure relief valve. The breather pressure relief valve vents overboard on the starboard side of the aft fuselage. See figure 1-35 for oil tank capacity and oil specification.

OIL PRESSURE INDICATOR

Engine oil pressure is shown on the oil pressure indicator (figure 1-7) on the instrument panel. Normal oil pressure is 40 to 50 psi. Minimum oil pressure for ground IDLE is 35 psi.

Note

• Maneuvers producing acceleration near zero "g" may cause a temporary loss of oil pressure. Absence of oil pressure for a maximum of 1 minute is permissible.

• Oil pressure indications are available on emergency generator.

FUEL SYSTEM

The internal fuel supply is carried in two tanks containing a total of 810 US gallons. These tanks can be serviced by means of two gravity fuel tank fillers for a single-point pressure fueling system. Three external drop tanks can be carried to increase the total fuel quantity to 1710 US gallons. Fuel is normally transferred from the drop tanks by tank pressurization and from the wing integral tank by an air-driven fuel transfer pump. In aircraft incorporating ASC 209, emergency wing fuel transfer may be accomplished by wing tank pressurization. All fuel is delivered to the fuselage tank, from which an electrically driven fuel boost pump delivers the fuel under pressure to the engine-driven fuel pump. A manual fuel shutoff control lever is provided in the cockpit. (See figure 1-35 for fuel grades and specifications of recommended and emergency fuels, and figure 1-9 for a schematic presentation of the fuel system.)

FUEL TANKS

INTERNAL TANKS

Internal tanks comprise an integral wing tank and a self-sealing type fuselage tank mounted between the cockpit and the engine bay. The fuselage tank contains the control valve for regulation of transfer fuel flow, the fuel boost pump which delivers fuel to the engine, and a fuel sump with flapper valves. The flapper valves assure a flow of fuel to the fuel pump regardless of attitude and during maneuvers involving negative g-loads and inverted flight for approximately 30 seconds.

Both fuel tanks are vented. The vent system exit is located aft of the right main landing gear strut and is designed to provide a small amount of ram air pressure in the fuel vent system to reduce the amount of collapse of the self-sealing type fuselage tank when it is partially full. Both tanks incorporate provisions for gravity filling, pressure fueling and defueling, and water and sediment drainage. (For information concerning total and usable fuel capacities of each tank, see figure 1-10.)

EXTERNAL TANKS

Provisions are made for carrying drop tanks singly or in combination. The inboard and centerline external stores racks will accommodate either 150-gallon or 300-gallon drop tanks. The centerline rack will also accommodate a 400-gallon drop tank. All drop tanks are vented, and contain provisions for gravity fueling, pressure fueling, and pressurization to effect fuel transfer to the integral wing tank at the option of the pilot. The drop tanks may be jettisoned in the same manner as other droppable external stores.

FUEL TRANSFER

WING TANK TRANSFER

The wing tank air turbine driven transfer pump utilizes engine compressor bleed air for power, and operates whenever the engine is running. Since the pump operates continuously, a float valve is placed in the fuselage tank to stop the transfer of fuel whenever the fuselage tank is full, in order to prevent transfer fuel from being pumped overboard through the fuel vent system. A fuel transfer failure caution light is provided on the left side of the instrument panel and comes on when wing tank fuel transfer pressure drops below 2 (+1/4, -1/8) psi. Steady illumination indicates fuel transfer pump failure or wing tank fuel depletion. Maneuvering flight may cause the pump to become temporarily unported, thereby inducing intermittent illumination of the fuel transfer caution light. Engine rpm settings below approximately 70 percent provide insufficient bleed air pressure to maintain the required fuel transfer pressure, thus causing the caution light to come on. In this situation, fuel may continue to transfer at a reduced rate. Increasing rpm above approximately 70 percent will cause the light to go out, indicating normal fuel transfer has resumed.

DROP TANK TRANSFER

Fuel transfer from the drop tanks to the integral wing tank and fuselage tank is effected by means of drop tank pressurization. Placing the drop tanks switch on the engine control panel (figure 1-6) at PRESS opens a solenoid-operated air shutoff valve which directs engine compressor bleed air to the drop tanks. Once the tanks are pressurized, the flow of fuel from the drop tanks to the wing tank is controlled by the dual float pilot valve in the wing tank, which stops the transfer of fuel when the wing tank is full or allows it to continue when space is available. If the wing tank is full and the fuselage tank is not (as in the case of wing tank transfer pump-failure), drop tank fuel will flow directly to the fuselage tank. Placing the drop tanks switch at OFF energizes the drop tank air shutoff valve, thereby closing the valve and discontinuing transfer of fuel from the drop tanks. If electrical failure occurs, the drop tank air shutoff valve is automatically opened, providing immediate and automatic transfer of drop tank fuel as wing tank space permits. To prevent drop tank pressurizing air from being exhausted overboard through the drop tank vent, each drop tank is equipped with a combination float and diaphragm vent shutoff valve. This valve acts to close the drop tank vent when the tank is full or pressurizing air is introduced.

Fuel transfer from the drop tanks, sea level to 5000 feet altitude, is 8000 PPH, and from 25,000 to 35,000 feet altitude, it is 4000 PPH (90 percent power setting).

NOTE

- When fuel is transferred from the center-line drop tank to wing or fuselage tank, leave the drop tank transfer switch in PRESS position. This will prevent wing tank fuel from being transferred to the centerline drop tank if the emergency transfer system is used. Should this occur, the fuel can be used by moving the drop tank transfer switch to PRESS.

- A noticeable thumping may be experienced during the latter stages of drop tank transfer.

EMERGENCY TRANSFER

After incorporation of A-4/ASC 209, emergency transfer of fuel from the wing rank to the fuselage tank is possible. A switch located on the engine control panel (figure 1-6) provides for the transfer of fuel by wing tank pressurization. Moving the switch to the EMER TRANS position actuates the wing tank pressure and vent valve closed, allowing engine compressor bleed air to pressurize the wing tank. Fuel is transferred to the fuselage tank through the pressure fueling line. If normal transfer failure was caused by a failure of the transfer pump, emergency transfer fuel will also flow through the regular transfer line as well as the pressure fueling line to the fuselage tank.

WARNING

- When the wing fuel dump switch is in EMER TRANS position, over-pressurization of wing is possible if fuel covers fuel vent outlet in tank due to 6-psi static pressure imposed on wing during emergency transfer. This condition will exist during negative g-flight and when aircraft is in nosedown attitude. Do not exceed 45-degree bank angle, or load factors of positive 2g, and avoid negative g or nosedown maneuvers during emergency transfer. When center drop tank is installed, following sequence should be used due to automatic transfer of wing tank fuel to center drop tank with a wing tank transfer failure. First, transfer all drop tank fuel that will fill the wing tank and then flow directly to fuselage tank. Then while maintaining drop tank pressurization, initiate emergency transfer. Air pressure in center drop tank will prevent flow of fuel from wing down into center drop tank, where it would be unavailable for immediate emergency transfer.

- The wing fuel dump switch must be in OFF position during air refueling and hot refueling operations. This will prevent dumping of fuel overboard through wing fuel dump valve.

WING TANK FUEL DUMP AND PRESSURE RELIEF

After incorporation of A-4/ASC 209, a valve installed in the wing tank will prevent over-pressurization of the tank and allows wing tank fuel to be dumped overboard if desired. Moving the wing tank fuel dump switch, located on the engine control panel (figure 1-6), to the DUMP position will allow wing fuel to flow by gravity out the dump mast on the right main landing gear fairing at the rate of approximately 100 gallons per minute.

NOTE

While dumping wing tank, monitor the fuel quantity indicator closely to preclude inadvertent dumping of fuel below the desired level.

FUEL TRANSFER BYPASS SWITCH

On aircraft incorporating A-4/AFC 317, a fuel transfer bypass switch has been installed on the rain removal panel located on the right console. When the switch is placed in the FUEL TRANS BYPASS position during in-flight refueling, fuel flows into the fuselage fuel tank only. The switch is normally used when the receiver aircraft has wing damage to prevent fuel from entering a damaged wing tank thus averting a fuel loss/fire hazard condition.

In-flight refueling of the drop tanks and fuselage fuel tank (bypassing the wing tanks) is possible by placing the DROP TANKS switch to the FLIGHT REFUEL position, in addition to placing the fuel transfer bypass switch to the FUEL TRANS BYPASS position.

WARNING

Damaged integral wing tanks may include damage of drop tank fuel transfer lines, which are routed through wing tanks. An attempt to fuel drop tanks with broken transfer lines will result in loss of fuel and will also create a fire hazard condition.

FUEL BOOST PUMP

An electrically driven fuel boost pump is submerged in the fuselage tank sump. The fuselage tank sump incorporates flapper valves which act to keep the boost pump fuel inlet supplied with fuel at all aircraft attitudes, including diving flight and negative g or inverted flight not to exceed 30 seconds duration. Operation of the fuel boost pump is automatic whenever the aircraft electrical system is energized by the main generator, by external power, or by external power through the ground test switch installed by A-4/AFC No. 207A, depending upon aircraft configuration. In the event of main generator failure, the fuel boost pump will be inoperative and will remain so even though the emergency generator is deployed.

FUEL BOOST PRESSURE INDICATOR

Loss of fuel boost pressure is indicated by a FUEL BOOST warning light located on the caution panel, left-hand side of the instrument panel (figure 1-7). The warning light will glow whenever fuel boost pressure falls below 4 psi and goes out at 6 psi.

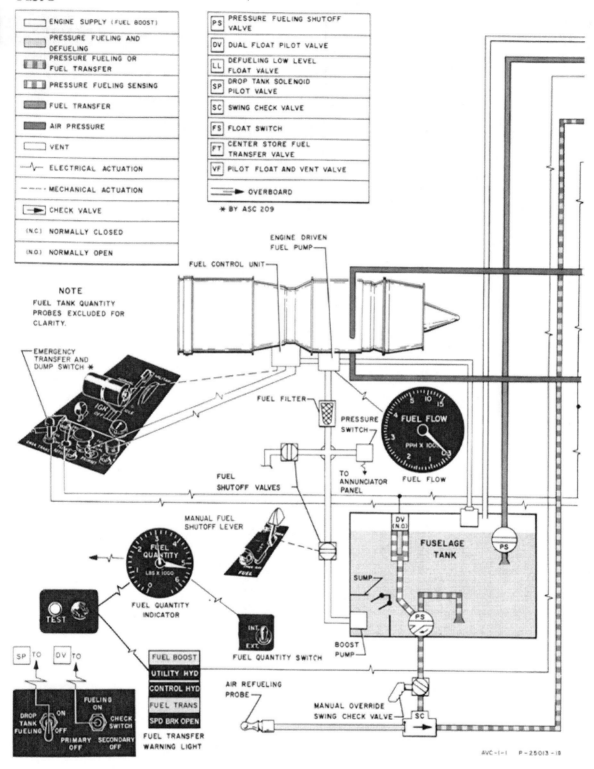

Figure 1-9. Fuel System (Sheet 1)

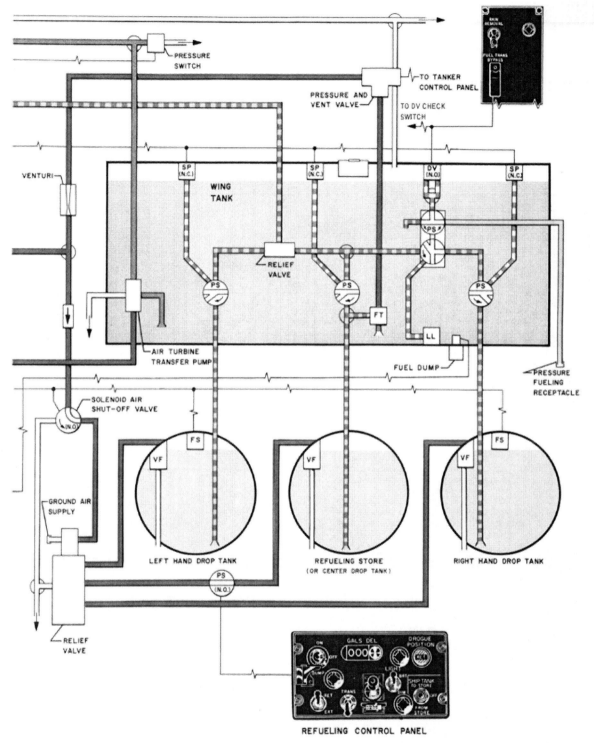

Figure 1-9. Fuel System (Sheet 2)

FUEL QUANTITY DATA
GALLONS — POUNDS

TANKS	USABLE FUEL			UNUSABLE FUEL LEVEL FLIGHT	EXPANSION SPACE	TOTAL VOLUME
	GALLONS	POUNDS				
		JP-4	JP-5			
PRESSURE FUELING INTEGRAL WING	560	3640	3803	6	9	585
GRAVITY FUELING	570	3705	3876			
PRESSURE FUELING FUSELAGE	230	1495	1564	0	0	240
GRAVITY FUELING	237	1541	1612			
L H WING (INBOARD WING RACK)						
150 GALLON DROP	147	956	1000	2	1	150
* 300 GALLON DROP	295	1918	2006	4	1	300
CENTERLINE						
150 GALLON DROP	147	956	1000	2	1	150
* 300 GALLON DROP	295	1918	2006	4	1	300
300 GALLON AIR REFUELING STORE	295	1918	2006	4	1	300
400 GALLON DROP	396	2574	2692	3	2	401
R H WING (INBOARD WING RACK)						
150 GALLON DROP	147	956	1000	2	1	150
* 300 GALLON DROP	295	1918	2006	4	1	300
* OR AERO 1D 300 GALLON DROP	295	1918	2006	4	1	300

TANKS	USABLE FUEL TOTALS					
	PRESSURE FUELING	* POUNDS		GRAVITY FUELING	* POUNDS	
		JP-4	JP-5		JP-4	JP-5
FUSELAGE, WING	790	5135	5372	807	5245	5487
FUSELAGE, WING, (150) CENTER DROP	937	6090	6371	954	6201	6487
FUSELAGE, WING, (300) CENTER DROP	1085	7052	7378	1102	7163	7493
FUSELAGE, WING, (300) AIR REFUELING STORE	1090	7085	7412	1107	7195	7527
FUSELAGE, WING, (400) CENTER DROP	1186	7709	8064	1203	7819	8179
FUSELAGE, WING, TWO (150) WING RACK DROP	1084	7046	7371	1101	7156	7486
FUSELAGE, WING, (150) CENTER, TWO (150) WING RACK DROP	1231	8001	8370	1248	8112	8486
FUSELAGE, WING, (300) CENTER, TWO (150) WING RACK DROP	1379	8963	9377	1396	9074	9492
FUSELAGE, WING, (400) CENTER, TWO (150) WING RACK DROP	1480	9620	10,063	1497	9730	10,178
FUSELAGE, WING, TWO (300) WING RACK DROP	1360	8970	9384	1397	9080	9499
FUSELAGE, WING, (150) CENTER, TWO (300) WING RACK DROP	1527	9926	10,383	1544	10,036	10,449
FUSELAGE, WING, (300) CENTER, TWO (300) WING RACK DROP	1675	10,887	11,390	1692	10,998	11,505
FUSELAGE, WING, (400) CENTER, TWO (300) WING RACK DROP	1776	11,544	12,076	1793	11,654	12,191

NOTE:
* Calculated for standard day conditions using 6.5 LB/GAL for JP-4
6.8 LB/GAL for JP-5

AVC-1-1 P-25012-1D

Figure 1-10. Fuel Quantity Data

MANUAL FUEL SHUTOFF CONTROL

The fuel system incorporates a manually operated fuel shutoff control lever (figure 1-6) located outboard of the left-hand console. This lever has two positions, NORMAL and EMER OFF. The EMER OFF position of the control stops all fuel flow from the airplane fuel system to the engine fuel control system. A spring-loaded lift-type guard is provided to prevent inadvertent movement of the lever to EMER OFF.

Note

To ensure complete fuel shutoff, the control lever must be moved fully aft into the EMER OFF detent.

FUEL QUANTITY INDICATING SYSTEM

The fuel quantity indicating system is comprised of capacitance-type fuel quantity probes, a fuel quantity indicator, a low-level

Changed 15 May 1966

switch, fuel quantity test switch, and associated wiring. The wing tank contains six fuel quantity probes. Each external fuel tank and the fuselage tank contains one fuel quantity probe. The probes are wired into the fuel quantity indicator in such a manner as to indicate the total quantity of fuel remaining in the internal tanks when the fuselage tank contains more than 170 gallons (1105 pounds). External fuel tanks quantity is checked by moving the internal-external fuel switch to EXT. The air refueling store does not have provisions for fuel gaging, and fuel contained in this tank (when carried) will not be indicated. The fuselage tank contains a low-level switch (thermistor bead) located approximately 1/3 of the distance down the length of the fuel quantity probe at about the 170-gallon level (approximately 1100 pounds). If the fuel supply in the fuselage tank falls below this level due to malfunction of the wing tank transfer system, or failure or mismanagement of the drop tank transfer system, the low-level switch will cause the reading of any remaining wing-tank transfer fuel to be dropped out, indicating to the pilot that approximately 170 gallons of usable fuselage fuel remains.

The effect of aircraft attitude on the relationship between indicated and actual total fuel quantity is shown on figure 1-11. When the fuselage tank indicated fuel quantity is at or below 1000 pounds, and the aircraft attitude is between 4 degrees noseup and 4 degrees nosedown, indicated quantity can be considered to be actual quantity. Indicated airspeed for most accurate fuel reading is 250 KIAS.

FUEL QUANTITY INDICATOR

The fuel quantity indicator (figure 1-7), located on the instrument panel, indicates the total fuel available in pounds multiplied by 1000. The range of indication is from 0 to 6400 pounds.

NOTE

● With failure of the transformer rectifier circuit, no dc power will be available to the fuel quantity control unit. As a result, the fuel quantity indicator will indicate only

fuel available in the fuselage fuel cell (fuel available in the wing tank will not be included). This fuel indication will be approximately 1400 pounds with the engine operating. As total usable fuel becomes less than 1400 pounds, the correct fuel quantity will be indicated.

● Maneuvering or accelerated flight causes erroneous fuel quantity indications.

The fuel quantity indicator gage, may be tested by the press-to-test button (figure 1-7) on the instrument panel. When the test button is depressed, the fuel quantity indicator pointer will rotate in a counterclockwise direction. When the button is released, the pointer will return to the original indication if all units of the fuel quantity measuring circuit are functioning properly.

Internal-External Fuel Switch. A toggle-type switch labeled INT-EXT is located on the instrument panel for checking external fuel load. The switch is spring loaded to the INT position. External fuel quantity will be indicated when the switch is held to the EXT position until the indicator needle stabilizes.

SINGLE-POINT FUELING AND DEFUELING SYSTEM

The pressure fueling system is designed to permit fueling at a rate of 200 gallons per minute through a single-point pressure fueling receptacle, located at the trailing edge of the wing just inside the aft engine compartment access door. The system may be defueled through the same receptacle at a rate of approximately 100 gallons a minute.

PRESSURE FUELING SWITCH PANEL

The pressure fueling switch panel is located on the right side of the aft engine access compartment just inside the access door. This panel has two switches: the check switch, and the drop tank fueling switch. The check switch has three positions, PRIMARY OFF, FUELING ON, and SECONDARY OFF and is used to test the operation of the dual float pressure fueling shutoff valves. The drop tank fueling switch has two positions, ON and OFF. The ON position of the drop tank fueling switch energizes the drop tanks solenoid pilot valves, permitting pressure fueling of the drop tanks.

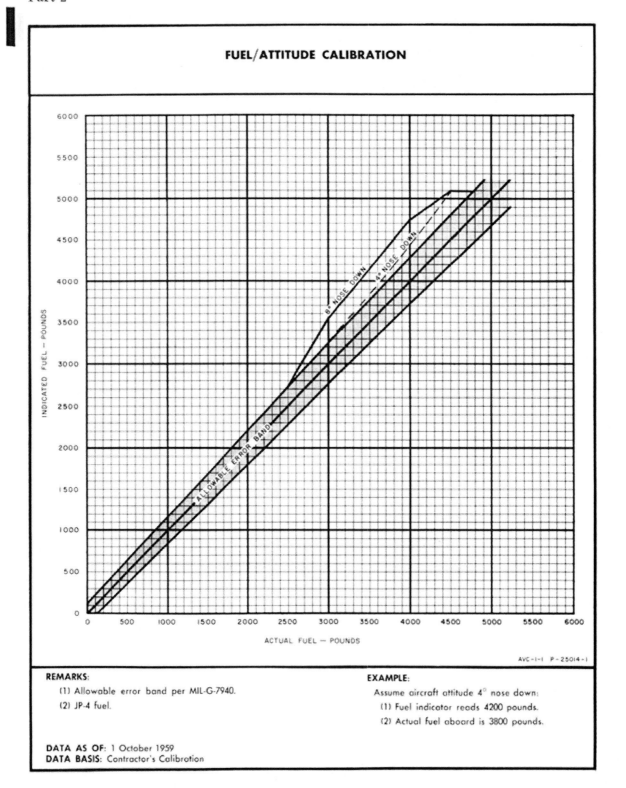

FUEL/ATTITUDE CALIBRATION

INDICATED FUEL – POUNDS

ACTUAL FUEL — POUNDS

AVC-1-1 P-25014-1

REMARKS:

(1) Allowable error band per MIL-G-7940.

(2) JP-4 fuel.

EXAMPLE:

Assume aircraft attitude 4° nose down:

(1) Fuel indicator reads 4200 pounds.

(2) Actual fuel aboard is 3800 pounds.

DATA AS OF: 1 October 1959
DATA BASIS: Contractor's Calibration

Figure 1-11. Fuel/Attitude Calibration Chart

PRESSURE FUELING

When the wing and fuselage tanks are being
fueled, fuel pressure opens the fueling shutoff valve in each tank, allowing fuel to enter
the tank and also to flow through the sensing
lines to the dual float pilot valve. When the
tank becomes full, the floats close the pilot
valve, causing pressure to increase behind
the diaphragm of the shutoff valve and close
it. Each shutoff valve consists of a primary
float, which is the pilot for the shutoff valve;
and a secondary float, which is a standby for
the shutoff valve. Moving the check switch
to either the PRIMARY OFF or SECONDARY
OFF position causes solenoids to raise the
respective float valve to simulate the normal
shutoff valve action at the maximum fuel
capacity level. This check can be made only
after the pressure fueling operation has
begun.

CAUTION

When external electrical power is
not available during pressure fueling of the airplane, the functional
tests of pressure fueling shutoff
components cannot be performed.
Therefore wing and fuselage tank
gravity filler caps must be removed
during fueling to prevent possible
damage to internal fuel tanks structure.

To fuel the drop tanks by means of the pressure fueling system, it is necessary to plug
in external electrical power. Placing the drop
tank fueling switch on the pressure fueling
switch panel at ON energizes the normally
closed solenoid pilot valve, permitting fuel
pressure to open the drop tanks shutoff valves
and, subsequently, flow to the drop tanks.
Under these conditions fuel also flows through
the sensing lines to the drop tanks solenoid
pilot valves. As each drop tank becomes full,
a float switch in the tank rises, breaking the
electrical circuit to the energized solenoid
pilot valve, causing the pilot valve to close
and pressure to build up behind the diaphragm
of the shutoff valve, which then also closes,
discontinuing the pressure fueling to that tank.

CAUTION

Unless the drop tank fueling switch
in the aft compartment is in the OFF
position after fueling the drop tanks
and prior to takeoff, fuel transfer
from the drop tanks will not be possible in the air. However, drop tank
fuel transfer may be accomplished
by extending the emergency generator.

Note

The drop tank shutoff valves allow
free flow of fuel from the drop
tank to the wing tank at any time.

When the air refueling store is installed instead of the center drop tank, it is fueled
through the pressure fueling receptacle on
the store.

PRESSURE DEFUELING

To defuel the integral wing tank requires no
procedure other than connecting the defueling
hose to the pressure fueling receptacle. To
defuel the fuselage tank it is necessary to
operate the manual override check valve between the wing and fuselage tanks. When the
defueling operation is begun, negative pressure in the pressure fueling shutoff valves
will open the valves and allow the fuel to be
removed. When either the fuselage or wing
tank becomes empty, the defueling low level
float valve opens, increasing the pressure
behind the diaphragm of the shutoff valve,
causing the valve to close. This prevents air
from entering the defueling line and breaking
the siphon when one tank empties ahead of the
other.

To defuel the drop tanks through the pressure
fueling system, it is necessary to connect a
source of air pressure to the capped tee in the
drop tanks pressurizing system, and first
transfer the drop tanks fuel into the integral
wing tank.

ELECTRICAL SYSTEM

Electrical power is normally supplied by a 10 kva engine-driven generator, which furnishes 115/200-volt, 3-phase 400-cycle, constant frequency a c power, and, through a transformer-rectifier, 28-volt dc power. No dc generator or battery is provided. An additional transformer modifies generator power to 26-volt a-c power for the operation of certain equipment. Eight busses serve to distribute power to the various electrical units. An airstream operated emergency generator provides electrical power to essential equipment in the event of main generator or engine failure. External power can be used to energize the system through an external power receptacle located in the lower forward plating of the left-hand wing root. Operation of the electrical system is completely automatic, with the exception of the emergency generator, which must be activated by the pilot upon failure of the main generator. (Refer to section V for emergency operation of the electrical system, and see figure 1-12 for schematic presentation of normal and emergency electrical power distribution.)

MAIN GENERATOR

The generator is driven at a steady state speed of 8000 rpm over the entire operating range of the engine from idle to maximum power by the constant speed drive unit. A test unit may be plugged into the receptacle on the fuse panel in the nosewheel well to ascertain that the generator is operating within prescribed limits. As a result of improved generator compartment cooling and the fact that the generator has no brushes, improved reliability in rain and icing conditions should be realized.

EXTERNAL POWER SWITCH

When the external power switch is in the EXTERNAL position, the aft monitored bus is disconnected from the main generator and is connected to the external power receptacle, so that power from an external source may be applied to the system. The external power receptacle door cannot be closed when the switch is in the EXTERNAL position.

EMERGENCY GENERATOR

The emergency generator, rated at 1.7 kilo-volt-amperes, is carried in a compartment in the lower right-hand side of the forward fuselage. When the generator is released into the airstream, a variable pitch propeller governs the speed of the generator at approximately 12,000 rpm to provide 400-cycle power to the primary and monitored primary bus.

EMERGENCY GENERATOR BYPASS SWITCH

An emergency generator bypass switch labeled NORMAL-BYPASS is located on the right-hand console (see figure 1-8). If the emergency generator is extended, placing this switch in BYPASS allows the pilot to return to main generator operation providing main generator power has been regained.

EMERGENCY GENERATOR RELEASE HANDLE

The emergency generator release T-handle (28, figure 1-5) on the extreme right side of the cockpit, above the right console, provides control of the emergency electrical system in the event of main generator failure. When the handle is pulled, the emergency generator drops into the airstream, the main generator becomes disconnected from the electrical system, and the primary and monitored primary bus are connected to the emergency generator. The emergency generator bypass switch must be in the NORMAL position.

Note

Electrical power will be provided by the emergency generator only if the emergency generator bypass switch is in NORMAL.

Once the emergency generator is extended, there is no way to retract it to the normal stowed position while in flight.

Changed 15 March 1965

A-C POWER DISTRIBUTION

NORMAL A-C POWER

Power from the main generator is sampled by a voltage regulator. The voltage regulator maintains a constant voltage output from the main generator by varying the current in the generator exciter field. The voltage-regulated power moves through the INTERNAL position of the external power switch.

EMERGENCY A-C POWER

Extending the emergency generator into the airstream breaks the main generator exciter field circuit, rendering the main generator inoperative, and transfers the primary bus and monitored primary bus from the aft monitored bus to the emergency generator. (See figure 1-12.) If the horizontal stabilizer manual override is actuated while operating on emergency generator the monitored primary bus will be lost as all emergency generator power is diverted to the primary bus. Upon release of the manual override, the output of the emergency generator is again directed to the monitored primary bus.

D-C POWER DISTRIBUTION

The primary bus supplied 115/200-volt, 3-phase, 400-cycle ac power to a single transformer-rectifier, which converts the ac power to 28-volt dc power.

ARMAMENT BUS

The armament bus receives dc power provided that the master armament switch is ON and the landing gear handle is UP. An armament safety switch, actuated by the DOWN position of the landing gear handle, deenergizes the armament bus as a safety feature to prevent inadvertent firing of the guns or

release of stores when the aircraft is on the ground or in the landing pattern with the wheels down.

ARMAMENT SAFETY DISABLING SWITCH

The armament safety disable switch is located on the outboard side of the right-hand wheel well for ground testing of the armament circuit. When the master armament switch is ON and the armament safety disable switch is momentarily depressed, an armament safety disabling relay is closed, allowing power to energize the armament bus. The relay is held closed until the master armament switch is turned off, or electrical power is disconnected from the airplane. When this occurs, the armament safety feature is automatically reinstated.

FUSE PANELS

All electrical circuits, with the exception of the all attitude indicating system, are protected by fuses in lieu of circuit breakers in order to save weight and provide better wire protection. The fuses are located on three panels, two in the nosewheel well, and the other in the forward engine compartment.

FIRE DETECTION SYSTEM

The fire detection system will indicate the existence of fire in the area surrounding the engine, tailpipe, and accessories section. If fire occurs in these locations, a push-to-test type FIRE warning light (21, figure 1-5) on the glareshield will glow. The fire detection system may be checked by depressing the press-to-test button (figure 1-7). When the button is depressed, the FIRE warning light will glow, indicating a properly functioning circuit. This system discriminates against short circuits and prevents illumination of the fire warning light by either the fire detection control unit or press-to-test button when a short exists.

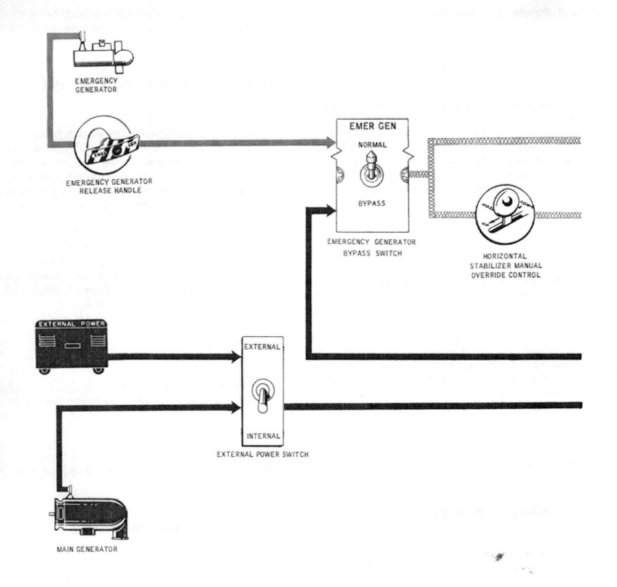

■■■	MAIN GENERATOR OR EXTERNAL POWER
▓▓▓	MAIN OR EMERGENCY GENERATOR POWER
■■■	EMERGENCY GENERATOR POWER
＼＼＼	28-VOLT-DC-POWER
ｌｌｌ	26-VOLT-AC-POWER

(1) INOPERATIVE ON EMERGENCY GENERATOR BECAUSE TRIM ACTUATOR POWER IS FROM AFT MONITORED BUS.

(2) INOPERATIVE ON EMERGENCY GENERATOR WHEN LANDING GEAR IS DOWN.

NOTE: ITEMS LISTED IN RED ALSO AVAILABLE ON EMERGENCY GENERATOR.

AVC-1-1 P-25015-1C

Figure 1-12. Electrical System (Sheet 1)

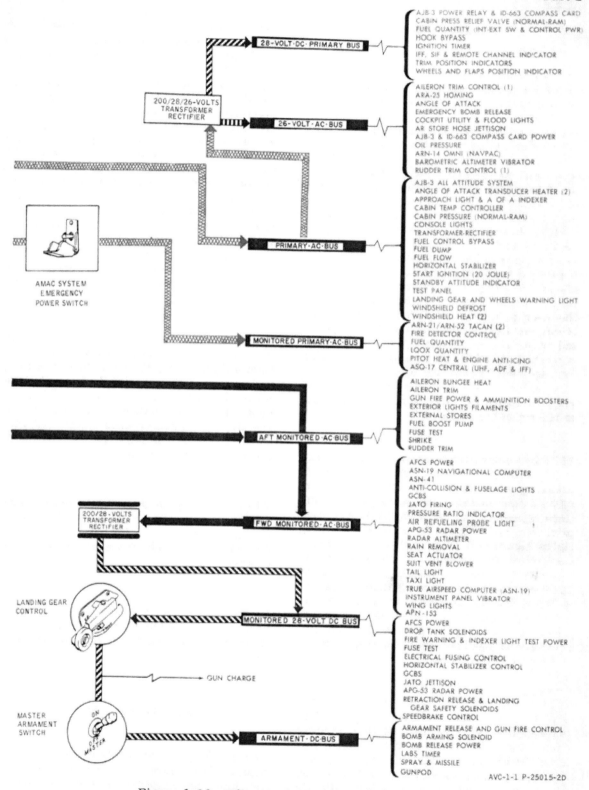

28-VOLT-DC-PRIMARY BUS
- AJB-3 POWER RELAY & ID-663 COMPASS CARD
- CABIN PRESS RELIEF VALVE (NORMAL-RAM)
- FUEL QUANTITY (INT-EXT SW & CONTROL PWR)
- HOOK BYPASS
- IGNITION TIMER
- IFF, SIF & REMOTE CHANNEL IND'CATOR
- TRIM POSITION INDICATORS
- WHEELS AND FLAPS POSITION INDICATOR

200/28/26-VOLTS TRANSFORMER RECTIFIER

26-VOLT-AC-BUS
- AILERON TRIM CONTROL (1)
- ARA-25 HOMING
- ANGLE OF ATTACK
- EMERGENCY BOMB RELEASE
- COCKPIT UTILITY & FLOOD LIGHTS
- AR STORE HOSE JETTISON
- AJB-3 & ID-663 COMPASS CARD POWER
- OIL PRESSURE
- ARN-14 OMNI (NAVPAC)
- BAROMETRIC ALTIMETER VIBRATOR
- RUDDER TRIM CONTROL (1)

PRIMARY-AC-BUS
- AJB-3 ALL ATTITUDE SYSTEM
- ANGLE OF ATTACK TRANSDUCER HEATER (2)
- APPROACH LIGHT & A OF A INDEXER
- CABIN TEMP CONTROLLER
- CABIN PRESSURE (NORMAL-RAM)
- CONSOLE LIGHTS
- TRANSFORMER-RECTIFIER
- FUEL CONTROL BYPASS
- FUEL DUMP
- FUEL FLOW
- HORIZONTAL STABILIZER
- START IGNITION (20 JOULE)
- STANDBY ATTITUDE INDICATOR
- TEST PANEL
- LANDING GEAR AND WHEELS WARNING LIGHT
- WINDSHIELD DEFROST
- WINDSHIELD HEAT (2)

AMAC SYSTEM EMERGENCY POWER SWITCH

MONITORED PRIMARY-AC-BUS
- ARN-21/ARN-52 TACAN (2)
- FIRE DETECTOR CONTROL
- FUEL QUANTITY
- LOOX QUANTITY
- PITOT HEAT & ENGINE ANTI-ICING
- ASQ-17 CENTRAL (UHF, ADF & IFF)

AFT MONITORED-AC-BUS
- AILERON BUNGEE HEAT
- AILERON TRIM
- GUN FIRE POWER & AMMUNITION BOOSTERS
- EXTERIOR LIGHTS FILAMENTS
- EXTERNAL STORES
- FUEL BOOST PUMP
- FUSE TEST
- SHRIKE
- RUDDER TRIM

200/28-VOLTS TRANSFORMER RECTIFIER

FWD MONITORED-AC-BUS
- AFCS POWER
- ASN-19 NAVIGATIONAL COMPUTER
- ASN-41
- ANTI-COLLISION & FUSELAGE LIGHTS
- GCBS
- JATO FIRING
- PRESSURE RATIO INDICATOR
- AIR REFUELING PROBE LIGHT
- APG-53 RADAR POWER
- RADAR ALTIMETER
- RAIN REMOVAL
- SEAT ACTUATOR
- SUIT VENT BLOWER
- TAIL LIGHT
- TAXI LIGHT
- TRUE AIRSPEED COMPUTER (ASN-19)
- INSTRUMENT PANEL VIBRATOR
- WING LIGHTS
- APN-153

LANDING GEAR CONTROL

MONITORED 28-VOLT DC BUS
- AFCS POWER
- DROP TANK SOLENOIDS
- FIRE WARNING & INDEXER LIGHT TEST POWER
- FUSE TEST
- ELECTRICAL FUSING CONTROL
- HORIZONTAL STABILIZER CONTROL
- GCBS
- JATO JETTISON
- APG-53 RADAR POWER
- RETRACTION RELEASE & LANDING GEAR SAFETY SOLENOIDS
- SPEEDBRAKE CONTROL

GUN CHARGE

MASTER ARMAMENT SWITCH

ARMAMENT-DC-BUS
- ARMAMENT RELEASE AND GUN FIRE CONTROL
- BOMB ARMING SOLENOID
- BOMB RELEASE POWER
- LABS TIMER
- SPRAY & MISSILE
- GUNPOD

AVC-1-1 P-25015-2D

Figure 1-12. Electrical System (Sheet 2)

HYDRAULIC SYSTEMS

The hydraulic systems consist of the utility hydraulic system and the flight control hydraulic system utilizing two self-pressurizing fluid reservoirs and two identical engine-driven variable displacement pumps. Both reservoirs are located in the upper right-hand side of the fuselage over the center of the wing, with the flight control system reservoir aft of the utility system reservoir. Capacity of the utility system reservoir is 1.25 gallons of hydraulic fluid, that of the flight control system, 0.30 gallon. Each system operates normally under a pressure of 3000 psi, and relief valves in each system open at 3650 psi to prevent damage to the lines and equipment, should the pump displacement compensator fail. Tandem power cylinders are used in the aileron, elevator and rudder power controls; one-half of each cylinder being operated by flight control system pressure, and the other half by utility system pressure. This arrangement allows the ailerons, elevator and rudder to be power-operated at reduced hinge moments by either system in the event of failure of the other.

The flight control system powers only its half of the aileron, elevator and rudder tandem actuating cylinders. The utility hydraulic system also operates the landing gear, wing flaps, speedbrakes, arresting hook, and auto-pilot servos. Hydraulic pressure warning lights (figure 1-7) are provided in the cockpit for each of the two systems. Pressure gages for both systems are installed in the right-hand wheelwell. There is no auxiliary pump, so no hydraulic pressure is available for ground operation unless the engine is running. Whenever the engine is running, normal pressure is supplied to both the flight control and the utility systems.

Both of the engine driven hydraulic pumps are of the constant pressure, variable displacement type. The flow of fluid through each system will vary in rate (gallons per minute) with the operating speed of the associated pump. As rate of fluid flow determines the speed at which the various hydraulically operated units respond to actuation of their individual controls, variation in rate of flow with power changes during normal operation might ordinarily produce objectionable characteristics in operation of the hydraulic systems. Therefore, flow restrictors have been installed in the subsystems to regulate the maximum rate of flow. The flow restrictors prevent the wing flaps, speedbrakes, and arresting hook from operating too fast when fluid flow is at its peak, yet do not affect the time of operation when flow is reduced at low engine speeds. As long as the engine is turning at IDLE rpm or greater, the hydraulically operated units will operate against the usual loads. However, at engine windmilling speeds, fluid flow is greatly reduced, and the time required for hydraulically operated units to respond fully is increased. (See figure 1-13 for a schematic diagram of the hydraulic systems.)

Either the utility hydraulic system warning light or the control hydraulic system warning light (ladder lights) will indicate loss of pressure to one or the other of the hydraulic systems. No stiffening of the control stick, except near full surface deflection at high speeds, will be encountered except with complete failure of both the flight control and the utility hydraulic systems.

When operating on the utility system alone, actuations of various units normally operated by utility pressure will cause a temporary decrease in the effectiveness of the flight controls.

No means are available for the pilot to correct hydraulic system failure. For action to be taken in the event of failure, refer to Section V.

FLIGHT CONTROL SYSTEM

The primary flight controls systems are tandem full power hydraulic systems with artificial feel supplied by bungee springs in parallel with the controls. Motion of the stick

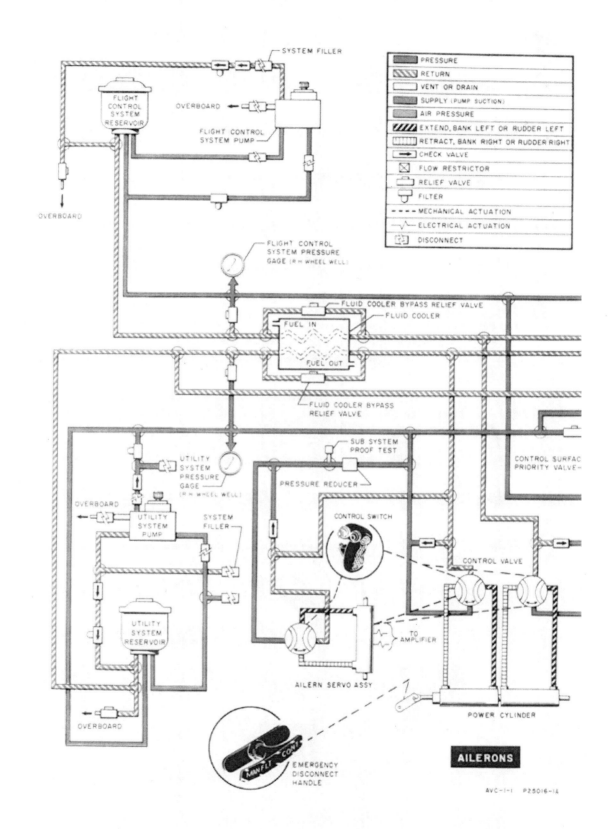

AILERONS

AVC-1-1   P25016-1A

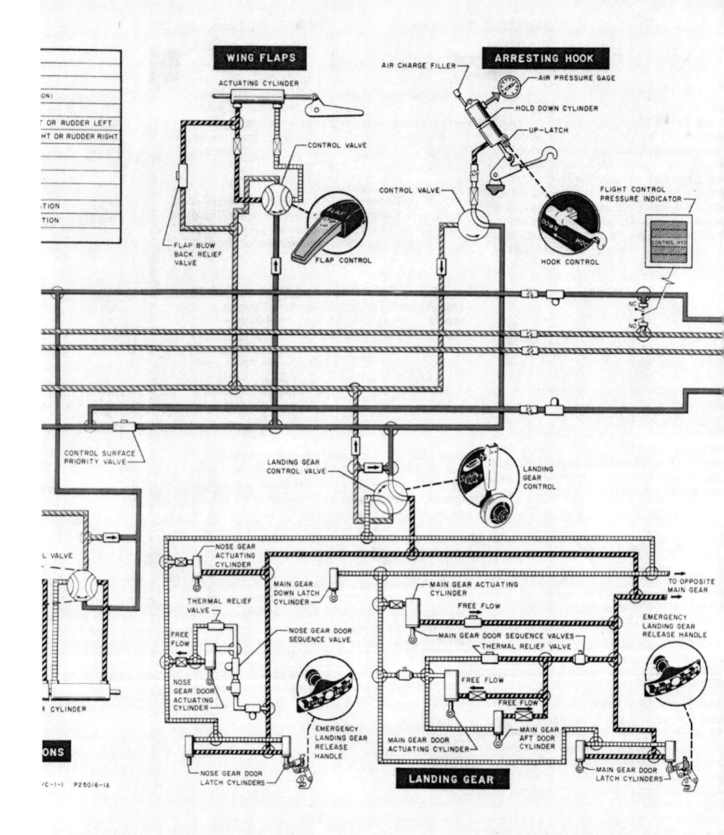

WING FLAPS

ACTUATING CYLINDER

CONTROL VALVE

FLAP BLOW BACK RELIEF VALVE

FLAP CONTROL

ARRESTING HOOK

AIR CHARGE FILLER

AIR PRESSURE GAGE

HOLD DOWN CYLINDER

UP-LATCH

CONTROL VALVE

HOOK CONTROL

FLIGHT CONTROL PRESSURE INDICATOR

CONTROL HY

T OR RUDDER LEFT
HT OR RUDDER RIGHT

TION
TION

CONTROL SURFACE PRIORITY VALVE

LANDING GEAR CONTROL VALVE

LANDING GEAR CONTROL

L VALVE

NC

NO

R CYLINDER

ONS

7C-1-1   P25016-1A

NOSE GEAR ACTUATING CYLINDER

THERMAL RELIEF VALVE

FREE FLOW

NOSE GEAR DOOR ACTUATING CYLINDER

NOSE GEAR DOOR SEQUENCE VALVE

NOSE GEAR DOOR LATCH CYLINDERS

MAIN GEAR DOWN LATCH CYLINDER

EMERGENCY LANDING GEAR RELEASE HANDLE

MAIN GEAR ACTUATING CYLINDER

FREE FLOW

MAIN GEAR DOOR SEQUENCE VALVES

THERMAL RELIEF VALVE

FREE FLOW

FREE FLOW

MAIN GEAR DOOR ACTUATING CYLINDER

MAIN GEAR AFT DOOR CYLINDER

LANDING GEAR

TO OPPOSITE MAIN GEAR

EMERGENCY LANDING GEAR RELEASE HANDLE

MAIN GEAR DOOR LATCH CYLINDERS

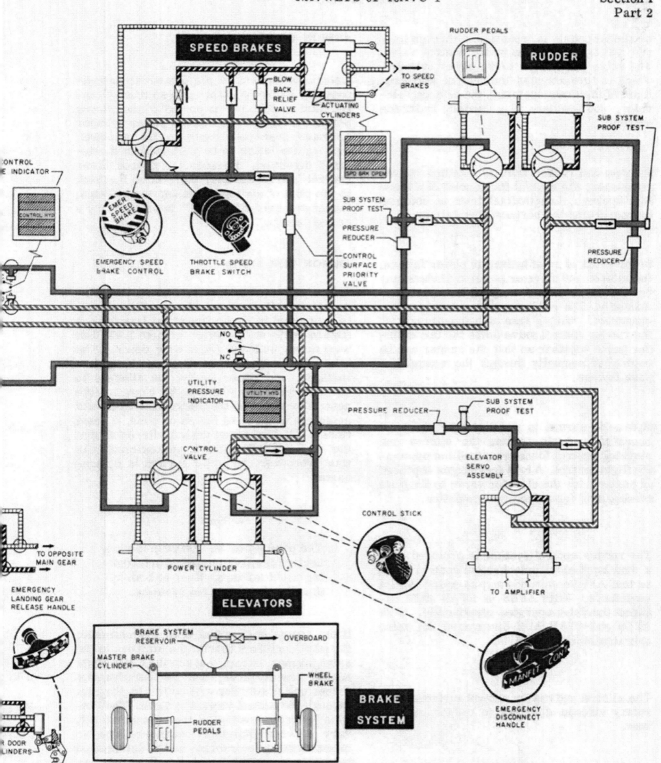

Figure 1-13. Hydraulic System

or rudder pedals is transmitted through linkage and cable systems to the control valve. The valve ports fluid to the power cylinder, which in turn actuates the control surfaces. Each of the three systems, the aileron, elevator, and rudder, is a tandem hydraulic system.

Aileron and rudder trim is obtained by repositioning the neutral force point of a load-feel bungee. Longitudinal trim is obtained by positioning the horizontal stabilizer.

In the event of total hydraulic power failure, the aileron and elevator power cylinders may be disconnected and control is maintained manually. The rudder system cannot be disconnected. With a loss of hydraulic power, the rudder control valve ports the two cylinder ports together so that the rudder can be controlled manually through the manual bypass linkage.

Hydraulic servos in parallel with the pilot operated controls provide the aileron and elevator control forces required for automatic flight control. A load feel bungee is placed in series with the elevator servo to limit its force output for structural protection.

The rudder control system is provided with a dual input electromechanical control valve so that AFCS commands may be added to pilot commands. With AFCS or STAB AUG engaged the valve operates electrically. With AFCS and STAB AUG disengaged the valve operates mechanically.

The aileron and rudder control surfaces have rotary viscous dampers to reduce surface buzz.

The rudder pedals are independently adjusted fore and aft by a lever located on the inboard side of each pedal.

AILERON CONTROL

Lateral movement of the control stick positions the aileron control valve so that hydraulic fluid at 3000 psi is ported to the aileron power cylinder. The aileron power cylinder operates push-pull tubes to the ailerons, causing the latter to be deflected in the desired direction. Because the aileron power control is irreversible, there is no feedback to the pilot of air loads against the ailerons; therefore, artificial "feel" is provided by a spring bungee.

AILERON TRIM SYSTEM

An electrically powered aileron trim actuator is controlled by movement of the trim switch (figure 1-29) on the stick grip to LWD (left wing down) or RWD (right wing down). The trim actuator moves the stick, power system linkages, and consequently, the ailerons to the desired trim position by changing the neutral position of the aileron load feel and centering bungee. At the same time, it positions a followup tab on the left aileron so that the airplane will remain approximately in trim whenever the power system is disconnected.

Note

The position of the followup tab has negligible effect on lateral trim during flight utilizing either or both hydraulic power control systems.

If the power system had been disconnected, the pilot continues to trim the ailerons in the same manner, except that now the tab is positioning the surfaces, and the aerodynamic forces on the ailerons will be felt by the pilot through the manual control system. The "in-trim" angular position of the aileron tab will vary between individual airplanes due to manufacturing tolerances, and is established by company test pilots prior to fleet delivery of each airplane. Theoretically this setting should not change during the service life of the airplane unless some change is made to its aerodynamic configuration. For safety of flight, it is mandatory that the "in-trim" position be reestablished after an aileron or wing change since this determines the range of action of the tab. Failure to do so may result in uncontrollable rolling tendencies when the power system is disconnected. (See Hydraulic Power Disconnect.)

The stick trim actuator is inoperative when the emergency generator is in use. No indicator is provided to show the trim position of the ailerons and tab, but the control stick is displaced from center to a new "neutral" position as the trim tab and ailerons are moved from their faired positions by the trim actuator.

ELEVATOR CONTROL

Fore and aft movement of the control stick moves a pushrod attached to the elevator control valve, which ports hydraulic pressure to the elevator power control cylinder. The cylinder then, through mechanical linkage, deflects the elevator surface as desired. The elevator power control is aerodynamically irreversible and pilots "feel" is induced by a spring bungee in the elevator control system. The forward and aft bob-weights also provide additional feel during vertical and longitudinal accelerations to prevent the pilot from over-stressing the empennage structure. The elevators are not equipped with trim tabs, as longitudinal trim is provided by a movable horizontal stabilizer. A bungee is installed in the elevator control system to provide longitudinal load feel. The bungee is linked to the horizontal stabilizer so that the elevator deflects upward (stick moves aft) while trimming noseup and deflect downward while trimming nosedown. The elevator moves approximately 8 degrees as the stabilizer travels from full-throw up to full-throw down. When elevator hydraulic power is lost, the elevator-stabilizer linkage is ineffective. The elevators are interconnected with the operation of the speedbrakes to assist the pilot in overcoming trim changes resulting from speedbrake operation. A system of cables and springs attached to the left speedbrake

actuates the control cables between the stick and the elevator control valve. When speedbrakes are opened, this system pulls the nose-down elevator cable, moving the stick forward and actuating the elevator to reduce a noseup pitch. When the speedbrakes are closed, the stick moves aft to its original trimmed position, thus reducing nosedown pitch.

HORIZONTAL STABILIZER TRIM SYSTEM

The entire surface of the horizontal stabilizer is moved by an electrically operated actuator to provide longitudinal trim. The actuator is controlled by forward and aft movement of the trim switch (figure 1-29) to NOSE DOWN or NOSE UP. Stabilizer travel is from 12 1/4 ± 1/4 degrees noseup to 1 degree nosedown. The position of the horizontal stabilizer is shown on the trim position indicator.

Note

Actuation of the horizontal stabilizer may require a percentage of the electrical power supply large enough to cause a momentary drop in volume of the UHF radio, a disturbed radar presentation and autopilot functioning, and a momentary dimming of the exterior and interior lights.

MANUAL OVERRIDE LEVER

A horizontal stabilizer manual override lever (see figure 1-6), on the left console outboard of the throttle, will operate the horizontal stabilizer in the event the trim switch becomes inoperative. The positions of the manual override lever correspond to those of the trim switch, and as the switch is spring loaded to the center or OFF position, it must be moved to the full extent of its travel in either direction to operate the horizontal stabilizer. When the emergency generator is operating, the manual override lever is the only means of actuating the horizontal stabilizer.

Do not run the actuator against the stops during the preflight check. Use of the horizontal stabilizer manual override lever does not cut out the actuator motor when the horizontal stabilizer reaches full travel. Continued operation of the manual override lever in one direction when the stabilizer is at the limit of travel will burn out the actuator motor and will cause complete loss of stabilizer control.

HORIZONTAL TRIM DISCONNECT SWITCH

Some A-4E aircraft will have COMNAVAIRPAC Aircraft Bulletin 11-63 incorporated. This provides for a trim disconnect switch located on the port bulkhead/glareshield, which will interrupt all electrical power to the horizontal stabilizer trim motor.

RUDDER CONTROL

The aircraft is equipped with a rudder system operating at a reduced hydraulic pressure of 1150 psi. The rudder power control is operated by the flight control system and the utility system at the same reduced pressure. Movement of the rudder pedals mechanically positions the rudder electromechanical dual input servo valve. The valve ports hydraulic pressure to the rudder actuating cylinder as required. Since there is no feedback of air loads on the control surface of a hydraulic power system, a spring bungee is installed in the fin to center and restrain the control valve and rudder pedals, and to provide artificial "feel."

RUDDER TRIM SYSTEM

Directional trimming is accomplished by displacing the entire rudder surface as a result of repositioning the center or neutral point of the spring bungee through the action of an electrical motor controlled by the rudder trim switch (see figure 1-6) on the left-hand console. Positions of the trim switch are NOSE LEFT and NOSE RIGHT. Rudder trim position is shown on the trim position indicator. Trim is not available during emergency generator operation.

Note

Loss of rudder hydraulic power results in loss of rudder trim.

HYDRAULIC POWER DISCONNECT

A manual flight control T-handle (see figure 1-7) on the lower right side of the instrument panel may be used to disconnect the elevator and aileron power cylinders from the flight controls in the event of complete hydraulic systems failure. After disconnect, stick forces are high, particularly for lateral deflections. At airspeeds in excess of 300 KIAS, stick forces become extremely high.

Note

• The rudder has no hydraulic disconnect in the system.

• As long as (normal) electrical power is available, the aircraft can be trimmed. Therefore, in the event of an actual hydraulic system failure, when the manual flight control handle is pulled, if the aircraft starts to roll, it should be trimmed immediately.

The flight procedure for checking the aileron tab rigged setting is set forth in Section IV, Flight Test Procedures. Additional information is available in the A-4E Maintenance Instruction Manual.

TRIM POSITION INDICATORS

The positions of the rudder trim and the horizontal stabilizer are shown on the trim position indicators (figure 1-8) at the forward end of the right-hand console. The rudder trim position indicator is graduated in 1-degree units to the L (left) and R (right) of 0. Total travel of the rudder trim position indicator represents 7 degrees of rudder travel left and right of center. All even degree marks are numbered from 0 through 6.

The scale for horizontal stabilizer position is graduated in 1-degree units from DN (down) through UP. All even numbered degree marks are identified numerically.

LANDING GEAR SYSTEM

The tricycle landing gear is retracted and extended by utility hydraulic system pressure during normal operation. The main gear retracts up and forward and the wheels rotate to fit flush into the wheelwells in the wings. The nosegear also retracts up and forward. The nose strut telescopes to allow the nosewheel to fit into the nosewheel well. When retracted, the landing gear is held up by utility hydraulic pressure and in the case of hydraulic system failure, the gear rests on the landing gear doors which are held closed by mechanical latches. For emergency extension of the landing gear, the door latches are manually released by the pilot.

LANDING GEAR HANDLE

The landing gear control handle (figure 1-5) forward of the left cockpit rail controls the normal operation of the landing gear system. The landing gear control handle has two positions, UP and DOWN, and is mechanically linked to the landing gear control valve. A mechanical guard attached to the control handle locks the handle in the UP or DOWN position. Depressing the guard permits movement of the handle to the desired position.

A warning light in the wheel-shaped handle of the control glows when the handle is moved to either of its two positions. The light remains on until the wheels are locked in either the up or down position. The position of the wheels is shown on the wheels and flaps position indicator on the left console. A flasher-type wheels warning light (figure 1-5) is installed beneath the upper left side of the glareshield adjacent to the LABS light. With the wing flap handle at any position other than the UP detent and the landing gear up or unsafe, retarding the throttle below approximately 92 percent rpm causes the WHEELS warning light to flash informing the pilot of a possible unsafe condition.

To prevent movement of the landing gear handle to UP when the aircraft is on the ground, the landing gear handle is latched in the DOWN position. In normal operation, the retraction release switch located on the left main landing gear strut, is actuated when the aircraft becomes airborne and the landing gear struts extend, energizing the safety solenoid. The solenoid then unlatches the handle. When the emergency generator is extended, the retraction release safety solenoid is deenergized. If the safety solenoid should malfunction, or if it should become necessary to retract the landing gear during emergency generator operation or while on the ground, the serrated end of the latch on the landing gear control panel must be moved aft to unlatch the landing gear handle.

EMERGENCY LANDING GEAR SYSTEM

In the event of utility hydraulic system failure, the landing gear may be lowered manually by means of the emergency landing gear release T-handle (figure 1-5) on the extreme left side of the cockpit, above the left console. When the landing gear control is moved to DOWN and the emergency landing gear release handle is pulled, the landing gear doors are unlatched, allowing the landing gear to drop into the airstream. The landing gear extends and locks by a combination of gravity and ram air force.

CAUTION

If the landing gear handle is raised after the emergency landing gear release T-handle is pulled, damage will be sustained to the bulkhead brackets and the landing gear handle ratchet.

WING FLAPS

Split flaps are installed on the trailing edges of the wings. Hydraulically actuated by a single cylinder, the wing flaps are mechanically controlled by the wing flap handle (12, figure 1-6) on the left console, outboard of the throttle. The wing flaps may be extended 50 degrees by moving the flap handle to DOWN, or may be stopped at any intermediate position by placing the flap handle at STOP. When UP is selected, the flaps will retract fully. The position of the flaps is shown on the flaps position indicator. A relief valve in the wing flap system allows the flaps to blowback to prevent structural damage when air loads cause the hydraulic pressure within the actuating cylinder to exceed the pressure at which the relief valve opens (3650 psi). This automatic retraction will begin at approximately 230 knots IAS.

Note

The flaps will not return automatically to the extended position if the flap handle is in the STOP position.

WHEELS AND FLAPS POSITION INDICATORS

The position of the landing gear and wing flaps is presented on the wheels and flaps position indicators (see figure 1-6) located on the left console. When the wheels are down and locked, the image of a wheel appears in a small window provided for each wheel on the instrument. When the landing gear is up and locked, the word UP appears in each window. During the period when the landing gear is transient, or when the wheels are not locked in position, diagonally striped signals are shown in the windows. The position of the wing flaps is shown in units with respect to the wing. Each unit corresponds to one-quarter of the total amount of extension possible. Labeled positions are UP, 1/2, and DOWN.

SPEEDBRAKES

Two flush-mounted speedbrakes (figure 1-4), one on each side of the fuselage, provide deceleration during flight. Hydraulically operated, the speedbrakes are electrically controlled by the speedbrake switch (see figure 1-6) on the inboard side of the throttle grip. Movement of the switch to either OPEN or CLOSE actuates a solenoid valve which controls the flow of hydraulic pressure to the speedbrake actuating cylinders. The speedbrakes cannot be stopped at intermediate positions between fully opened and fully closed.

The SPD BRK OPEN warning light, located on caution panel (23, figure 1-7) illuminates whenever the speedbrakes are in any position other than fully closed. A blowback feature allows the speedbrakes to begin closing when the airload against them causes the hydraulic pressure in the actuating cylinders to exceed the pressure at which the blowback relief valve opens (3650 psi), thus preventing damage to the speedbrake system. The speedbrakes begin to blow back at an indicated airspeed of approximately 490 knots. The speedbrakes will not open fully above 440 knots IAS.

Three flush-mounted JATO hooks are attached to each speedbrake for mounting a JATO bottle when required for assisted takeoffs.

Changed 15 March 1965

Note

When JATO bottles are attached to the speedbrakes, an interlock in the speedbrake electrical circuit will prevent the speedbrakes from opening when the speedbrake switch is in OPEN position. Ascertain that the speedbrake switch is in the CLOSED position prior to takeoff to prevent inadvertent opening of the speedbrakes when the JATO bottles are jettisoned.

SPEEDBRAKE-ELEVATOR INTERCONNECT

Speedbrake-elevator interconnect springs minimize aircraft pitchup during speedbrake actuation by automatically providing nosedown elevator when the speedbrakes are opened.

EMERGENCY SPEEDBRAKE CONTROL

The airplane is equipped with an emergency speedbrake solenoid valve override control. The emergency speedbrake control (9, figure 1-6) is a push-pull knob located at the aft end of the left-hand console can be used to open or close the speedbrakes in the event of dc electrical failure, or failure of one of the speedbrake control valve solenoids. The emergency speedbrake control knob is held in a "neutral" position by the action of a spring bungee and must be pulled up or pushed down to open or close the speedbrakes, respectively.

In the event of electrical failure, the speedbrakes may be opened or closed by momentary operation of the emergency speedbrake control push-pull knob.

WING SLATS

Aerodynamically controlled slats are installed on the leading edges of the wings to improve airflow characteristics over the wing surfaces at high angles of attack, primarily during approach and landing. The wing slats will open and close independently and automatically as the aerodynamic loading on them dictates. Because so many variables — airspeed, gross weight, and applied load factor-affect the operation of the wing slats, no fixed

airspeeds can be established as the points at which the slats begin to open or close. In general, however, they begin to open at some airspeed below 200 knots, and are fully opened at stalling speed.

BARRICADE STRAP DETENTS

Three barricade strap detents (30, figure 1-4), are installed on each leading edge to insure proper barricade engagement. Two of the detents are spaced evenly on the wing slat; the third is on the leading edge of the wing, inboard of the slat.

VORTEX GENERATORS

To combat buffet and random wing drop at high altitude, vortex generators, which are small metal vanes set at various fixed angles relative to the normal airflow, are installed along the span of the slats and on the upper surface of the wing.

ARRESTING HOOK

An externally mounted arresting hook (33, figure 1-4) is installed on the lower aft fuselage. Retraction and extension of the hook are accomplished by a pneumatic-hydraulic holddown cylinder in the aft engine compartment. The holddown unit is essentially a reservoir which is divided into two chambers by a relief valve and orifice arrangement. The upper chamber is filled with hydraulic fluid to the full level and then charged with compressed air to 900 ± 50 psi with the hook retracted. The lower chamber contains the actuating piston which is attached to the arresting hook. Utility hydraulic system pressure is applied to the lower side of the piston to effect retraction of the arresting hook, which is then held in the retracted position by a mechanical latch. Compressed air pressure and the weight of the arresting hook cause extension when the latch is released. With the arresting hook extended, the relief valve and orifice provide snubbing action to keep the hook on the deck during arrested landings by restricting the flow of fluid between the lower and upper chambers of the holddown unit when external forces tend to bounce the hook toward the retracted position.

Changed 15 March 1965

ARRESTING HOOK CONTROL

An arresting hook handle (27, figure 1-5) on the right cockpit rail controls the operation of the arresting hook. When the handle is moved to DOWN, the arresting hook is manually unlatched, allowing pressure from the holddown unit and the force of gravity to extend the hook.

> **CAUTION**
>
> The arresting hook handle should be firmly placed into position, not flipped nor slammed.

A light in the hook handle will glow when the handle is moved to DOWN and will go out before the hook reaches the fully extended position. The UP position of the handle manually positions the arresting hook control valve so that utility hydraulic fluid at 3000 psi flows into lower part of the arresting hook holddown cylinder overriding the air pressure, and causing the hook to be retracted and latched against the lower surface of the fuselage. The arresting hook system employs a "fail-safe" feature which allows the hook to be extended in the event of cable system failure or hydraulic pressure failure.

When the utility hydraulic pressure is lost, compressed air pressure and the weight of the arresting hook will cause the hook to extend when the hook handle is moved to the down position. However, the pilot cannot retract the arresting hook without hydraulic pressure.

Should the arresting hook control cable part, the uplatch will be released allowing the hook to move to the down position.

WHEEL BRAKES

Single-disc, spot-type brakes are installed on the main wheels only. The brake system includes a separate hydraulic reservoir (figure 1-13) located in the nose section of the airplane. Two master brake cylinders, operated by toe pressure on the upper part of the rudder pedals, provide the pressure necessary for operation of the brakes.

Note

The wheelbrakes are a completely independent hydraulic system. Accordingly, the pilot should realize that he will have brakes even though he makes a field landing with complete hydraulic system failure.

COCKPIT ENCLOSURE

The cockpit enclosure consists of a fixed, three-piece windshield and a hinged "clamshell" canopy. The two windshield side panels are of molded plastic, and the center panel is constructed of alternating layers of glass and vinyl.

CANOPY

The cockpit canopy is hinged at the aft end and moves back and up when opened. When closed, the canopy is held in place on both sides of the canopy rail by latch hooks which engage fixed rollers on the cockpit rails. An air bungee cylinder (figure 1-35), mounted aft of the ejection seat, counterbalances the canopy during normal operation and provides snubbing action. The canopy is closed by grasping the ledge on either side and by pulling down, overriding the air bungee cylinder pressure. The canopy may then be closed and locked by moving the canopy lever forward. Confirmation of the canopy being closed and latched can best be made by insuring that the canopy handle snaps forward when the mechanism is in the overcenter position and by checking latch for proper hook engagement.

CANOPY CONTROLS

CANOPY LEVER

The canopy lever (10, figure 1-6) on the left console, is mechanically linked to the canopy mechanism. Moving the lever forward slides the canopy forward, causing the latch hooks to engage the latch rollers. Moving the lever aft slides the canopy aft, disengaging the latch hooks and allowing air bungee pressure to open the canopy. The canopy mechanism includes an overcenter device, which causes a noticeable increase in lever load as the lever approaches the locked position. This load drops off abruptly as the lever is moved past the overcenter position to the locked position. If the lever load does not drop off as the handle is moved overcenter, canopy rigging should be checked.

EXTERNAL CANOPY RELEASE HANDLE

An external canopy release handle (figure 5-9), which can be reached from the ground, is set flush in the left side of the fuselage below the cockpit. Pulling the external canopy release handle out and forward unlatches the canopy, allowing it to open in the normal manner. To be closed and locked from the outside, the canopy must be manually held down and the external handle moved aft and in until it is flush with the fuselage.

INTERIOR CANOPY JETTISONING

CANOPY-JETTISON HANDLE

The canopy may be jettisoned by pulling the canopy-jettison T-handle (figure 1-5) on the right side above the console. On aircraft incorporating A-4/AFC 310, the canopy-jettison handle is a circular-shaped handle. At airspeed of 125 knots or above, the canopy will shear when it is opened by the normal canopy opening lever. However, use of the canopy-jettison handle to jettison the canopy is recommended. When the canopy-jettison handle is pulled, the canopy slides slightly aft to unlatch, swings open, and shears at the hinges. To fire the initiator, the canopy-jettison handle must be pulled with a force of 20 to 35 pounds. The handle will extend 3/4 of an inch and then fall free after the initiator has fired.

WARNING

When canopy is jettisoned in flight by any means, rapid rearward movement of manual canopy lever occurs as wind raises and shears canopy. To avoid possible injury, ensure that hand and arm are clear of this area during canopy-jettison.

CANOPY JETTISON SAFETY PINS

To prevent the cockpit enclosure air bungee from being inadvertently fired while on the ground, safety pins are provided for the canopy jettison initiators and are connected by a red streamer stenciled REMOVE BEFORE FLIGHT.

EXTERIOR CANOPY JETTISONING

An emergency canopy-jettison handle (figure 5-9) is provided on each side of the fuselage, just forward of the wing root, for jettisoning the canopy during rescue. The control is a red handle, marked PULL CANOPY JETTISON, and is installed in a recess behind a spring-loaded door. The door is pointed out by a RESCUE arrow. When the door is pushed in, the handle extends and may be grasped and pulled to fire the air bungee cylinder. The canopy will jettison regardless of position.

WARNING

Seat catapult is armed during removal of canopy by this means.

Note

To jettison, canopy must be closed on airplanes not incorporating ASC 204 (nitrogen bottle).

UNDERWATER CANOPY-JETTISON RELIEF VALVE

The aircraft has an underwater canopy-jettison relief valve which will allow water to flow into the cockpit after a ditching. The pilot can recognize the installation of the relief valve by a circular insert in the outer skin on the left side of the fuselage, alongside the ejection seat, just under the canopy rail and by a circular pad of upholstery above the left console.

The underwater canopy-jettison relief valve is a door, normally sealed and held in place by a torsion rod, and designed to open when the outside water pressure head is approximately 2 psi. The flow of water into the cockpit reduces the effective pressure head on the canopy. The use of the canopy-jettison handle is recommended to obtain the power of the bungee. The use of the manual canopy lever should be considered an alternative, last resort method of underwater canopy opening.

EJECTION SEAT SYSTEM

The aircraft is equipped with a rocket catapult seat which utilizes rocket thrust to propel the seat from the aircraft. The seat provides ground level escape capability during takeoff and landing emergencies at 90 KIAS and above. It also provides safe escape throughout the remainder of the flight envelope of the aircraft except for very unusual flight conditions such as inverted flight or steep angles of bank or dives at low altitudes (see figure 5-5). The seat accommodates a back-type parachute, a modified PK-2 pararaft kit and seat pan, and is designed for use with an integrated torso harness. A nonadjustable headrest is part of the seat structure and houses the face curtain. The front surface of the seat bucket serves as a buffer for the calves of the legs, and the sides of the bucket extend above the pilot's thighs to protect the legs and minimize flailing during high speed ejection. The ejection sequence is started by pulling the face curtain with both hands over the helmet in front of the pilot's face. The sequence may also be started by pulling the secondary ejection handle. Partial travel of the face curtain jettisons the canopy and removes the canopy interlock.

This allows the face curtain further travel, firing the catapult which ejects the seat. As the seat travels up the guide rails, the bailout oxygen bottle is actuated. The seat also contacts a striker plate which trips the harness-release actuator sear and causes the harness-release actuator to fire. After a 1.0 second delay, the harness-release actuator automatically frees the seat belts and shoulder harness, releases the face curtain, and inflates the separation bladders which separate the pilot from the seat. The delayed action of the harness-release actuator provides protection for the pilot, retaining him in the seat during the period of ejection. The parachute is equipped with an automatic barometric parachute actuator which incorporates a 2-second delay feature (MK 5 MOD 0 cartridge) to prevent premature opening of the parachute. Premature opening of the parachute could cause damage to the parachute from high velocity windblast and severe opening shock to the pilot. During the delay period, the pilot and seat will decelerate to a speed where the stresses placed upon the pilot and parachute are reduced from the critical stage. As the pilot descends below 10,000 feet or if ejection occurs below 10,000 feet, the parachute is opened automatically at the end of the delay period.

FUNCTIONAL COMPONENTS

HARNESS-RELEASE ACTUATOR

The harness-release actuator is essentially a cylinder containing a piston, a slow burning MK 86 MOD 0 cartridge, and a firing mechanism. The firing mechanism is spring loaded and is held in a safe position by a sear in the firing pin assembly. The actuator piston rod is connected to a bellcrank attached to the seat structure. Thus, when the seat is ejected, the actuator arming pin sear is tripped by the striker plate allowing the firing mechanism to detonate the cartridge which, 1.0 second later, exerts enough force to actuate the piston. The piston extends and rotates the bellcrank causing the seat belts, shoulder harness, and face curtain (or secondary handle) to pull free, and puncture the nitrogen storage bottle releasing pressure to the separation bladders, thus separating pilot and seat.

Changed 15 May 1966

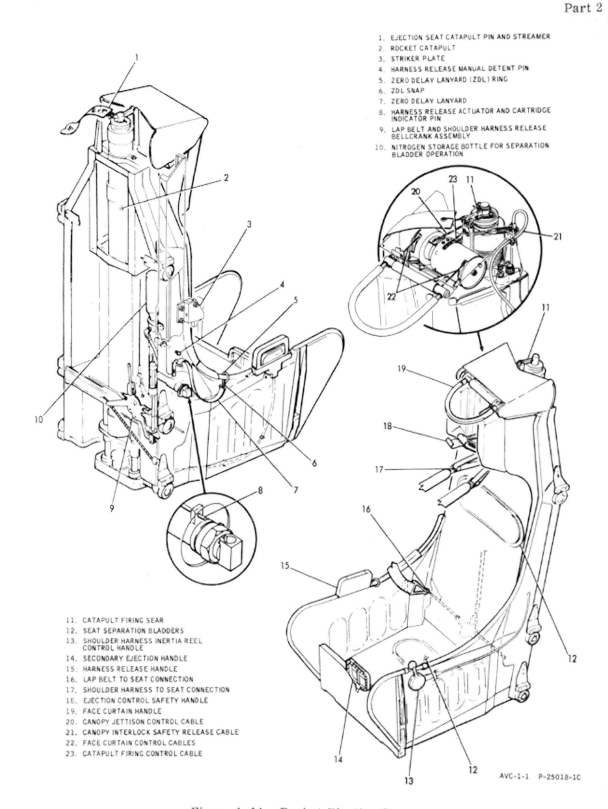

1. EJECTION SEAT CATAPULT PIN AND STREAMER
2. ROCKET CATAPULT
3. STRIKER PLATE
4. HARNESS RELEASE MANUAL DETENT PIN
5. ZERO DELAY LANYARD (ZDL) RING
6. ZDL SNAP
7. ZERO DELAY LANYARD
8. HARNESS RELEASE ACTUATOR AND CARTRIDGE INDICATOR PIN
9. LAP BELT AND SHOULDER HARNESS RELEASE BELLCRANK ASSEMBLY
10. NITROGEN STORAGE BOTTLE FOR SEPARATION BLADDER OPERATION

11. CATAPULT FIRING SEAR
12. SEAT SEPARATION BLADDERS
13. SHOULDER HARNESS INERTIA REEL CONTROL HANDLE
14. SECONDARY EJECTION HANDLE
15. HARNESS RELEASE HANDLE
16. LAP BELT TO SEAT CONNECTION
17. SHOULDER HARNESS TO SEAT CONNECTION
18. EJECTION CONTROL SAFETY HANDLE
19. FACE CURTAIN HANDLE
20. CANOPY JETTISON CONTROL CABLE
21. CANOPY INTERLOCK SAFETY RELEASE CABLE
22. FACE CURTAIN CONTROL CABLES
23. CATAPULT FIRING CONTROL CABLE

AVC-1-1   P-25018-1C

Figure 1-14.   Rocket Ejection Seat

AUTOMATIC BAROMETRIC PARACHUTE ACTUATOR

Parachutes used with the integrated torso harness are equipped with a barometrically controlled parachute actuator. The actuator is designed to deploy the parachute automatically at a predetermined altitude, in the event of pilot incapacitation. The actuator provides a 2-second delay before opening the parachute after reaching the preset altitude. When ejection is made below, at, or slightly above, the altitude for which the actuator is set, the delay allows the pilot to decelerate prior to parachute opening, thus reducing or eliminating pilot injury or parachute damage from opening shock. The delay also prevents the parachute from fouling on the seat when ejection is made at altitudes below that for which the actuator is set, where deployment would occur immediately upon separation from the seat. The automatic parachute actuator interferes in no way with the manual parachute release ripcord grip (D-ring) which may be pulled at any time to open the parachute.

An arming pin is inserted through the actuator mechanism to prevent inadvertent release of the parachute during normal operation when the aircraft descends through the altitude for which the actuator is set. The arming pin is anchored by the automatic parachute actuator arming lanyard (see figure 1-15) to the harness-release handle. For aircraft equipped with the zero-delay-lanyard (ZDL), the arming pin is pulled and the actuator armed as the seat moves up the guide rails. If the automatic harness-release mechanism fails to operate and the harness-release handle is used to free the pilot from the seat, the parachute will deploy automatically since the actuator was armed by the zero-delay-lanyard. On aircraft not equipped with ZDL, the arming pin is automatically pulled and the actuator armed when the pilot separates from the seat after ejection.

WARNING

If the automatic harness-release fails to operate, on aircraft not equipped with ZDL, and the harness-release handle is used to free the pilot from the seat, the arming pin will not be extracted and the parachute must be opened manually.

Other features of the rocket catapult ejection seat include a load limiting energy absorbing device to reduce the possibility of back injuries from survivable crashes or hard arrested landings. A secondary ejection control handle (to be used when adverse conditions prevent the pilot from reaching the face curtain) is located on the seat bucket between the pilot's legs. An ejection control safety handle, located in the center of the headrest, locks the ejection mechanism in a safe condition during ground operation. A dual strap inertia reel allows for mobility while seated. A cartridge indicator is incorporated in the harness release actuator allowing the pilot to visually check for cartridge installation.

SEAT ATTACHMENTS

The pilot is held in the seat by attachments to the integrated torso harness (see figure 1-15.) This torso harness incorporates within its structure a seat belt, shoulder straps and a parachute harness, thus leaving the pilot with few of the usual encumbrances. The shoulder harness straps are sewn to the parachute risers and attach to the inertia reel connection just below the headrest. The loose ends of the parachute risers have quick-disconnect fittings which engage other fittings that extend from the front shoulders of the torso harness. Short seat belts, which are sewn to the parachute harness on each side, and attached to the seat structure at the after corners of the seat bucket, are adjustable in length. The loose ends of the seat belts have quick-action fittings which engage fittings protruding from the hip region of the torso harness.

SEAT CONTROLS

SEAT SWITCH. The seat is electrically adjusted in the vertical plane by movement of the 3-position seat switch located on the miscellaneous switches panel (see figure 1-8) to either UP or DOWN, and is stopped at the desired position by releasing the switch to the center, or off position.

SHOULDER HARNESS INERTIA REEL CONTROL. The shoulder harness inertia reel control handle (see figure 1-14), on the left side of the seat bucket, locks the inertia reel drum to prevent playout of the webbing from the inertia reel. When the control is in the LOCKED position, the shoulder will not extend

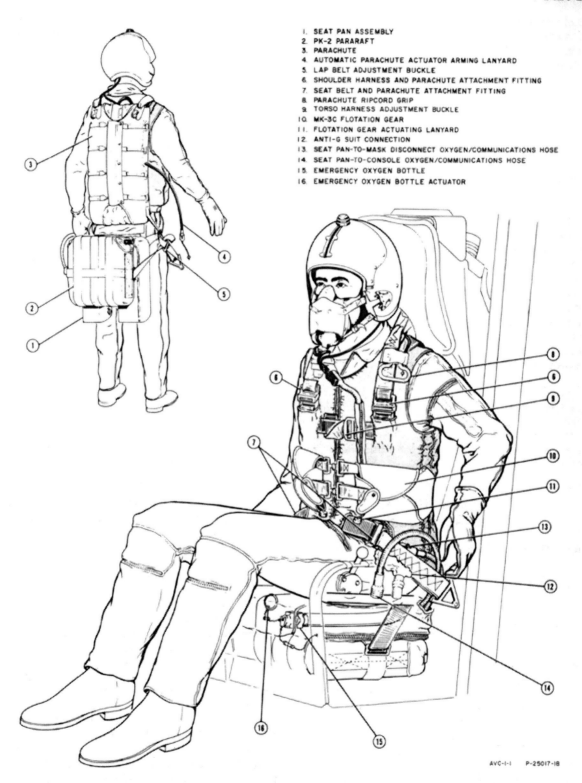

1. SEAT PAN ASSEMBLY
2. PK-2 PARARAFT
3. PARACHUTE
4. AUTOMATIC PARACHUTE ACTUATOR ARMING LANYARD
5. LAP BELT ADJUSTMENT BUCKLE
6. SHOULDER HARNESS AND PARACHUTE ATTACHMENT FITTING
7. SEAT BELT AND PARACHUTE ATTACHMENT FITTING
8. PARACHUTE RIPCORD GRIP
9. TORSO HARNESS ADJUSTMENT BUCKLE
10. MK-3C FLOTATION GEAR
11. FLOTATION GEAR ACTUATING LANYARD
12. ANTI-G SUIT CONNECTION
13. SEAT PAN-TO-MASK DISCONNECT OXYGEN/COMMUNICATIONS HOSE
14. SEAT PAN-TO-CONSOLE OXYGEN/COMMUNICATIONS HOSE
15. EMERGENCY OXYGEN BOTTLE
16. EMERGENCY OXYGEN BOTTLE ACTUATOR

AVC-1-1   P-25017-18

Figure 1-15.   Integrated Torso Harness

and the pilot's freedom of movement is restricted. The UNLOCKED position allows the shoulder harness to extend or retract as the pilot moves about. The reel will lock automatically if the aircraft is subjected to a deceleration in excess of 2.5 ± 0.5g along the thrust line. This safety feature helps to prevent injuries if the shoulder harness is not locked prior to an arrested landing or a crash. If the inertia reel fails to unlock while any load is being applied to the cable, relax the load and recycle the handle.

HARNESS-RELEASE HANDLE. A D-handle (see figure 1-14), labeled HARNESS RELEASE is mounted on the right side of the seat. A pin protrudes from the aft end of the handle, which extends down through the edge of the ejection seat to anchor the arming lanyard of the barometric parachute opener. A spring-loaded latch, which is grasped in conjunction with the harness release handle, retains the handle in the proper position and must be squeezed before the latter can be pulled. When the handle is pulled up, the barometric parachute opener lanyard and the shoulder harness and seat belt attachments are released from the seat, allowing the pilot to leave the cockpit with the parachute and pararaft kit still attached to the integrated torso harness (see figure 1-15).

WARNING

- The harness release D-handle should not be pulled while the aircraft is airborne or until it comes to a complete stop after landing. Pulling the D-handle releases the shoulder harness and lapbelt end fittings, which cannot be reengaged in flight.

- Disconnect the barometric parachute opener arming lanyard from the harness release handle before removing the parachute from the seat. If this is not done, the arming pin will be pulled and the parachute will open.

FACE CURTAIN. The ejection seat face curtain handle (see figure 1-14) is automatically adjustable to maintain a suitable handle position relative to the pilot's helmet. It serves not only as a control for ejecting the seat, but also as a support for the pilot during ejection. The face curtain, which is housed in the headrest structure with the handle protruding, is mechanically connected to the canopy jettison system and the seat catapult firing mechanism. When the face curtain is pulled downward, the first portion of travel jettisons the canopy and the last portion causes the seat to be ejected. The seat will not eject until the canopy is clear of the ejection path.

WARNING

Canopy jettisoning by means of partial face curtain extension should not be attempted except during the ejection sequence since no positive stops are provided to prevent seat ejection after the canopy has jettisoned.

SECONDARY EJECTION HANDLE. The secondary ejection handle (see figure 1-14) provides an alternate means for initiation of ejection.

EJECTION SEQUENCE

1. The pilot initiates the ejection sequence by pulling the face curtain handle or secondary ejection handle.

2. The canopy jettisons.

3. The seat is accelerated initially by the launch stage of the MK 1 MOD 0 or MOD 1 rocket catapult to a velocity of 40 feet-per-second as it leaves the ejection guide rails. On aircraft equipped with the zero-delay-lanyard, the arming pin is pulled and the actuator armed as the seat moves up the guide rails. Then the rocket propellant is ignited, further accelerating the seat by a thrust forward and upward through the seat-pilot center of gravity, which provides an effective end velocity of approximately 103 feet-per-second, which gives a vertical height of 200 feet. The maximum design acceleration along the pilot's spine is a safe 12 g.

Changed 1 November 1965

4. After a 1.0 second delay, the harness-release actuator releases the pilot from the seat, disconnects the ejection handles and inflates the separation bladders.

5. Drag differential and the separation bladders separate the pilot from the seat, thereby arming the parachute opener on aircraft not equipped with zero-delay-lanyard.

6. After 2 -second delay, on aircraft not equipped with zero-delay-lanyard, the parachute pack opens if below the preset altitude. (With zero-delay-lanyard, parachute pack opens 2-seconds after ejection, if below preset altitude.)

7. The parachute deploys and fills, and a steady rate of descent is achieved from 160 to 100 feet above the flight path.

8. Pilot must remove ripcord grip D-ring and the end of the ripcord housing from the pocket assembly on the riser duration descent to ensure subsequent jettisoning of the parachute upon landing.

OXYGEN SYSTEM

Oxygen is supplied by a vacuum bottle liquid oxygen converter mounted in a vented compartment in the aft fuselage section. The converter filler valve is reached through an access door on the right side of the fuselage for servicing. The bottle contains 10 liters of liquid oxygen when serviced to capacity. Evaporation loss is constant when the system is not in use, and this loss is used to pressurize the system. By venting any excess pressure overboard through relief valves, pressure is maintained at 70 ± 5 psi. Venting pressure may increase to 100 ± 10 psi when the liquid oxygen system is not being used.

LIQUID OXYGEN QUANTITY INDICATOR

A liquid oxygen quantity indicator (see figure 1-7) is located on the left center of the instrument panel, and is graduated with markings of 10, 8, 6, 4, 2, and 0. The quantity indicator is electrically operated and has a small OFF window to show that the indicator is inaccurate when electrical power is lost. A red low level warning light on the indicator face illuminates when the quantity falls below

1 liter. Depressing the TEST button (see figure 1-7) tests the operation of the liquid oxygen quantity indicator causing the needle to move counterclockwise. The low level warning light will go on when the needle passes the 1 liter mark. When the TEST button is released, the needle should return to its previous position.

CONTROLS AND EQUIPMENT

A lift-type toggle switch installed at the rear of the left console on the anti-g and oxygen panel (see figure 1-6) places the oxygen system in operation when moved from OFF to ON.

When the oxygen switch is turned on, oxygen is delivered from the supply system at a pressure of 70 psi to the oxygen receptacle located on the oxygen and anti-g panel (see figure 1-6) on the left console. The pilot's supply tube is plugged into the receptacle to allow the oxygen to flow to the oxygen mask regulator, installed just below the pilot's face mask. The mask regulator reduces the 70 psi converter oxygen pressure and delivers 100 percent oxygen to the mask under a positive pressure of about 1-inch water pressure at all cabin altitudes below approximately 35,000 feet. At higher cabin altitudes the delivered pressure is automatically increased to allow the pilot adequate oxygen absorption.

> **WARNING**
>
> The Type A-13A face mask used with this oxygen system must be properly fitted to the pilot's face. Relatively small leaks around a mask are cumulative in effect and result in considerable oxygen loss over long periods of operation.

EMERGENCY OXYGEN SUPPLY

Emergency oxygen is contained in a cylindrical U-shaped bottle (see figure 1-15), installed in the seat pan. A pressure gage, which extends through the lower forward right-hand corner of the seat pan, should register 1800 psi when the bottle is filled. The duration of the emergency oxygen supply is approximately 4 to 20 minutes, dependent upon the altitude (the higher the altitude, the longer the duration) since the oxygen is delivered by the mask regulator only upon demand. Oxygen from the emergency oxygen bottle is supplied by the release of a valve in the pressure regulator at the forward left corner of the seat pan. Two keeper yokes on the valve shaft keep the valve in the closed position until emergency oxygen is required. One of these yokes is attached by a cable to the manual release (16, figure 1-15) (green ring) which is stowed in a pocket of the seat pan. The other is attached by a cable, through a quick-disconnect fitting, to the left console. Either cable will dislodge a yoke and actuate the emergency oxygen supply valve to provide oxygen from the bottle and shut off the regular supply. When the seat is ejected or the pilot leaves the airplane still attached to his survival gear, the cable attached to the airplane structure is pulled and emergency oxygen is supplied automatically. Manually pulling the green ring provides emergency oxygen at any time. The pressure reducer allows the oxygen to flow at a reduced pressure of 60 psi through the supply tube to the oxygen regulator for delivery to the face mask. A check valve in the segment of supply tube which plugs into the OXYGEN receptacle on the left console prevents loss of oxygen when the emergency oxygen bottle is actuated.

To ensure the automatic supply of emergency oxygen, during ejection or bailout:

1. Check pressure gage for adequate supply (1800 psi).

2. Be sure the automatic release cable is attached to the console quick-disconnect fitting.

3. Determine that release keeper yokes have not been unintentionally dislodged.

Note

With the mask-to-seat pan hoses connected and the console supply shut off or disconnected, there should be no oxygen flow.

OXYGEN DURATION

Figure 1-16 is a tabulation of hours remaining for various altitude oxygen quantity combinations for the liquid oxygen supply system. It will be noted that although 100 percent oxygen is used at all times, duration is greater at high altitudes. Due to the physical property of gases as affected by pressure, the volume of oxygen increases in direct proportion to the decrease in atmospheric pressure as altitude increases. Thus, while the volume of oxygen required by the pilot is approximately the same at any altitude, the oxygen delivered in reduced cockpit pressure is lower in density and less of the supply is required to satisfy the demand.

NORMAL OPERATION

BEFORE FLIGHT

Before each flight the oxygen system and mask shall be checked for proper operation.

LIQUID OXYGEN DURATION

10 LITER SYSTEM

HOURS REMAINING

CABIN PRESSURE ALTITUDE —FEET—	GAGE READING (LITERS)					
	10	8	6	4	2	1
40,000 UP ▶	60.6	48.5	36.4	24.2	12.0	4.8
35,000 ▶	37.0	29.6	22.2	14.8	7.4	3.6
30,000 ▶	27.2	21.8	16.4	10.8	5.4	2.8
25,000 ▶	20.4	16.4	12.4	8.2	4.0	2.0
20,000 ▶	16.0	12.8	9.6	6.4	3.2	1.6
15,000 ▶	12.8	10.2	7.6	5.2	2.6	1.2
10,000 ▶	10.0	8.0	6.0	4.0	2.0	1.0
5,000 ▶	8.4	6.6	5.0	3.2	1.6	0.8
SEA LEVEL ▶	7.0	5.6	4.2	2.8	1.4	0.6

P-25042-1

REMARKS:

(1) Based on 800 liters of gaseous oxygen per liter of liquid oxygen.

(2) Data assume the use of a properly fitted mask.

DATA AS OF: 1 February 1962
DATA BASIS: Specification MIL-I-19326(Aer)

Figure 1-16. Liquid Oxygen Duration

Connect the oxygen supply tube to the connector on the seat cushion with the mask turned away from the face. Turn the oxygen switch ON. Listen for free flow of oxygen. Don the mask. Inhalation should be almost effortless if the regulator is delivering oxygen at a slight positive pressure. Exhalation should also be possible but will require some effort in order to close the inhalation valve.

Note

If exhalation is difficult, there is inhalation valve leakage.

DURING FLIGHT

Oxygen quantity should be checked periodically during flight.

Note

- Separation of the oxygen hose coup-
lings will be immediately apparent
as oxygen flow and radio communication will cease.

- A transient odor which is not repeated should not be cause for alarm.

FLIGHT INSTRUMENTS

The airspeed indicator, rate-of-climb indicator, and altimeter are connected to the
pitot-static system. The turn and bank indicator is operated by engine compressor bleed
air pressure. The attitude gyro, standby attitude gyro, bearing-distance-heading indicator (BDHI), angle-of-attack-system, and
radar altimeter are electrically operated.
The 8-day clock and accelerometer are independent of other systems in operation.

AIRSPEED INDICATOR

A combination airspeed indicator and Mach
meter (24, figure 1-7) is mounted on the instrument panel. The airspeed portion of the
dial is fixed in position, and is calibrated from
80 to 650 knots. The Mach meter scale is a
rotating disc, marked from 0.50 to 2.9, turning beneath the airspeed dial. Only a portion
of the disc can be seen through a cutout in the
airspeed dial. Airspeed and corresponding
Mach number are indicated simultaneously by
a single needle pointer. On the Mach number
disc is a movable index which is used to set
a Mach reference by depressing and turning
a set knob on the lower left corner of the instrument case. On the edge of the airspeed
dial is an airspeed index pointer, which is adjustable through a range of 80 to 145 knots
merely by turning the set knob.

RATE-OF-CLIMB INDICATOR

A rate-of-climb indicator (20, figure 1-7) is
located on the pilot's instrument panel. The
indicator shows the rate of ascent or descent
of the aircraft and is so sensitive that it can
register a rate of gain or loss of altitude which
would be too small to cause a noticeable change
in the altimeter reading. The upper half of
the indicator face is graduated in 500 foot units
from 0 to 6000 feet with 100 foot scale divisions
from 0 to 1000 feet. The upper half of the instrument indicates rate of climb in thousands
of feet per minute. The lower half of the indicator face is identical to the upper half except
that it indicates rate of descent. The rate-of-
climb indicator is connected to the static pressure system of the aircraft and measures the
change in atmospheric pressure as the aircraft climbs or descends.

ALTIMETER

The pressure altimeter (21, figure 1-7) indicates the altitude of the airplane above sea
level to a height of 50,000 feet. The dial face
is marked in increments of 100 feet, each
complete revolution of the pointer indicating
change in altitude of 1000 feet. On the left of
the center of the instrument is a window containing two rotating counters: the inner
counter registers altitude in thousands of feet,
while the outer registers ten thousands of feet.
When the altimeter pointer makes twelve rev-
olutions, for instance, the outer counter will
indicate 1, and the inner counter will indicate 2, thus showing that the aircraft is at an
altitude of 12,000 feet above sea level. Whenever the airplane is below 10,000 feet, a yoke
flag appears in the outer counter. At the extreme right side of the altimeter face is the
barometric pressure window. The barometric
pressure dial seen through the window is
marked from 28.10 to 31.00 inches of mer-
cury, and used to correct for variations in
sea level barometric pressure by means of a
knob on the lower left corner of the instrument
case.

Changed 1 November 1965

RADAR ALTIMETER

The AN/APN-141 radar altimeter (12, figure 1-7) employs the pulse radar technique to furnish accurate instantaneous altitude information to the pilot from 0 to 5000 feet terrain clearance. Aircraft height is determined by measuring the elapsed transit time of a radar pulse, which is converted directly to altitude in feet and displayed on the cockpit indicator. The indicator dial face is marked in 10-foot increments up to 200 feet, 50-foot increments from 200 to 600 feet, 100-foot increments from 600 to 2000 feet, and 500-foot increments from 2000 to 5000 feet. A control knob on the front of the indicator controls power to the indicator and is used for setting the low-limit indexer. It also provides for preflight and inflight test of the equipment with a push-to-test type control knob feature. A low-limit warning light (figure 1-7), located on the instrument panel adjacent to the radar altimeter, comes on when the actual altitude goes below the preselected altitude. An OFF flag on the indicator face appears when signal strength becomes inadequate to provide reliable altitude information, when power to the system is lost, or when the system is turned OFF.

NOTE

- Leave the AN/APN-11 radar altimeter in the OFF position until power is applied to the aircraft and return equipment to OFF before power is removed. At altitudes above 5000 feet terrain clearance, the OFF flag will appear and the pointer will move behind the masked portion of the indicator dial. The pointer will resume normal operation when the aircraft descends below 5000 feet.

The radar altimeter operates normally during 50-degree angles of climb or dive and 30-degree angles of bank right or left. Beyond these points the indications on the radar altimeter become unreliable but will resume normal operation when the aircraft returns to normal flight.

AN/AJB-3 ALL-ATTITUDE INDICATOR

The aircraft is equipped with an all-attitude indicator located on the instrument panel (figure 1-7), which provides the pilot with a pictorial presentation of the aircraft pitch and roll attitude, plus heading information. Aircraft attitude reference signals are supplied to the indicator by electrical connection with the remotely mounted master reference platform. Pitch, roll, and heading is presented by the orientation of the all-attitude indicator sphere which provides the background for a miniature reference aircraft attached on the instrument face. The horizon is presented on the sphere as a white line dividing the top and bottom halves of the sphere. The upper half, symbolizing sky, is indicated by a light grey area

above the horizon line; the lower half, symbolizing earth, is indicated by a dull black area below the horizon line. The sphere is graduated every 5 degrees in azimuth around the horizon line and every 30 degrees around the rest of the sphere. The sphere is graduated every 10 degrees of climb and dive. The sphere is free to move a full 300 degrees in pitch, roll, or heading without obstruction. Bank angles can be read by reference to roll indices located around the periphery of the instrument lens.

A pitch trim adjusting knob sets the potentiometer, controlling the sphere setting to line up the horizon line on the sphere with the reference aircraft to accommodate different trim and loading conditions of the aircraft.

A maximum of 90 seconds may be required for gyro erection and amplifier warmup. Complete loss of electrical power to the gyro and/or indicator will cause the OFF flag to appear.

WARNING

- Indicator is not reliable for flight indications if OFF flag is visible.

- It is possible to receive erroneous indications on gyro indicator without OFF flag showing.

A combination g-programmer and g-indicator is mounted on the left-hand side of the face of the all-attitude indicator for use with the indicator in performing loft bombing maneuvers. (Refer to Section I, Part 2, ARMAMENT EQUIPMENT.)

During the left bombing maneuver, the horizontal director pointer will move towards the top of the indicator if the climb is not meeting the programmed g's; if pullup is too fast, the pointer will move towards the bottom of the indicator. The vertical director pointer will deflect left for right wing down and right for left wing down. If the vertical director pointer deflects to the left, the stick should be moved to the left for correction; if the pointer deflects to the right, the stick should be moved to the right for correction. During the left bombing maneuver, the aircraft should be flown to keep the director pointers centered.

AN/AJB-3A ALL-ATTITUDE INDICATOR

The all-attitude indicator for the AN/AJB-3A system is called the attitude director indicator, indicator-programmer (g-programmer), and turn-and-slip indicator. The new indicator is the main visual difference between the AN/AJB-3 and the AN/AJB-3A systems. The vertical and horizontal director pointers on the attitude director indicator replace the indicator-programmed used in pullup in the bombing maneuver on the AN/AJB-3 system. During the loft bombing maneuver, the horizontal director pointer will move towards the top of the indicator if the climb is not meeting the programmed g's; if pullup is too fast, the pointer will move towards the bottom of the indicator. The vertical director pointer will deflect left for right wing down and right for left wing down. If the vertical director pointer deflects to the left, the stick should be moved to the left for correction; if the pointer deflects to the right, the stick should be moved to the right for correction. During the loft bombing maneuver, the aircraft should be flown to keep the director pointers centered. A bank inclinometer and rate-of-turn pointer, under the sphere on the attitude director indicator, replace the turn-and-slip indicator. The rate-of-turn pointer is electrically driven and will operate on the emergency generator. A 1/2-needle width turn will result in a 4-minute, 360-degree turn. A 1-needle width turn will result in a standard rate 2-minute, 360-degree turn. A 2-needle width (full deflection) turn will result in a 1-minute, 360-degree turn. The sphere indications, for all-attitude indicating are essentially the same on the new attitude director indicator and the old all-attitude indicator. Several indicating flags and pointers are incorporated in the instrument that are not used by this system. All of the flags and indicators are biased out of sight at the end of the 60-second start period, and only the horizontal and vertical director pointers, used in bombing, are later brought into view. The OFF flag disappears at the end of the 60-second start period and should not reappear until the system is turned off. If the OFF flag does appear, it indicates a power failure in the system. The roll indices are on the top and bottom of the new indicator.

GYRO CUTOUT SWITCH

On aircraft incorporating A-4/AFC 258, a gyro cutout switch has been installed in the left-hand side of the forward engine compartment. In the normal position, maintenance and servicing requirements involving power application to the aircraft may be accomplished without energizing the AJB-3/AJB-3A. Gyro damage will be prevented by allowing uninterrupted rundown subsequent to flight and preventing unnecessary brief turnups.

BEARING DISTANCE HEADING INDICATOR (BDHI)

The BDHI (figure 1-7) displays magnetic heading by rotation of the compass card dial. Distance and relative/magnetic bearings, in relation to a ground or shipboard station, are also displayed by the instrument.

Magnetic heading information from the compass compensator adaptor is provided to the rotating compass card which indicates magnetic heading in degrees. A fixed index at the top of the indicator denotes the reference heading of the aircraft.

A central window in the indicator face shows a 3-digit display, indicating distance in nautical miles for TACAN operation. An OFF flag is displayed when distance information is not present.

Displayed on the face of the indicator are two pointers, needle 1 (a single-bar pointer for ARA-25 operation) and needle 2 (a double-bar pointer for OMNI or TACAN). Both pointers will indicate relative and magnetic bearing information if the compass card is in synchronization (sync).

The rate-of-turn pointer is electrically driven and will operate on the emergency generator.

NOTE

Needle 1 will always indicate relative bearing from the aircraft. However, if the compass card is out of sync, needle 2 will "follow" the compass card and indicate magnetic bearing only.

STANDBY ATTITUDE INDICATOR

A remote indicating standby attitude indicator (figure 1-7) provides an alternate system for the all-weather instrumentation of the aircraft in the event of malfunction or failure of

lights show all readings in a red glow, compatible with night flying accommodation. Dimming is provided automatically when the exterior lights are turned ON. Intensity is further adjustable by the indexer dimming control wheel. The press-to-test button located on the instrument panel checks the lighting integrity of the indexer by illuminating all three bulbs of the indexer when depressed.

ANGLE-OF-ATTACK INDICATOR

The indicator registers units of angle-of-attack to the relative airstream, from 0 to 30 on the face of the dial. (These increments are not absolute angles-of-attack but are arbitrary indicated units grouped around the optimum.) An OFF flag becomes visible when ac power is lost. The dial is adjustable by means of an Allen wrench receptacle at the lower left-hand corner of the indicator to set the optimum unit setting at the 3 o'clock position. All switching is referenced to the 3 o'clock position regardless of dial setting. If the angle-of-attack indication of 17 1/2 units does not produce the indicated airspeed for the configuration computed from figure 11-37, recheck the aircraft configuration. If the appropriate configuration is established, disregard the angle-of-attack indication and make the approach at the computed airspeed from figure 11-37.

The angle-of-attack system may be used for cruise control in the event of failure of the airspeed system. It should be recognized that angle-of-attack indications are normally inadequate to use as a prime cruise control system, since small variations in angle-of-attack result in relatively large changes in airspeed at optimum cruise conditions. Sample angle-of-attack readings for this condition are as follows:

CONDITION	ANGLE-OF-ATTACK COCKPIT INDICATOR UNITS
Maximum range climb	6.8

CONDITION	ANGLE-OF-ATTACK COCKPIT INDICATOR UNITS
Maximum range descent or maximum endurance at all altitudes	10.5
Cruise at 5000 feet	7.0
Cruise at 35,000 feet	8.5
250-knot descent with speedbrakes extended (15,000 ft)	6.8

The above data are based on an aircraft configured with two 300-gallon external tanks and a 2,000-pound store on the centerline station. For aircraft without external stores, these angle-of-attack indicator readings should be decreased one unit.

NOTE

When above speeds of 200 knots, an angle-of-attack error of 0.5 unit is equal to an airspeed error of 25 knots.

EXTERNAL APPROACH LIGHT

The external approach lights unit located in the leading edge of the left wing behind a transparent section has three separate lamps covered by red, amber, and green lenses. The corresponding angle-of-attack conditions are shown to the LSO, as green for angle-of-attack too high; as amber for angle-of-attack optimum (or approaching or departing optimum); and as red for angle-of-attack too low.

The external approach lights unit glows bright in the daytime and dims automatically at night when the master exterior lights switch is activated for night flying.

The indicator in the cockpit will be in operation during the entire flight to present angle-of-attack information. The transducer is

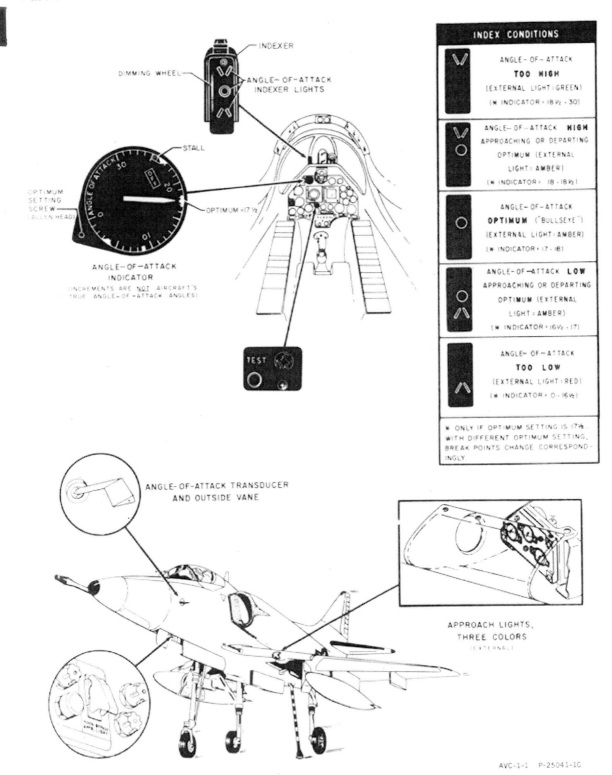

Figure 1-17.   Angle-of-Attack —Approach Light System

Changed 1 November 1965

also connected to the AN/APG-53A radar system. The indexer lights and the external approach lights, powered by the a-c primary bus, operate automatically when the landing gear is down and locked, the arresting hook is extended, and the airplane is in flight or up on jacks. All approach lights go out, upon landing, by means of a landing gear strut compress switch (squat switch). An approach light arresting hook bypass switch for field mirror landing practice with arresting hook retracted is provided.

APPROACH LIGHT ARRESTING HOOK BYPASS

A momentary contact toggle switch, labeled HOOK BYPASS, is located in the nosewheel well. This guarded switch is used to bypass the arresting hook circuit of the approach light system during field mirror landing practice. To provide approach lights during field landings without using the arresting hook, a ground crewman "flicks" the HOOK BYPASS switch to the BYPASS position. The approach lights stay on as long as the landing gear is down and the landing gear struts are not compressed enough to actuate the struts compress switch (squat switch). Normal operation of the approach light circuit is re-established by moving the arresting hook lever to the DOWN position, or interrupting electrical power to the approach light circuit.

WARNING

If "bounce drill" on the carrier is conducted using the approach light arresting hook bypass, extra precaution must be taken to insure that the arresting hook is extended before an arrested landing.

COMMUNICATIONS AND ASSOCIATED ELECTRONIC EQUIPMENT

GENERAL

All communications and associated electronic equipment is listed in the Table of Electronic

Equipment, figure 1-18. Major units of the AN/ARC-27A UHF radio, the AN/ARA-25 direction finder, and the AN/APX-6B IFF equipment are mounted in an integrated electronics central, which is designated AN/ASQ-17B and located in the nose section of the airplane, along with the AN/APA-89 coder group. Also installed in the nose section is the AN/ARN-21B or the AN/ARN-52(V)TACAN radio. Auxiliary navigation equipment, the AN/ARN-14E VOR radio and the AN/ARN-12 marker beacon receiver, can be carried as an external store in a navigation package (NAVPAC). The function selector switch of the AN/ARC-27A UHF radio is used as a master radio switch, and must be turned on to apply power to the AN/ARC-27A, AN/ARA-25, or AN/APX-6B. In addition, each piece of equipment must be turned on at the associated control panel with the exception of the AN/ARN-12 marker beacon receiver (when NAVPAC is installed), which is energized when the main generator is operating or external power is applied to the airplane.

Note

During extended ground operation (in excess of 30 minutes) cooling air for the AN/ASQ-17 electronics package must be provided by the air conditioning system. Consequently, the canopy must be closed and locked and pressurization switch must be in NORMAL.

UHF RADIO

The AN/ARC-27A UHF radio equipment provides two-way voice communications with other aircraft and with surface stations. The equipment can transmit or receive through the same antenna on any one of the 1750 channels within a frequency range of 225.0 through 399.9 megacycles.

UHF RADIO CONTROL PANEL

The C-3657/ARC-27A control panel (figure 1-8) is located on the right console. The

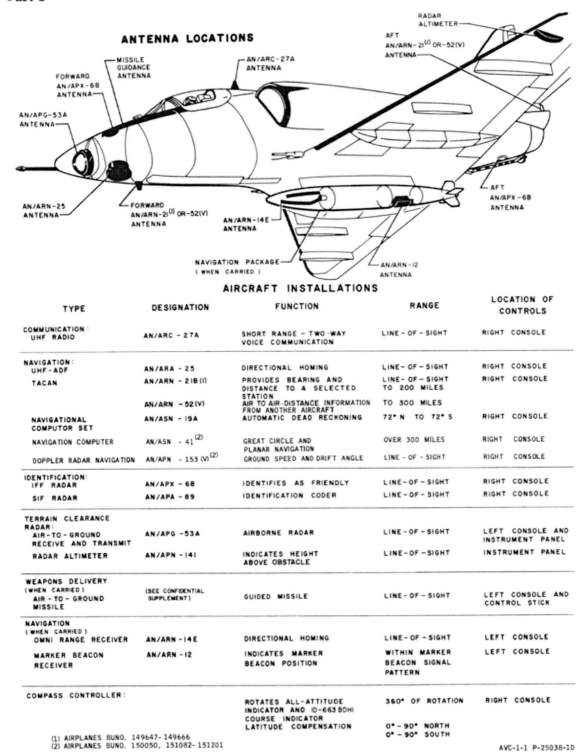

ANTENNA LOCATIONS

AIRCRAFT INSTALLATIONS

TYPE	DESIGNATION	FUNCTION	RANGE	LOCATION OF CONTROLS
COMMUNICATION: UHF RADIO	AN/ARC - 27A	SHORT RANGE - TWO-WAY VOICE COMMUNICATION	LINE - OF - SIGHT	RIGHT CONSOLE
NAVIGATION: UHF - ADF	AN/ARA - 25	DIRECTIONAL HOMING	LINE- OF - SIGHT	RIGHT CONSOLE
TACAN	AN/ARN - 21B (1)	PROVIDES BEARING AND DISTANCE TO A SELECTED STATION	LINE- OF - SIGHT TO 200 MILES	RIGHT CONSOLE
	AN/ARN - 52 (V)	AIR TO AIR-DISTANCE INFORMATION FROM ANOTHER AIRCRAFT	TO 300 MILES	
NAVIGATIONAL COMPUTOR SET	AN/ASN - 19A	AUTOMATIC DEAD RECKONING	72° N TO 72° S	RIGHT CONSOLE
NAVIGATION COMPUTER	AN/ASN - 41 (2)	GREAT CIRCLE AND PLANAR NAVIGATION	OVER 300 MILES	RIGHT CONSOLE
DOPPLER RADAR NAVIGATION	AN/APN - 153 (V) (2)	GROUND SPEED AND DRIFT ANGLE	LINE - OF - SIGHT	RIGHT CONSOLE
IDENTIFICATION: IFF RADAR	AN/APX - 68	IDENTIFIES AS FRIENDLY	LINE - OF - SIGHT	RIGHT CONSOLE
SIF RADAR	AN/APA - 89	IDENTIFICATION CODER	LINE - OF - SIGHT	RIGHT CONSOLE
TERRAIN CLEARANCE RADAR: AIR-TO - GROUND RECEIVE AND TRANSMIT	AN/APG - 53A	AIRBORNE RADAR	LINE - OF - SIGHT	LEFT CONSOLE AND INSTRUMENT PANEL
RADAR ALTIMETER	AN/APN - 141	INDICATES HEIGHT ABOVE OBSTACLE	LINE - OF - SIGHT	INSTRUMENT PANEL
WEAPONS DELIVERY (WHEN CARRIED) AIR - TO - GROUND MISSILE	(SEE CONFIDENTIAL SUPPLEMENT)	GUIDED MISSILE	LINE - OF - SIGHT	LEFT CONSOLE AND CONTROL STICK
NAVIGATION (WHEN CARRIED) OMNI RANGE RECEIVER	AN/ARN - 14E	DIRECTIONAL HOMING	LINE- OF - SIGHT	LEFT CONSOLE
MARKER BEACON RECEIVER	AN/ARN - 12	INDICATES MARKER BEACON POSITION	WITHIN MARKER BEACON SIGNAL PATTERN	LEFT CONSOLE
COMPASS CONTROLLER:		ROTATES ALL-ATTITUDE INDICATOR AND ID-663 BDHI COURSE INDICATOR LATITUDE COMPENSATION	360° OF ROTATION 0° - 90° NORTH 0° - 90° SOUTH	RIGHT CONSOLE

(1) AIRPLANES BUNO. 149647- 149666
(2) AIRPLANES BUNO. 150050, 151082- 151201

AVC-1-1 P-25038-1D

Figure 1-18. Table of Electronic Equipment

Changed 15 March 1965

panel contains a volume control, a vernier sensitivity control, function selector switch, channel selector switch, a manual tuning control and a channel PUSH TO SET CHAN button. The volume control regulates the volume of incoming signals, and the sensitivity control provides a vernier adjustment of the sensitivity. The channel selector switch has twenty channel positions, numbered 1 through 20, a G (guard) position, and an M (manual) position.

MANUAL TUNING CONTROL. The manual tuning control consists of three concentric dials. The outer dial is used to select the first two digits of the desired frequency, the center dial selects the third digit, and the inner dial selects the digit to the right of the decimal point. The channel selector switch must be placed at M before the selected frequency can be used.

FUNCTION SELECTOR SWITCH. The function selector switch is used to place the set in operation, and has four positions marked as follows:

Position	Function
OFF	Deenergized
T/R	Transmitter operable and receiver in operation.
T/R + G	Same as T/R plus reception on the guard.
ADF	Transmitter on standby and AN/ARA-25 direction finding equipment in operation through receiver.

SENSITIVITY CONTROL. To ensure peak reception of UHF signals, the sensitivity-control on the UHF control box should be set immediately below the point at which background noise occurs. This normally occurs with the SENS-knob index near the 1 o'clock position. If unable to create noise by a clockwise movement of this knob, or if unable to eliminate it by a counterclockwise movement,

the ASQ-17 sensitivity is not adjusted properly. The guard receiver has a separate sensitivity-control which eliminates background noise on the guard receiver. The pilot has no control of this setting.

PUSH TO SET CHAN BUTTON. The push to set chan button is provided to permit the pilot or ground crewman to change frequencies for the twenty channel positions. To accomplish this, increase the receiver sensitivity until there is noticeable background noise. Set the channel selector to the desired channel. Dial in the new frequency on the manual tuning control. Rotate the push to set chan button and depress it momentarily. Lift the press to set button to its original position and release. Upon completion of channeling, background noise should again be heard.

UHF REMOTE CHANNEL INDICATOR. A UHF remote channel indicator (19, figure 1-5) is located on the top right side of the glareshield for a quick visual check of the channel selected on the channel selector on the UHF control panel.

Note

The remote channel indicator is powered through the APX-6B rotary selector switch and that switch must be at some position other than OFF to energize the indicator.

OPERATION OF THE UHF RADIO

1. Function selector switch ... T/R + G

2. Channel selector switch. ... DESIRED CHANNEL

3. Throttle microphone switch .... DEPRESS

CAUTION

Allow 60-second warmup period before depressing microphone switch to transmit in order to prevent damage to the transmitter tube filaments.

RADAR IDENTIFICATION EQUIPMENT

The airplane radar identification equipment consists of the AN/APX-6B transponder (IFF) and the AN/APA-89 selective identification equipment (SIF).

AN/APX-6B TRANSPONDER (IFF)

The radar identification set AN/APX-6B is an airborne transponder which may be operated to provide a system of electronic identification and recognition. Its purpose is to identify the airplane in which it is installed as friendly when challenged by friendly radar, and to permit surface tracking control of the airplane. Functionally, the receiver portion of the AN/APX 6B equipment receives the challenges initiated by an interrogator - responder and applies a single pulse corresponding to each interrogation to the AN/APA-89 coder. In response to interrogations in MODES 1, 2, or 3, the AN/APA-89 coder provides coded pulse train replies, the coding of which can be selected for each of three modes, back to the AN/APX-6B. This pulse train is then transmitted by the transmitter portion of the AN/APX-6B to the interrogator-responder where proper replies, decoded or as raw video, are displayed along with the associated radar targets on the radar indicator. When a radar echo is accompanied by a proper IFF reply, that target is considered friendly.

IFF CONTROL PANEL C-1159 APX-6B

The IFF control panel (figure 1-8) is installed on the right console. The panel contains a rotary selector switch labeled MASTER with five designated positions; OFF, STBY, LOW, NORM and EMERGENCY. Two MODE switches are located adjacent to the MASTER switch to enable pilot selection of modes of response; either 1, 1 and 2, 1 and 3, or 1, 2, and 3 may be selected. A third toggle switch provides selection of I/P and MIC. The equipment is placed in operation when the AN/ARC-27A function selector switch is placed in an operating position and the IFF

Master switch is rotated out of the OFF position. The APX-6B can be operated from the main generator, external power or the emergency generator.

OPERATION OF THE APX-6B

The system is energized when the function selector knob (MASTER switch) on the IFF control panel is set to any position other than OFF. A red dial stop button below and to the left of the MASTER switch must be pressed before the switch can be rotated into the EMERGENCY position. This prevents inadvertent entry into the EMERGENCY position. Two lights on the panel provide illumination of the selector knob and the three toggle switches.

APX-6B FUNCTION SELECTOR. The functions of the selector knob are as follows:

Position	Function
OFF	Set is inoperative.
STDBY	Set is ready for operation but the transmitter receiver is not sensitized and replies cannot be transmitted.
LOW	Receiver sensitivity to interrogations is reduced. Transmitted response is the same as NORM.
NORM	Receiver is given full sensitivity and the transmitter operates with maximum power.
EMERGENCY	Mode I emergency replies are transmitted upon receipt of any IFF interrogation regardless of the mode of interrogation or the settings of the MODE toggle switches on the control panel.

Note

To enter the EMERGENCY position it is necessary to depress the red dial stop button.

I/P-OUT-MIC SWITCH. The I/P-OUT-MIC switch is a 3-position switch which allows identification of individual airplanes. This switch is functional only with the Mode 3 selector switch forward. The I/P position is momentary and, when actuated, initiates a two train coded Mode 3 response to any MODE 3 interrogations received for approximately 30 seconds. When the switch is placed in the MIC position, the 30 second period is commenced each time the UHF microphone button is depressed and the same two train coded Mode 3 response occurs as in the I/P position.

AN/APA-89 CODER (SIF)

The AN/APA-89 coder is used in conjunction with the AN/APX-6B transponder to supply multiple coded replies to the transmitter portion of the AN/APX-6B. By such means selective and individual identification of aircraft is possible, thus facilitating ground control and providing flexibility to the identification process. The AN/APA-89 coder accepts the decoded output of the AN/APX-6B transponder and generates coded information pulse trains, enabling the transponder to reply on SIF.

The AN/APA-89 has two supplementary functions. First, to provide two train coded modes replies automatically for I/P and MIC purposes; and, second, to provide four train coded Mode 1 emergency replies.

SIF CONTROL PANEL. The C-1272 APA-89 SIF control panel (figure 1-8) is installed on the right console aft of the IFF control panel. The panel contains two concentric dial type knobs identified as MODE 1 and MODE 3. Each knob has an inner and outer rotary dial. On MODE 1 the inner dial is numbered from one to three and the outer dial is numbered from one to seven. The MODE 3 selector knob has both the inner and outer dials numbered from one to seven. Positioning of these knobs provides the pilot with a selection of various codes in MODE 1 or MODE 3. Controls for the selection of codes in MODE 2 are located behind a door on the face of the

AN/APA-89 coder. They consist of a series of toggle switches that must be preset on the ground.

NAVIGATION EQUIPMENT

COMPASS CONTROLLER

Controls for the operation of the compass system are located on the compass controller (figure 1-8) on the right console. The switch marked SLAVED and FREE permits selection of either function. A push-to-set-heading knob is provided to rotate the ID-663 BDHI (bearing-distance-heading indicator) and the all-attitude indicator to any desired heading. This also may be used to synchronize the compass system with the magnetic flux valve. The rate of rotation is proportional to the amount of displacement of the set heading knob.

The PUSH TO SYNC button will do the synchronizing automatically. The compass synchronization needle is energized only when the system is operated as a slaved directional gyro. The synchronization indicator functions as a null indicator with heading information being obtained from either the BDHI or the all-attitude indicator.

If the average needle position is the center line of the synchronization indicator when the system is operated in the SLAVED mode, the compass card is synchronized with the magnetic flux valve. Any small deviation from the null position will be slaved out in a period of time from one to three minutes after the initial heading is set.

A compass card error of ±2 degrees will peg the needle. If the sync needle stays pegged after prolonged straight and level flight (more than 5 minutes), a possible malfunction of the system is indicated.

During flight, the sync needle will oscillate about the null position because of the motion of the flux valve. This oscillation is normal and indicates that correct integration of inputs from the flux valve is being accomplished (as long as the average position of the sync needle is the null position).

The directional gyro will integrate or smooth out these oscillations on the BDHI compass card. To synchronize the compass proceed as follows: if the sync needle is left of center, clockwise rotation of the set heading control should move the sync needle from left to right and rotate the compass card clockwise; if the sync needle is right of center, counterclockwise rotation of the set heading control should move the needle from right to left and rotate the compass card counterclockwise. For fast centering of the sync needle, push the PUSH TO SYNC button and hold it until the needle is centered. To move the sync needle slowly, depress and turn the set heading knob left or right until the desired slew rate is achieved.

The latitude setting dial is used to control the apparent drift of the gyro when operating as a free gyro. This dial is marked for each two degrees from 0 to 90. The dial should be set to the approximate latitude of the airplane. If the latitude changes as the flight progresses, the dial should be reset to the new latitude.

SLAVED OPERATION

When electrical power is initially applied to the system in the SLAVED mode, allow 100 seconds for warmup; then the auto sync cycle (approximately 12 seconds) will rotate the all attitude indicator and the BDHI compass card to the airplane's magnetic heading.

The heading indicator should show the correct magnetic heading when the synchronization needle stabilizes.

FREE GYRO OPERATION

To operate the system as a free gyro allow 90 seconds for the system to warm up, then:

1. Place the SLAVED-FREE switch to FREE.

2. Rotate the latitude setting dial to the latitude of the airplane.

3. Rotate the compass card of the BDHI to the desired heading by the use of the set heading knob.

Note

The compass synchronization needle nulls and is inoperative when the system is used as a free gyro.

TACAN BEARING-DISTANCE EQUIPMENT

The AN/ARN-21B or AN/ARN-52(V) TACAN airborne equipment operates in conjunction with surface navigation beacons to provide continuous directional and distance information to the pilot. Visual indication of magnetic bearing to a selected station is provided by the number 2 pointer of the ID-663-BDHI (19, figure 1-7), and distance information is indicated in the range window. Beacon identification tone signals are received through the regular headset.

TACAN CONTROL PANEL

The control panel (12, figure 1-8), is identified as TACAN and is located on the right-hand console. Operating controls include the power switch with OFF, REC, T/R, and A/A positions, two channel selector knobs, and a volume control. The REC and T/R positions give bearing information on the number 2 needle of the ID-663-BDHI. In the T/R position, distance information in the range window of the instrument is also given. When the AN/ARN-52(V) TACAN equipment is installed, the A/A position gives air-to-air distance information from another cooperative airplane.

Air-to-air (A/A) ranging requires cooperating aircraft to be within line of sight distance. This mode enables the TACAN installation to provide range indications between one aircraft and up to five others. TACAN displays normal range and azimuth information in the T/R mode and range information only in the A/A mode. (The azimuth indicator, No. 2 needle, rotates continuously.)

If A/A operation is desired between two aircraft, the channels selected must be separated by exactly 63 channels, i.e., number 1 aircraft is set to channel 64, number 2 aircraft is set at channel 1. Both aircraft must then select A/A on the TACAN function switch with the range between aircraft being displayed on the DME indicator. The maximum lock-on range is 198 miles. However, due to the relative motion of the aircraft, the initial lock-on range will usually be less.

If A/A operation is desired between one lead aircraft and five others, the channel selected by the lead aircraft may be 64, for example. The other five aircraft must be separated by exactly 63 channels, and would be on channel 1. The A/A mode must then be selected on the TACAN selector switch.

TACAN ANTENNA SWITCH

A 3-position TACAN antenna switch (see figure 1-8) is located on the right console adjacent to the emergency generator bypass switch for utilizing the forward or aft antenna. The switch is labeled AUTO, FWD, and AFT. The AUTO position provides automatic selection of the antenna which permits station lockon to be achieved.

TACAN TRANSFER RELAY

Because the ID-663-BDHI is common to both the AN/ARN-14 OMNI and the TACAN, a

switching means is provided for the selection of proper receiver-indicator combinations to meet specific navigational requirements. The TACAN transfer relay is energized by either the REC or T/R position of the power switch on the TACAN control panel, automatically disconnecting the OMNI and connecting the TACAN to the BDHI. Thus, if both radio sets are inadvertently turned on at the same time, the TACAN bearing is the one that will be presented on the BDHI number 2 needle.

OPERATION OF TACAN EQUIPMENT

To operate the TACAN radio, proceed as follows:

1. Power switch . . . . REC or T/R

NOTE

An automatic warmup period of about 90 seconds is provided after the power switch is moved from OFF.

2. Channel selector switch . . . . . . SET CHANNEL NUMBER.

3. Identify beacon by tone signals in headset and read magnetic bearing to station at the number 2 pointer of the BDHI.

4. For distance information, the power switch must be turned to T/R. Read slant range distance to the beacon in nautical miles in the range window.

AUTOMATIC DIRECTION FINDING EQUIPMENT

The AN/ARA-25 automatic direction finding equipment operates in conjunction with the

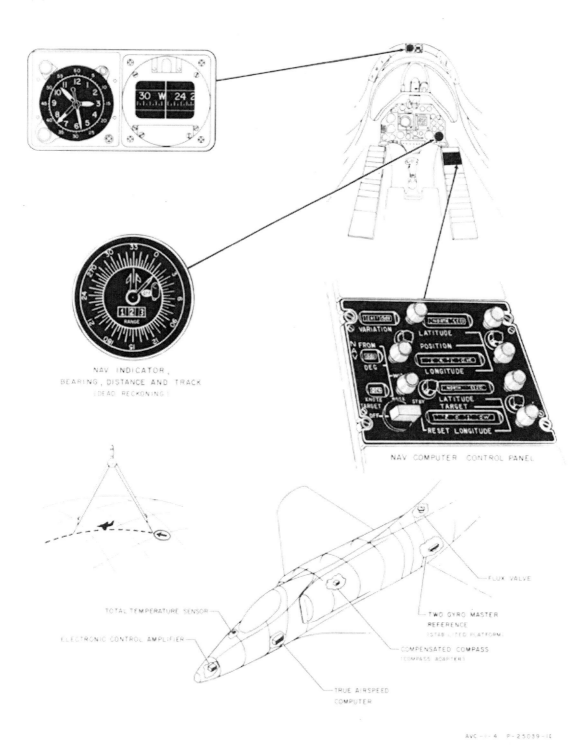

Figure 1-19. Navigational Computer Set

AN/ARC-27A UHF radio to provide a continuous directional indication of the source of signals received in the 225- to 400-megacycle band. Source indication in relative bearing for homing or navigational purposes is provided by needle 1 of the ID-633/U BDHI course indicator.

OPERATION OF THE AN/ARA-25

The AN/ARA-25 ADF equipment is energized when the aircraft electrical system is energized, and is placed in operation by moving the function selector switch on the UHF radio control panel to the ADF position.

NOTE

- When the UHF radio is left in the ADF position, transmission and reception are garbled.

- When the emergency generator is extended, ARN-52(V), APX-6B, ARA-25, ARC-27A, and the compass system are the only navigational aids available to the pilot. ARN-52(V) is inoperative when the landing gear is DOWN.

AN/ASN-19A NAVIGATIONAL COMPUTER SET

The AN/ASN-19A automatic dead reckoning set (figure 1-19) continuously computes and

- If the aircraft is to be abandoned and its equipment is likely to fall into the hands of an unfriendly nation, the function switch should be placed in the RESET position in order to erase base reference.

- The system will not operate on the emergency generator.

FLIGHTS GREATER THAN 1000 MILES

1. Set into the target counters an intermediate fix which lies on the desired flight path and which is less than 1000 miles from the starting position. The intermediate fix may be an arbitrary point along the flight path. If possible, however, employ a recognizable location in order to correct the present position readings if necessary.

2. When the intermediate fix is approached, set into the target counters another intermediate fix which is less than 1000 miles away.

3. When within 1000 miles of the target, set the target coordinates in on the target counters.

4. When returning from the target, use the same procedure as above except turn the selector switch to BASE when within 1000 miles of the base position.

Note

The use of intermediate fixes does not affect the accuracy of the dead reckoning set but is merely a convenient method for performing long range flights.

FLIGHTS USING DOGLEGS. The most convenient method of flying doglegs is as follows:

1. Set the target coordinates on the target counters.

2. Before the flight, determine the ground track angle and time required for each leg.

3. Fly each leg using the ground track angle presented by the dead reckoning set indicator and the predetermined time of flight. Since the dead reckoning set continuously computes present position, intermediate legs need not be flown accurately.

4. After entering the last leg, align the bearing pointer with the fiducial mark to obtain the correct path to the target.

If it is necessary for the legs to be flown accurately, set in the end point of each leg in turn into the target counters. This procedure will not result in any increase in accuracy over that obtainable from the first method unless the end points are recognizable locations and are used as check points.

AN/ASN-41 NAVIGATION COMPUTER SYSTEM

The AN/ASN-41 navigation system will supply to the pilot information on his position, windspeed and direction, distance to destination, bearing and ground track relative to true heading. It can store two target destinations without loss of primary data. The navigational system computes and provides outputs of great circle distance and bearing (relative to heading) to either of two selected targets. A great circle solution is employed for distances greater than 200 miles. A planar solution is employed for distances of less than 200 miles. Present position of the aircraft in latitude and longitude coordinates is continuously computed and displayed on the AN/ASN-41 control indicator (see figure 1-19A). The magnetic heading ground track bearing to the target and distance-to-go is displayed on the ID-663/U BDHI (bearing-distance-heading-indicator).

Three modes of operation are available for system operation: they are doppler, memory, and air mass mode.

Doppler mode: the system receives inputs of groundspeed, drift angle, true airspeed and magnetic heading to compute the groundspeed and airspeed vectors. The comparison

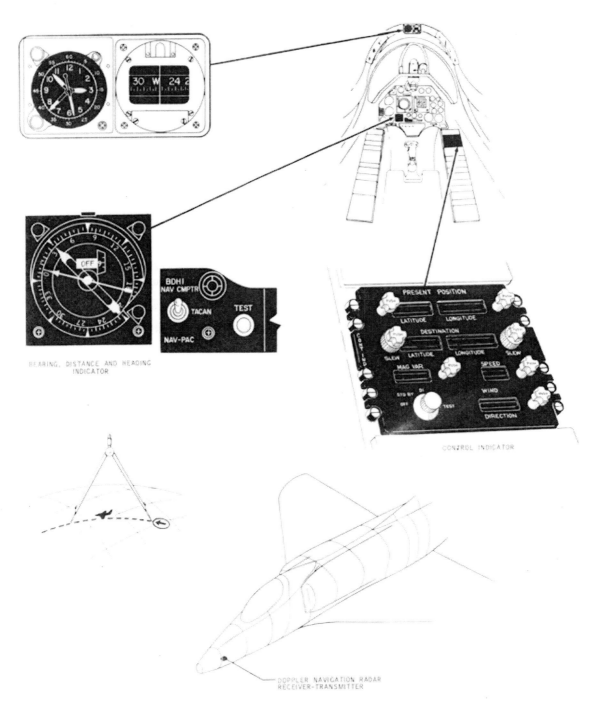

Figure 1-19A. AN/ASN-41 Navigation Computer System

Changed 15 November 1966

of groundspeed and airspeed vectors provides a continuous solution of wind direction and windspeed.

Memory mode: This mode, whenever there is a temporary loss of doppler information, will automatically actuate the wind memory portion of the AN/ASN-41 computer. The computer retains the last value of wind vector computed and combines the vector with the current airspeed vector to form a new groundspeed.

Air Mass Mode: When the doppler is completely inoperative, manually inserted wind settings are updated to combine with current airspeed to solve for groundspeed vector.

NAVIGATION COMPUTER SET CONTROLS

The controls indicator panel, on the right console, contains the controls and display windows to indicate:

1. PRESENT POSITION -- LATITUDE counter (in degrees and minutes) with a mechanical push-to-set knob.

2. PRESENT POSITION -- LONGITUDE counter (in degrees and minutes) with a mechanical push-to-set knob

3. DESTINATION -- LATITUDE counter (in degrees and minutes) with a mechanical and electrical set knob

4. DESTINATION -- LONGITUDE counter (in degrees and minutes) with a mechanical and electrical set knob

5. MAG VAR (magnetic variation) counter (in degrees) with a mechanical set knob

6. WIND SPEED counter (0 to 300 knots) with a mechanical set knob

7. WIND DIRECTION (in degrees) with a mechanical set knob.

8. The selector switch on the control indicator (CONT IND) panel, performs the following functions:

POSITION	FUNCTION
1. OFF	The navigation computer system is deenergized. The destination and present position counters can be manually set in preparation for a mission.
2. STBY	Power is applied to the set. Destination one (D1) is displayed on the counters and is also stored in the computer memory circuit.
3. D1 (Destination 1)	This position supplies course and distance information for integration of present position counters on the first leg of the mission. This information can be updated at any time using the push-to-set knobs.
4. D2 (Destination 2)	This position provides course and distance information for destination two (D2) on the second leg of the mission. Destination two (D2) can be updated by use of the push-to-set knobs.
5. TEST	This position inserts a presolved problem into the navigation computer whose solution is displayed by the control indicator counter and the ID-663/U (BDHI) bearing, distance heading indicator.

OPERATIONAL PROCEDURES

PRIOR TO FLIGHT

1. Rotate the ASN-41 selector switch to TEST.

2. BDHI switch to NAV CMPTR position.

WIND SPEED indicates 223.6 +1.5 knots.

WIND DIRECTION indicates 0.091 +1 degree.

LATITUDE PRESENT POSITION shows South integration.

BDHI shows smooth change in distance indication.

BDHI No. 2 pointer indicates 30-degrees right.

BDHI No. 1 pointer indication depends on present position and destination data set in.

3. Rotate function switch to STBY.

NOTE

In the STBY position, power is applied to all circuits except the present position integrator.

4. Rotate function switch to D2. Using the electrical slew knobs, set in latitude and longitude destination counters to a destination. If the destination is starting point, insert present position coordinates.

5. Rotate function switch to STBY and set in destination latitude and longitude counters to primary target coordinates using push-to-set knobs.

6. Set in latitude and longitude of present position on present position counters using push-to-set knobs.

7. Set in magnetic variation with push-to-set knob.

8. Set in wind direction and velocity.

9. Leave function switch in STBY.

NOTE

If the AN/APN-153 doppler radar is to be used with AN/ASN-41, step 8 need not be set in. This function will be automatically computed by the doppler.

10. Set function switch on doppler control to STBY. Allow approximately 5-minute warmup.

(a) Place function switch to test. If the system is operating properly, it will lock on to the left signal within 1 minute. The memory light will go off, the ground speed indicator will read 121 +5 knots, and the drift angle indicator will show 0 degree +2 degree.

NOTE

If above doppler test function is not acceptable, insert step 8 for AN/ASN-41 operation.

TAKEOFF

1. Leave function selector switch (AN/ASN-41) in STBY.

2. Set (AN/APN-153) function switch to either LAND or SEA position depending on the terrain over which the aircraft is flying.

3. When doppler operation locks on (memory light out), the computer switches to doppler mode and wind information is automatically computed.

4. When the aircraft is airborne and over the computed starting point, set function switch (AN/ASN-41) to D1 (see figure 1-19B). The present position counters start to integrate towards the primary target and the wind vector is computed and displayed.

5. To fly great circle route (shortest route) to target, adjust aircraft heading to align with pointer 1 on BDHI. Ground track (drift angle) is displayed by pointer 2. The distance counter on the BDHI indicates ground range to target or destination.

6. In order to precisely set preset position, upon completion of mission over target (D1), make a long enough turn to approach the entry point of the second leg with a minimum of 2 minutes of level flight and the two pointers on BDHI aligned. Make any changes necessary to make present position coordinates the same as the longitude and latitude of target 1. At crossover of the entry to second leg, rotate function switch to D2, keeping the pointers of BDHI aligned and fly to final target.

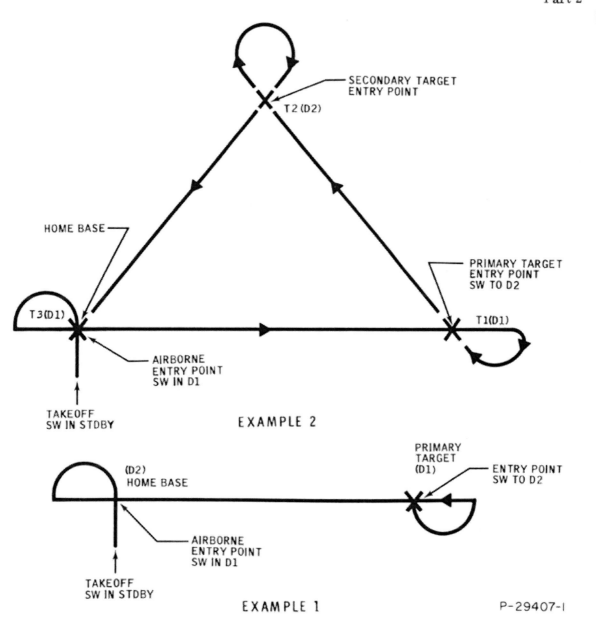

Figure 1-19B.   Example Course

Note

While the pilot is flying the pre-selected target (D1, destination two (D2) can be changed by selecting D2 with the function switch and inserting a new destination with the push-to-set knobs. Switching back to D1 enables the pilot to fly the initial leg of his mission. Upon completion of target on (D1) and while flying to the second target a third leg of the mission can be inserted in the (D1) position to complete the flight plan.

INFLIGHT

The pilot should monitor the navigation system and if necessary to update the following situations:

1. If the doppler radar is off for a considerable time, the wind data can be manually updated, using the predicted wind information from his flight plan.

2. If present position counters are incorrect while flying over a known check point, the counters can be updated.

NOTE

The destination counters will always display the coordinate of the destination as selected by the selector switch. Flexibility has been provided by permitting either destination to be changed at any time, or as often as required, for any specific mission.

3. Magnetic variation (MAG VAR) is to be updated as required throughout the flight.

AN/APN-153(V) RADAR NAVIGATION SET (DOPPLER)

The AN/APN-153(V) is a miniaturized radar navigation set that uses the doppler principle for continuous measurement of groundspeed and drift angle. The radar set transmits rf energy to the ground and measures the shift in frequency of the returned energy to determine aircraft groundspeed and through use of a special beam, drift angle. The AN/APN-153(V) doppler radar set is contained completely within the aircraft and does not depend on ground aids for navigation purposes. The radar set automatically acquires doppler information and computes groundspeed and drift angle within about 1 minute after it is turned ON. The AN/APN-153(V) doppler radar set operates in conjunction with the AN/ASN-41 computer to provide navigation to and from preselected targets.

SYSTEM OPERATION

The AN/APN-153(V) doppler radar navigation set, controls, and indicators are on the C-4418/APN-153(V) control indicator panel (figure 1-19C), labeled NAV and located on the pilot's right console. To operate the AN/APN-153(V) doppler radar set, the selector switch must be turned ON to either the LAND or SEA position depending on the terrain over which the aircraft will be flying. In the SEA position, the scale factor calibration network is altered to compensate for the apparent increase in antenna-looking angle when the aircraft is flying over water, thus providing proper groundspeed calibration. Circuits within the frequency tracker automatically sweep over the operating groundspeed range, seeking a usable return signal. When the reflected rf energy is of sufficient power to permit measurement of groundspeed and drift angle, the set is switched to the normal mode of operation. Until this change takes place, the set is in the memory mode and the MEMORY light on the C-4418 control indicator panel is on. While the doppler radar set is in the memory mode, the groundspeed and drift angle readings on the C-4418 control indicator panel are the values computed when the doppler radar set was in the normal mode. Drift angle (DA) and groundspeed (GS) push-to-turn control knobs are provided to enable the pilot to change groundspeed and drift angle when the doppler radar set is in the memory mode. If a malfunction should occur in the doppler radar set while it is connected to the AN/ASN-41 computer, the pilot can use the DA and GS knobs to insert approximate drift angle and groundspeed value, to enable the computer to continue operating. In the LAND position, the preceding conditions can also be handled.

The system may go into the memory mode under any of the following conditions:

1. Selector switch is at STBY, and transmitter will be off.

2. The period after the system has been turned on and before a signal has been acquired, will be about 1 minute.

3. During operation over smooth glassy seas.

4. During operation over extremely hilly terrain, where coherence may be lost despite broad antenna beams.

Changed 15 May 1966

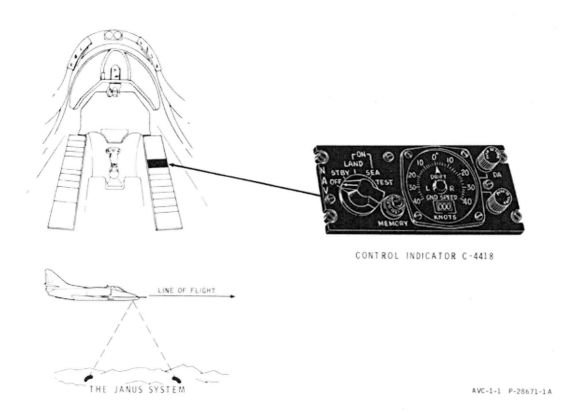

CONTROL INDICATOR C-4418

THE JANUS SYSTEM

AVC-1-1 P-28671-1A

Figure 1-19C. AN/APN-153 Radar Navigation Set (Doppler)

5. During periods when the aircraft is maneuvering beyond the antenna's limits of operation.

In the STBY position, all power except the modulator power required to drive the magnetron is applied to the AN/APN-153(V), doppler radar set. This position is used when observing radar silence or when maintenance personnel wish to check the system. When the selector switch is on STBY, the system goes into memory mode and the amber MEMORY light turns on.

PRIOR TO FLIGHT

1. Place selector switch to the "test" position. After 5 minutes warmup time the memory light should be extinguished, the ground speed dial should read 121 ±5 knots, and the drift angle dial should read 0 ±2 degree.

2. Rotate selector switch to STBY.

PRIOR TO TAKEOFF

1. Place selector switch to the ON-LAND or ON-SEA position depending upon the terrain to be flown over.

AFTER TAKEOFF

1. Within approximately 30 seconds after the airplane has reached 150 knots and an altitude of 40 feet, the memory light should go out.

2. After cruise altitude is attained, ground speed and drift angle should be observed to read within ±50 knots and ±10 degrees respectively for the known condition of flight.

NOTE

It may be necessary to use the push-to-set knob and set the doppler to 150 knots after test and prior to takeoff.

3. Bank and turns are limited to 30 degrees roll in right or left and/or to type of terrain being flown over. If the above limitations are exceeded, memory light will come on, indicating loss of tracking signal.

4. Climbing and descending maneuvers should be observed. High angle climbs and descents should be at approximately 25-degree pitch attitude, since 25-degree pitch angle is near the operating limits. The memory light may be illuminated for periods of time, not to exceed 3 seconds.

5. At combat ceiling and at lowest mission altitude (not below 40 feet) the memory light should remain extinguished, indicating doppler signal lock-on and tracking.

AN/APG-53A RADAR SYSTEM

The AN/APG-53A radar system (figure 1-20) is designed primarily to provide improved navigation and terrain clearance capabilities and to provide air-to-ground ranging, obstacle warning, and limited ground mapping. The system does not provide automatic fire control.

Operating controls are provided on the radar control panel located on the left hand console, on a small radar switch panel installed near the center of the bottom edge of the instrument panel, and around the perimeter of the azimuth-elevation-range indicator (scope) mounted in the instrument panel.

Four radar scope presentations or modes of operation are available for pilot selection: search, two obstacle modes (terrain clearance plan and terrain clearance-profile), and air-to-ground ranging. Only the profile mode gives a visual and aural obstacle warning.

RADAR COMPONENTS

Figure 1-20 illustrates the components of the radar set. The pilot actuated controls, azimuth-elevation-range indicator (scope) and

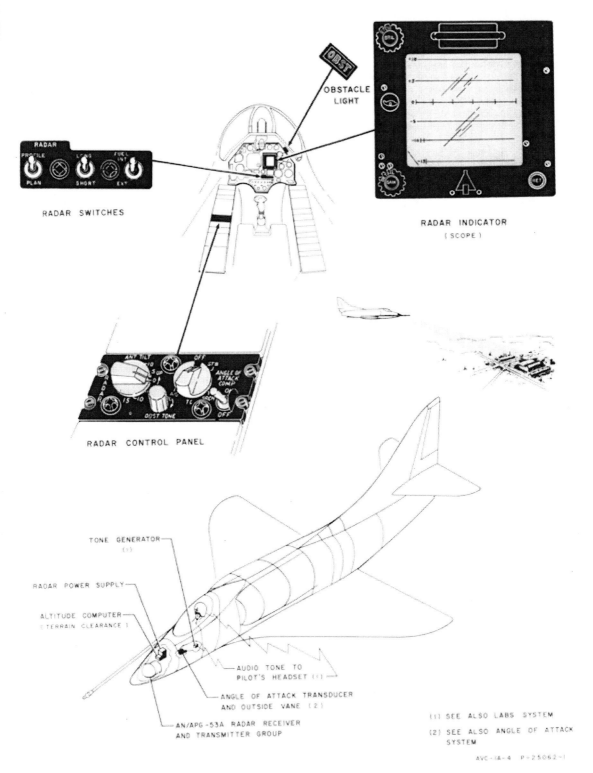

Figure 1-20. AN/APG-53A Radar System

lights are shown at the top of the figure. Remotely located components are shown in the lower portion. The radar set operates on a 3-phase, 115-volt, 400-cycle, a-c power supplied by the airplane generator.

Note

The radar system will not operate on emergency generator.

RADAR CONTROLS

RADAR CONTROL PANEL. Located on the lefthand console is the radar control panel, labeled RADAR. This panel contains a rotary antenna elevation control, a mode selector switch, an angle of attack compensation switch, and a volume control for the aural warning tone.

The antenna elevation control provides the pilot with manual control of the antenna elevation angle. The normal elevation limits of the antenna are plus 10 degrees and minus 15 degrees with respect to the elevation zero position. In the terrain clearance-profile mode of operation the antenna tilt control has no effect since the programming circuits in the altitude computer control the antenna and cause it to sweep between the lower and upper position limits.

A rotary mode selector switch provides application or removal of primary power and selection of the type of operation. In the standby position, the selector switch causes energizing of all primary power relays and initiates the modulator time delay (warmup) period. When placed in one of the operating positions, the selector switch sets up the system for performing the required functions in the mode selected and also allows energizing of the modulator if the normal 3-minute time delay period has elapsed.

A guarded angle of attack switch of the two-position toggle type enables the pilot to remove the angle of attack compensation if the

airflow sensor becomes inoperative. When the switch is in the OFF position, the zero reference line of antenna elevation is the armament datum line rather than the flight path.

RANGE SELECTOR SWITCH

The range selector switch is located in the center of the instrument panel (see figure 1-20). The switch has two positions labeled LONG and SHORT. Ranges provided are:

Mode	Short	Long
SRCH	20 miles	40 miles
T/C	10 miles	20 miles
A/G	15,000 yards	15,000 yards

TERRAIN CLEARANCE MODE SELECTOR SWITCH. The switch is located in the center of the instrument panel adjacent to the range selector switch and has two positions marked PLAN and PROFILE. The switch is functional when the mode selector switch (on the left console) is at T/C, and is used to select an E-scope presentation (profile mode) or a B-scope presentation, (plan mode) (see figure 1-21).

OBSTACLE LIGHT

Located beneath the right side of the glare-shield is a yellow caution light labeled OBST. This light functions only when in terrain clearance-profile mode operation.

The OBST light flashes whenever a target projects above the electronically produced line displayed on the scope which represents an imaginary plane 1000 feet below the antenna 0 degree reference line. (Provisions are available for wiring the OBST light in the plan mode.)

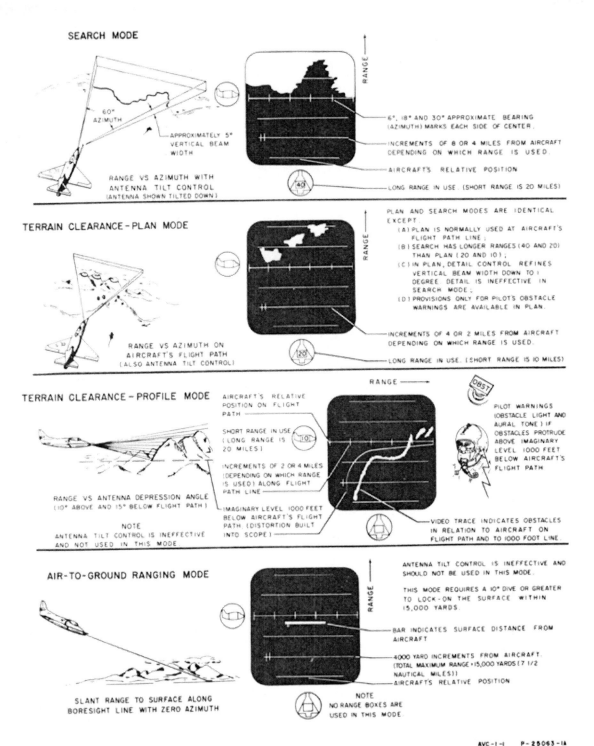

Figure 1-21. Radar Scope Presentations

AURAL WARNING TONE

In terrain clearance-profile mode operation, an aural warning tone is heard in the pilot's headset at the same time that the obstacle light comes on. A volume control for the aural warning tone is located on the radar control panel on the left console. (Provisions are available for wiring the aural tone in the plan mode.)

RADAR INDICATOR (SCOPE)

Located in the center area of the instrument panel is the radar indicator, designed to display targets with a brilliance sufficient to permit viewing without the use of a hood. In addition to the iatron tube, the indicator contains the necessary sweep circuits and the high-voltage power supply. Flag type indicators, one on the left side in a horizontal airplane and the other at the bottom in a plan-view airplane, show the range scale being used. (See figure 1-20.)

Front panel controls permit adjustment of brilliance, storage, gain, and detail. Brilliance and storage controls are on concentric shafts, and regulate the brightness and storage time (how long the picture lasts) of the indicator display. Gain and detail controls are also concentric. The gain control varies the amplitude of the signals applied to the indicator, and therefore, the sensitivity of the radar. It is the strength or "sum" of the picture signal. The normal setting of the gain control is approximately three-quarters of its clockwise travel. The detail control has the effect of varying the effective vertical beam width in the terrain clearance modes. It governs the sharpness or "difference" of the picture. This control is used in conjunction with the gain control to obtain 1 degree resolution of vertical beam width in the profile mode, and is determined by reference to the horizontal elevation markings on the scope reticle. The reticle knob controls the illumination of range-elevation-azimuth reference lines on the scope reticle for operation of radar in night lighting conditions.

Note

- Gain and detail controls have no effect in the air-to-ground mode.

- Detail control has no effect in the SEARCH mode.

- Dimming of radar scope is completely independent of interior lights controls.

A red filter plate to cover the face of the scope is a Douglas addition to the AN/APG-53A Radar Set. The filter is a red acrylic plate permanently secured to a spring-loaded hinge. It is used in the down position for night flying, to change the yellow-green target display to a red display to coincide with the red instrument lighting. During daytime flying, the plate is manually raised away from the face of the indicator (scope) so that a normal (yellow-green) display is seen.

Note

Always use the tab on the bottom to raise or lower the filter plate; never use the side tab.

OPERATING MODES

SEARCH MODE. The search mode presentation displays range versus azimuth. Either 0 to 20 or 0 to 40 mile range in nautical miles may be selected. The range in use is shown by a flag-type marker in the plan-view airplane at the bottom of the scope. The indicator face is divided by horizontal lines, each representing one-fifth of the total range.

With the range switch in the LONG position, the bottom (-15°) line is zero range and the top (+10°) line is 40 miles. This gives a calibration line every 8 miles.

With the switch at the SHORT position, each division represents 4 miles.

In SRCH, the radar antenna is programmed to sweep 60 degrees in azimuth using a 5 degree cone of radiation at the elevation angle (antenna tilt) selected by the pilot. Vertical marks on the zero elevation line of the reticle show the approximate bearing to any point on the display. The marks represent 6, 18, and 30 degrees each side of center. The antenna elevation is set by the pilot and may be varied from 10 degrees above to 15 degrees below the flight path (angle of attack switch ON).

Turning the antenna tilt control moves the radar antenna up or down. This function is an aid to search and ground mapping procedures. In the search mode, the antenna will remain in the position indicated by the antenna tilt control. A friction device prevents the tilt control from returning to zero until the pilot manually repositions it or the mode selector on the control panel is moved from SRCH to the T/C position.

The search mode display is a B-scope presentation (range-vs-azimuth) of the terrain ahead of the airplane.

Targets will appear on the scope as bright yellow-green spots. Surfaces which reflect little energy back to the radar, such as smooth water, appear on the scope as dark or unlighted areas. The result is a maplike display which is linear in the range coordinate but distorted in azimuth by a factor which is inversely proportional to range. This distortion is due to presentation of the conical radiation pattern as a rectangular display on the scope. (See figure 1-22.) Coast lines, islands, lakes, wide rivers, and highly reflective areas such as cities or factory complexes may be used to aid navigation when operating above an overcast or in reduced visibility, and at an altitude which insures safe terrain clearance. The 40-mile range provides for long range identification of coastlines. The 20-mile range permits detailed examination of closer objects. Range is attenuated as altitude is reduced so that at 1000 feet above level terrain, target return is reduced to about 18 miles except for specific targets at greater range with significant vertical development.

Brilliance and storage, can be changed at any time to get the best picture, depending upon varying cockpit lighting conditions. Normally, the gain setting should be established by "snowing" the scope, then reducing the setting to a point where only a trace of "snow" remains. As tilt control is changed, usually gain control will require readjustment to create the desired scope sensitivity for the range (tilt) selected. As the antenna is depressed, the gain must be reduced (counterclockwise). If only the highly reflective areas are of interest, the gain setting is reduced until only such areas are displayed.

TERRAIN CLEARANCE-PLAN MODE. With the profile-plan switch in the PLAN position, the rotary mode selector switch in the T/C position, and the angle-of-attack switch ON, the indicator (scope) provides a B-scope (range-versus-azimuth) presentation of obstacles in the projected flight path of the aircraft.

The terrain clearance-plan display is provided to enable the pilot to maneuver around obstacles rather than over them.

Azimuth scan is 60 degrees using a beam width of 5 degrees and a vertical beam width effectively reduced to 1 degree by means of the detail control on the scope.

The vertical width of the beam is determined by the setting of the detail knob on the indicator. With the knob fully counterclockwise, beam width is approximately 5 degrees; fully clockwise, beam width is approximates 1/2 of 1 degree. The scope will display only those obstacles, which are within the beam. If the antenna tilt control is at 0 and the angle-of-attack switch is on, the objects shown will be in a plane which contains the projected flight path and is parallel to the lateral axis of the airplane. With the angle-of-attack switch OFF, the objects will be in the plane of the armament datum line. Only radar return from the near slope of mountains is received so the presentation is usually patchy as shown in figure 1-21.

Changed 15 March 1965

The pilot may examine terrain above or below the flight path (or ADL) by manually adjusting the tilt control to the desired setting (from plus 10 to minus 15 degrees). However, the tilt control knob is spring-loaded in the T/C modes and will return to 0 when released.

Available for selection are ranges of 0 to 20 or 0 to 10 nautical miles (LONG or SHORT).

The range in use is indicated by a flag type marker in the plan-view airplane at the bottom of the scope as in SRCH mode. The horizontal lines on the indicator face each represent one-fifth of the total range. With the range switch at LONG, each calibration line represents 4 miles; in the SHORT position, 2 miles. Azimuth markings are identical to search mode; 6, 18, and 30 degrees to the left or right of the aircraft heading.

TERRAIN CLEARANCE — PROFILE MODE

With the presentation switch at PROFILE and the rotary mode selector switch at T/C, the indicator (scope) provides an E-scope (range-versus-antenna depression angle) display of the terrain profile ahead of the airplane. The radar beam automatically locks in azimuth and sweeps in elevation from plus 10 degrees to minus 15 degrees using a beam width of 5 degrees and a vertical beam width effectively reduced to 1 degree by means of the detail control on the scope.

The elevation zero is normally referenced to the flight line by including an angle of attack correction in the servo loop. This provides for an extended antenna sweep up to a maximum of plus 11 degrees to minus 19 degrees from the armament datum line (antenna sweep limits). In the event the angle of attack sensor vane becomes damaged, frozen, or inoperative, the angle of attack switch is provided to lock the zero reference line with the armament datum line. The antenna tilt control does not function in this mode.

The long-short range switch provides either 20 or 10-mile ranges for sufficient detail under various conditions. Vertical marks on the horizontal 0-degree elevation line divide the display into 2- or 4-mile segments according to the range in use. A flag type marker in the airplane silhouette at the left of the scope shows which range is in use.

A solid line representing an imaginary plane 1000 feet below the antenna 0 degree elevation line is electronically displayed on the indicator as an aid to low level navigation. This is the terrain clearance scribe line (see figure 1-21) and is synchronized with the elevation sweep. The zero elevation line of the indicator reticle represents the instantaneous forward projection of the airplane flight or armament datum line depending on the position of the angle of attack switch. Since the vertical calibration is in degrees of antenna depression angle rather than in feet of altitude, the resulting expansion of the conical radiation pattern into a rectangular display causes the 1000-foot marker and radar target return to curve downward at the low range end of the indicator. (See figure 1-21.)

An irregular line display is the radar return. Assuming level terrain and by flying so that the radar return presentation is parallel to the 1000-foot marker, it is possible to fly at a constant altitude above level terrain.

The profile function also incorporates visual and aural warning to the pilot when obstacles protrude above a horizontal plane positioned 1000-feet below and parallel to the antenna 0 degree reference plane.

The obstacle alarm consists of both the obstacle light and the pilot's headset signal, warning the pilot that a potential hazard exists.

The alarm is controlled by the same circuits that control the 1000-foot terrain clearance scribe line and warns if any obstacle appears above it. A rough indication of the range to the target is provided by the percentage of time that the alarm is actuated. Targets

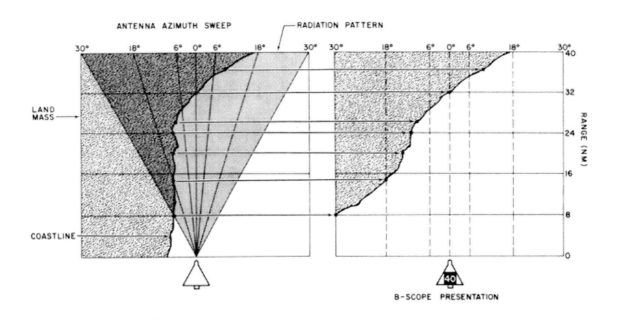

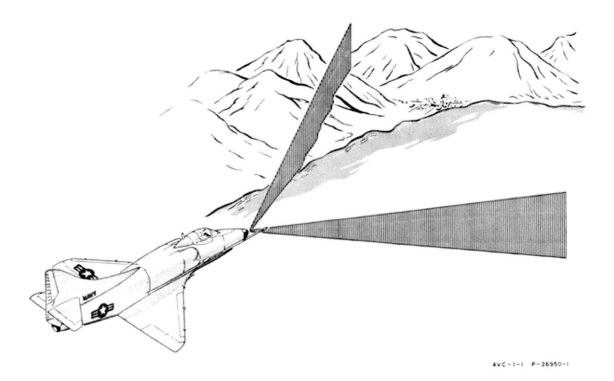

Figure 1-22. Radar Scope Distortion (Sheet 1)

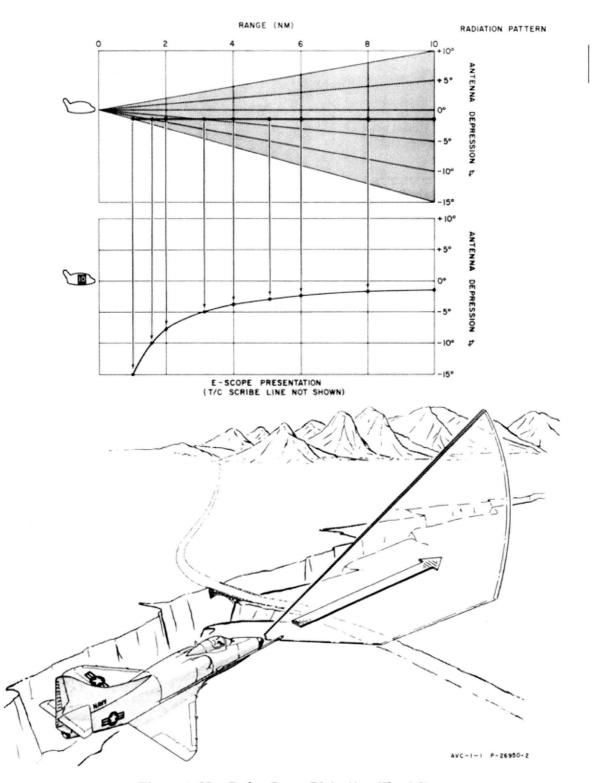

Figure 1-22. Radar Scope Distortion (Sheet 2)

AVC-1-1 P-26950-2

near maximum range will give short blinks and as the target comes closer, the light will remain on for longer periods.

Note

By comparing the presentations in the plan and the profile modes, the pilot can quickly decide whether to change elevation or bearing to avoid obstacles.

WARNING

- When flying 1000-feet terrain clearance at normal low level airspeeds, crosswind component of 9 knots or more can cause a drift rate which would preclude displaying obstacles in the ground track of the airplane in profile mode. To prevent inadvertent collision with an obstacle, it is necessary to shift to PLAN mode to scan the 60° forward sector at intervals of one minute or less unless flying over known level terrain.

- Whenever possible, boresight should be checked at 1000-feet above terrain after each radar mission takeoff.

The profile display also provides an aid to letdown under conditions of reduced visibility. The letdown is accomplished simply by descending at the desired schedule until the radar return intersects the 1000-foot terrain clearance scribe line at a range of six miles. The dive angle is then continuously readjusted to maintain the intersection of radar return and T/C scribe line at 6 miles. This results in a gradual reduction in dive angle (and rate of descent) until in straight and level flight 1000 feet above the terrain.

AIR-TO-GROUND MODE

Note

At the present time, this mode is in no way functionally related to the armament system in this airplane.

With the mode selector switch in the A/G position, the indicator (scope) shows the distance to the ground dead ahead. The antenna is automatically fixed in the azimuth zero position and is parallel to the armament datum line in the elevation coordinate. When the antenna boresight line and the sight line are made parallel (0 mil lead), the range indication will show the distance to the point on the ground at which the sight is aimed. The angle between the ground and the antenna boresight line should be at least 10 degrees to provide adequate radar return for ranging lockon.

If the distance to the ground exceeds the radar lockon range, the horizontal line will search from the top of the scope to the bottom. When ground lockon occurs the line will stop cycling and, as the slant range decreases, the bar will move downward. The solid horizontal bar gives the pilot the approximate slant range in yards. The total maximum range in the air-to-ground mode is 15,000 yards (approximately 7 1/2 nautical miles. The airplane relative position is at the bottom line on the scope (-15 degree elevation line). After range lockon of the horizontal bar, slant range can be read by reference to the horizontal lines etched on the reticle each of which represents a range increment of 4000 yards.

PREFLIGHT PROCEDURE

Position controls as follows:

1. Radar Control Panel
   Mode selector switch . . . . OFF
   Antenna tilt control . . . . 0°
   Angle-of-attack switch . . . . . . OFF

2. Radar Indicator
   Brilliance knob . . FULL-CLOCKWISE
   Gain knob . . . . FULL
            COUNTERCLOCKWISE
   Storage knob . . . . FULL-CLOCKWISE
   Detail knob . . . . FULL
            COUNTERCLOCKWISE
   Reticle knob . . . . FULL
            COUNTERCLOCKWISE

Changed 15 March 1965

3. Radar Switch Panel
    Range switch . . . . LONG
    T/C Plan-profile switch . . PROFILE

BEFORE TAKEOFF

Test the scope presentations as follows:

1. Mode selector switch . . . . STBY
(Allow 3 minutes for equipment warmup.)

2. Mode selector switch . . . . SRCH

3. Antenna tilt switch . . . . MINUS 6°

4. Turn gain control knob clockwise until targets appear.

5. Position range switch at SHORT. Presentation should double in size. Confirm that flag indicates 20 miles.

6. Position mode selector switch at T/C. Confirm that flag indicates 10 miles. Antenna tilt control should zero. Turn gain knob clockwise until targets appear to be 5 degrees in vertical dimension. Turn detail knob clockwise until targets are reduced to 1 degree in vertical dimension. Tails should be disregarded in any 1 degree analysis. These may be observed on late model radar sets as shown on figure 1-21.

7. Observe terrain clearance line on scope. Position range selector switch to LONG. Confirm that terrain clearance line moves to the left and slightly up.

8. Position mode selector switch to A/G and confirm that horizontal line on scope sweeps from top to near bottom.

9. Position the mode selector switch to OFF.

INFLIGHT TEST. A brief operational check during the first part of each tactical flight is recommended.

INFLIGHT PROCEDURE

SEARCH MODE. Make sure that a-c power is available (note that the all-attitude indicator flag is not visible after a 90-second warmup).

1. Mode selector switch . . . . STBY

Note

A 3-minute warmup procedure is required.

2. Angle-of-attack switch . . . . ON

3. Antenna tilt control. . . . . . . DESIRED
                                        SETTING

4. LONG-SHORT range switch . . . .
                                   DESIRED RANGE

5. Mode selector switch . . . . SRCH

6. Brilliance, storage, and gain knobs. .
                                   DESIRED PICTURE

Note

●   The profile-plan switch is not functional in search mode.

●   There is no obstacle alarm in the search mode.

TERRAIN CLEARANCE-PROFILE MODE

After observing the radar set operating properly in search mode, or after performing step 1 of the search mode procedure, perform the following steps:

1. Angle-of-attack switch . . . . OFF

2. Mode selector switch . . . . T/C

3. Profile-plan switch . . . . . . PROFILE

4. Long-short range switch .... SHORT

5. Brilliance and storage knobs ......
DESIRED PICTURE

6. Gain and detail knobs .. ADJUST FOR
1 DEGREE BEAM RESOLUTION
(DISREGARD TAILS)

7. Angle-of-attack switch .... ON
(TARGET RETURN SHOULD SHIFT
DEPENDENT UPON AIRPLANE
ANGLE OF ATTACK.)

TERRAIN CLEARANCE-PLAN MODE

After tuning set in PROFILE and observing the radar set operating properly, shift to PLAN. Point the aircraft at an obstacle or at the ground to provide a target within the range selected and note proper display on the indicator.

Note

No change in gain, detail, brilliance, or storage is required when changing between PLAN and PROFILE operation or between LONG and SHORT range.

AIR-TO-GROUND MODE

After observing the radar set operating properly in search, or the T/C modes, or after performing step 1 of the search mode procedure, perform the following steps:

1. Mode selector switch .... A/G

2. Brilliance and storage knobs ......
DESIRED PICTURE

3. Initiate a dive of 10 degrees or greater so that the optical sight line intercepts the ground within 7-1/2 nautical miles. The horizontal bar on the scope should stop sweeping and begin to indicate the slant range between the nose of the airplane and the intersection of the optical boresight line with the ground. Any type of terrain or choppy water is an acceptable target.

Note

● The long-short switch, the profile-plan switch and the gain and detail knobs are not functional in the air-to-ground mode.

● There is no obstacle warning in the air-to-ground mode.

EMERGENCY OPERATION AND MALFUNCTIONS

The angle-of-attack switch enables the pilot to remove the angle-of-attack compensation for line-of-flight reference for the various modes if the airflow sensor becomes inoperative. With the angle-of-attack switch in the OFF position, the zero line on the indicator is referenced to the armament datum line rather than to the flight path.

Because of its importance to the execution of the mission, the radar system has been designed so that many inflight failures may be compensated for by normal pilot control adjustments. At any instant, the terrain clearance-profile mode presentation will indicate whether the equipment is transmitting, the location of the obstacle warning horizontal plane (normally positioned 1000 feet below the airplane), and the instantaneous beam width of the system. For example, if the terrain return has widened, it can be corrected by advancing the detail knob clockwise. In the event of trouble in this channel which the detail knob will not compensate, the system may still be flown with the widened beam; but the widened video trace will cause the pilot to fly the airplane higher than normal.

OMNIRANGE RADIO

The AN/ARN-14E omnirange radio includes an R-540/ARN-14C VHF receiver, an ID-251/ARN indicator control, and an antenna; all are contained in the NAVPAC external store. The omnirange radio provides for the reception of VOR and localizer signals in a frequency spectrum of 108.0 to 136.0 megacycles. Use of the equipment in this airplane is described as follows:

1. Indication of the magnetic bearing of the VHF omnirange station from the aircraft by the number 2 needle of the ID-663 BDHI.

2. Reception of voice facilities on communications frequencies or superimposed on navigation signals in the localizer or omnirange channels.

OMNIRANGE RADIO CONTROL PANEL. The omnirange receiver is remotely tuned by means of a C-760 R/A ARN-14 control panel (when carried) labeled VHF navigation. The panel contains a power switch with ON TONE and OFF positions, a volume control, and a frequency selector which consists of two concentric dials. A window is provided to show the selected frequency.

OPERATION OF THE OMNIRANGE RADIO

1. Power switch . . . . ON TONE

2. Frequency selector . . . . DESIRED FREQUENCY

3. Read the magnetic bearing to the station on the number 2 needle of the BDHI.

Note

The power switch on the TACAN control panel must be turned OFF for the AN/ARN-14E radio to be connected to the BDHI.

MARKER BEACON EQUIPMENT

The AN/ARN-14 marker beacon equipment, which is placed in operation when the airplane electrical system is energized, is located in the external navigation package. Functionally, the system receives a 75-megacycle signal, modulated at 400, 1300, or 3000 cycles, from marker beacon transmitters. From the signals, the relative position of the airplane can be checked in respect to specific marker beacon stations. An aural indication of marker beacon interception is provided by the airplane audio system. In addition, a marker beacon indicating light (13, figure 1-5) located beneath the glareshield glows an amber color to give visual indication of marker beacon interception.

Note

The marker beacon indicating light is also used in conjunction with certain special weapon installations when the NAVPAC is not carried. In this event, a red lens cover should be placed over the light by the ground crew.

MARKER BEACON CONTROL PANEL

A marker beacon control panel (when carried) on the left console forward of the throttle, contains two toggle switches, an audio switch with ON and OFF positions, and a sensitivity switch with positions marked BELOW 20,000 FT and ABOVE 20,000 FT. Since no volume control is provided, the audio switch is used to continue or discontinue the reception of aural signals when their volume level interferes with other radio receptions. Regardless of the position of the audio switch, visual indication of marker beacon interception will be provided by the indicator light. The sensitivity switch should be placed in the position corresponding to the general altitude level at which the aircraft is flying to achieve the best reception.

AUTOMATIC FLIGHT CONTROL SYSTEM (AFCS)

The automatic flight control system (AFCS) is a completely transistorized system designed to provide pilot relief from routine control of the aircraft. (See figure 1-23.) The AFCS will maintain heading, altitude, and pitch and bank angles, and perform a coordinated turn to a preselected heading without use of the pilot control stick. These functions utilize attitude and direction information from the AN/AJB-3/3A all attitude flight reference and bombing system. Without moving a switch or disconnecting the AFCS, the pilot can maneuver the aircraft in an unlimited manner throughout the AFCS envelope by using the control stick as in normal flight. Directional stability augmentation is active during AFCS operation or can be selected separately while on normal flight control. This yaw damping action is independent of pilot movement of the rudder pedals.

The AFCS has safety features which function automatically to insure satisfactory operation and to prevent a system malfunction from damaging the aircraft or displacing the ailerons excessively. There are operating components which sense aircraft attitude and performance, and convert electrical control and correction input signals to mechanical signals for use by the aircraft hydraulic control system that moves the aerodynamic control surfaces.

The AFCS is an electro-hydraulic system requiring all three phases of the 115/200-volt, 400 cycle, ac power and 28-volt dc power. Normal hydraulic system pressure of 3000 psi is reduced to 1500 plus 75 or minus 50 psi for the aileron and elevator servos and to 1150 plus 450 or minus 50 psi for the dual input rudder valve.

Note

- The AFCS will not operate on the emergency generator.

- The hydraulic servos require utility system hydraulic power.

- The AFCS will not engage unless proper electrical and hydraulic power is available and it will disengage automatically if the electrical or hydraulic power fails.

AUTOMATIC FLIGHT CONTROL PANEL

The control panel (6, Figure 1-6) is labeled AFCS and is located on the left hand console.

STANDBY SWITCH. Movement of the standby switch to STANDBY provides electrical power to the AFCS for warmup and automatic control synchronization to prevent engage transients. This switch should be in STANDBY at least 30 seconds prior to engaging the stability augmentation switch or the AFCS main engage switch. When this switch is moved to the OFF position, all toggle switches on the panel return to the OFF position.

ENGAGE SWITCH

Movement of the engage switch to the ENGAGE position turns on the AFCS in one of two modes; attitude hold or heading hold, depending on flight attitude.

In addition, the pilot can further select any one of three modes: control stick steering, altitude hold and/or heading hold.

The switch may be moved to the OFF position at any time. The switch should not be moved to ENGAGE position until the standby switch has been in STANDBY position for 30 seconds.

The AFCS will not engage until the all attitude indicator OFF flag disappears.

When this switch is moved to the OFF position both the heading select switch and the altitude switch return to the OFF position. An abrupt lateral stick force of 40 pounds causes the aileron servo to bypass, which effectively

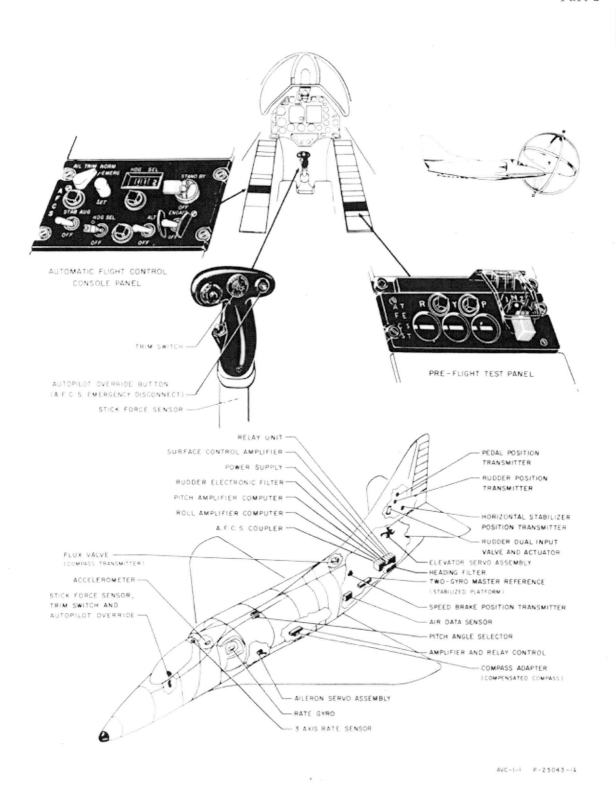

Figure 1-23. Automatic Flight Control System

disengages the AFCS lateral controls. The engage switch does not move from the ENGAGE position. Lateral control of the aircraft is then provided by the normal control system. To reengage the lateral servo, cycle the engage switch to the OFF position and then return to the ENGAGE position. This operation may be performed at any time.

Pressing the AFCS override button (AP) on the control stick causes the mode switches to move automatically to the OFF position. The AFCS can be reengaged by moving the engage switch to ENGAGE.

HEADING SELECT SWITCH

Movement of the heading select switch to the HDG SEL position starts the aircraft turning by the shortest route toward the heading selected on the heading select indicator by use of the SET knob. The heading select switch may be moved to the OFF position at any time. If moved to the OFF position prior to the completion of a turn, the aircraft will roll smoothly to a level attitude and maintain the compass heading indicated at that time. If the SET knob is used to change the heading on the indicator while the switch is in the HDG SEL position, the following can occur:

1. If the aircraft is in level flight, sudden SET knob movement will result in abrupt aircraft lateral movement. If the SET knob is moved very slowly, small heading changes can be made satisfactorily.

2. If the aircraft is already in a preselect heading turn, the SET knob may be moved at any rate if the new selected heading is in the same direction as the turn and is less than 180 degrees away from the compass heading at the time of selection. Selection of a heading reciprocal to the present aircraft heading will cause the aircraft to reverse the turn abruptly.

The heading select switch will automatically move to the OFF position if the control stick steering mode is engaged.

Note

Pilot use of the SET knob within 5 seconds after moving the heading select switch to the OFF position will cause an abrupt roll transient.

Upon engaging the HDG SEL switch, the approximate pitch attitude will be maintained during the turn. If a level turn is desired, the altitude hold mode should be engaged by moving the altitude switch to ALT.

ALTITUDE HOLD SWITCH

Movement of the altitude switch to the ALT position causes the aircraft to maintain the barometric altitude at actuation. If the mode is engaged in a climb or dive, the aircraft will return to the barometric altitude existing at the time of altitude hold engagement. Altitude hold cannot be engaged in climbs or descents in excess of 4000 feet per minute. The mode cannot be engaged if any force is being applied to the control stick. The switch will move automatically to the OFF position whenever control stick steering mode is engaged.

STABILITY AUGMENTATION SWITCH

Yaw damping action is provided when the engage switch is in the ENGAGE position or the stability augmentation switch is in the STAB AUG position.

AILERON TRIM NORM-EMERGENCY SWITCH

The aileron trim switch has two positions NORM and EMER. This switch is usually in the NORM position, but may be moved to the EMER position to provide aileron trim after the AFCS is disengaged, if aileron trim is not available in NORM. Movement of this switch to the EMER position also disengages and prevents reengagement of the AFCS, except stability augmentation, while in the EMER position. The AFCS can be reengaged after returning the switch to the NORM position.

Changed 15 May 1966

PREFLIGHT TEST PANEL

This panel is the AFCS test panel on the aft right hand console. The three indicators R, Y and P measure d-c control current to the AFCS servos for roll, yaw and pitch respectively. The 1-N-2 switch is provided to obtain two test conditions. The switch is spring loaded in the N (normal) position and must be held in either test position 1 or test position 2. All test procedures are covered in PRE-FLIGHT PROCEDURE.

Note

The 1-N-2 switch must be in N position for normal AFCS operation.

CONTROL STICK

AUTOPILOT OVERRIDE BUTTON. The control stick has an AFCS override button labeled AP. Pressing this button immediately disengages the entire AFCS.

SENSOR

Within the control stick is a force sensor which transmits signals of pilot applied stick forces to the control stick steering function of the AFCS.

STICK TRIM SWITCH

The control stick trim button, which is used to trim the airplane in roll and pitch during normal flight, is inoperative during all AFCS modes except control stick steering. During the control stick steering mode, the lateral trim signal causes a trimming adjustment within the autopilot and not within the aileron power control as in normal control system use. All pitch trim signals operate the horizontal stabilizer whether on control stick steering mode or normal flight controls.

Note

The control stick trim button should be used with normal technique when control stick steering mode is engaged. Transients are minimized during disengagement or reengagement of control stick steering if the airplane is correctly trimmed at that time.

AFCS MODES

The following modes of operation provide automatic flight control.

CONTROL STICK STEERING (CSS) MODE

This mode provides for longitudinal and lateral control of the airplane through the AFCS by pilot movement of the stick as in normal flight. This mode is engaged regardless of other modes selected or in operation by applying a force on the control stick grip of 2 pounds or more. Preselect heading and altitude hold modes are disengaged by use of control stick steering and they must be reengaged to be used again. The AFCS reverts from control stick steering mode to either attitude hold or heading hold mode when pilot force on the control stick is reduced below 2 pounds. The airplane is controllable in all attitudes in control stick steering throughout the AFCS flight envelope, which is $4 \pm 1/2$ positive g, $1-1/2 \pm 1/2$ negative g, and one-half aileron deflection left or right. If these limits are exceeded, the AFCS disengages. The AFCS will not switch out of control stick steering at bank angles exceeding 70 degrees or pitch angles exceeding 60 degrees noseup or nosedown unless limits of acceleration or aileron deflection are exceeded.

CAUTION

The control stick should not be released while in control stick steering if the pull or push force at the time exceeds 12 pounds because of large disengage transients. These transients are minimized if the airplane is properly trimmed at the time of release.

ATTITUDE HOLD MODE

With an airplane bank angle between 5 degrees and 70 degrees and a pitch angle less than 60 degrees noseup or nosedown, the airplane lateral and longitudinal attitude at time of engagement of the AFCS or reversion from the control stick steering mode will be maintained.

HEADING HOLD MODE

If the pitch angle is within 60 degrees noseup or nosedown and the bank angle of the airplane is less than 5 degrees upon engagement of the AFCS or reversion from control stick steering mode, the airplane will be rolled to a level attitude and the heading and pitch angles at that time will be maintained.

PRESELECT HEADING MODE

Upon engagement of this mode after the heading has been preselected on the indicator, the airplane will roll into a smooth turn to the preselected heading and then roll out on this heading. The turn will always be in the direction of the shortest route to the preselected heading. The bank angle will be maintained at 27 ± 5 degrees under all conditions.

Note

The fixed bank angle of 27 ± 5 degrees may cause the airplane to buffet in an approach to stall if the preselect heading mode is selected below airspeeds ranging from 160 KIAS at 10,000 to 200 KIAS at 40,000 feet.

STABILITY AUGMENTATION MODE

The stability augmentation mode provides rudder yaw damping action which is independent of pilot movement of the rudder pedals. The mode can be selected at any time without other AFCS functions. It is also in operation automatically during all other AFCS functions.

Note

The pilot must trim the airplane directionally while using the AFCS in the same manner as he would when on the normal flight control system. If the airplane is out of trim directionally, the following will occur:

1. A lateral engage transient will occur during change to the control stick steering mode.

2. The airplane will be in a steady heading side slip in the heading hold mode.

ALTITUDE HOLD MODE

This mode may be engaged when the rate of change of altitude is less then 4,000 ± 500 feet per minute. The airplane will maintain the altitude at engagement. The airplane automatically will pull out of its climb or dive and return to and maintain the engage altitude.

GROUND CONTROL BOMBING MODE

Refer to GROUND CONTROLLED BOMBING SYSTEM, this section.

AUTOMATIC SAFETY FEATURES

The following automatic major safety features are incorporated in the AFCS.

AIRPLANE STRUCTURAL PROTECTION

The AFCS is automatically disengaged and the engage switch automatically moved to the OFF position when normal load factor approaches 4 ± 1/2 positive g or 1-1/2 ± 1/2 negative g, or when the aileron surface displacement exceeds 20 degrees, one half lateral stick displacement from neutral. Normal acceleration values are reduced to 3-1/2 ± 1/2 positive g and 1 ± 1/2 negative g when a centerline store is carried, except when operating in CSS mode. (Refer to CONTROL STICK STEERING MODE.)

Note

The system in response to hardover signals disengages the AFCS with negligible upset in either noseup or nosedown attitudes. The incremental load factors, as a result of hardover signal, will vary between 0 g and 0.6 g for airspeeds up to Mach 0.85. Elevator surface rates in excess of 20 degrees/second disengage the AFCS with the same characteristics as hardover signals. For displacement rates of 5 degrees/second to 20 degrees/second at speeds in excess of 300 knots, structural limits are not exceeded. Altitude change from hardover to disconnect is less than 100 feet. This does not include the additional altitude necessary to recover to level flight.

AFCS TEMPORARY OVERPOWER

The AFCS can be overpowered temporarily laterally and longitudinally. Pilot application of 15 pounds longitudinal stick force will overpower the AFCS longitudinal control without affecting AFCS lateral or directional control. In the same manner a 35-pound lateral stick force will overpower the AFCS lateral control without affecting AFCS controls and will remain overpowered as long as the stick forces as noted are maintained.

Note

The only occasion to use the overpower feature will probably be to counteract a failure within the AFCS that would cause large deflection of the elevator or aileron. Unless prevented by the failure noted above, the AFCS will engage the control stick steering mode when the stick force is applied, and will disengage this mode when the stick force is reduced below 2 pounds.

AFCS LATERAL HYDRAULIC DISENGAGE

The lateral AFCS control can be disengaged by applying a sudden sharp force laterally to the control stick. This lateral disengagement allows the pilot to provide lateral control through the normal system but does not affect AFCS longitudinal control. AFCS lateral control may be reengaged by cycling the engage switch to OFF and then returning it to the ENGAGE position.

CONTROL STICK DISENGAGE

Pressing the AP button on the control stick will disconnect the AFCS electrically. The AFCS can be reengaged in the normal manner.

PREFLIGHT PROCEDURE

The following preflight test procedure is recommended:

1. Landing gear handle . . . . DOWN

2. Engine rpm . . . . IDLE

3. All-attitude indicator power warning flag not visible.

4. Observe hydraulic power from movement of control surfaces and caution panel lights.

5. Standby switch . . . . STANDBY

6. Aileron trim emergency switch . . . . NORM

7. Stability augmentation switch . . . OFF

8. Heading select switch . . . . OFF

9. Altitude switch . . . . OFF

10. Engage switch . . . . OFF

11. 1-N-2 switch . . . . N

12. Heading select counter and
set knob . . . . ANY PRE-
SELECTED
HEADING OR
POSITION DESIRED

Note

Two sets of preflight performance checks are provided here. The pilot should make the following four MANDATORY CHECKS before each flight when time is limited. If there is sufficient time available or after reworking or overhauling of the autopilot system, the COMPLETE PERFORMANCE CHECKS consisting of seventeen items should be made.

MANDATORY CHECKS

These four checks are made in test position 2 and with the engage switch at ENGAGE.

1. Move the stick right. At about half deflection, the autopilot should disengage and the engage switch will be seen to slip to its OFF position. Recycle the engage switch to its ENGAGE position after centering the stick. Repeat the same check to the left. The results should be the same. This is the aileron limit switch check.

2. Move the trim button right. The auto pilot should disengage and the engage switch will be seen to flip to its OFF position. Recycle the engage switch to its ENGAGE position after centering the trim button. Repeat the same check to the left. The results should be the same. This is the load factor monitor limit switch check.

3. Move the stick aft (noseup) and move the horizontal stabilizer trim toward NOSEUP. The autopilot should disengage and the engage switch will be seen to "flip" to its OFF position. Recycle the engage switch to its ENGAGE position after centering the stick. Move the stick forward (nosedown) and move the horizontal stabilizer trim toward NOSEUP. The results should be the same. This is the trim monitor switch check.

4. Depress AP button. The autopilot should engage and the engage switch will be seen to flip to its OFF position.

The pilot will know from the above tests that he has electrical power to the AFCS servos and that the safety circuits are operating.

Note

If all four AFCS mandatory checks are not satisfactorily completed, the AFCS STANDBY-OFF switch should be placed in the OFF position. STAB-AUG will not be available with the STANDBY switch in the OFF position.

COMPLETE PERFORMANCE CHECKS

It is recommended that these checks be made in the sequence given. These are 4 checks in "TEST POSITION 1" and 13 checks in "TEST POSITION 2". These 17 checks should be made if there is adequate time or after reworking or overhauling the autopilot system.

TEST POSITION 1 CHECKS. Hold the spring-loaded 1-N-2 switch in the test position 1 until the following four tests have been completed: (The AFCS is unsynchronized.)

1. All three pointers (R, Y, and P) should deflect upward and remain positioned upward. This shows dc control current to the autopilot servos and indicates proper direction for surface movement.

2. Push on the right rudder pedal. The indicator needle in the Y (yaw) window should move from the upward position to a full down position. Sluggish rudder operation will be apparent, but is normal.

3. Actuate the engage switch to the ENGAGE position: It should not engage, because the AFCS should never engage while in an unsynchronized condition. If the switch does not "flip" back to the OFF position, report the trouble.

4. Actuate the stability augmentation switch to the STAB AUG position: It should remain engaged rather than "flipping" back to OFF. Return switch to OFF position when test is completed.

Changed 15 March 1965

TEST POSITION 2 CHECKS: Hold the spring-loaded 1-N-2 switch in position 2 until the following thirteen tests have been completed. (The AFCS is still unsynchronized.)

1. All three pointers (R, Y and P) should again deflect upward and remain positioned upward.

2. Actuate the stability augmentation switch to the STAB AUG position: It should engage, but the (Y) indicator for rudder should "null" (go to the center) because test position 2 closes the rudder loop. Leave the switch in the STAB AUG position for later checks.

3. Actuate the engage switch to the ENGAGE position: It should engage and the switch should remain there because test position 2 allows engagement in the unsynchronized condition by bypassing the synchronizing monitors that normally protect the aircraft from engage transients (jumping). A small stick jump or movement normally accompanies engagement in position 2.

4. With the engage switch in the ENGAGE position (as in step 3), the P and R indicators for pitch (elevator) and roll (aileron) should "null" (go to the center) because the pitch and roll loops have been closed in test position 2.

5. Move the control stick for roll and pitch: It should "feel" normal.

6. Move the control stick hardover to the right. The engage switch should flip to the OFF position but the stability augmentation switch should remain engaged, because the aileron has reached a position greater than half-travel from faired and the protection circuit has caused the AFCS system to disengage.

7. Move the engage switch back to ENGAGE position. Move the control stick hardover to the left. The results should be the same as in step 6.

8. Move the engage switch back to ENGAGE position. Move the trim button to the right for right aileron. The results should be the same as in steps 6 and 7, because test position 2 feeds a test signal into the structural protection circuit.

9. Move the engage switch back to ENGAGE position. Move the trim button to the left for left aileron. The results should be the same as in step 8.

10. Move the engage switch back to the ENGAGE position. Actuate the aileron trim emergency switch to the EMER position. The engage switch should flip to the OFF position, but the stability augmentation switch should remain in the STAB AUG position. The emergency trim switch is to be used only with the AFCS disengaged, and this switch interlocks the AFCS engage switch as a protective measure.

11. Return the aileron trim emergency switch to the NORM position, but do not move the engage switch to its ENGAGE position at this time. Engage the AFCS by actuating the engage switch to the ENGAGE position. Then move the stick aft and, while holding an aft force on the stick, operate the stick trim button to trim the aircraft NOSEUP. The result should be that the autopilot disengages, the engage switch should flip to its OFF position and the stability augmentation switch should remain in its STAB AUG position. The test simulates the automatic trim circuit working improperly (making an out-of-trim condition worse).

12. With the switches left in the positions resulting from the check of step 11, engage the AFCS and make a similar test as in step 11, but push the stick forward and trim for a NOSEUP condition. The results should be the same as in step 11.

13. Reengage the engage switch, and then depress the AP button on the stickgrip. The ENGAGE switch and the stability augmentation switch should flip to their OFF positions. This emergency switch removes all AFCS authority from the airplane control system.

14. Turn standby switch to OFF. Leave switch OFF for takeoff.

WARNING
Positioning AFCS test switch to TEST POSITION 2 may change the longitudinal trim setting. Takeoff trim should always be checked after completion of AFCS preflight check.

NORMAL INFLIGHT OPERATION

TO ENGAGE STABILITY AUGMENTATION

1. Standby switch . . . . STANDBY

2. Warmup period . . . . 30 to 90
   SECONDS

3. Aileron trim emergency
   switch . . . . NORM

4. Heading select switch . . . . . . OFF

5. Altitude switch . . . . OFF

6. Engage switch . . . . OFF

7. 1-N-2 switch . . . . N

CAUTION

Do not use the 1-N-2 switch while
in flight

8. Stability augmentation
   switch . . . . STAB AUG

TO ENGAGE AFCS

Perform the above steps, then actuate the
engage switch to the ENGAGE position.

Note

Engagement by use of the engage
switch can be made without first
using stability augmentation (STAB
AUG). However, stability augmentation actuation is recommended
first so that the pilot will have the
stability augmentation mode after he
disengages the AFCS.

TO DISENGAGE AFCS

The pilot may disengage the AFCS in the fol-
owing ways:

1. Pressing control stick button AP will
disengage the AFCS.

2. Moving the standby switch to its OFF
position.

3. Moving both the engage and the stability
augmentation switches to their OFF position.

4. Depressing the PUSH TO SYNC button
on the compass controller.

5. Moving the SET HDG switch on the compass controller.

6. Moving the aileron trim NORM/EMER-
GENCY switch to EMERG position. In the
event the switchover from automatic trim to
manual trim malfunctions, or upon disengagement, the EMRG position gives an additional
switchover and will disengage the AFCS.

7. Moving the horizontal stabilizer manual
override lever on the left-hand console will
manually overcome malfunction of the automatic pitch trimmer.

Note

Up to 4 seconds of override lever
actuation may be required before
disengagement occurs.

8. Pulling the emergency generator release handle.

LIGHTING EQUIPMENT

INTERIOR LIGHTS

The interior lighting system includes all instrument and console lights, and cockpit
floodlights. A light is mounted in each instrument lens (except the oil pressure gage)
to provide equal illumination over the entire
face of the instrument. Two floodlights are

mounted on each side of the gunsight beneath the glareshield to provide auxiliary or emergency lighting of the instrument panel. A white kneeboard floodlight incorporating a red filter is mounted on the gunsight support on the right-hand side to provide lighting for the pilot's kneeboard. Six red floodlights are installed to provide auxiliary or emergency console lighting. Four white floodlights are provided for auxiliary cockpit lighting for use with the thermal radiation closure. Instrument and console lights are operative on emergency generator.

INTERIOR LIGHTS CONTROL PANEL

An interior lights (INT LTS) control panel (figure 1-24) mounted on the right console, contains switches for the operation of all interior lights except the four high intensity white floodlights. Two rotary switches, marked INST and CONSOLES are rotated clockwise from OFF to turn on the instrument lights and console lights, respectively. Further rotation in a clockwise direction toward the BRIGHT position increases the intensity of the light.

Note

When the instrument lights switch is any position other than OFF, the ladder lights are dimmed for night operations and may not be visible in daylight

A toggle switch with three positions, BRIGHT, DIM, and MEDIUM, controls the intensity of the red floodlights after the CONSOLES switch is rotated from the OFF position. The pilot's kneeboard floodlight has separate intensity control on the case.

The four high intensity white floodlights, two for the instrument panel and one for each console, have a common control installed above the right-hand console on the fuselage skin. Clockwise rotation from the OFF position turns the floodlights on dimly and further clockwise rotation increases the intensity.

EXTERIOR LIGHTS

The exterior lights system includes position lights, fuselage wing lights, air refueling probe light, an approach light, and a taxi light. A semiflush white high intensity gas discharge and low intensity filament fuselage wing light is located under the leading edge of each wing and one is mounted on top of the fuselage. The aircraft has two flashing red anticollision beacons; one is mounted on the top of the fuselage and the other on the left main landing gear strut fairing. The angle-of-attack approach lights are mounted in the leading edge of the left wing (see figure 1-25). The taxi light is installed on the right hand main landing gear door.

The air refueling probe light is located on the right-hand intake duct forward outboard lip. (See figure 1-25)

Wing tip, tail, and fuselage lights are actually double lights, as both filament and gas discharge types are provided. The BRT (bright) position directs power to the gas discharge lights; the DIM position directs power to the filament lights.

WARNING

Exterior lights do not operate on emergency generator power.

EXTERIOR LIGHTS CONTROLS

MASTER EXTERIOR LIGHTS SWITCH. A master exterior lights switch (figure 1-25) on the outboard side of the throttle grip, controls power to the exterior lights. The switch has a forward ON position, a center OFF position, and an aft momentary ON position. The master exterior lights switch is spring loaded from the aft to the center position, providing a means of signaling with the exterior lights.

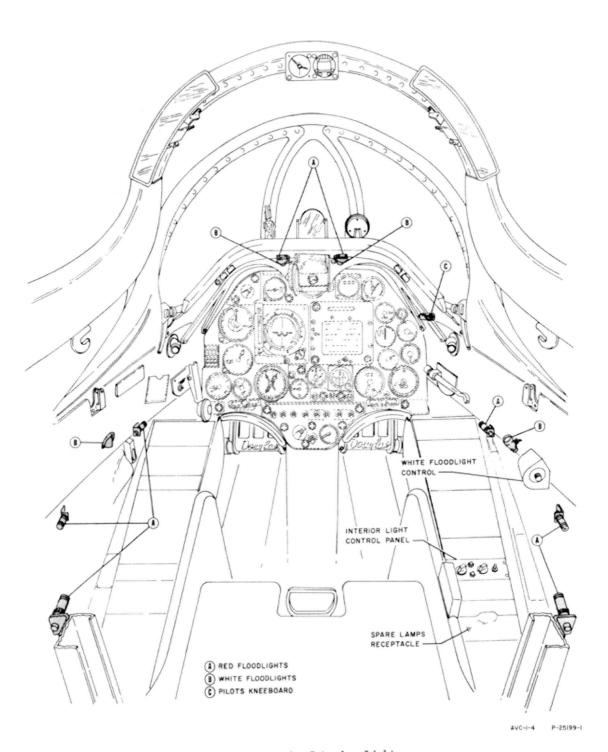

WHITE FLOODLIGHT
CONTROL

INTERIOR LIGHT
CONTROL PANEL

SPARE LAMPS
RECEPTACLE

(A) RED FLOODLIGHTS
(B) WHITE FLOODLIGHTS
(C) PILOTS KNEEBOARD

AVC-1-4   P-25199-1

Figure 1-24. Interior Lights

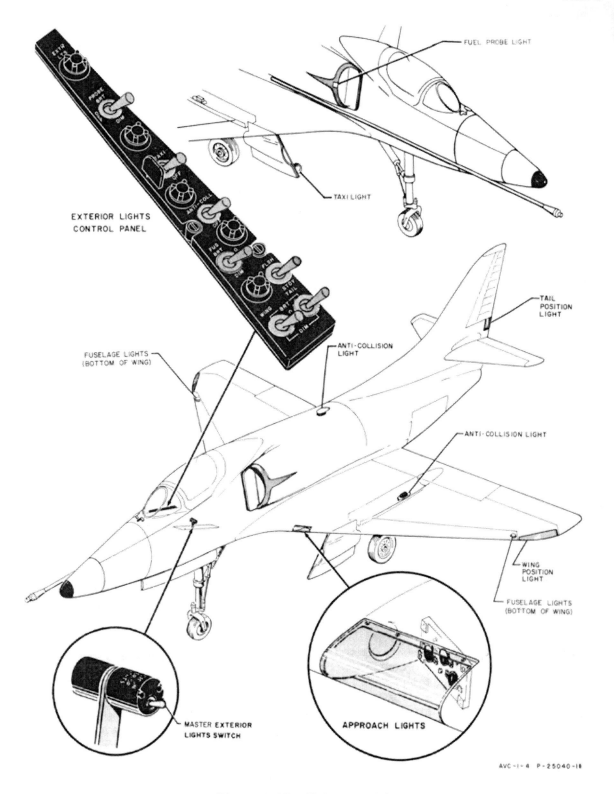

EXTERIOR LIGHTS
CONTROL PANEL

FUEL PROBE LIGHT

TAXI LIGHT

TAIL
POSITION
LIGHT

FUSELAGE LIGHTS
(BOTTOM OF WING)

ANTI-COLLISION
LIGHT

ANTI-COLLISION LIGHT

WING
POSITION
LIGHT

FUSELAGE LIGHTS
(BOTTOM OF WING)

MASTER EXTERIOR
LIGHTS SWITCH

APPROACH LIGHTS

AVC-1-4 P-25040-18

Figure 1-25. Exterior Lights

EXTERIOR LIGHTS CONTROL PANEL. An exterior lights control panel (figure 1-25) on the right console contains switches for functional control of the exterior lights.

APPROACH LIGHT OPERATION

The approach light circuit is controlled by a tailhook switch, a landing gear microswitch, and by a manually operated tailhook bypass switch. When the master exterior lights switch on the throttle is ON, the approach lights are automatically dimmed for night operations. Approach lights will operate on emergency generator power.

AIR CONDITIONING AND PRESSURIZATION SYSTEM

A combination air conditioning and pressurization system heats, cools, ventilates, and pressurizes the cockpit. The system comprises an air cycle system refrigeration unit, cockpit pressure regulator, pressure relief valve, and temperature control components. (See figure 1-26 for a schematic of the air conditioning and pressurization system.)

AIR CONDITIONING

Hot high pressure air is bled from the engine compressor section, and is ducted either through or around the refrigeration unit, as governed by a cockpit temperature controller. Air passing through the refrigeration unit is directed through a heat exchanger and turbine, where it is expanded and cooled. The cooled air from the refrigeration unit is further mixed with hot air which has bypassed the unit, and is delivered to the cockpit. The degree of mixing of the conditioned air is controlled automatically by an air temperature control valve, which maintains the air at the temperature selected from the cockpit.

The air conditioning system is a delivered air temperature control system. Since the console control calls for a fixed temperature of the air as it enters the cockpit, the pilot must change the setting as cockpit heating and cooling loads change. Position of the temperature control knob is not an indicator for pilot comfort. Under certain flight conditions full cold will provide comfort; under other conditions, full hot may be required. The pilot, therefore, must adjust the control to maintain a comfortable cockpit.

PRESSURIZATION

When the air conditioning system is in normal operation, the air provided for heating, cooling, and ventilation is also used to pressurize the cockpit. The pressurizing schedule (figure 1-27) provides for cockpit pressure to equal atmospheric pressure from sea level to 8000 feet altitude. The cockpit pressure at 8000 feet is then maintained to an altitude of 17,000 feet. From this point on, the cockpit pressure is maintained at 3.3 psi above the existing atmosphere pressure. Cockpit pressure is shown in terms of altitude by the cabin altimeter (figure 1-26), located on the right side of the armament panel.

In order to prevent excessive positive or negative pressure differentials because of possible malfunctioning of the pressure regulator, a pressure relief valve opens at a positive pressure differential of 3.6 psi and at a negative differential of minus 0.10 psi. The pressure relief valve also incorporates an emergency feature which allows it to dump cockpit pressure when the cockpit pressurization switch is placed in the RAM position.

AIR CONDITIONING CONTROL PANEL

The air conditioning control panel (3, figure 1-8) is located outboard of the right-hand console. It contains a two-position lever lock toggle switch for operation of the cabin pressurization system, a rotary cabin temperature control knob, and a 3-position windshield defrost switch.

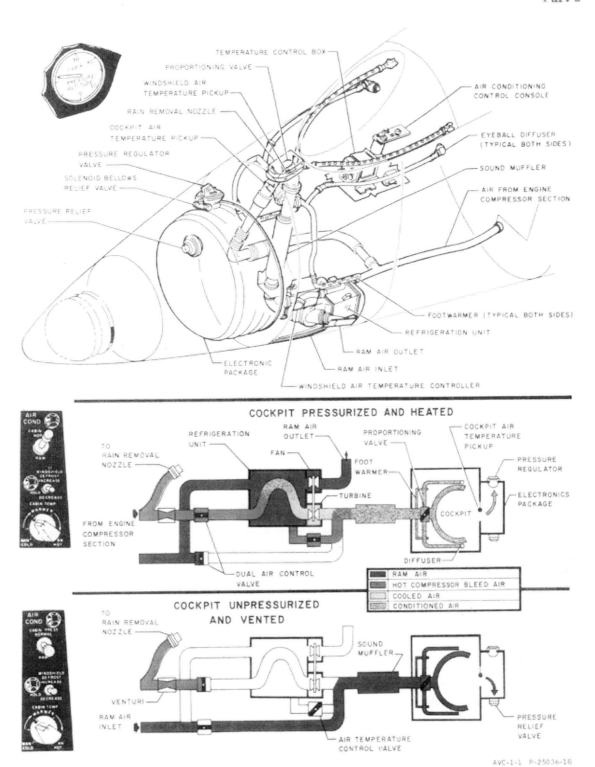

Figure 1-26. Air Conditioning and Pressurization System

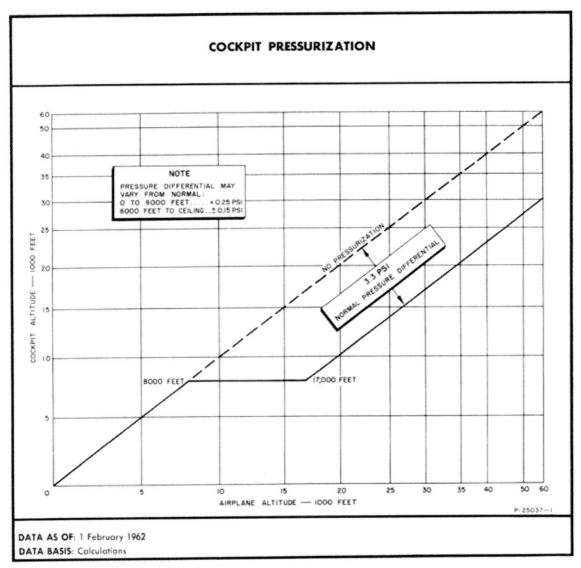

Figure 1-27. Cockpit Pressurization Chart

CABIN PRESSURE SWITCH

The cabin pressure switch is marked RAM and NORMAL. When NORMAL is selected, and the canopy is closed, the cockpit is sealed and pressurized by engine compressor bleed air. Pressurization is automatically maintained at a predetermined schedule by the cockpit pressure regulator. The RAM position electrically opens a pressure relief valve to dump cockpit pressure and opens a motor-driven valve in the ram air line allowing outside air to ventilate the cockpit. Selecting RAM also closes off engine bleed air to the air conditioning system.

CABIN TEMPERATURE CONTROL

Marked positions of the rotary cabin temperature control are MAN COLD, MAN HOT, and

Changed 15 March 1965

WARMER. The control is functional whenever the cockpit pressurization switch is in the NORMAL position. In normal operation, the control is set in the arc (from 10 o'clock to 2 o'clock) designated WARMER which provides the desired cockpit temperature. In the vent of a malfunction in the normal temperature control circuitry, manual temperature control is provided by rotating the temperature control past a detent to the MAN COLD or MAN HOT positions. These positions bypass the automatic temperature control circuitry and changes the mixing of hot and refrigerated air in the selected direction as long as the control is held in position.

Note

- The temperature control is spring loaded away from the MAN COLD and MAN HOT positions (7 o'clock and 4 o'clock, respectively) and must be held firmly in the desired position against this pressure.

- When released from the MAN COLD or MAN HOT positions, the temperature control is in a "hold" condition and the mixing valve motor is deenergized. If the air conditioning unit fails or loses electrical power, the cockpit air temperature control valves will remain in the same position and the cockpit pressure will remain as is.

WINDSHIELD DEFROST SWITCH

The windshield defrost switch is marked INCREASE, HOLD, and DECREASE and controls a motor-driven proportioning valve which serves to proportion air between the windshield defrost manifold and the footwarmers. Air directed to the footwarmers is also shared with the "eyeball" diffusers. The "eyeball" diffusers may be turned on, off or to any intermediate position by rotation of the diffuser nozzle and may be directed to provide air flow in the most comfortable direction by manual adjustment of the diffuser in its ball-socket base. When the defrost switch is

placed in INCREASE, the proportioning valve is operated to a position which increases the proportional air flow to the windshield. If allowed to remain in this position for several seconds, all air entering the cockpit will be directed to the windshield defrost manifold. When the defrost switch is moved to its momentary DECREASE position, the proportioning valve decreases the air flow to the windshield and increases the air flow to the footwarmers (and eyeball diffusers if opened) as long as the switch is held in DECREASE, or until the proportioning valve reaches its limit. At this time, all air is bypassing the windshield defrost manifold and is directed into the footwarmers (and eyeball diffusers if opened). The HOLD position allows the proportioning valve to remain as is.

DEFROST

Defrosting of the windshield side panels is accomplished by windshield defrost air as above.

Frosting of the bullet resistant glass center panel of the windshield is prevented by electrical means. This system is energized when the main generator is operating or when external power is supplied. A transparent layer within the glass panel provides resistance for electrical heating, and a sensing element contained in the panel causes a heating controller to regulate automatically the temperature of the surface to maintain it between two predetermined limits.

Windshield center panel defrosting also functions when the emergency generator is extended. With the emergency generator extended, a switch in the system automatically shuts off the heating element when the landing gear handle is moved to the DOWN position. To minimize fogging of the center panel when the emergency generator is extended, delay lowering the landing gear as long as possible in the landing sequence.

COCKPIT FOG AND SNOW SUPPRESSION

Small quantities of fog, light snow, or ice will frequently appear at the air conditioning outlets. A screen has been added to the manifold connection to prevent ice from being emitted from the distribution system. While this is a normal condition resulting from rapid cooling of air by the air conditioning unit, an excessively large volume of fog which obstructs vision can occur under extreme conditions of high humidity and high ambient air temperatures at low altitude. This fog may be eliminated by adjusting the cockpit temperature control knob for higher cockpit temperature, or by adjusting the windshield defrost switch to decrease the flow of air to the windshield defrost ducts and closing the "eyeball" diffusers, thereby dumping the fog and snow to the footwarmers. In some cases the ducting may have cooled to a point where fog will persist for a short time after the cockpit temperature has been increased. After the fog has been suppressed, a temperature setting should be selected that will provide the most comfortable temperature above the fogging point.

ANTIBLACKOUT SYSTEM

The antiblackout system utilizes high pressure engine bleed air. Air is filtered and directed through a line to the valve located on the anti-g and oxygen panel on the left-hand console (figure 1-6). The valve control knob can be turned to HI or LO to regulate the amount of air pressure increase in the anti-g suit. As g-forces are reduced, the valve will automatically reduce the pressure in the suit. A push button on the top of the valve control knob may be manually operated to test the system. If the valve has any tendency to stick or fails to return to the closed position, it should be replaced. On long flights this system makes it possible for the pilot to inflate the suit occasionally for body massage to lessen fatigue. The antiblackout suit connection plugs into a receptacle adjacent to the control knob.

Note

In the event of inadvertent g-suit hose disconnect, noticeable chattering in the valve may occur during accelerated flight.

ANTI-ICING SYSTEM

ENGINE

The engine anti-icing system is designed to prevent ice formation, and safe operation requires that the pilot anticipate the possibility of ice formation whenever these weather conditions exist.

Ice formation in the engine air inlet section is prevented by an integral power plant system which utilizes high pressure, hot bleed air from the compressor section. Air bled from both sides of the compressor discharge is piped forward through external lines and distributed through the inlet guide vanes from which it is ported into the engine inlet airstream.

ANTI-ICING CONTROL

Electrical control of the anti-icing system is accomplished by placing the anti-icing switch (figure 1-8), located outboard of the right-hand console, to the ALL position. The switch in this position directs power to the anti-icing valve and regulator mechanism on the external lines. It also actuates the heating element of the pitot tube.

CAUTION

Operation below approximately 75 percent rpm may not supply sufficient heat to keep the engine air inlet ducts clear of ice. Whenever severe icing conditions are encountered or anticipated, operate engine at or above 75 percent rpm.

Changed 15 May 1966

PITOT AND ANGLE-OF-ATTACK VANE

When the aircraft becomes airborne and the landing gear struts extend, the retraction release switch is actuated, completing the circuit to the outside sensing vane heater to prevent icing. Heating is provided for the pitot tube by placing the anti-icing switch to the PITOT position.

RAIN REMOVAL SYSTEM

The rain removal system utilizes high-pressure engine bleed air to remove rain from the bullet-resistant glass center panel of the windshield. Hot, high-pressure bleed air is ducted to the rain removal automatic pressure regulating unit. The pressure regulating unit allows constant pressure air to be delivered to the jet pump unit. The jet pump unit mixes the hot bleed air with ambient air and delivers it to a nozzle which directs the high-velocity, hot air over the windshield surface. Electrical control of the system is maintained by the rain removal control panel located on the wedge outboard of the right-hand console. The rain removal system is inoperative on emergency generator.

RAIN REMOVAL CONTROL PANEL

The rain removal control panel (figure 1-8) has two switch positions labeled RAIN REMOVAL and OFF. When the switch is placed at the RAIN REMOVAL position, hot high-pressure air is directed over the windshield surface. The OFF position of the switch cuts off the air. In the event of electrical power failure, the valve in the pressure regulating unit automatically closes, shutting off the system.

NORMAL OPERATION

ON THE GROUND

Rain removal airblast temperatures are a function of engine power setting. At IDLE power, airblast temperature is not sufficiently hot to cause damage to the windshield and the system may be operated continuously. However, at MILITARY, the temperature becomes extremely hot, and the operation at

high-power settings is limited to a maximum of 3 minutes.

CAUTION

Exceeding this limit could cause bubbling of vinyl layers and cracking of glass.

The pilot may check the rain removal system after engine starting by noting the warm air-blast over the top of the windshield. The rain removal switch should always be returned to the OFF position immediately after the pre-flight check to prevent inadvertent operation at high-power settings and subsequent damage to the windshield. On takeoff, if the rain removal system may be required, the switch should be placed at RAIN REMOVAL just prior to the takeoff roll.

IN THE AIR

The rain removal system may be used for extended periods of time during approach and landing due to the lower power settings usually required for this phase of flight.

ARMAMENT EQUIPMENT

All stores are carried externally on five racks. Stores which may be carried are listed in NAVWEPS 01-40AVC-1A. A 4-hook ejector-type bomb rack is installed on the centerline (fuselage) station and 2-hook ejector racks are provided on the wing stations. The centerline rack, which is limited to a load of 3575 pounds, can be used to carry stores which require either 30-inch or 14-inch suspension. Inboard wing racks are provided with 14-inch suspension, and have a load limit of 1200 pounds each, except when carrying the 300-gallon external fuel tanks or multiple bomb racks. Outer wing racks are restricted to a load limit of approximately 500 pounds.

Control of all armament is effected through the armament panel located below the instrument panel. When various special stores which require timing and fuzing devices for proper operation are carried, additional control panels (see figure 1-30) may be installed in the left-hand console. Electrical release of stores is controlled directly by the pilot.

ARMAMENT PANEL

MASTER ARMAMENT SWITCH. All armament equipment is controlled by the master armament switch (figure 1-28) except gun charging and emergency jettisoning of stores. The armament circuits can be energized only when this switch is ON. An armament safety circuit prevents operation of the armament system when the landing gear handle is down.

STATIONS SELECTOR SWITCHES

Five stations selector switches (figure 1-28) are provided for armament release. Each switch has READY, OFF, and SALVO positions providing single or multiple release of stores with the armament firing switches.

Note

The SALVO position no longer serves any useful purpose and should not be used.

FUNCTION SELECTOR SWITCH

A rotary select switch (figure 1-28) is provided for selecting the type of armament to be released. The switch may be set on any one of six separate detents which are labeled LABS, BOMBS & GM ARM, ROCKETS, GM UNARM, OFF and SPRAY TANK.

ARMAMENT SAFETY CIRCUIT DISABLING SWITCH

When the airplane is on the ground, an alternate circuit may be energized for the purpose of checking the armament system. This circuit is engaged by momentarily closing the

armament safety disable switch, located on the outboard side of the right-hand wheelwell. Raising the landing gear or moving the master armament switch to OFF will restore the armament safety circuit to normal operation.

GUNSIGHT

A lighted gunsight (figure 1-28) is provided for gunnery and for rocket and bomb aiming. The gunsight, mounted on the top center of the glareshield, contains one ladder-type reticle and a glass reflector to super-impose the reticle image upon the target.

GUNSIGHT ELEVATION CONTROL

A sight elevation knob (figure 1-28) on the left-hand side of the gunsight controls the glass reflector angle for increasing or decreasing the lead of the reticle. The locking yoke must be lifted before setting the sight elevation knob.

CAUTION

Be sure to unlock the yoke before attempting to rotate the elevation control knob. Failure to do so may damage the mechanism and result in sight elevation errors.

After setting the knob to the desired lead, press the locking yoke firmly against the sight body to lock the reflector plate struts.

CAUTION

Press on the yoke proper, do not press on the guard attached to the locking yoke.

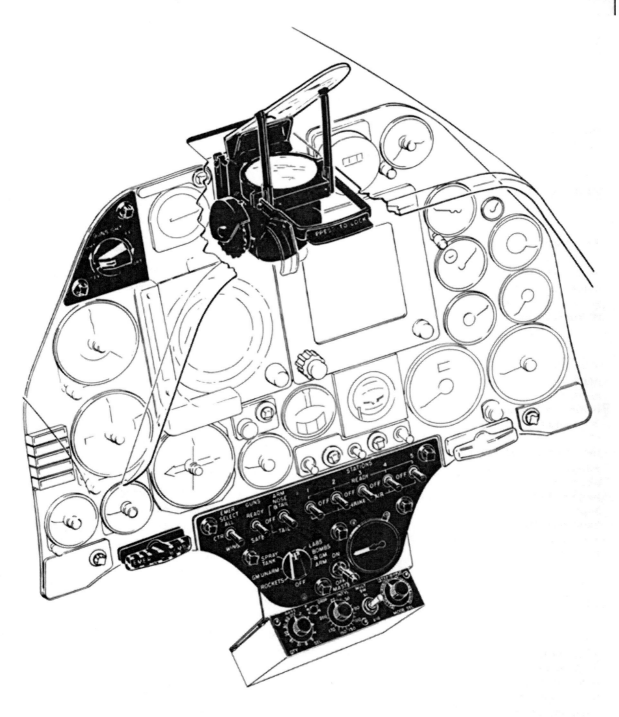

Figure 1-28. Gunsight and Armament Panel

GUNSIGHT RETICLE LIGHT CONTROL

A single rotary knob located on the upper left-hand corner of the instrument panel (figure 1-28) identified as gunsight serves as the gunsight reticle light control. By rotating the knob, either of two filaments may be selected for lighting. Light intensity can be adjusted between the OFF and BRIGHT positions for either filament.

GUNNERY EQUIPMENT

Two forward firing MK 12 Mod 0 20-millimeter guns can be installed in the airplane as alternate armament. Ammunition boxes, located in the main access area between the guns, can be loaded with one hundred rounds of ammunition for each gun.

The MK 12 Mod 0 gun is a combination blowback and gas-operated weapon which fires ammunition electrically. The weapon, which is air-cooled, has a rate of fire of 1000 rounds per minute in short bursts. A pneumatic charger mechanism operates the breechblock for first round loading. Although firing is simultaneous from both guns, individual compressed air tanks, filled to 3200 ±200 psi, permit each gun to be remotely charged as a separate unit. The gun electropneumatic packages are located in the right-hand wheelwell, and in the forward engine compartment and accessory section.

GUN CHARGING SWITCH

The gun charging switch (figure 1-28) on the armament panel is identified as guns and has two positions, SAFE and READY. The breechblock is retracted by pneumatic pressure in the charger cylinder and held aft as long as the switch remains on SAFE. When the switch is moved to READY, the breechblock and a round of ammunition are brought forward to charge the gun.

| WARNING |

DO NOT CYCLE THE GUN CHARGER. Movement of the gun selector switch from READY to SAFE and back to READY can cause an explosion by ramming a new round against a jammed one. The Master Armament Switch should be used to interrupt the trigger circuit between runs.

Always keep the charging switch in the SAFE position until guns must be readied, and return it to that position after final run.

| WARNING |

Always SAFE guns in an authorized area to prevent injury to ground personnel from ejected cartridges or links.

The armament safety circuit functions when the landing gear is lowered, deenergizing the guncharging circuits and causing the breechblock to be retracted to the safe position.

| WARNING |

Do not fly behind or below any aircraft that is in or has previously completed a firing run to prevent damage from ejected cartridges links.

GUN-ROCKET TRIGGER

The gun-rocket trigger on the control stick grip is used to fire both guns and rockets. The trigger is on the front of the stick grip. (See figure 1-29.) The guns will fire when the trigger is depressed, providing the master armament switch is turned ON and the guns charging switch is at READY.

Changed 15 March 1965

Note

To prevent rockets from firing when operating the guns, the function select switch should be set on the OFF position or the stations selector switches turned OFF.

FIRING GUNS

1. Function select switch or stations selector switch . . . . . . OFF

2. Guns switch . . . . READY

3. Master armament switch . . . . ON

4. Gun-rocket trigger . . . . . . SQUEEZE

MK 4 GUN POD

The MK 4 gun pod is a 20 MM gun system. There are provisions for installation of MK 4 guns pods at ejector rack stations 2, 3, and 4 on aircraft 151142 and subsequent. The provisions (refer to figure 1-29A) consist of a gun pod control panel for installation in the left-hand console and permanent gun pod wiring from the left-hand console to the center, and left- and right-hand inboard ejector racks.

MK 4 GUN POD CONTROL PANEL

The gun pod control panel provides the means to electrically control operation of the MK 4 gun pod from the cockpit. Firing of the gun pod system is controlled by the gun-rocket trigger on the control stick grip. The control panel contains three STATION selector switches and a CHARGE-OFF-CLEAR switch. The STATION selector switches are single-throw, triple-pole, toggle switches and provide SAFE and READY switch positions for the LH, CTR, and RH gun pod installations. The CHARGE-OFF-CLEAR switch is a double-throw, triple-pole toggle switch and electrically controls charging and clearing functions of the guns.

> **CAUTION**
>
> Do not attempt carrier landings with fully loaded gun pods, as maximum allowable gross weight (14,500 pounds) may be exceeded. Each gun pod weighs 1400 pounds fully loaded and 797 pounds empty. When carrying three fully loaded gun pods, the total complement of ammunition for two gun pods (1206 pounds) must be expended in order to obtain desired aircraft arrested landing weight.

ROCKET EQUIPMENT

Forward firing air-to-ground rockets of two sizes can be carried in rocket launchers suspended from the bomb racks. The rockets are carried in the package launchers in any combination of the following configurations:

Each Wing Station	Centerline Station
7 . . 2.75-inch rockets	7 . . 2.75-inch rockets
19 . . 2.75-inch rockets	19 . . 2.75-inch rockets
4 . . 5.00-inch rockets	

FIRING ROCKETS

Release of rockets from packages is accomplished by ripple fire. To fire the rockets, observe the following procedure:

1. Function select switch . . . . ROCKETS

2. Stations selector switches   READY ON EACH STATION AS REQUIRED

3. Guns switch . . . . SAFE

4. Master armament switch . . . . . . ON

5. Gun-rocket trigger . . . . . SQUEEZE

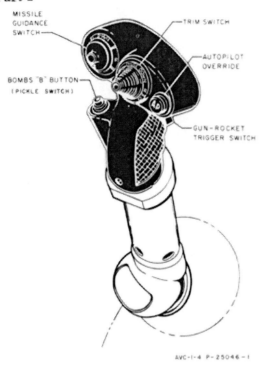

MISSILE
GUIDANCE
SWITCH

TRIM SWITCH

AUTOPILOT
OVERRIDE

BOMBS "B" BUTTON
(PICKLE SWITCH)

GUN-ROCKET
TRIGGER SWITCH

AVC-1-4 P-25046-1

Figure 1-29. Control Stick Switches

Note

Make certain that the gun charging switch is on SAFE, to prevent the guns from firing simultaneously with the rockets.

JETTISONING ROCKETS

Rockets are carried only in packages hung directly on the bomb racks. The packages may be jettisoned in the same manner as other external stores, using either the normal bomb releasing methods or the emergency releasing controls. (Refer to RELEASING BOMBS.)

BOMBING EQUIPMENT

DESCRIPTION

Release of bombs and other stores from the ejector-type racks is accomplished by electrical detonation of cartridges. When car-

tridges are fired by pressing the bomb release switch, the initial force is an upward thrust which opens the hooks, followed by a downward ejector thrust of several inches which forces the bomb clear of the airplane. The ejector foot is located aft of center on the bomb rack in order to counteract the twisting moment on the bomb caused by drag forces in high speed flight. Each rack contains two cartridges. One firing circuit is for normal release and the second is for emergency release.

BOMB ARMING SWITCH

The bomb arming switch (figure 1-28), identified as ARM is located adjacent to the function select switch. The 3-position arm switch can be set at NOSE & TAIL or TAIL depending on arming requirements, or can be placed in the OFF position for releasing stores in an unarmed condition.

BOMB RELEASE BUTTON

The "pickle" (figure 1-29) used for releasing bombs and other external stores, is located on the left side of the control stick grip and is identified by the letter "B". This switch is also used with alternate installations, such as the chemical spray tank, the practice bomb container, the Bullpup missile and the multiple bomb rack. The "pickle" functions only when operating on the main generator.

EMERGENCY SELECTOR SWITCH

The emergency select switch (figure 1-28), located adjacent to the emergency bomb release handle, provides selection of WINGS, CENTER, or ALL stations when jettisoning stores with the emergency bomb release handle. This switch functions with the main or emergency generator in operation.

EMERGENCY BOMB RELEASE HANDLE

An emergency bomb release T-handle (figure 1-28) on the lower left-hand side of the instrument panel is used to jettison external stores.

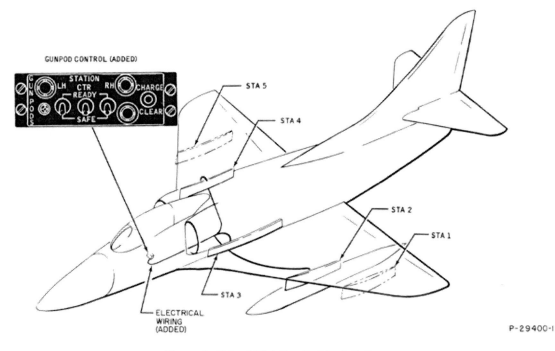

Figure 1-29A. MK 4 Gun Pod Installation

Pulling the handle closes a switch in the emergency release circuit, bypassing the normal release controls. Power to the emergency circuit is supplied by the primary bus, which is energized by either the main or the emergency generator. Stores selected by the emergency selector switch may be released irrespective of the position of the landing gear control or master armament switch.

RELEASING BOMBS

NORMAL RELEASE

1. Arming Switch . . . . . TAIL OR NOSE & TAIL

2. Function select
switch . . . . BOMBS & GM ARM

3. Stations selector
switches . . . . READY

4. Master armament
switch . . . . ON

5. Bomb release
button . . . . DEPRESS

NOTE

Do not use the SALVO position of the station selector switch.

EMERGENCY RELEASE

1. Emergency select   WING, CENTER OR
switch . . . .   ALL (AS REQUIRED)

2. Emergency bomb
release handle. . . . . PULL

CAUTION

When emergency bomb release handle is used to release wing stores only (emergency select switch set on WING), make sure center station selector switch is in OFF position to prevent an electrical feedback through normal bomb release circuit and inadvertent release of center store.

WARNING

Do not jettison bombs below maximum fragmentation envelope whether in armed or safe condition.

AIRCRAFT WEAPONS RELEASE SYSTEM (AWRS)

The aircraft weapons release system allows the pilot to control the quantity of weapons for release and the interval between releases. The quantity of weapons, drop interval, and delivery mode can be changed without affecting system operation. The weapons stations, on the armament panel, can be selected and deselected and the system will retain the memory of the stations and weapons remaining or released providing the AWRS is not turned OFF. The AWRS, if turned OFF, will lose the memory of stations used and weapons released and could send release pulses to empty weapons stations. Whenever the bomb

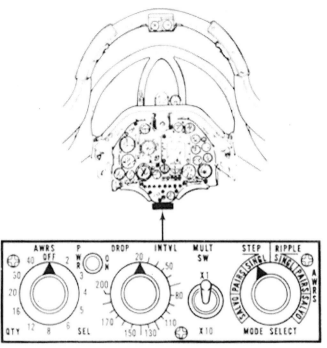

AVC-1-1 P-29992-1

Figure 1-29B. Aircraft Weapons Release System Panel

release button or rocket trigger is depressed, the
LABS light turns on and an aural tone is heard in the
pilots headset. The stations that receive the release
pulses are selected, by the pilot, with armament
panel STATIONS select switch. The aural tone stops
after the last weapon is dropped (AWRS ripple mode
only).

The AWRS consists of an AN/AWE-1 control panel,
a programmer, a tone generator, a system operation
light (LABS light), associated wiring, a single point
test receptacle, and a system bypass cable. When
the AN/AWE-1 control panel is in the OFF position,
a bypass allows release capabilities to all other armament systems. A harness assembly bypass must
be installed on the programmer bracket when the
programmer is not in the aircraft.

RELEASE MODES

The pilot may choose one of the two basic release
modes, ripple release or step release.

The AWRS in the ripple mode, releases weapons at a
selected drop interval until the selected number of
weapons have been released. In the ripple mode the
LABS light will stay on and the aural tone will be
heard until the selected number of weapons are
released. When the AWRS is in the step mode the
weapons release will be at a rate determined by the
pilot. One release signal is generated each time the
bomb release button is depressed. In the step mode
the LABS light will stay on and the aural tone will be
heard as long as the bomb release button is held down.

The release modes can be selected as follows:

STEP SINGLES

Turn the mode select switch to STEP SINGLES and
the quantity select switch to 2. One weapon will be
released for each depression of the bomb release
button. The AWRS will alternate the weapons releases
from left to right outboard to inboard wing stations if
all stations are selected. In the step modes the drop
interval is determined by the frequency of the bomb
release button depressions.

STEP PAIRS

Turn the mode select switch to STEP PAIRS and the
quantity select switch to 2 or to the number of weapons to be released. One weapon will be released
simultaneously from each station of equal priority
with each depression of the bomb release button. The
station priority will be outboard to inboard (see figure 1-29B). No weapons will be released from the
centerline station in the STEP PAIRS mode because
the centerline station does not have a station of equal
priority. If stations of different priority are selected,
no weapon release pulses will be generated by the
AWRS. No aural tone will be heard in the pilot's
headset.

STEP SALVO

Turn the mode select switch to STEP SALVO and the
quantity select switch to 2. One weapon will be

released simultaneously from each station selected with each depression of the bomb release button. The interval select control is not applicable as the interval of each salvo is determined by the frequency of the bomb release button depressions. The salvo mode has no station priority.

RIPPLE SINGLES

Select the quantity of weapons to be released with the quantity select switch. The interval select control and multiplier switch must be set to the desired interval between releases. The weapons will be released, upon depressing the bomb release button, from left to right outboard to inboard until the quantity of weapons selected has been released. The aural tone will be heard in the pilot's headset when the bomb button is depressed and go off when the quantity selected is released. Then the pilot can release the bomb release button. If, during the drop sequence, the bomb release button is inadvertently released and depressed again the AWRS will not complete the interrupted sequence, but start at the beginning of a new sequence. The aural tone will cease after the selected number of weapons have been released or when the last weapon has been released, whichever occurs first.

RIPPLE PAIRS

Set the quantity select switch to the number of pairs of weapons to be released. Set the drop interval control and multiplier switch to the desired interval between releases. The aural tone will be heard in the pilot's headset when the bomb release button is depressed and will cease when the selected pairs of weapons are released or the last pair of weapons on equal priority stations is released, whichever occurs first. If there are no weapons on pairs of equal priority stations, the aural tone will not be heard when the bomb release button is depressed. If stations of different priority are selected, no release pulses will be generated and the aural tone will not be heard when the bomb release button is depressed.

RIPPLE SALVO

Set the quantity select switch to the number of weapons to be released simultaneously from each selected station when the bomb release button is depressed. The interval select control and the multiplier switch must be set for the desired interval between salvo releases. The aural tone will be heard in the headset when the bomb release button is depressed. The aural tone will go off when the selected number of salvo release pulses have been delivered or all weapons on the aircraft have been released, whichever occurs first.

PRIORITY OF RELEASE

The AWRS generates release signals in the following priority:

1. Outboard stations have priority over inboard stations. As long as an outboard station is selected and contains stores, it receives the release

signals before any inboard selected station regardless of its left or right location.

2. Opposite wing stations of equal outboard to inboard priority receive release signals alternately in step singles until one is depleted. At this time the release signals are directed to the other station and continue until that station is depleted. Then priority reverts inboard in the same manner.

AWRS STATION PRIORITY

Station	Priority
1 and 5	1
2 and 4	2
Center	3

AN/AWE-1 CONTROL PANEL

The AN/AWE-1 control panel, labeled AWRS, is located below the armament panel and contains the following switches: QTY SEL switch, PWR ON light, DROP INTVL control, MULT SW, and the MODE SELECT switch.

1. The quantity select control and power on - off switch serves as an OFF/ON switch for the AWRS and provides selection of weapon release quantity. The AWRS is removed from the aircraft armament system when the quantity select switch is in the OFF position. The quantity select positions of 2, 3, 4, 5, 6, 8, 12, 16, 20, 30, and 40 indicate the quantity of weapons that can be selected and also turns the AWRS ON.

2. The power on light will turn on when the QTY SEL switch is moved to any of the quantity select positions, other than OFF, and indicates power to the AWRS.

3. The drop interval control is used in conjunction with the multiplier switch to determine the drop interval between weapons. The drop interval control has positions of 20 to 200 milliseconds when used in conjunction with the X 1 position of the multiplier switch. When the multiplier switch is placed in the X 10 position, drop interval becomes 200 to 2000 milliseconds.

4. The multiplier switch is used with the drop interval switch to increase the drop interval range.

5. The mode select control provides the following modes of operation: Step Singles, Step Pairs, Step Salvo, Ripple Single, Ripple Pairs, and Ripple Salvo.

AWRS PILOT OPERATION

The pilot must use the following steps to operate the AWRS:

1. Function Selector   ROCKETS OR
   Switch (armament panel) . . . . BOMBS & GM ARM

2. Station Select
   Switches (armament panel) . . . . desired stations

WARNING

- Always select stations of equal priority (both LH and RH stations must be selected) in the step pairs or ripple pairs mode or no release will occur.

- Never select the centerline station in the step pairs or ripple pairs mode as no release will occur.

- Do not de-select and then reselect the RH station after firing the LH station. (Next firing would return to the LH station and would result in the last two firings, in sequence, from the RH station. This could cause Snakeye weapons to collide if the time interval is too short.)

- If it is necessary to de-select the wing stations prior to selecting the centerline station, always de-select the RH wing station before the LH wing station.

3. Arm Switch (armament panel) . . . . NOSE & TAIL

Note

- The nose and tail arm switch must be placed in the NOSE & TAIL position when the MER 7 and TER 7 racks are used. This provides power for the MER 7 and TER 7 stepping function.

Note

- The preceding step will not be required after wiring changes are incorporated in the MER 7 and TER 7 racks.

4. Quantity Select
   Switch . . . . set quantity of pulses

Note

- Operation of the quantity select switch activates the AWRS and sets the quantity of pulses delivered to the selected stations.

- Do not turn the AWRS quantity select switch OFF, except for recycling during partial rocket pod firing. The AWRS programmer will lose the memory of what stations have been released and could send release pulses to empty stations. This could mean either no bomb drop or holes in the bombing pattern.

- When selecting the ROCKET mode for partial rocket pod firing from single pods on the aircraft: After the selected aircraft stations have received release signals, the pilot must then reset the quantity select switch, on the AWRS panel, to the OFF position and then back to a selected quantity in order to continue partial

rocket firing from these stations. Partial pod firing from MER 7 and TER 7 racks is not recommended until wiring changes are incorporated.

5. Drop Interval Control
   and Multiplier Switch . . . . set proper drop interval

Note

- Whenever a multiple rack on the centerline station is selected in the ripple mode, sufficient interval must be selected to allow adequate bomb-to-bomb clearance between weapons launched successively from the same multiple rack.

- The pilot selects the proper drop interval ranging from 20 to 2000 milliseconds.

- Never select a time interval less than ~~70~~ milliseconds when a MER 7, TER 7 or MBR is installed on the aircraft (200 milliseconds for PMBR). A drop interval of less than ~~70~~ milliseconds could result in failure to drop the bombs or fire the rockets.

6. Mode select
   Switch . . . . desired mode of release

WARNING

- Do not select the centerline station simultaneously with the wing stations when releasing Snakeye weapons from the MER 7, TER 7, or PMBR racks in the ripple mode. The release sequence from the centerline station could cause the Snakeye weapons to collide because of too short a time interval between releases. (The bomb drop spacing on the wing stations is twice the distance of the centerline station for the same selected drop interval setting.) The wing stations alternate starting from left to right for release and therefore successive drops from the same wing station have a bomb-to-bomb clearance which is double the selected interval.

- Whenever an uneven number of stores are released from multiple bomb racks on the wing stations, the right wing will retain one more than the left wing. Since the programmer always causes the left wing to release first, release of another stick having an uneven number of stores will result in retention of two more stores on the right wing than on the left. When all weapons on the left wing nave been released, any weapons remaining to be released from the right wing will be provided with only a single interval of clearance. Adequate interval for single station bomb-to-bomb clearance must be selected under these circumstances.

7. Master Armament Switch
(armament panel). . . . . ON

CAUTION

The AWRS power is not controlled by the master armament switch. It is possible to turn the master armament switch ON or OFF to arm or safe the armament system, and not reset the AWRS.

Note

The pilot must turn the master armament switch ON to activate the armament system.

8. Bomb Release Button
or Rocket Trigger
(pilot's control stick) . . . . depress

Note

• The pilot must depress the bomb release button or rocket trigger to initiate weapon delivery. The pilot will hear an aural tone and see the LABS light turn ON when the bomb button or rocket trigger is depressed. When the mode select switch is in the STEP MODE position a continuous pulse is delivered to each selected station for the period of time the pilot depresses the bomb button or rocket trigger. The aural tone and LABS light will remain on until the pilot releases the button or trigger, when the STEP MODE is selected. This means one release from each selected station would occur for each depression of the bomb button or one rocket pod firing from each selected station would occur for each depression of the rocket trigger. In the ripple mode, the preset number and length of pulses are sent to the selected stations. The pilot will hear the aural tone and see the LABS light ON when the bomb button or rocket trigger is depressed until the quantity selected is completed. The bomb button should be released after the aural tone and LABS light are off.

• Never interrupt the bomb release sequence once the sequence is initiated. If at any time during a drop sequence the bomb release button is inadvertently released and then depressed again, the AWRS will start the count sequence anew without interrupting the release sequence. The AWRS will not complete the interrupted sequence.

• The aural tone will always go off when the last weapon is released even when a larger quantity of weapons are selected than the number of weapons on board.

• The PMBR and A/A 37 B1 MBR adapter cables must be changed, as noted in AAC 393 Amendment No. 3, to increment 1 to operate with the AWE-1 system. This change provides a ground for the 2 - 6 station transfer function.

• Ten extra release pulses will occur between the release of stations 2 and 4 and the release of station 3 when single weapons are loaded on the 3 stations. This could result in failure to release the centerline station and a hole in the bombing pattern. Stations 2 - 4 and station 3 should not be selected for stick release with single weapons until AAC 393 Amendment No. 3 to increment 1, is incorporated. This will eliminate the 10 extra pulses between stations 2 - 4 and station 3. This only occurs with single weapon loadings and does not occur when multiple racks are installed.

• It is recommended that only full rocket pods be fired until wiring changes are incorporated in the MER 7 and TER 7 racks, to provide full partial pod capability.

• The "firing on" time is 50% of the drop interval selected in the ripple mode of the AWRS. (Twice the rocket pod firing time must be selected to assure pod fire out.)

9. Rocket pod jettison from multiple racks. Change the function select switch to the "BOMBS & GM ARM" position, set the AWRS quantity select switch and power ON - OFF switch to the OFF position. A maximum of eleven (11) depressions of the bomb button is required to jettison the launchers (depending on stepper switch position).

Note

• The recommended procedure is to fire out all rockets before jettisoning the pods.

• It is recommended that jettisoning of the rocket pods should only occur after rockets are fired. Turn the AWRS switch to the OFF position, select all empty rocket pods stations and pulse the bomb button eleven (11) times. A wiring change will be incorporated in the MER 7 and TER 7 racks, at a later date, that will eliminate the necessity of the eleven (11) pulses.

A/A37B-1 BOMB RACK (MBR)

The multiple bomb rack assembly is designed for installation on the Aero 7A and Aero 20A

ejector racks. The MBR provides for the carrying and release of six bombs or stores from each wing rack and the centerline rack. The bombs may be released in single, dual, or train release at timing intervals of 15, 30, or 60 milliseconds. Each of the six bomb racks on the MBR has its own integral wiring, breech mechanism, and a nose and tail arming unit for mechanically armed bombs; and provisions for a bomb arming unit for electrically fuzed bombs (AN/AWW-1 electrical fuzing system). Releasing a "hung" bomb from an individual bomb rack station is not possible. However, bombs and multiple bomb racks may be jettisoned by pulling the EMER BOMB release handle.

RELEASE MODE SELECTOR SWITCH

A rotary release mode selector switch is located in the tail cone assembly of the MBR and must be preset prior to takeoff. The switch may be set at SINGLE, DUAL, 0.015 SEC., 0.030 SEC., or 0.060 SEC., depending on arming requirements.

When SINGLE or DUAL is preselected on the mode selector switch the bombs B (pickle) button must be pressed each time for the desired number of releases. If 0.015 SEC., 0.030 SEC. or 0.060 SEC. is preselected, hold the bombs B button for 1 second and the bombs will release in train at the interval selected.

Bombs are released from the MBR in the following sequence regardless of mode selections.

Position 1	Aft Center
Position 2	Forward center
Position 3	Aft left
Position 4	Forward left
Position 5	Aft right
Position 6	Forward right

Safety pins are provided to prevent accidental bomb release when the bomb rack is loaded and must be removed before flight.

AN/AWW-1 FUZE FUNCTION CONTROL SYSTEM

WARNING

Oscillator plug-in units and the retaining fuzing templates of the fuze function control set AN/AWW-1 should be removed from the aircraft when it is intended to employ electric fuzes only in the dc modes. Removing these units will prevent inadvertent selection of any available rf modes from resulting in possible hazardous change in arming and/or functioning time.

The aircraft has provisions for the installation of the AN/AWW-1 fuze function control system. (See figure 1-31.) The provisions include a safety interlock and modified bomb racks. This system permits inflight selection of any one of five different arming delay and impact delay times for radio frequency (rf) and four different options for direct current (dc) types of conventional bomb and rocket fuzes. The four options (specific arming delay and impact delay times) for dc types of fuzes are always available. Of the total of 28 different options available for rf types, only 5 chosen on the ground can be selected during a flight.

C2612/AWW-1 FUZE FUNCTION CONTROL PANEL

The fuze function control panel labeled AN/AWW-1, is located on the left-hand console. The panel is supplied as loose equipment, to be installed and used for electrically fuzed weapons missions. The fuze function control panel provides continuity for input power, selects the option to be used in charging fuzes and provides a check of system readiness.

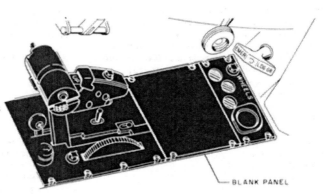

NO STORES CARRIED

EIGHT ALTERNATIVE CONFIGURATIONS
FIT BLANK PANEL DEPENDING
ON WHICH STORES CARRIED.

BLANK PANEL

OMNI RANGE (AN/ARN-14E),
MARKER BEACON (AN/ARN-12)
(NAVPAC) AND BLANK PANEL.

AIR REFUELING (TANKER)
CONTROL AND BLANK
PANEL.

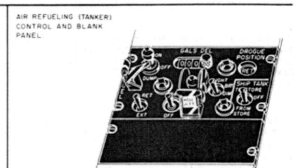

(DCU-75/A) WITH LABS
CONTROL PANEL.

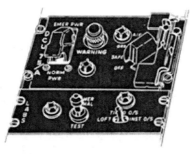

ARMAMENT FUZE PANEL
C-2612/AWW-1 (AERO 5A)
AND BLANK PANEL.

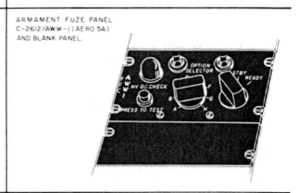

GROUND CONTROLLED
BOMBING SYSTEM
CONTROL PANEL.

SPRAY TANK (AERO 14-B)
CONTROL AND BLANK
PANEL

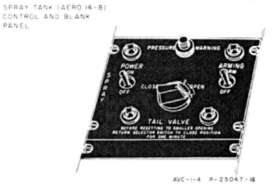

AVC-1-4   P-25047-18

Figure 1-30. Alternate Control Panels

Changed 15 March 1965

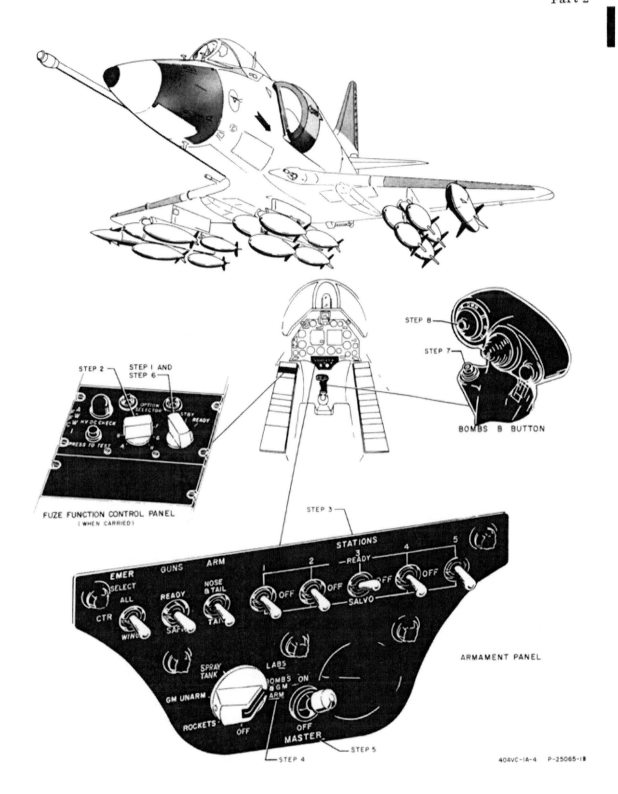

Figure 1-31. AN/AWW-1 Fuze Function Control System

MISSILE SAFE STBY-READY CONTROL SWITCH

The three-position rotary fuze function control switch controls the application of power to the system. In the SAFE position, it disconnects all power. In the STBY position, it supplies power to the vacuum tube filaments and the thermal delay relay, which operates after being energized for a minimum of 20 to 30 seconds and which delays the energizing of the high voltage circuits until the vacuum tube filaments have reached operating temperatures. In the READY position, power is applied to all circuits when the option selector switch is in any rf option position; but only to the dc circuits if the option selector switch is in a dc option position.

On a tactical mission, the fuze function control switch should be kept in the STBY position for at least 30 seconds prior to using the system so that high voltage will be available as soon as the switch is rotated to READY.

OPTION SELECTOR SWITCH

The option selector switch, an eight-position rotary type, selects the arming delay and impact delay times used in charging rf and dc types of fuzes. Positions A through E are used to charge rf types; E through H are used to charge dc types of bomb fuzes and certain fuzes for the bullpup missile.

Note

Position E is used to charge both dc and rf type fuzes. In some rf type fuzes, only 300 volts dc and no rf power is required to obtain certain options. When this is true, position E is used.

PRESS TO TEST SWITCH

The press-to-test switch is used to bypass the interlock system and permit a check of system readiness.

WARNING

Do not press the control stick pickle switch and the press-to-test switch simultaneously except when necessary to override the ground safety interlock.

HV D.C. CHECK LAMP

System readiness is indicated if the HV D.C. CHECK lamp comes on when the switch is in the READY position and the press-to-test switch is pressed. The internal lights switch, controls the lighting of the panel edge.

GROUND CONTROLLED BOMBING SYSTEM

The combined functions of the AN/TPQ-10 ground radar and an aircraft equipped with the GCBS installation provides an all weather close support weapon system capability. The TPQ-10 Radar Course Directing Central is a mobile ground based radar with analog computer, designed to locate, track, and guide an aircraft to the proper point in space and to release stores to effect a hit on a predetermined target.

The GCBS airborne components are the AN/ARW-67 command link receiver and antenna, the AN/APN-132 radar beacon with two antennas, pilot's control panel, and three cockpit indicator lights. Command signals from the TPQ-10 are received by the command link receiver and integrated into the AFCS for automatic heading control. When a turn signal is received the cockpit turn indicator light comes on (left or right) and remains on for the duration of the turn signal. In the absence of turn commands the AFCS returns the aircraft to straight and level flight. The amber arm ordnance light, located adjacent to the right turn indicator light on the glareshield, is actuated by a command signal from the TPQ-10 and is a visual indication to the pilot to select the proper arming and station select switches for release of the external stores.

Changed 15 May 1966

Ground command signals automatically release the external stores. In normal operation, the pilot merely monitors GCBS operation.

```
CAUTION
```

In the event of erratic operation or systems malfunction, it is recommended that the control stick AP button (see figure 1-29) be depressed to disengage the GCBS to minimize possible disengage transients.

The GCBS operates on 115-volt ac and 28-volt dc power received through the ENGAGE position on the AFCS control panel. The AFCS preflight test panel (see figure 1-32) on the right-hand console is used for preflight checking the AFCS system prior to engaging GCBS.

GROUND CONTROLLED BOMBING SYSTEM CONTROL PANEL

The GCBS control panel (see figure 1-32) is located on the left-hand console. The panel contains the switches for control and checking the GCBS functions. The switches are labeled power, system, beacon, pulse, step turn, code, channel, and pitch.

POWER SWITCH

The power switch has ON and OFF positions. The ON position makes electrical power available at the GCBS control panel.

SYSTEM SWITCH

The system switch has two positions, STANDBY and ENGAGE. The ENGAGE position applies electrical power to the GCBS providing the channel switch is in some position other than 0 and the AFCS is engaged.

BEACON SWITCH

The beacon switch has an ON and OFF position. In the OFF position, with the channel switch at any position other than 0, the beacon is in the standby mode.

STEP TURN SWITCH

The step turn switch has OFF, L and R positions and is used to check system response without ground station signal indications and for turn control in the GCBS mode of operation.

PULSE SWITCH

The pulse switch has two positions, SINGLE and DOUBLE. It controls the mode of operation of the radar beacon.

CODE SWITCH

The rotary code switch is labeled 0, 1, 2, and 3, and selects the proper coded arrangements for response to command signals from the TPQ-10.

CHANNEL SWITCH

The rotary channel switch has five positions labeled 0, 1, 2, 3, and 4, and selects the channel on which the AN/ARW-67 receives signals from the TPQ-10. It also controls 115-volt a-c power for the AN/ARW-67 receiver and the AN/APN-132 radar beacon when in any position other than 0.

PITCH SWITCH

The pitch switch has two positions, OFF and AFCS NORMAL. The OFF position disconnects the pitch channel of the AFCS system. The AFCS NORMAL position allows the pitch channel to function normally.

PREFLIGHT PROCEDURE

Preflight the GCBS in the following manner by placing the cockpit console switches in the positions specified:

GCBS Control Panel

    Power switch . . . . OFF

    System switch . . . . STANDBY

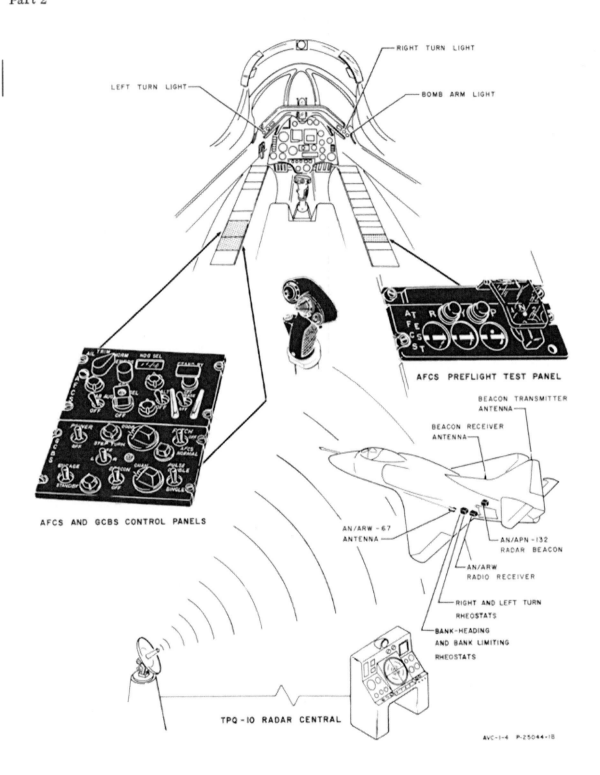

RIGHT TURN LIGHT

LEFT TURN LIGHT

BOMB ARM LIGHT

AFCS PREFLIGHT TEST PANEL

BEACON TRANSMITTER
ANTENNA

BEACON RECEIVER
ANTENNA

AFCS AND GCBS CONTROL PANELS

AN/ARW-67
ANTENNA

AN/APN-132
RADAR BEACON

AN/ARW
RADIO RECEIVER

RIGHT AND LEFT TURN
RHEOSTATS

BANK-HEADING
AND BANK LIMITING
RHEOSTATS

TPQ-10 RADAR CENTRAL

AVC-1-4 P-25044-1B

Figure 1-32. Ground Controlled Bombing System

Changed 15 March 1965

Beacon switch . . . . OFF

Step turn switch . . . . OFF

Pulse switch . . . . SINGLE

Code switch 0

Channel switch 0

AFCS Control Panel

Standby switch . . . . . STANDBY

Engage switch . . . . OFF

The following checks should be made with the AFCS test panel switch in the number 2 position.

Note

Check that compass controller free-slaved switch is in FREE prior to operating in the GCBS mode.

1. Place the GCBS power switch to the ON position.

2. Place the GCBS system switch to ENGAGE. It should not hold this position since the AFCS is not engaged.

3. Place the AFCS panel switches in the following positions.

   a. Engage switch . . . . ENGAGE

   b. Heading select switch . . . . HDG SEL

   c. Altitude hold switch . . . . ALT

4. Place the GCBS system switch to ENGAGE. It should hold this position. The AFCS heading select switch should turn to OFF and the altitude hold switch should remain at ALT.

5. Place GCBS step turn switch at R. Right turn light comes ON and stick moves to right.

6. Place step turn switch at L. Left turn light comes ON and stick moves to left.

7. Return step turn switch to OFF.

INFLIGHT OPERATION

For airborne operation of the GCBS, the pilot will set up the AFCS and GCBS control panels in the following prescribed sequence:

Note

The compass controller free-slaved switch must be in the FREE position prior to operating in the GCBS mode. This eliminates short term transients introduced by the compass slaving system.

AFCS Control

Standby switch . . . . . . STANDBY

Note

The standby switch should be in STANDBY at least 30 seconds prior to engaging other AFCS control switches.

Engage switch . . . . ENGAGE

Altitude hold switch . . . . . . ALT

GCBS Control

Power switch . . . . ON

System switch . . . . . . ENGAGED

Pulse switch . . . . . AS BRIEFED

Code switch . . . . . AS BRIEFED

Channel switch . . . AS BRIEFED

A periodic inflight operational check of the GCBS may be made in the following manner. Establish an airspeed of Mach 0.6 at 20,000 feet altitude. Using the step turn switch, make a 90-degree turn to the right and a 90-degree turn to the left and note the steady-state bank angle obtained for each turn. The steady-state bank angles should be the same within 5 degrees. The rollout from the turns should begin within 2 seconds after returning the step turn switch to OFF. Again using the step turn switch, start a turn either right or left, and note the time taken to obtain 2/3 of the previously established steady-state bank angle. This is the airplane response time. The airplane response time should be 3.8 seconds + .4 second.

When the pilot informs the strike controller by radio of his "ready" status the TPQ-10 takes over control of the airplane and will guide it to the point of store release. Turn signals from the TPQ-10 will cause the airplane to turn and the turn indicator light to glow. When the turn signal is interrupted the turn indicator light goes out and the airplane returns to straight and level flight. Turns are made at the rate of approximately 3 degrees per second. When the bomb arm light comes on the pilot then selects the proper fuzing switches for store release. A TPQ-10 signal will release the store automatically and store release is indicated by an audio tone in the headset.

On aircraft without AFC 263, the following applies. When the airplane is operating in the GCBS mode the autopilot control stick steering feature is completely locked out of the system. Whenever altitude hold difficulties are encountered that necessitate altitude corrections, disengage the AFCS and GCBS with the control stick AP button, manually adjust for proper altitude, then re-engage the GCBS.

Note

Until such time as a pitch axis disconnect feature is incorporated, no GCBS operations should be accomplished below 1000 feet altitude terrain clearance.

On aircraft with AFC 263 installed, the following procedures should be used when attitude and/or altitude changes are required. The PITCH switch on the GCBS control panel should be placed in the OFF position. After the desired attitude and/or altitude changes are obtained the pitch attitude can be re-engaged by placing the PITCH switch on the GCBS control panel in the AFCS NORMAL position or by placing the ALTITUDE switch on the AFCS control panel in the ALTITUDE position.

EMERGENCY OPERATION

The pilot may at any time discontinue the GCBS function by depressing the control stick AP button. This method of disengage is recommended in lieu of disengaging the GCBS system switch on the GCBS control system because of the faster reaction time due to the close proximity of the pilot's hand to the control stick release button, and to minimize disengage transients.

CAUTION

Overpowering the system while in the GCBS mode of operation is possible but should only be done under emergency conditions. If overpowering becomes necessary, disconnect as soon as possible using the control stick AP button. The forces required to overpower the system are approximately 15 pounds pressure longitudinally and 35 pounds pressure laterally.

Manual release of stores while on the GCBS mode of operation may be effected by the pilot by merely depressing the bombs B (pickle) button on the control stick, providing the master armament switch is ON and the stations selector switches are at READY. Emergency release of the stores may be effected by placing the emergency select switch to WING,

CENTER or ALL and then pulling the emergency bomb release handle.

SPRAY TANK

A chemical spray tank, designated Aero 14B, can be installed on the fuselage station only.

OPERATION

The following steps are required to operate the Aero 14B spray tank:

1. Function select
   switch . . . . SPRAY TANK

2. Spray power switch . . . . ON

LABS MODE SWITCH. The LABS mode switch is a three-position toggle switch. In the LOFT position, timed low or medium angle release is obtained. The TIMED O/S position selects a high angle loft release using the time interval measuring feature of the LABS timer, and the internally located pitch angle selector. The INST O/S position selects a high angle release resulting in an untimed instantaneous, high angle, over-the-shoulder bomb drop.

LABS TIMER TEST SWITCH. The LABS timer switch is a two-position toggle switch marked NORMAL and TEST. The switch remains in the NORMAL position for LABS operation and may be actuated to the TEST position to check timer, the LABS light and the aural tone operation.

ALL-ATTITUDE INDICATOR

A remotely controlled all-attitude indicator, located at the center of the instrument panel, provides easily read indications of heading, pitch, and roll. (See FLIGHT INSTRUMENTS, this section, for a complete description of this part of the ALL-ATTITUDE INDICATOR.) Also incorporated with the all-attitude indicator are two novel features for programming and executing the proper g schedule for loft bombing. Along the left edge of the instrument the desired g is programmed by a motor-driven g-programmer, while the actual g resulting from the execution of the Immelmann turn is shown on the g-indicator. By matching the index of the g-indicator with the index of the g-programmer, the optimum flight path for the loft is maintained.

Note

The 4g mark is next to the wings level horizon, and the LABS light is observable while the pilot flies a coordinated Immelmann by maintaining alignment of the sphere horizon, the g-programmer, and the g-indicator within the small scanning area.

FUNCTION SELECTOR SWITCH

The function selector switch is located on the armament panel. With this rotary type switch in its LABS position, power is supplied to the LABS timer motor and circuits are closed to the bomb release button.

LABS TIMER

The LABS timer (figure 1-33) is located at the top of the instrument panel. It is used to set in the time from IP to pullup in seconds in 0.1 second increments over a range of 0.1 to 30 seconds. The instrument begins the timing countdown as soon as the "pickle" is depressed at the initial point.

CAUTION

Rotating the timer knob when the pickle is depressed or pulling out the timer knob when rotating it will damage the timer.

LABS LIGHT

The LABS light is located just below the glareshield on the left side of the instrument panel. It provides the pilot with the following information:

Light off when pickle is depressed at beginning of timing period.

Light on momentarily 1 second from pullup point.

Light on continuously at pullup point.

Light off at bomb release.

AURAL TONE

The aural tone is a 1200-cycle per-second signal received in the pilot's headset. When the timer runs down to 1 second, a three-tenths (0.3) second aural burst warns the pilot to prepare for pullup. At the end of the timing period (pullup point) a constant tone is heard which continues until store releases. The tone is generated by the tone generator of the control panel, and is transmitted through the AN/ARC-27A radio set.

Note

When the armament selector switch is in BOMBS & GM ARM position, depressing the bomb release switch will energize the tone generator of the radar control panel in the left-hand console. While the bomb release switch is held depressed, the aural tone will be audible in the pilot's headset. When the S2 switch on the radar console is in the training position, the tone will also be transmitted on the AN/ARC-27A transmitter to ground monitoring stations.

STATION SELECTOR SWITCHES

Five station selector switches (see figure 1-33) are located at the top of the armament panel. The switches select station armament releases. Each switch has READY, SALVO, and OFF positions, providing single or multiple release of stores.

Note

The SALVO position no longer serves any useful purpose and should not be used.

BOMBS RELEASE BUTTON

Located on the side of the control stick grip (see figure 1-33) is the bomb "pickle" button,

labeled B. This button is depressed at the initial point and held until the bomb is released in the loft maneuver.

LOFT BOMBING RELEASE PROCEDURE

If the loft mode of release is selected, make the bombing run as follows:

1. Rotate the function select switch to LABS.

2. Move the LABS mode switch to LOFT.

3. Select the proper bomb release station by moving the proper stations switch from OFF to READY.

4. Move the master armament switch to ON.

5. When the airplane passes over the IP, heading toward the target at the desired altitude and speed, depress the "pickle" button. This puts LABS in readiness and starts the LABS timer. Hold the "pickle" button depressed until after bomb release.

WARNING

Releasing the "pickle" button prior to bomb release will abort the LABS bombing run.

Note

If a loft release must be aborted for some reason, INST O/S can be selected during the run-in and the mission accomplished since no IP or time setting is required in this mode.

6. One second before the pullup point, the LABS light on the glareshield will light momentarily and the aural tone will "beep" momentarily. This is the signal for the pilot to

ensure that the aircraft is on the intended track and to anticipate the pullup.

7. At the pullup point, the LABS timer circuitry initiates the maneuver command, sounding a steady aural tone in the pilot's headset, the LABS light comes on, starting the command index marker on the vertical accelerometer (g-programmer pointer) moving down the left edge of the all-attitude indicator.

8. Execute the pullup at the g indicated on the g-programmer, by maneuvering in pitch so that the small index of the g-indicator matches the moving position of the g-programmer. The desired g-acceleration is to reach 4g in 2 seconds. Maintain wings level to prevent any change of aircraft heading. Yaw maneuver error is displayed as roll. Both roll/yaw maneuver errors are corrected by rolling the aircraft back to wings-level attitude. The bomb will release automatically when the preselected pitch angle is reached if the "pickle" button has been held depressed since the IP point. The LABS light will go off and the aural tone will stop, indicating bomb release. Release "pickle" button.

9. Complete the Immelmann turn or other delivery maneuver, referring continually to the all-attitude indicator for the escape maneuver. If succeeding LABS maneuvers are to be made, the aircraft should be flown unaccelerated in straight and level flight on the run-in path for a minimum of 1 minute prior to pullup to allow the gyro erection system to remove any accrued errors.

10. Upon completion of the final LABS maneuver, move the function select, station selector, and master armament switches to the OFF position.

LOFT BOMBING RELEASE PROCEDURE, AN/AJB-3A

The procedure for loft bombing on the AN/AJB-3A (figure 1-34) configuration is the same as for the AN/AJB-3 configuration, except for the method of programming the pullup in the bombing maneuver. The indicator-programmer (g-programmer) is no longer attached to the side of the all-attitude indicator. The g-programmer has been replaced by the vertical and horizontal director pointers on the face of the attitude director indicator. The vertical and horizontal director pointers are biased out of sight until the bomb run is started. The procedure for setting up the bomb run is the same as in the old system. When the identification point is reached and the bomb release (pickle) switch is depressed, the horizontal and vertical director pointers spring into view in a centered position on the indicator. At the end of the time interval, at the point when the old g-programmer would start to drive, the horizontal director pointer would, if the aircraft continued on a level flight path, drive toward the top of the indicator. However, pullup should commence at this point, and the pilot should fly the aircraft so that the horizontal director pointer stays in a centered position on the indicator. If the pilot pulls up too fast, the horizontal pointer will move toward the bottom of the indicator. If the climb is not meeting the programmed g's, the pointer will be above the centerline on the indicator. Any roll or yaw deviation is shown on the vertical director pointer. Left deflection of the vertical director pointer is corrected by moving the stick to the left; right deflection is corrected by moving the stick to the right. Both the vertical and horizontal director pointers should stay centered and the pilot should fly the aircraft to keep the pointers centered. The vertical director pointer is the more sensitive of the two, and is more difficult to keep centered. When the bomb is released, the two pointers disappear. If the aircraft exceeds the yaw tolerance the yaw cancel relay operates as in the AN/AJB-3 configuration, and the two pointers will disappear, indicating that the bomb run has been aborted.

TIMED OVER-THE-SHOULDER RELEASE PROCEDURE

The procedure for timed over-the-shoulder bombing is the same as for LOFT BOMBING PROCEDURE, except that in step (2) the LABS mode switch is set to TIMED O/S.

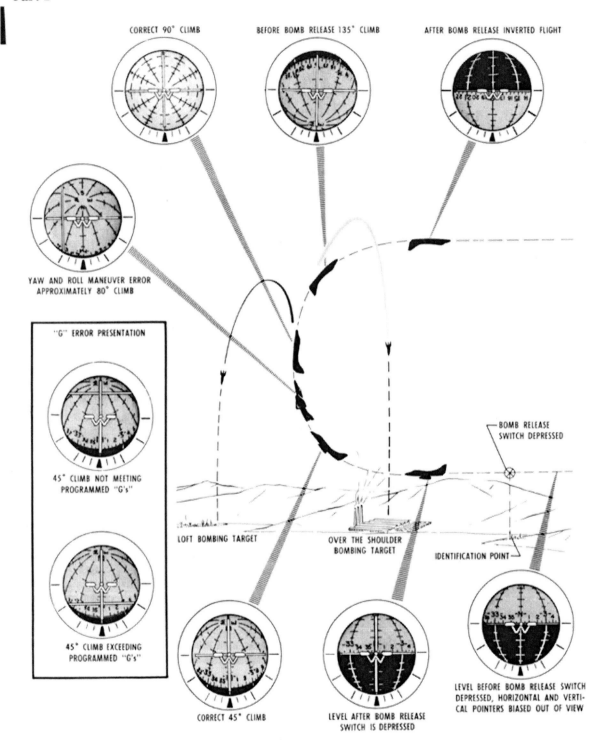

CORRECT 90° CLIMB

BEFORE BOMB RELEASE 135° CLIMB

AFTER BOMB RELEASE INVERTED FLIGHT

YAW AND ROLL MANEUVER ERROR
APPROXIMATELY 80° CLIMB

"G" ERROR PRESENTATION

45° CLIMB NOT MEETING
PROGRAMMED "G's"

45° CLIMB EXCEEDING
PROGRAMMED "G's"

LOFT BOMBING TARGET

OVER THE SHOULDER
BOMBING TARGET

BOMB RELEASE
SWITCH DEPRESSED

IDENTIFICATION POINT

CORRECT 45° CLIMB

LEVEL AFTER BOMB RELEASE
SWITCH IS DEPRESSED

LEVEL BEFORE BOMB RELEASE SWITCH
DEPRESSED, HORIZONTAL AND VERTI-
CAL POINTERS BIASED OUT OF VIEW

AVC-1-1 P-28457-1

Figure 1-34. AN/AJB-3A Bombing Presentations

Changed 15 March 1965

NOTE

At a pitch angle of approximately 70 degrees or more, the minor roll indices are blanked out.

INSTANTANEOUS OVER-THE-SHOULDER RELEASE PROCEDURE

In the event that the IP is missed or cannot be used, or should the mission require it, the bomb may be released by the procedure for instantaneous over-the-shoulder bombing. This procedure is the same as for LOFT BOMBING, except that in step 2 the LABS mode switch is set to INST O/S, and the IP and the target are identical. Therefore, the bomb release button should be depressed and pullup commenced when over the target. The remainder of the operation is the same as for LOFT or TIMED O/S releases.

NOTE

In aircraft incorporating the AN/AJB-3A system, the g-programmer, g-indicator, and yaw-roll indicator are incorporated in the face of the attitude director indicator. Yaw-roll and "g" indicators are presented by horizontal and vertical needles, which move into view when the bomb release button is depressed and remain in view until bomb release.

NOTE

- The operation of the LABS release mechanism may be stopped at any time during the maneuver by releasing the bomb release button.

- Before entering the aircraft, be sure that the desired bomb release angles for both loft and/or over-the-shoulder runs are set into the pitch angle selector control (access door on top of the fuselage aft of cockpit). (See figure 1-33.)

CP-741/A WEAPON RELEASE COMPUTER

COMPUTER CAPABILITIES

The CP-741/A weapon release computer referenced in this writeup as the CP-741/A computer, (figure 1-34A) is a solid-state analog computer utilizing magnetic amplifiers. It is of plug-in modular construction, including the chassis. In conjunction with the aircraft's various data systems, the CP-741/A computer takes over the task of complex computations essential to accurate delivery of weapons. The CP-741/A computer is capable of weapon delivery in four modes, toss, stik, loft, and O/S, and can deliver either nuclear weapons, conventional ordnance, or the Shrike missile.

DESCRIPTION OF MATERIEL

The CP-741/A bombing system consists of the following associated subsystems:

1. Air Data Computer AXC-666.

2. AN/APG-53A Radar. (Radar modified in accordance with Avionics Change No. 343.)

3. CN-494A/AJB-3 Displacement Gyroscope Assembly (Vertical Gyro).

4. Accelerometer Transducer 24171S and 24171S-3.

5. Relative Wind Transducer.

6. Optical Sight MK 17-0.

7. Cockpit indicator lights.

8. CP-741/A Weapon Release Computer.

9. Weapon Control Panel.

SYSTEMS OPERATION

The CP-741/A weapons release computer has the capability of calculating release angles for the delivery of both conventional and nuclear bombs during toss maneuvers. In performing this function, the CP-741/A computer, in conjunction with the aircraft air data system, makes many of the observations, measurements, and complex computations essential to the accurate delivery of ordnance. It can also be used for LOFT and O/S attacks.

TOSS MODE. In the TOSS mode of operation, the pilot tracks the target with the pipper. When the pull-up angle required to place the bomb on target is less than 45 degrees and the horizontal range to target is within the limits of the CP-741/A computer capability to provide a valid solution, an IN-RANGE signal in the cockpit is illuminated and pull-up may be initiated. To release the weapon, the pilot depresses the bomb release button on the stick, pulls up with an indicated acceleration of 2 to 6 g's, and the bomb is automatically released at the correct pullup angle. The theoretical altitude/horizontal range envelopes within which the computer is designed to provide valid bombing solutions are shown in figures 1-34B and 1-34C.

STIK MODE. This mode is used for the toss delivery of sticks of bombs. It provides an early release

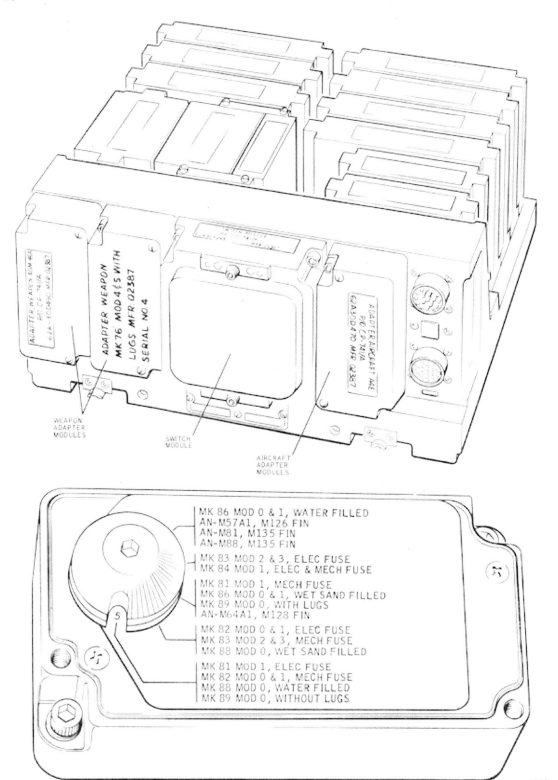

WEAPON
ADAPTER
MODULES

SWITCH
MODULE

AIRCRAFT
ADAPTER
MODULES

MK 86 MOD 0 & 1, WATER FILLED
AN-M57A1, M126 FIN
AN-M81, M135 FIN
AN-M88, M135 FIN

MK 83 MOD 2 & 3, ELEC FUSE
MK 84 MOD 1, ELEC & MECH FUSE

MK 81 MOD 1, MECH FUSE
MK 86 MOD 0 & 1, WET SAND FILLED
MK 89 MOD 0, WITH LUGS
AN-M64A1, M128 FIN

MK 82 MOD 0 & 1, ELEC FUSE
MK 83 MOD 2 & 3, MECH FUSE
MK 88 MOD 0, WET SAND FILLED

MK 81 MOD 1, ELEC FUSE
MK 82 MOD 0 & 1, MECH FUSE
MK 88 MOD 0, WATER FILLED
MK 89 MOD 0, WITHOUT LUGS

Figure 1-34A. CP-741/A Weapon Release Computer

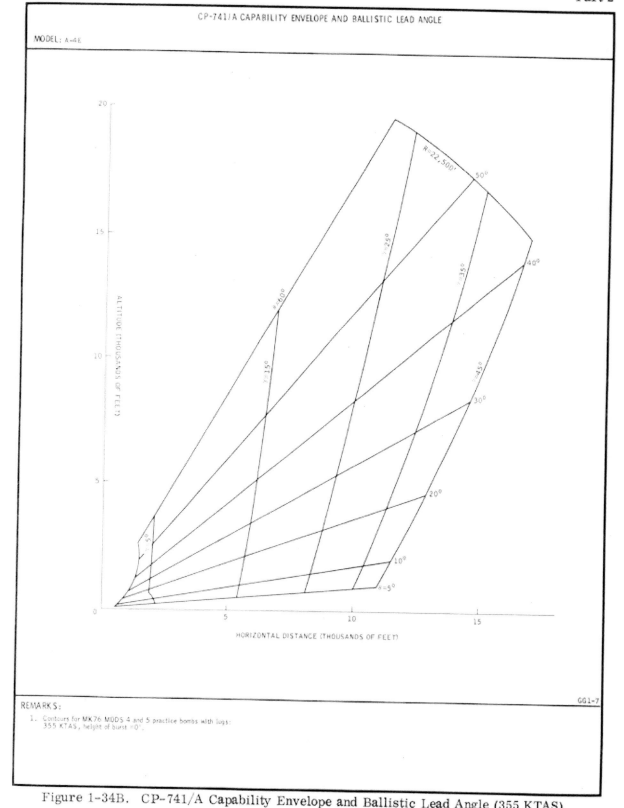

Figure 1-34B. CP-741/A Capability Envelope and Ballistic Lead Angle (355 KTAS)

Changed 15 November 1966

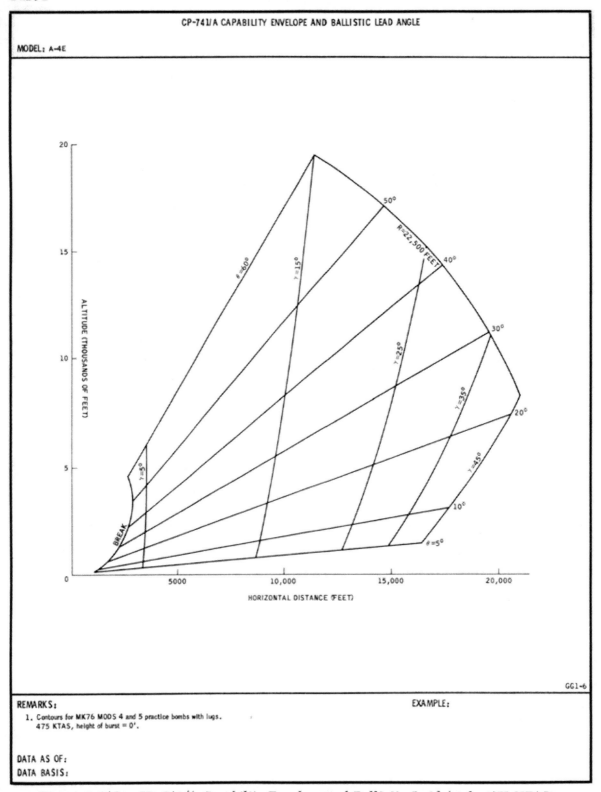

CP-741/A CAPABILITY ENVELOPE AND BALLISTIC LEAD ANGLE

MODEL: A-4E

REMARKS:
 1. Contours for MK76 MODS 4 and 5 practice bombs with lugs.
    475 KTAS, height of burst = 0'.

DATA AS OF:
DATA BASIS:

EXAMPLE:

GG1-6

Figure 1-34C. CP-741/A Capability Envelope and Ballistic Lead Angle (475 KTAS)

signal which, coupled with an intervalometer, will space a number of weapons along a linear target or in position to straddle the aim point. It should be noted that the CP-741/A computer does not perform intervalometer functions. The series of firing signals necessary for stick bombing must be provided by a separate aircraft (AWRS) or rack intervalometer.

LOFT MODE. Delivery in this mode is a canned maneuver in that the LOFT RUN-IN distance from IP to the desired pull-up point and the LOFT ANGLE must be set in prior to takeoff. The LOFT ANGLE is the angle between the velocity vector at "pickle" and the velocity vector at release. The LOFT ANGLE is not equal to the LABS sector setting. When the aircraft covers the preselected LOFT RUN-IN distance from the IP, a pull-up signal is given to the pilot. The pilot pulls up, using a programed g and velocity schedule. When the pull-up angle is equal to the preselected LOFT ANGLE, the weapon is automatically released. In this mode, the CP-741/A computer corrects only for the errors in pull-up point that would accumulate if incorrect run-in speeds were flown.

O/S MODE. In this mode, the pilot depresses the bomb release button as he flies over the target and immediately commences a programed pull-up. As in conventional LABS deliveries, an automatic release occurs when the preselected O/S ANGLE is reached. Again, the angle is not equal to the LABS sector setting.

NOTE

There is no timed O/S available with the LABS or CP-741/A with a CP-741/A weapon control panel installed.

In its toss bombing mode, the CP-741/A computer bombing system provides an automatic release signal at the proper angle during pull-up to place the bomb on target. The CP-741/A weapons release computer calculates this release angle using inputs from the auxiliary equipment of the bombing system and combining them to determine the lead angle required for the release conditions encountered.

1. The aircraft air data computer provides aircraft barometric altitude, true airspeed, and Mach number information.

2. The AN/APG-53A radar measures the slant range from aircraft to target and provides an indication of radar lock-on to the pilot.

3. The vertical gyro measures aircraft pitch angle.

4. The relative wind transducer provides aircraft angle-of-attack information or indication.

5. The accelerometer transducer measures acceleration normal to the aircraft longitudinal axis. This acceleration is used in the computation of the angle through which the aircraft rotates during pull-up.

6. The weapon control panel allows the pilot to "make" the circuit to the CP-741/A computer, to select the mode of attack and the proper weapon adapter module, and to make certain other inputs to the computer from the cockpit.

7. The CP-741/A weapon release computer calculates from all of these inputs the proper pull-up angle at which a bomb release signal should be initiated. When the CP-741/A computer uses radar ranging to determine slant range to target, it is said to be operating in the RADAR mode. When radar range inputs are not available (radar not locked-on), the CP-741/A computer uses preset values derived from target altitude, aircraft barometric altitude, corrections for deviations from standard atmospheric conditions, and aircraft pitch angle to compute slant range to target. In this case, the system is operating in its BARO mode.

MODULES DESCRIPTION

The CP-741/A computer is composed of 17 sealed modules, which include:

1. The aircraft adapter module, which provides information to the computer concerning the performance characteristics of the delivery aircraft.

2. Two weapon adapter modules, each of which can provide specific inputs to the computer to describe the ballistics of the weapons being carried. The pilot can select from the cockpit the weapon adapter module appropriate to the type of ordnance he plans to deliver on each pass.

3. The switch module controls (figure 1-34D), should be set during preflight.

a. O/S ANGLE. Angles up to 120 degrees may be selected for O/S delivery. This is a potentiometer adjustment and for accuracy must be set with the module tester ASM-152. Calibration information for voltages versus release angles above 90 degrees is not presently available.

b. SAFE STANDOFF. This 10-position switch was designed for use with special weapons to provide a safe standoff signal. Time of flight from 12 to 30 seconds is provided in 2-second increments. Currently the A-4E aircraft are not being wired to furnish this signal, and this setting is not used.

c. SET RANGE. This setting is to provide the pilot with a visual light signal when a preselected horizontal range to the target is reached. Ranges for the AGM-45A missile may be selected on

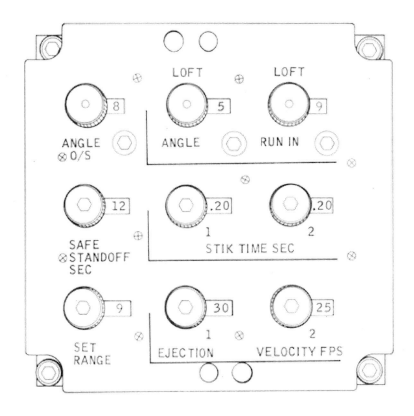

Figure 1-34D. Switch Module (Front Cover Removed)

a 10-position switch. For bombs, only the first six positions provide meaningful ranges out to 20,270 feet.

d. LOFT ANGLE. Angles up to 120 degrees may be selected with this setting. This is a potentiometer adjustment and for accuracy must be set with the module tester ASM-152.

e. LOFT RUN-IN. This is a potentiometer setting for run-in distances from 2000 to 20,000 feet. For accuracy, this setting must be made with the module tester ASM-152.

f. STIK TIME. This setting is used in the STIK mode to provide an early release signal to place the bomb stick in a position straddling the aim point. The early release settings range from 0.03 second to a maximum value of 0.25 second. Two knobs are provided to set in STIK TIME - one for each weapon adapter module position. This feature permits a different setting for each of the two weapon adapter modules. The STIK mode on the weapon control panel must be selected to use STIK TIME. When a stik length of greater than 0.5 second is desired, the pilot must aim short of the center of the target.

g. EJECTION VELOCITY. These selections modify the release angle computed for TOSS and STIK deliveries to compensate for ejected launching effects. Since the CP-741/A computer does not use the values set into this position during LOFT and O/S modes of attack, the pilot must compensate for the effects of ejection velocity in his choice of release angles. For TOSS and STIK deliveries, the value of ejection velocity set in should correspond to the component of the ejection velocity that is perpendicular to the aircraft velocity vector at time of release. The settings are from 0 to 45 feet-per-second in 5 foot-per-second increments. As with STIK time, this value is set for each weapon adapter module separately.

WEAPON CONTROL PANEL

The weapon control panel has five selector switches for selecting modes of operating the bombing system and of supplying inputs to the computer. (See figure 1-34E.)

BURST HEIGHT. Available settings are 0, 50, 100, 400, 700, 900, 1300, 1600, 2000, and 3000 feet AGL. This function only used for TOSS or STIK bombing.

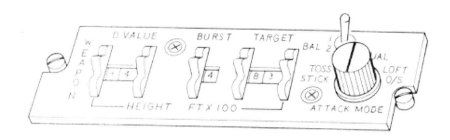

GG1-3

Figure 1-34E.   Weapon Control Panel

D-VALUE.   A D-value may be selected by the pilot to provide corrections to barometric altitude for deviations from standard atmospheric conditions. This correction is used when aircraft pitch angle and barometric altitude are being used to determine slant range (BARO mode). The correction may be made in 100-foot increments from minus 1900 feet to plus 1900 feet. Determination of the value to be set in is discussed under OPERATING PROCEDURES.

TARGET HEIGHT.   Target elevation above mean sea level is selected for BARO mode deliveries in 100-foot increments from 0 to 9900 feet.

BALLISTIC SELECTOR (BAL).   This is a two-position switch by which the pilot may select the weapon adapter module on the CP-741/A computer to match the weapon to be delivered.

ATTACK MODE.   This switch serves as an OFF-ON switch for the system and as an attack mode selector. The positions are MANUAL, TOSS, STIK, LOFT, and O/S. If this switch is in the MANUAL position or if a signal is not available from the CP-741/A computer to the computer power relay, the normal release circuit is completed when the armament selector switch is in BOMBS & GM ARM. When the armament selector switch is in LABS, the armament control panel is used to choose between the LOFT and O/S modes in aircraft LAB system.

WARNING

- Operation of the CP-741/A computer system cannot ensure avoidance of ground collision or safe separation between delivery aircraft and detonation of conventional bombs. Minimum release heights must be observed according to weapon/delivery tactic combination being employed.

Changed 15 November 1966

- To ensure prevention of bomb-to-aircraft and bomb-to-bomb collision refer to Aircraft Stores Carriage and Release Limitations and Weight Section, Confidential Supplement to NATOPS. Station loading applies. Release interval for the CP-741/A computer was promulgated by NATC message 281659Z Oct 1966.

- If power input or certain components of the CP-741/A computer fail, the bombing system reverts to a manual release. Weapon will release when the bomb release button is pressed. This could result in a low g release in the TOSS and STIK Modes and a release in the LOFT and O/S modes when the bomb button is depressed.

CP-741/A WEAPONS RELEASE COMPUTER OPERATING PROCEDURES IN TOSS OR STIK MODES

The step-by-step procedures for dive toss bombing utilizing computer will be in sequence from prior to manning the aircraft through the delivery maneuver.

PRIOR TO MANNING AIRCRAFT

Pilots should be prepared to deliver their bombs in the BARO modes (radar off), as well as RADAR mode. Therefore, the pilot must be aware of target altitude and D-values for the target area and desired burst height for the target/fuze combination.

D-VALUES.   Table 1-1 is a worksheet for determining D-values. Aerology provides the existing atmospheric pressure, in millibars, at the target area for the proposed pullup altitudes. These values

1	2 MINUS	3 EQUALS	4 TIMES	5 EQUALS	6	TARGET AREA	
ALTITUDE (Ft/MSL)	PRESSURE (mb)	STANDARD (mb)	P-S (mb)	D-FACTOR (ft/mb)	D-VALUE (ft)	WIND DIR	WIND VEL
S/L		1013		27			
1000		979		28			
2000		942		29			
3000		908		30			
4000		875		31			
5000		843		32			
6000		812		33			
7000		782		34			
8000		753		35			
9000		724		36			
10,000		697		38			
11,000		670		39			
12,000		644		40			
13,000		619		42			
14,000		595		43			
15,000		572		44			
16,000		549		45			
17,000		527		47			
18,000		506		48			
19,000		485		50			
20,000		466		51			

TABLE 1-1. WORKSHEET FOR THE DETERMINATION OF D-VALUES

are inserted in column 2. The values listed in column 3, standard atmospheric pressures, are subtracted from the corresponding value in column 2, and the difference is inserted in column 4. The numbers in column 4 will be positive if the number in column 2 is larger than the number in column 3. The number inserted in column 4 is multiplied by the value in column 5 to convert the "D-factor" (ft/mb) to the "D-value" (feet).

By following this procedure, a set of D-values corresponding to each 1000 feet of altitude above mean sea level can be calculated. This D-value

(corresponding to the anticipated pullup altitude above mean sea level) is the value set into the weapon control panel in the D-value window. Select proper "+" or "-" values.

STIK TIME. The STIK mode provides an early release signal in STIK mode which allows the first bomb off to impact short of the target and the stick to straddle the target. The amount of time required for the early release is the "STIK Time". Figures 1-34F and 1-34G are nomographs for determining STIK Time for various release conditions.

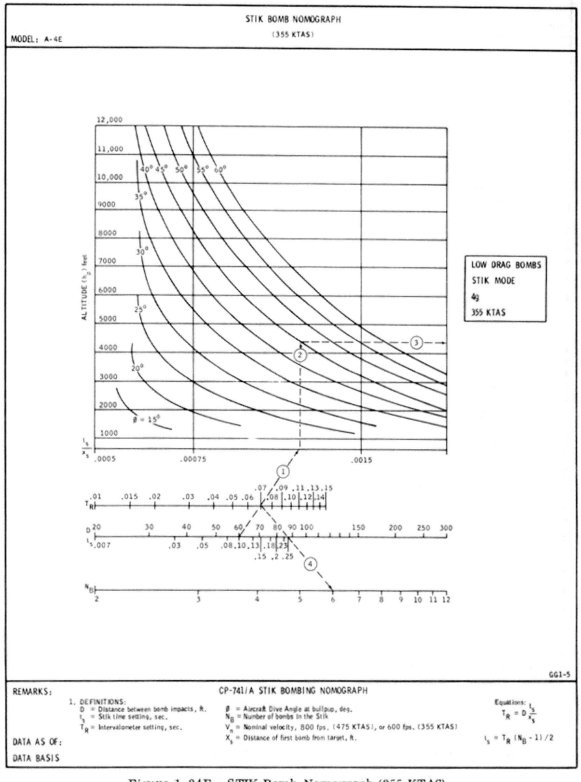

Figure 1-34F. STIK Bomb Nomograph (355 KTAS)

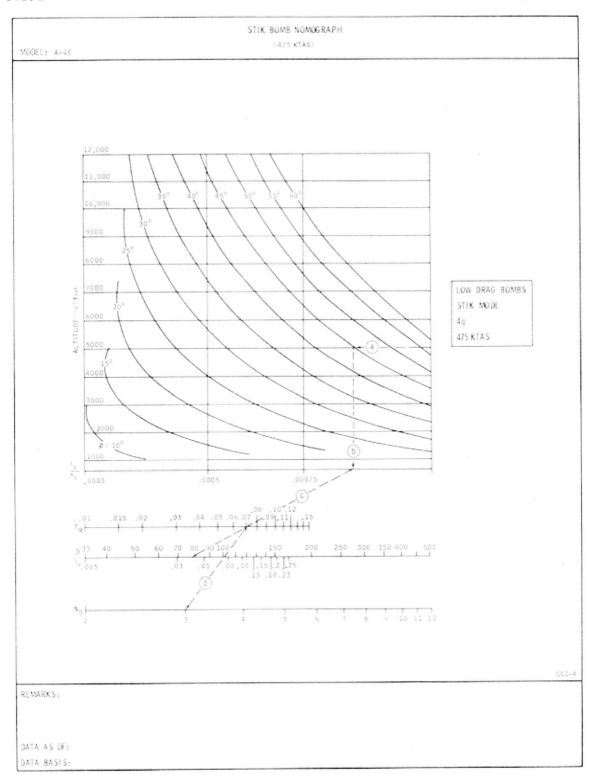

Figure 1-34G. STIK Bomb Nomograph (475 KTAS)

NOTE

AWE-1 must be set to RIPPLE mode, and
proper release interval. MER/TER release mode selector switch must be on
SINGLE when using AWE-1. If SALVO is
selected on the rack, the AWE-1 can be
OFF.

Racks without automatic homing must be
homed.

SAMPLE PROBLEM A:

Stik Time Setting   (V_a = 355 KTAS)

(For figure 1-34F)

1. Draw a straight line connecting the desired
distance between bomb impact, D = 60 feet and the
available Intervalometer Time T_R = 0.07 second, to
obtain a value for t_S/x_S (0.0013 sec/ft).

2. From this point in the t_S/x_S scale, rise vertically to intersect the anticipated dive angle,
φ = 45 degrees.

3. From this point of intersection with the dive
angle contour, obtain the altitude, h_p = 4300 feet,
desired at the start of pullup.

4. Draw a straight line from the selected
T_R = 0.07 second to the desired number of bombs,
N_B = 6.

5. Read the corresponding value for the STIK
Time setting in the CP-741/A switch module,
t_S = 0.25 second, from the t_S scale.

SAMPLE PROBLEM B:

Stik Time Setting   (V_a = 475 KTAS)

(For figure 1-34G)

Known: STIK mode delivery.
        Start pullup at 5000 feet AGL.
        Dive angle 45 degrees.
        Airspeed 475 KTAS.

(a) Enter figure 1-34G at h_p = 5000 feet and move
right to the 45-degree contour.

(b) Move down to the $\frac{ts}{xs}$ line.

(c) Draw a straight line from this point on the $\frac{ts}{xs}$
line through the desired intervalometer setting,
T_r = 0.07 second. The distance between bomb
impact, D, should be 80 feet.

NOTE

This line, c, can be drawn through any
T_r setting to get a desired interbomb
spacing. Care must be taken not to
exceed any minimum intervalometer/
rack limitations.

(d) Draw a straight line from the intervalometer
setting, T_r, to the desired number of bombs,
N_B = 3, and read the corresponding t_s value for the
STIK Time setting of the CP-741/A switch module.
In this example, the t_s value lies between the two
available times of 0.05 and 0.08 second. Since
interpolation between settings is not possible, it is
recommended the higher time (earlier release) be
selected. Bombs impacting short of the target will
inflict more damage due to the fragmentation and
blast pattern than those impacting long.

PRIOR TO ENTERING THE COCKPIT

Check connections of CP-741/A and ensure proper
loading of weapons.

Ensure that the correct values are set into the switch
module:

1. Set Range corresponding to the horizontal range
at which the pilot desires visual warning by the SET
RANGE light.

2. Ensure that the ejection velocity is set into the
EJECTION VELOCITY FPS window that corresponds
to the weapon adapter module that is to be used.
Ejection velocity appropriate to the rack/firing
cartridge/ordnance combination installed on the aircraft. See table 1-2 for ejection velocities.

3. Set the proper value for the STIK TIME setting,
if STIK mode is to be used.

4. Replace and secure the cover of the switch
module and the aircraft covering panel.

5. Check for correct Weapon Adapter
Modules and note position.

NOTE

LOFT ANGLE O/S, LOFT ANGLE, and
LOFT RUNIN are potentiometer adjustments set in the module tester. SAFE
STANDOFF SEC is for nuclear weapons
and is not presently wired in the aircraft.

AFTER ENTERING COCKPIT

The controls on the weapon control panel can be set
either before or after engine startup. They may also
be reset in flight. Parameters which are set into the
weapon control panel for dive-toss bombing are:

1. ATTACK MODE switch to TOSS or STIK.

2. Ballistic selector switch to the module corresponding to the ordnance to be released.

3. BURST height appropriate to the ordnance/
fuzing/target combination.

4. TARGET height above mean sea level.

5. D-VALUE as determined from worksheet.
Settings in steps 4 and 5 are used only in BARO
mode toss bombing and perform no function during

TABLE 1-2. EJECTION VELOCITIES

Rack	Store Weight (lb)	Ejection Velocity (fps)	Recommended CP-741/A Eject Velocity (fps)
MER/TER-7	All	*	5
PMBR/MBR	All	0	0
Aero 7A-1 (1 MK 1 Mod 2 and MK2 Mod 0 Cartridges)	250	35	35
	500	29.5	30
	750	25.5	25
	1000	22.7	20
	2000	16.5	15
Aero 20A-1	250	24	25
	500	19.5	20
	750	15.4	15
	1000	12.5	10

*The MER/TER-7 ejection velocity normal to fuselage reference plane varies with rack station and store weight. This variance is from 4.3 fps to 9.3 fps. By using an average 5 fps (switch module ejection velocities are set in 5-fps increments from 0 to 45 fps), setting the maximum system error due to the ejection velocity will be less than 5 mils.

RADAR mode attacks. However, radar malfunction or failure to achieve lock-on is an ever-present possibility. If no radar ranging information is provided to the CP-741/A computer, the CP-741/A computer will automatically use the values set into the weapon control panel to compute a BARO solution. Therefore, pilots should set into these controls the best available information for an alternative BARO mode attack in case the radar does not function as planned.

The preflight procedure for preparing the AN/APG-53A radar to function in its air-to-ground mode is described in Section I of this manual.

Turn on the gunsight, set it at the desired brilliance, conduct optical boresight, check and ensure that the sight drum is set at 0 mils sight depression.

If multiple releases are planned, the AWE-1 cockpit intervalometer should be set up for stick bombing. (RIPPLE mode and interval.) The CP-741/A sends out the first release signal and the intervalometer sends out all additional releases. The release signal (aural tone) from the computer continues until the last bomb is released. In STEP mode, tone ceases when bomb button is released.

AFTER ENGINE START

Turn the Radar Mode Selector Switch to STANDBY. Allow at least 3 minutes for equipment warmup prior to selecting an operating mode of the radar.

THE DELIVERY

The armament switches are set up as follows:

1. AWE-1 QUANTITY, INTERVAL AND MODE . . . . SELECTED

2. NOSE/TAIL ARM or AWW-1 . . . SELECTED

3. MIL Setting . . . . ZERO

4. CP-741/A Weapon Control Panel. SET

5. Radar . . . . A/G

6. Station Selector Switch . . . . DESIRED STATIONS

7. Armament Selector Switch . . . . . BOMBS & GM ARM

8. Master Armament Switch . . . . . ON.

NOTE

If IAAC 444 is not incorporated in AWE-1, position master arm switch to ON before turning AWE-1 on.

Maneuver the aircraft to be within the capability envelope of the computer bombing system at time of pullup (figures 1-34B, 1-34C). Maximum slant range is 22,500 feet, or a maximum altitude of 15,000 feet in the BARO mode.

After ensuring that the IN RANGE light is illuminated, the pilot may initiate his release at any time he desires. To release the bombs, put the pipper on the target, depress the bomb release button and establish a 2- to 6-g pullup. It is not necessary to fly a g schedule during the pullup. However, a higher g during pullup will provide a more rapid release and reduce the down range travel of the aircraft. These factors will tend to improve the accuracy of delivery. Therefore, fly the maneuver at the highest g load that is comfortable. The bomb release tone will come on when the bomb release button is depressed and go off when the last bomb selected is automatically released. If a step mode of the AWE-1 is used, the tone will go off at bomb button release.

When repeated passes are planned, a straight and level leg of at least 1 minute will permit precession of the AJB-3 Gyro to be corrected.

The CP-741/A bombing system does not provide corrections for the effects of the existing wind. Either of two approaches can be used to correct for these effects:

1. Offset the aim point into the wind a distance that will compensate for the effects of the wind at release altitude.

2. Track the target with the pipper. Crosswind effects will require the upwind wing low to keep the pipper on target in coordinated flight. Depress the bomb button while maintaining the pipper on target and pull up in the plane perpendicular to the plane of the wings at the time of pickle. This maneuver corrects for one-half of the effects of crosswind. To correct also for the effects of range wind, keep the pipper vertically aligned with the target but offset the aim point along the run-in track into the range wind component.

Large impact errors can be expected when making repeated runs in the BARO mode at low dive angles. Vertical gyro precession will result in slant range error input to the computer.

For best accuracy a 2- to 4-second tracking time is recommended. The recommended tracking time is not mandatory but will improve accuracy. The two most important items are (1) "In-Range" light illumination and (2) steady pipper tracking.

Accuracy is seriously degraded if bomb release button is depressed while pipper is sweeping through the target.

CAUTION

Do not release bombs if the "In-Range" light is not illuminated. This light indicates the computer has a bombing solution. Release at slant ranges near 10,000 feet without an "In-Range" light can result in impact errors up to 3000 feet.

NOTE

The information in Table 1-3 will allow additional use of the MK 76 series and the MK 76 weapon adapter modules until specific modules are available.

STATION LOADING

Refer to External Stores Limitations, Section I, part 4, Confidential Supplement.

MISSILE, AIR-TO-GROUND

Refer to Section I, part 2, Confidential Supplement.

AIR REFUELING (TANKER) SYSTEM

The air refueling system enables the aircraft to serve as a tanker for other aircraft. Fuel from the wing tank and the drop tanks may be transferred to the refueling store. All fuel in the tanker aircraft except that contained in the fuselage tank may be transferred to the receiver aircraft.

AIR REFUELING STORE

The refueling store carried on the centerline rack contains a 300-gallon fuel cell; a constant-speed,

TABLE 1-3. MK 80 SERIES AND BANDED AN SERIES BOMB ADAPTER MODULE

Switch Position	Bomb
1	MK 86 Mod 0 and 1, Water Filled
	AN-M57A1, M126 Fin
	AN-M81, M135 Fin
	*MK 81 Mod 0 and 1, MK 14 Fin, Mech Fuze, Unretarded
2	MK 83 Mod 2 and 3, Elec Fuze
	MK 84 Mod 1, Elec and Mech Fuze
3	MK 81 Mod 1, Mech Fuze
	MK 86 Mod 0 and 1, Wet Sand Filled
	MK 89 Mod 0, with Lugs
	AN-M64A1, M 128 Fin
	*MK 82 Mod 0 and 1, MK 15, Mech Fuze Unretarded
	*MK 79 Mod 1 Fire Bomb
4	MK 82 Mod 0 and 1, Elec Fuze
	MK 83 Mod 2 and 3, Mech Fuze
	MK 88 Mod 0, Wet Sand Filled
	*MK 28 EX Mod 0 and 1
	*MK 104 Mod 0 and 1
5	MK 81 Mod 1, Elec Fuze
	MK 82 Mod 0 and 1, Mech Fuze
	MK 88 Mod 0, Water Filled
	MK 89 Mod 0, Without Lugs

*These bombs are not listed on the module face. When releasing these stores with the CP-741/A weapon release computer, use the indicated MK 80 weapon adapter module switch position.

MK 76 MOD 4 AND 5 WITH LUGS BOMB ADAPTER MODULE

AN-M57A1, MK 14 Fin, Unretarded

AN-M81, MK 14 Fin, Unretarded

AN-M88, MK 14 Fin, Unretarded

Use the MK 76 weapon adapter module with any of the above listed bombs when using the CP-741/A weapon release computer.

ram air turbine-driven hydraulic pump; a hydraulically driven fuel pump; a hydraulically operated hose reel; and 50 feet of refueling hose with a drogue. The store is capable of transferring fuel to the receiver aircraft at approximately 180 gallons per minute. (See figure 4-7.) Provisions are made for dumping fuel overboard if necessary.

The operational envelope of the store with the drogue extended is limited to 300 KIAS or 0.80 Mach, whichever is lower, at altitudes up to 35,000 feet. See

Section XI, Part 6, for the complete operational envelope and fuel available for transfer.

AIR REFUELING STORE LIGHTS

At the aft end of the refueling store are two lights, amber (left side) and green (right side). These lights are of use only to the receiver aircraft. The amber light comes on when the hose is extended, indicating that the receiver aircraft may now engage the drogue. After engagement is accomplished the receiver must move forward (3 to 6 feet) until the amber light goes out. Illumination of the green lights indicates that fuel is actually flowing from the tanker to the receiver.

AIR REFUELING CONTROL PANEL

The refueling control panel located forward on the left console contains all the indicators and switches used to operate the system (except the drop tank pressurization switch). The system is designed so that any sequence of switch positioning is possible without causing damage or malfunction to the tanker store.

DROGUE POSITION INDICATOR

The drogue position indicator has 3 possible indications: RET (retracted), EXT (extended), or TRA (transfer). The indication will be RET only when the drogue is fully retracted or during drogue extension. The indicator indicates EXT only when the drogue is fully extended and ready for receiver engagement. TRA is indicated only when the hose and drogue has been engaged and approximately 4 feet of hose retracted on to the store reel and also during hose retraction until the drogue is fully retracted.

GALLONS DELIVERED COUNTER

The gallons delivered counter registers the gallons of fuel transferred through the hose and drogue to the receiver in increments of 2 gallons. A reset knob is provided to reset counters to 0 when desired.

REFUELING MASTER SWITCH

The refueling master switch has three positions: ON, OFF, and DUMP. When the refueling master switch is placed ON, it unlocks and unfeathers the air driven propeller

at the forward end of the refueling store. When placed to OFF it feathers and locks the propeller. When the switch is placed at DUMP, an electrically operated fuel dump valve in the bottom of the refueling store opens to dump fuel. To place it in DUMP, first depress the spring-loaded lever guard then lift the switch from its spring-loaded safety position.

DROGUE SWITCH

The drogue switch controls the hose and drogue positioning and is marked RET and EXT. When the refueling master switch is ON and the drogue switch is positioned at EXT, the hose will extend to trail position. Extension of the drogue energizes a bypass relay. This relay prevents feathering of the air turbine regardless of the position of the refueling master switch until the drogue is fully retracted. When the drogue switch is positioned at RET, the hose will retract.

FUEL TRANSFER SWITCH

The fuel transfer switch controls the flow of fuel after proper hookup is made. The switch must be at TRANS before fuel will transfer. Fuel flow will stop any time this switch is positioned at OFF. A holding relay is provided which causes the switch to remain in the TRANS position until store fuel is depleted or the pilot moves it to OFF.

LIGHT SWITCH

The light switch determines the brightness or the amber and green lights at the aft end of the refueling store. The switch has two positions: BRT for daylight fueling, and DIM for night. With the switch in DIM, store lights will not be visible during daylight.

SHIP-TANK SWITCH

The ship-tank switch has three positions: TO STORE, OFF, and FROM STORE. The TO STORE position permits fuel to flow from the wing tank to the refueling store. When the switch is placed at FROM STORE, fuel will flow under engine air pressurization from the air refueling store and drop tanks to the wing tank.

HOSE JETTISON SWITCH

The hose jettison switch is provided to cut and crimp the store hose in the event of a store malfunction which precludes drogue retraction. It also removes all electrical power from the store controls except for the refueling master switch. The hose jettison switch must be kept in the forward OFF position at all times unless jettisoning of the hose and drogue is required during an inflight emergency. To move the hose jettison switch to HOSE JETTISON, first hold back the spring-loaded channel guard then lift the switch from its spring-loaded safety position. Be sure that this switch is in its forward OFF position before electrical power is applied. Once the HOSE JETTISON position is selected, do not return it to its forward OFF position as the turbine will unfeather and cause the hose to be pulled from the guillotine crimper spilling fuel in the store and creating a fire hazard.

DROP TANK TRANSFER DURING AIR REFUELING

To use the fuel in the drop tanks for air refueling, place the drop tank pressurizing switch at PRESS. This provides normal drop tank transfer to the wing where it may then be used for transfer to the store by means of the SHIP-TANK switch.

Note

When the SHIP-TANK switch is in the FROM STORE position, fuel in the drop tanks will automatically be transferred to the wing regardless of the position of the drop tank transfer switch on the engine control panel.

AIR REFUELING (RECEIVER) SYSTEM

During air refueling, fuel flows through the receiver airplane's probe nozzle under pressure and is distributed to each tank in the same manner as it is through the pressure fueling receptacle.

JET-ASSISTED TAKEOFF SYSTEM

A two-bottle JATO system provides the airplane with additional thrust during takeoff. A JATO bottle is mounted on each speedbrake (35, figure 1-4). Each bottle is capable of producing 4500 pounds of thrust for a period of 5 seconds. The bottles are fired electrically and jettisoned hydraulically by utility system hydraulic pressure controlled through a solenoid operated selector valve.

JATO CONTROL PANEL

The JATO control panel, located outboard of the left-hand console (figure 1-6), contains the following controls for arming and jettisoning of the JATO bottles; the JATO arming switch, the JATO jettison switch and a press-to-test type JATO arming caution light.

JATO ARMING SWITCH. The JATO arming switch is a tow-position lever-lock toggle switch labeled ARMED and OFF. To place the switch in the ARMED position, the spring-loaded toggle lever must be lifted. This arms the JATO firing circuit by energizing the JATO firing button on the catapult handgrip and the jettison circuit to the jettison switch.

JATO ARMED INDICATOR LIGHT. A JATO armed indicator light on the control panel comes on when the arming switch is energized. The press-to-test feature of this light provides a means for preflight checking of JATO arming and firing circuit continuity.

JATO JETTISON SWITCH. The JATO jettison switch on the control panel is a guarded, momentary-contact toggle switch, spring loaded to the SAFE position. In the JATO JETT position the switch energizes a solenoid-controlled hydraulic selector valve which directs hydraulic pressure to the JATO mounting hook actuating cylinders. The mounting hooks are actuated to release both JATO bottles simultaneously.

> **CAUTION**
>
> An interlock in the speedbrake electrical circuit prevents the speedbrakes from operating with the JATO bottles attached. Be sure the speedbrake switch on the throttle is in the CLOSED position prior to jettisoning the JATO bottles; otherwise, upon release of the JATO bottles the speedbrakes will open.

JATO FIRING BUTTON. The JATO firing button (figure 1-5), located at the end of the catapult handgrip energizes a relay which completes the circuit to the firing mechanism. Refer to Section XI, Performance Data, for additional information on takeoff airspeeds with JATO and distances at which the JATO bottles are fired.

> **WARNING**
>
> To prevent possible JATO system accidents, the JATO arming switch in the cockpit must be at OFF and a no-voltage test should be made at the airplane igniter terminals prior to attaching the JATO igniter leads to the bottles.

BANNER TOW TARGET EQUIPMENT

Equipment consists of a banner target, towline, and Mark 51 bomb rack and adapter suspended from an AERO 7A-1 bomb rack on the aircraft centerline station.

TARGETS

Standard Navy or Air Force 7-1/2 foot by 40 foot or 6 foot by 30 foot banner targets may be utilized.

TOWLINE

Recommended towline configuration is 1950 feet of 7/16-inch nylon towline attached to 50 feet of 7/32-inch armored cable leader. The armored cable leader is required at the tow plane end of the towline to prevent burn through which will occur if an all nylon towline is used.

AIRCRAFT TOWLINE ATTACHMENT

For detail on the Mark 51 bomb rack and adapter installation on the AERO 7A-1 bomb rack, refer to the pertinent aircraft armament bulletin.

MISCELLANEOUS EQUIPMENT

THERMAL RADIATION CLOSURE

A thermal radiation closure may be installed on the canopy structure for use on missions requiring pilot protection from the heat and light produced by nuclear explosions.

Changed 15 May 1966

The closure consists of fixed fiberglas panels and a manually actuated segmented telescoping hood (buggy top) attached to the canopy. the glareshield installation includes light seals and an extension on the aft end. When the canopy is closed, the fixed panel on the canopy matches the glareshield in contour and forms a glareshield extension. The buggy top pivots down and forms a light seal with the fixed panel completely sealing the pilot within a thermal protective covering. Attached to the forward segment of the buggy top are right and left handholds for opening and closing as required. The right handhold contains a latching mechanism for locking the buggy top in the open (stowed) position. Two detent "ready positions" hold the buggy top partially open for forward visibility. This affords the pilot partial protection in the event of a surprise burst and shortens the time required to go from the ready position to fully closed. Buggy top should stay in detented positions if subjected to turbulence or acceleration forces of 5g or less.

OPERATION

To close the buggy top, reach back with either hand and pull forward on the right handhold to release the locking mechanism.

In cases when "hands on stick" flight is required the recommended procedure for unlatching the buggy top is to reach across the chest with the left arm while holding the stick with the right hand. Pull it forward to the "ready" position checking by feel to assure it centers in both detents simultaneously. To fully close the buggy top, firmly grasp the handholds with both hands and slam it shut to preclude the possibility of light leaks by seating the detents firmly on both sides.

Note

It is recommended that pilots gain proficiency in operation of the thermal radiation closure on short practice missions at safe altitudes. It is also pointed out that the closure may be used as an instrument training hood.

To open, pull back on the handholds to override the detent pressure and telescope the closure back into its stowed and locked position.

WARNING

Ascertain that the closure locks in the stowed position to prevent its slamming shut inadvertently. This may be checked by pulling forward on the hood.

The pilot should familiarize himself with the operation of the thermal radiation closure prior to flight.

The following method is suggested:

1. Adjust seat to its lowest position.

2. Close and latch the canopy.

3. Check the accessibility of the face curtain handle.

4. Adjust seat upward exercising care not to strike enclosure.

WARNING

When the thermal radiation closure is installed, the secondary ejection handle is recommended for ejection.

5. Unlock buggy top and pull it forward to its detent "ready" position. Operation should be smooth and without binding. Even fingertip pressure on each handhold should assure buggy top is firmly held in both right and left detent positions. A pull of approximately 10 pounds is required to override the detent pressure.

6. Close buggy top by slamming firmly down using both handholds. Check for light leaks.

Note

In direct sunlight or equivalent there should be no outside light directly visible to the pilot.

7. Check the accessibility of the face curtain handle.

8. Return buggy top to the open (stowed) position and check for positive latch.

9. Inspect all exposed surfaces of the thermal radiation closure for cleanliness.

EMERGENCY OPERATION

The thermal radiation closure will be jettisoned along with the canopy in emergencies. The extended aft portion of the glareshield is flexible and will deflect if contacted during ejection.

ANTI-EXPOSURE SUIT VENTILATION

An anti-exposure suit ventilation control panel is installed on the left-hand console (8, figure 1-6) for use with the Mark 5 anti-exposure suit.

The control panel contains the EXPOSURE SUIT VENT and OFF toggle switch, a ventilation blower, and a quick-disconnect flexible hose for connection to the anti-exposure suit. The suit hose disconnect coupling contains a butterfly valve to control the flow of ventilating air to the anti-exposure suit or to close off the opening when the suit is not used.

MAP POCKET

A map pocket is provided on the right side of the cockpit.

SPARE LAMPS RECEPTACLE

Replacement lamps are contained in the SPARE LAMPS receptacle (5, figure 1-8) on the right-hand console.

RELIEF CONTAINER

The relief provisions for this airplane consist of disposable plastic bags. The storage compartment for the bags is located on the left-hand side of the canted bulkhead. (Refer to EMERGENCIES, Section V.)

REAR VIEW MIRRORS

A rear view mirror is installed on each side of the canopy bow and provides limited rearward vision during flight and taxiing.

Changed 15 March 1965

AVC-I-I   P-26943-X

PART 3

AIRCRAFT SERVICING

TABLE OF CONTENTS

TEXT

ILLUSTRATIONS

GENERAL

The following part describes the minimum servicing information the pilot should know.

The A-4E Maintenance Instruction Manual (General Information and Servicing) contains a complete description of all servicing procedures.

Changed 1 November 1965

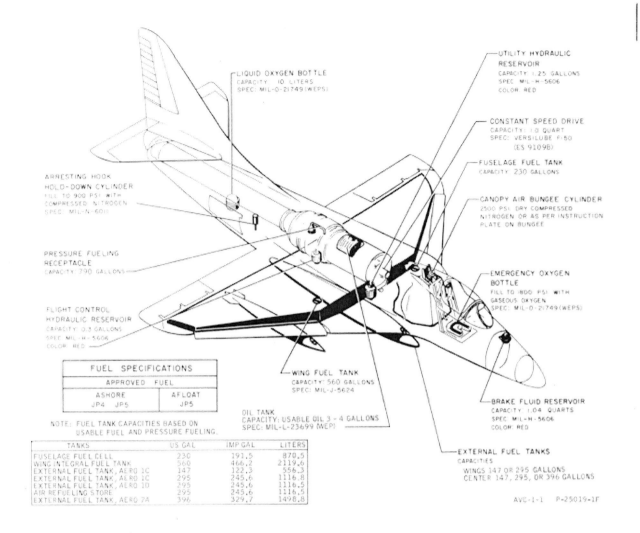

Figure 1-35. Servicing Diagram

PRESSURE FUELING

Normal Pressure Fueling of Aircraft And External
Fuel Tanks

(See figure 1-36.)

WARNING

• Follow procedure only when external electrical power is available and more than
100 gallons of fuel is to be delivered. Use
alternate method when external electrical
power is not available. Use top-off method
if adding less than 100 gallons of fuel.

• Make certain that fuel vent is not obstructed.

• Ensure that aircraft and pressure fueling
equipment are properly grounded.

• All maintenance on aircraft must stop
during pressure fueling; adequate fire
fighting equipment must be available in
immediate area.

• Do not start fueling operations within 100
feet of aircraft with radar equipment being
operated.

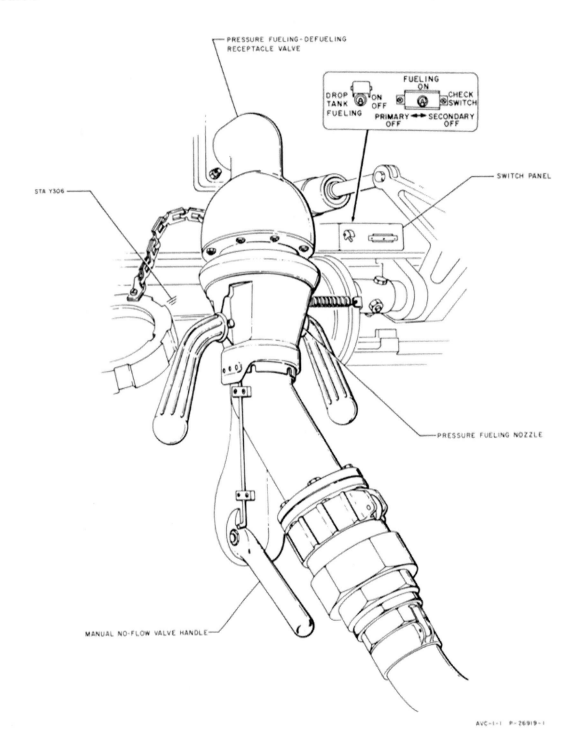

Figure 1-36. Pressure Fueling Airplane and External Fuel Tanks

Note

Airplane should be in 6-degrees noseup attitude during pressure fueling to allow maximum amount of fuel to enter aircraft tanks.

PROCEDURE

a. Open engine aft compartment access door.

b. Remove pressure fueling-defueling receptacle valve cap.

c. Connect pressure fueling nozzle to pressure fueling-defueling receptacle valve.

Note

When the nozzle is connected to the valve, the airplane is grounded automatically through the connection and no further grounding of individual fuel tanks is necessary.

d. On switch adjacent to receptacle valve, check DROP TANK FUELING switch OFF.

e. Connect external electrical power to airplane.

WARNING

Proper connection of a-c external power cable plug to airplane external power receptacle must be made. Failure to insert plug completely in receptacle can result in presence of high voltage on airplane metal surfaces.

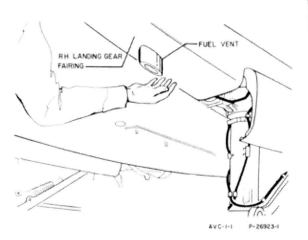

AVC-1-1   P-26923-1

Figure 1-37. Fuel Vent System Outlet Mast

Note

Two methods of applying external a-c power are possible. The first method utilizes the ground start and refueling adapter cable, which permits a-c power to be applied through the engine starter access door. The second method is performed by applying a-c power through the external power receptacle. (Refer to External Power Application this section.)

f. Energize external electrical power.

g. Open manual no-flow valve on fueling nozzle and commence pressure fueling.

CAUTION

Maximum no-flow pressure must not exceed 55 psig at any time at fueling nozzle.

h. Immediately after pressure fueling has started, test the fuel vent system for proper functioning by holding the hand beneath fuel vent mast at the right-hand main gear fairing. (See figure 1-37.)

CAUTION

Air should be exhausted from fuel vent mast during pressure fueling. If air cannot be felt exhausting from the mast, stop pressure fueling operations immediately and investigate fuel vent system.

i. During the initial stage of pressure fueling operations, perform functional test of pressure fueling shutoff components by actuating switches on switch panel as follows:

CAUTION

If fuel flow does not stop when noted in following test, stop pressure fueling operations immediately and investigate. Replace any defective component.

NOTE

When it is specified that fuel flow should stop during following test, an apparent leakage of 2 gpm maximum is permissible registered on pressure fueling meter. Leakage is due to flow of fuel through pilot lines of float valves. When pressure fueling is completed (all tanks full) leakage must not exceed 1 gpm.

j. Place CHECK SWITCH in PRIMARY OFF position. Fuel flow should stop in 1 to 3 seconds.

k. With DROP TANK FUELING switch remaining in OFF position, return CHECK SWITCH to FUELING ON position. Fuel flow should resume.

l. Place CHECK SWITCH in SECONDARY OFF position. Fuel flow should stop in 1 to 3 seconds.

m. Hold CHECK SWITCH in SECONDARY OFF position, and place DROP TANK FUELING switch in ON position. Fuel flow should start into external fuel tanks only. Place DROP TANK FUELING switch OFF unless drop tanks are to be filled.

n. Return CHECK SWITCH to FUELING ON position. Fuel flow should start into wing integral fuel tank and fuselage fuel cell; fuel flow should continue into external fuel tanks if DROP TANK FUELING switch is ON.

NOTE

During pressure fueling, drop tanks may fill unevenly.

o. Continue pressure fueling.

p. During pressure fueling, inspect for evidence of fuel leakage. Correct if required.

q. When pressure fueling has been completed, place DROP TANK FUELING switch in OFF position.

r. Close manual no-flow valve on fueling nozzle.

s. Disconnect nozzle from receptacle valve.

t. Install receptacle valve cap.

u. Disconnect external electrical power from aircraft.

v. Close engine aft compartment access door.

PRESSURE FUELING TOP-OFF METHOD

Top-off procedure is used when less than 100 gallons of fuel is required to complete filling of tanks and when external electrical power is available. The alternate method outlined in this section must be used when external electrical power is not available. Because of the short time required to pressure fuel less than 100 gallons, strict adherence to all steps is mandatory to prevent possible rupture of the wing integral tank. The procedure is as follows:

WARNING

- Stop all maintenance on airplane during fueling operation.

- Insure that adequate fire fighting equipment is available in immediate area.

- Do not fuel airplane within 100 feet of airplane with radar equipment being operated.

- Make certain that fuel vent mast is not obstructed.

a. Open aft engine compartment access door.

b. Remove pressure fueling-defueling receptacle valve cap.

c. Remove fuselage fuel cell and wing integral tank gravity filler caps.

d. Connect pressure fueling nozzle to receptacle valve.

Note

When the pressure fueling nozzle is connected to the valve, the airplane is grounded automatically through the connection and no further grounding of individual fuel tanks is necessary.

e. Connect external electrical power to airplane.

WARNING

Proper connection of a-c external power cable plug to airplane external power receptacle must be made. Failure to insert plug completely in receptacle can result in presence of high voltage on airplane metal surfaces.

f. Energize external electrical power.

g. Place and hold CHECK SWITCH, on switch panel adjacent to receptacle valve, in "PRIMARY OFF" position.

h. Open manual no-flow valve on fueling nozzle and observe fuel supply meter for 1 minute. Fuel flow must not be indicated; maximum allowable leakage is 2 gpm.

i. Place CHECK SWITCH in "FUELING ON" position for 2 to 3 seconds. Fuel supply meter must indicate normal fuel flow.

CAUTION

Maximum no-flow pressure at fueling nozzle must not exceed 55 psig.

j. Place and hold CHECK SWITCH in "SECONDARY OFF" position. Fuel flow must cease within 5 seconds. Observe fuel supply meter: maximum allowable leakage is 2 gpm.

WARNING

If valves fail to function properly, stop fueling immediately and investigate. Remove and replace defective components.

k. If surveillance check indicates satisfactory valve operation, place CHECK SWITCH in "FUELING ON" position and resume fueling. If drop tanks are to be topped off place DROP TANK FUELING switch ON.

l. When topping-off is completed, close no-flow valve on fueling nozzle and disconnect nozzle from receptacle.

m. Verify that DROP TANK FUELING switch is OFF.

n. Install receptacle valve cap.

o. Disconnect external electrical power from aircraft.

p. Install fuselage fuel cell and wing integral tank gravity filler caps.

q. Close or reinstall engine aft compartment access door.

PRESSURE FUELING — ALTERNATE METHOD

External fuel tanks cannot be pressure fueled using the alternate procedure. The following procedure is used when external electrical power is not available. Because of the short time required to pressure fuel less than 100 gallons, strict adherence to all steps is mandatory to prevent possible rupture of the wing integral tank.

WARNING

- Make certain that fuel vent mast is not obstructed.

- Airplane and pressure fueling equipment must be properly grounded during pressure fueling.

- All maintenance on airplane must stop during pressure fueling.

- Adequate fire fighting equipment must be available in immediate area.

a. Open engine aft compartment access door.

b. Remove pressure fueling-defueling receptacle valve cap.

c. Remove fuselage fuel cell gravity filler cap.

d. Remove wing integral fuel tank gravity filler cap.

WARNING

Gravity filler caps must be removed as instructed in steps c and d to prevent possible damage to wing integral fuel tank structure.

e. Connect pressure fueling nozzle to pressure fueling-defueling receptacle valve.

Note

When the pressure fueling nozzle is connected to the valve, the airplane is grounded through the connection and no further grounding of individual fuel tanks is necessary.

f. Open manual no-flow valve on fueling nozzle and commence pressure fueling.

CAUTION

One man should stand ready to stop pressure fueling equipment immediately should any pressure fueling shutoff component fail to stop fuel flow when tanks are full. This will be manifested by fuel flow from the filler ports.

g. During pressure fueling, inspect for evidence of fuel leakage. Also inspect fuel vent mast and external fuel tank overboard vent line for evidence of fuel leakage. Correct if leakage is evident.

h. When pressure fueling has been completed, close manual no-flow valve on fueling nozzle and disconnect nozzle from receptacle valve.

i. Install receptacle valve cap.

j. Install fuselage fuel cell gravity filler cap.

k. Install wing tank gravity filler cap.

l. Close or reinstall aft engine compartment access door.

HOT REFUELING

Refer to procedures in Section III, Part 5 for refueling of aircraft with the engine running.

GRAVITY FUELING

WARNING

- Ground aircraft and fueling equipment during all fueling operations.

- Stop all maintenance on aircraft during fueling.

- Ensure that adequate firefighting equipment is available in immediate area.

- Make certain that proper fuel is used for refueling. (Refer to servicing diagram.)

- Do not connect external electrical power to aircraft when gravity fueling.

- Do not start fueling or defueling operations within 100 feet of aircraft operating with radar equipment.

GRAVITY FUELING FUSELAGE FUEL CELL

(See figure 1-38.)

a. Open fuselage cell gravity filler access door; remove cap from gravity filler port.

b. Insert nozzle grounding jack in grounding receptacle directly aft and outboard of access door; insert refueling nozzle in gravity filler port.

c. Fill fuselage cell until fuel level is at bottom of gravity filler port neck.

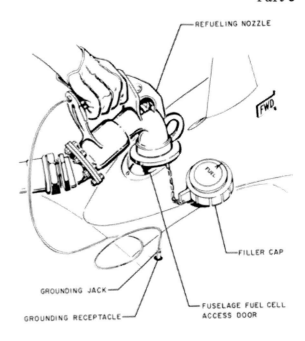

AVC-1-1 P-26920-1

Figure 1-38. Gravity Fueling Fuselage Fuel Cell

d. Remove refueling nozzle from gravity filler port; disconnect grounding jack from receptacle.

e. Install gravity filler port cap and secure access door.

GRAVITY FUELING WING INTEGRAL FUEL TANK

(See figure 1-39.)

a. Remove wing integral fuel tank filler cap.

b. Insert refueling nozzle grounding jack in grounding receptacle on wing nose.

WARNING

Do not drop fueling nozzle in wing tank filler port because nozzle will damage lower surface of tank. Do not pull fueling hose over wing slats.

c. Insert refueling nozzle in gravity filler port. Hold refueling nozzle in one hand and support refueling hose with other hand.

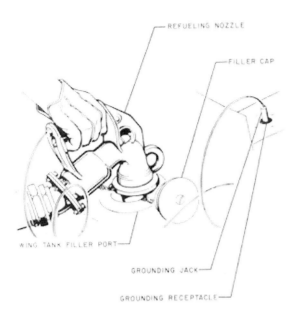

Figure 1-39. Gravity Fueling Wing
Integral Tank

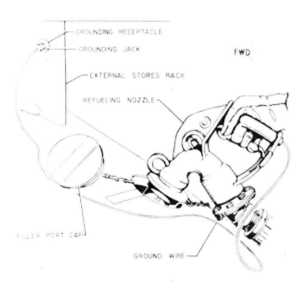

Figure 1-40. Gravity Fueling External
Fuel Tank or Air Refueling Store

d. Fill wing fuel tank until fuel is at bottom of gravity filler port neck.

e. Remove refueling nozzle from gravity filler port; disconnect grounding jack from receptacle.

f. Install wing fuel tank gravity filler port cap and lock securely in place.

GRAVITY FUELING EXTERNAL FUEL TANK OR AIR REFUELING STORE

(See figure 1-40.)

a. Remove tank or store filler cap.

b. Insert refueling nozzle grounding jack in grounding receptacle on left-hand side of external stores rack.

c. Insert refueling nozzle into filler port. Hold refueling nozzle in one hand and support refueling hose with other hand.

d. Fill tank or store until fuel level is approximately 1 inch below filler port to allow for thermal expansion.

e. Remove refueling nozzle from filler port; disconnect refueling nozzle grounding jack from receptacle.

f. Install tank or store filler cap.

FUEL CONTROL FUEL SELECTOR

For extended operations, the fuel grade selector on the engine fuel control should correspond to the grade of fuel being used. For one time use of fuel other than that selected, the pilot must monitor EGT to ensure full throttle operation remains within the prescribed limits. (See figure 1-41.)

ADJUSTMENT

a. Open engine forward compartment left-hand access door.

b. Remove retaining nut securing locking bracket to retaining stud on housing.

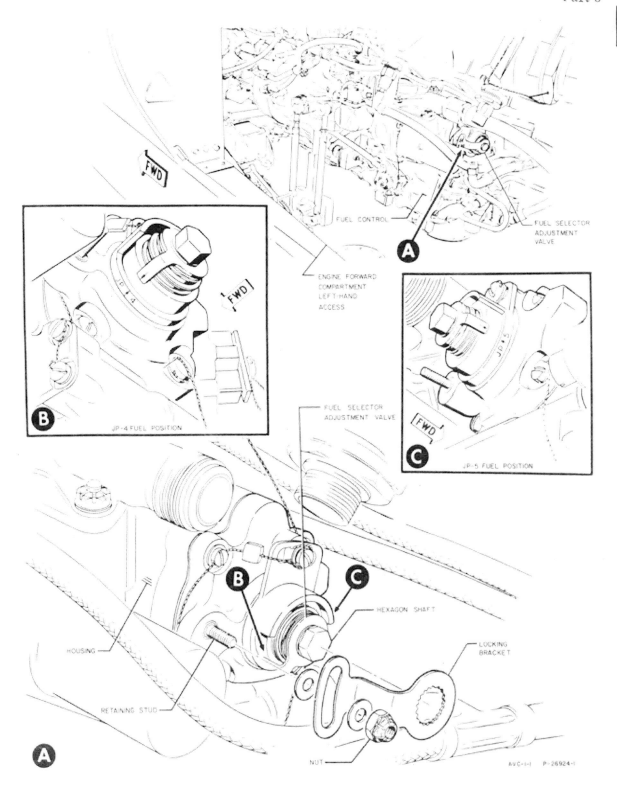

Figure 1-41. Fuel Control Fuel Selector Adjustment

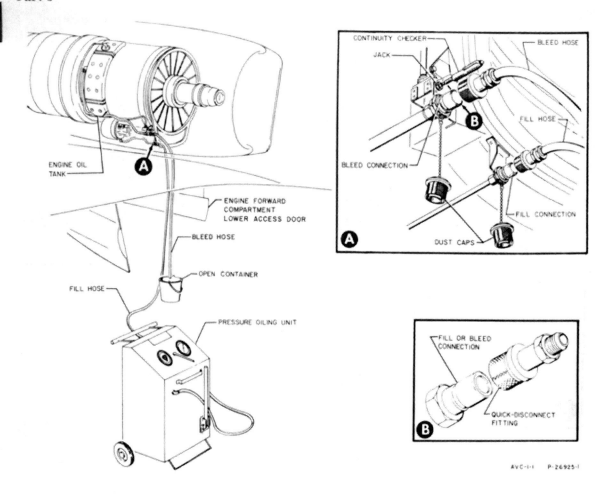

Figure 1-42.   Engine Oil System — Pressure Filling

c.   Remove locking bracket from stud.

d.   Invert locking bracket and insert over hexagon shaft.

e.   Using locking bracket as a wrench, rotate hexagon shaft until pointer on outside of valve is aligned with index for grade of fuel to be used.

f.   Replace locking bracket over hexagon shaft so that slotted end fits over retaining stud on housing.

g.   Secure bracket to retaining stud with washer and nut.

h.   Close engine forward compartment left-hand access door.

ENGINE OIL SYSTEM SERVICING

Servicing provisions are accessible through the engine forward compartment lower access doors.   The PON-5A pressure oiling unit is recommended for servicing the engine oil tank.   This unit is equipped with a penlite continuity checker which, when plugged into the engine oil tank pressure switch circuit, indicates whether the oil level is adequate for safe engine operation.

CHECKING OIL LEVEL

(See figure 1-42.)

a.   Open engine forward compartment lower access doors.

b. Insert continuity checker plug into jack marked CHECK on pressure filling panel located on forward right-hand side of engine. If continuity checker does not light, oil in the tank may be below the level required for safe engine operation and oil must be added.

Note

Checking or filling the engine oil system should be accomplished within 3 hours after engine shutdown. If engine is not serviced within 3 hours, engine must be turned up at 75% rpm or more for 30 seconds to establish actual oil tank level.

c. If checker indicates continuity, remove plug from jack; oil level is adequate for safe engine operation.

ENGINE OIL SYSTEM PRESSURE FILLING

(See figure 1-42.)

a. Remove oil fill and oil bleed dust caps.

b. Connect pressure oiling unit hose to fill connection.

c. Connect 3-foot hose with Roylyn 7776 3/4-inch (MS24475-2) quick-disconnect fitting to bleed connection.

Note

Bleed hose should be not more than 3 feet in length to prevent back pressure in bleed line.

d. Allow bleed hose to empty into open container.

e. Pump oil (MIL-L-23699(WEP) into tank until a continuous stream of oil runs out the bleed line.

CONSTANT SPEED DRIVE (CSD) SERVICING

The constant speed drive (see figure 1-43) is located on the forward end of the engine. It is mounted on an adapter bolted to the engine pad and secured by a V-band coupling. The drive unit and components should be inspected daily. Access to the constant speed drive is through the engine forward compartment lower right-hand access door and the constant speed drive outer and inner access doors. Servicing consists of inspecting for fluid level and adding fluid.

DAILY INSPECTION

The following inspection should be made:

a. Open engine forward compartment right-hand access door and constant speed drive outer and inner access doors.

b. Using a flashlight and an inspection mirror, inspect constant speed drive for signs of fluid leakage.

c. Inspect fluid level on sight gage.

FILLING

(See figure 1-43.)

a. Open engine forward compartment right-hand access door, and constant speed drive outer and inner doors.

b. Remove lockwire and filler plug located at top right-hand side of pump.

CAUTION

Use only Versilube, F-50 silicone fluid. Mixing or the use of other than an approved fluid will cause constant speed drive failure.

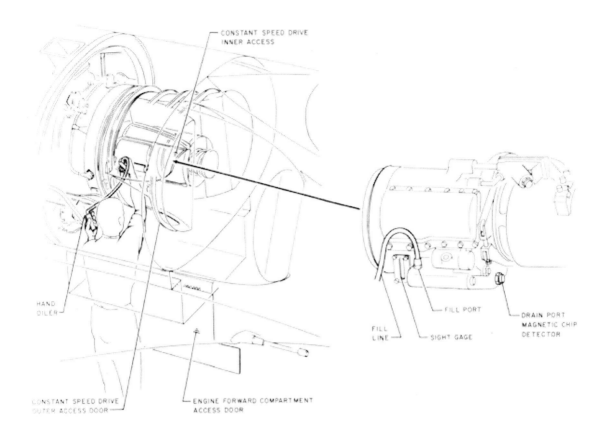

Figure 1-43.   Constant Speed Drive Filling

c.   Add fluid (F-50 Versilube silicone fluid) until fluid level is at "FULL" mark on sight gage.

Note

The capacity of the constant speed drive is 1 quart.

d.   Replace filler plug and secure with lock-wire.

e.   Replace access doors.

HYDRAULIC SYSTEM SERVICING

The utility hydraulic system and the flight control hydraulic system are serviced separately.

UTILITY HYDRAULIC SYSTEM FILLING

(See figure 1-44.)

a.   Open engine forward compartment access doors and utility hydraulic reservoir access door.

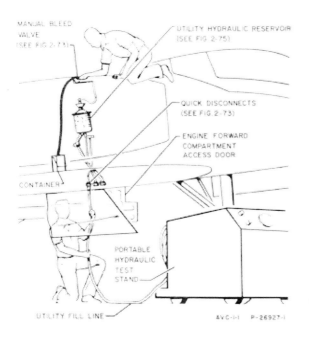

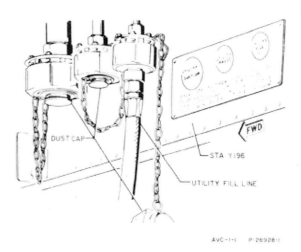

Figure 1-45. Utility Hydraulic
Quick-Disconnect

Figure 1-44. Utility Hydraulic
System Filling

b. Remove dust caps and connect source of hydraulic fluid to FILL quick-disconnect on right-hand side of engine compartment. (See figure 1-45.)

c. Remove utility hydraulic bleed line from retaining clips; pass free end of line through utility hydraulic reservoir access door and place end in suitable container on wing to receive any possible overflow of fluid when bleeding.

d. Fill reservoir until piston registers "FULL" on sight gage. (Gage is viewed through utility hydraulic reservoir access door.) (See figure 1-46.)

f. Disconnect external supply source when reservoir has been filled and bled.

g. Install dust cap on FILL quick-disconnect.

h. Reinstall bleed line in retaining clips.

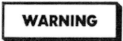

Do not allow pressure applied to FILL port to exceed 65 psi.

e. Depress manual bleed valve until sight gage is free of air bubbles. (See figure 1-47.)

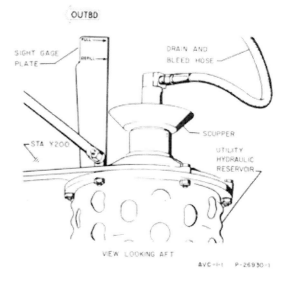

Figure 1-46. Utility Hydraulic
Reservoir Sight Gage

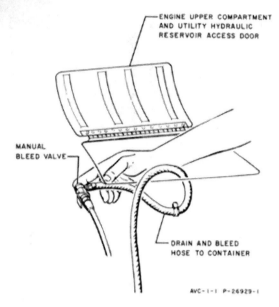

Figure 1-47. Utility Hydraulic
Manual Bleed Valve

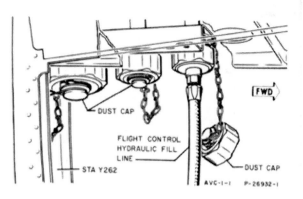

Figure 1-49. Flight Control Hydraulic
Quick-Disconnect Panel

FLIGHT CONTROL HYDRAULIC SYSTEM FILLING

(See figure 1-48.)

a. Open engine control access door and flight control hydraulic reservoir access door.

b. Disconnect hydraulic pump line from quick-disconnect identified as FILL. (See figure 1-49.)

c. Connect source of hydraulic fluid (MIL-H-5606A) supply to FILL quick-disconnect.

d. Remove flight control hydraulic bleed line from retaining clip, pass free end of line through flight control hydraulic reservoir access door, and place free end in suitable container on wing to receive any possible overflow of fluid when bleeding. (See figure 1-50.)

e. Fill reservoir until piston registers full on sight gage. (Gage is viewed through flight control hydraulic reservior access door.) (See figure 1-51.)

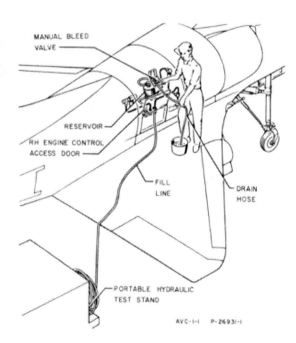

Figure 1-48. Flight Control Hydraulic
System Filling

WARNING

Do not allow pressure applied to FILL port to exceed 100 psi.

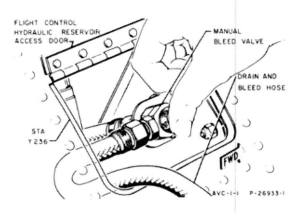

Figure 1-50. Flight Control Hydraulic
Manual Bleed Valve

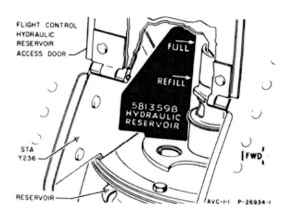

Figure 1-51. Flight Control Hydraulic
Reservoir Sight Gage

f. Depress manual bleed valve until sight gage is free of air bubbles.

g. Disconnect external supply source when reservoir has been filled and bled.

h. Reconnect hydraulic pump line to FILL quick-disconnect.

i. Reinstall bleed line in retaining clamps; secure engine fuel control and flight control hydraulic reservoir doors.

BRAKE RESERVOIR SERVICING

(See figure 1-51A.)

a. Open nose section.

Note

Aircraft should be in a 6 degree nose up attitude for servicing.

b. Remove filler plug from brake reservoir.

c. Insert filler nozzle of hydraulic servicing tank into reservoir filler port.

d. Fill reservoir with hydraulic fluid until gage indicates full.

Note

When sight gage indicates reservoir is full, do not add more fluid; if reservoir is filled to level of port, excess fluid will be vented overboard during flight maneuvers.

e. Install reservoir filler plug.

Note

If brakes are bled, reservice reservoir as necessary.

g. Close nose section.

LIQUID OXYGEN SYSTEM SERVICING

Servicing of the A-4E 10-liter liquid oxygen system (see figure 1-53) is accomplished by means of a portable external source. Liquid oxygen from an insulated servicing trailer is transferred under pressure to the airplane system. Because of the nature of liquid oxygen no external pressure source is required, as evaporation builds up sufficient pressure within the servicing trailer to complete the operation.

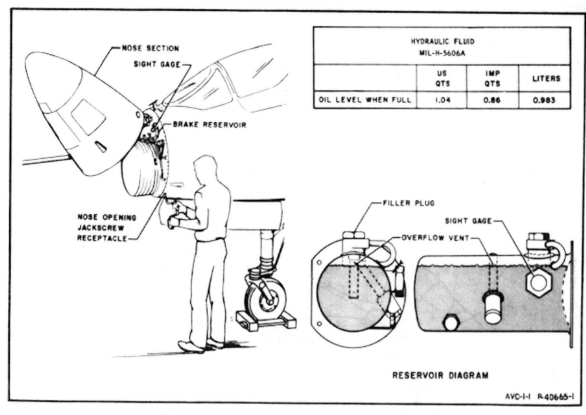

	HYDRAULIC FLUID MIL-H-5606A		
	US QTS	IMP QTS	LITERS
OIL LEVEL WHEN FULL	1.04	0.86	0.983

RESERVOIR DIAGRAM

AVC-I-I R.40665-I

Figure 1-51A. Brake Reservoir Servicing

FILLING CONVERTER

a. Make certain oxygen switch in cockpit is in "OFF" position.

b. Open liquid oxygen compartment access door.

c. Remove filler valve cap from filler valve.

d. Purge filler hose on servicing trailer until oxygen flows in steady uninterrupted stream.

e. Connect filler hose immediately to converter filler valve and commence filling.

Note

Any prolonged delay in connecting filler hose may allow liquid oxygen in hose to change to gaseous oxygen. Pressure in servicing trailer should be between 45 to 50 psi.

f. When liquid oxygen flows from overflow vent port in steady stream, close fill drain valve on servicing trailer; disconnect filler hose from filler valve which will automatically return converter to "BUILDUP" position.

WARNING

Warn all personnel working on aircraft and in area to stay clear of liquid oxygen overflow. (See figure 1-52.)

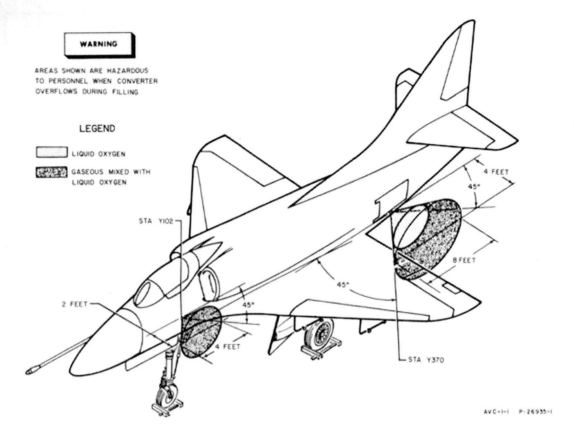

WARNING

AREAS SHOWN ARE HAZARDOUS
TO PERSONNEL WHEN CONVERTER
OVERFLOWS DURING FILLING

LEGEND

LIQUID OXYGEN

GASEOUS MIXED WITH
LIQUID OXYGEN

STA Y102

2 FEET

45°

4 FEET

45°

45°

4 FEET

45°

8 FEET

STA Y370

AVC-3-1   P-26935-1

Figure 1-52.   Liquid Oxygen Handling Precautions

Note

If the converter filler valve freezes
during filling, remove filler hose and
install filler valve cap. Recheck filler valve after approximately 10
minutes.

g. Relieve pressure in servicing trailer
filler hose by engaging filler nozzle in purg-
ing device on trailer.

h. Install dust cap on filler valve.

Note

Prior to installing filler valve dust
cap, inspect cap closely for evi-
dance of water. If water or moisture
is noted, dry thoroughly with compressed air because water in cap
may freeze in filler valve.

i. Install dust cap on filler hose nozzle.

j. Secure liquid oxygen compartment door.

EMERGENCY OXYGEN BOTTLE SERVICING
(See figure 1-52A.)

a. Remove parachute and seat pan assembly from the aircraft.

b. Place parachute and seat pan assembly
on clean work table.

c. Unzip seat pan cover and fold cover
back for access to filler valve.

d. Connect source of gaseous oxygen and
charge bottle to correct pressure compensated for ambient air temperature.

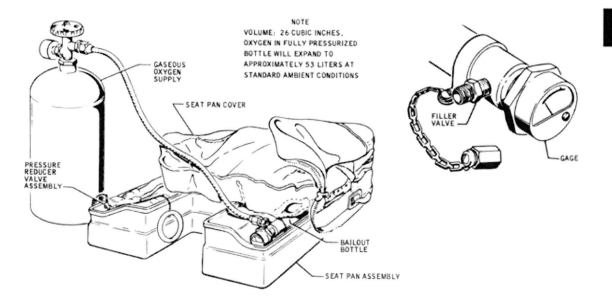

NOTE
VOLUME: 26 CUBIC INCHES.
OXYGEN IN FULLY PRESSURIZED
BOTTLE WILL EXPAND TO
APPROXIMATELY 53 LITERS AT
STANDARD AMBIENT CONDITIONS

GASEOUS
OXYGEN
SUPPLY

SEAT PAN COVER

FILLER
VALVE

GAGE

PRESSURE
REDUCER
VALVE
ASSEMBLY

BAILOUT
BOTTLE

SEAT PAN ASSEMBLY

WARNING

MAKE CERTAIN PRESSURE REDUCER
VALVE ASSEMBLY AND LOCKWIRE
ARE NOT DAMAGED OR BROKEN DUR-
ING SERVICING. (REFER TO SECTION IV).

EMERGENCY OXYGEN BOTTLE CHARGING PRESSURE					
AMBIENT AIR TEMPERATURE		CHARGING PRESSURE	AMBIENT AIR TEMPERATURE		CHARGING PRESSURE
F°	C°	(psi)	F°	C°	(psi)
0	-18	1600	70	21	1925
10	-12	1650	80	27	1950
20	-7	1675	90	32	2000
30	-1	1725	100	38	2050
40	5	1775	110	43	2100
50	10	1825	120	49	2150
60	16	1875	130	54	2200

AVC-1-1   P-40652-1

Figure 1-52A.   Emergency Oxygen Bottle Servicing

e. Disconnect oxygen supply from filler valve and check valve for leakage.

f.   Zip seat pan cover closed.

g.   Install parachute and seat pan assembly in ejection seat.

EXTERNAL POWER APPLICATION

Two methods of applying ac external electrical power to the aircraft are available. The primary or standard method utilizes an ac mobile electric power plant (NC-5 or equivalent). (See figure 1-54.) The second method enables a ground crewman to apply ac power, dc power, and starter air through the engine starter access door, utilizing the aircraft ground start disconnect cable. The ground starting method is not an alternative to the standard method of applying ac electrical power.

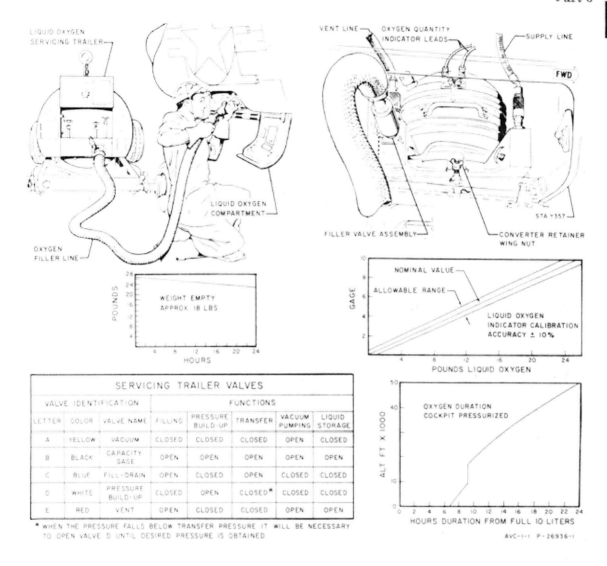

SERVICING TRAILER VALVES							
VALVE IDENTIFICATION			FUNCTIONS				
LETTER	COLOR	VALVE NAME	FILLING	PRESSURE BUILD-UP	TRANSFER	VACUUM PUMPING	LIQUID STORAGE
A	YELLOW	VACUUM	CLOSED	CLOSED	CLOSED	OPEN	CLOSED
B	BLACK	CAPACITY GAGE	OPEN	OPEN	OPEN	OPEN	OPEN
C	BLUE	FILL-DRAIN	OPEN	CLOSED	OPEN	CLOSED	CLOSED
D	WHITE	PRESSURE BUILD-UP	CLOSED	OPEN	CLOSED*	CLOSED	CLOSED
E	RED	VENT	OPEN	CLOSED	CLOSED	OPEN	OPEN

* WHEN THE PRESSURE FALLS BELOW TRANSFER PRESSURE IT WILL BE NECESSARY
TO OPEN VALVE D UNTIL DESIRED PRESSURE IS OBTAINED

AVC-1-1 P-26936-1

Figure 1-53.   Liquid Oxygen System Servicing

STARTING REQUIREMENTS

A high pressure air supply to the air turbine
starter (installed in the aircraft) and external electrical power is required for starting
the A4E.   Approved starter units are listed
below:

SUITABLE STARTER UNITS

Suitable starter units for A-4 aircraft are:

GTC-85 (USN) , GTCE-85-1-1

MA-1TA (Palouste and Continential)

MA-1A (AiResearch and Continential)

MD-1A (Hough Tractor with GTC-85 unit)

MD-2A (with GTC-85 unit)

ME-1A (with GTC-85 unit)

GTCE-85-1 (with GTC-85 unit)

GTC-15

GTC-24

GTC-28

Changed 15 March 1965

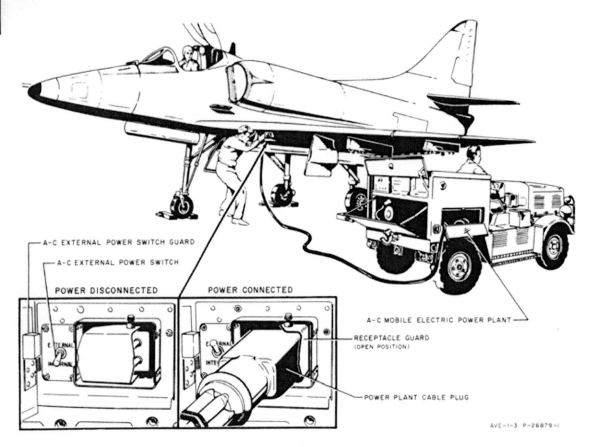

Figure 1-54. External Power Application

The GTC-24 unit can be used; however, at minimum temperatures (-65° F), this unit develops torque high enough to damage the starter.

A source of 115 volt ac power is required for ignition. 28 volt dc power is required if a cockpit controlled start is desired. Ac power can be provided through the external power receptacle (see figure 1-54) or through the aircraft ground start disconnect (see figure 1-55). Dc power (for cockpit controlled start) can only be supplied through the aircraft ground start disconnect.

Note

If 28-volt dc power is not available, a ground start must be accomplished.

DANGER AREAS

During ground operation certain hazardous areas exist. These areas are depicted in figures 1-52, 1-53, and 1-56.

TURNING RADII

For turning radii of the A-4E aircraft, see figure 1-57.

Changed 1 November 1965

2. Align nosewheel fore and aft, secure nose and main gear wheels fore and aft with chocks.

Note

Use adjustable chocks if available.

WARNING

Minimum and maximum angles of tiedown chain in relation to aircraft and ground or deck must be strictly adhered to.

3. Attach chain assemblies to tiedown points indicated for normal weather tiedown and tighten chains.

4. Make certain throttle lever is in OFF position and tighten THROTTLE FRICTION AND LOCK CONTROL.

5. Close canopy.

6. Install cockpit enclosure cover.

7. Install pitot and temperature probe covers.

8. Install manifold exhaust cover.

9. Install aft compartment cooling duct plugs.

10. Install aileron gust lock.

11. Install wing slat locks.

12. Install engine air inlet covers.

13. Install angle of attack vane guard.

14. Install nose compartment cooling duct plugs.

15. Install air conditioning ram air duct plugs.

16. Install engine exhaust cover.

17. Remove entrance ladder, if installed.

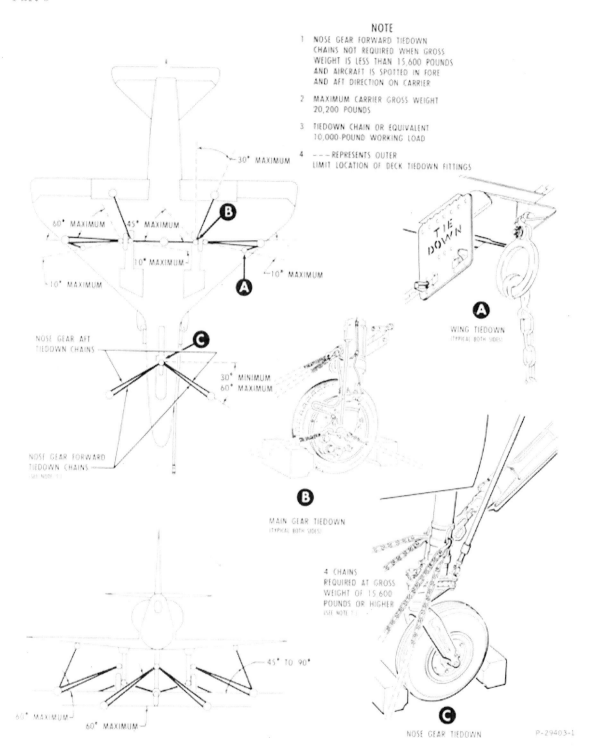

Figure 1-60. Normal Weather Tiedown

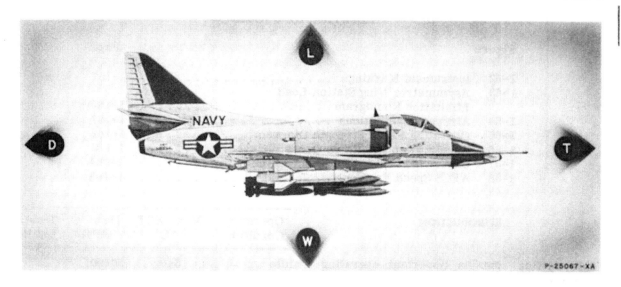

P-25067-XA

PART 4

OPERATING LIMITATIONS

TABLE OF CONTENTS

TEXT

ILLUSTRATIONS

ILLUSTRATIONS (Cont)

INTRODUCTION

This section contains important operating limitations which shall be observed during normal operation of the aircraft. Additional limitations are covered in Section I, Part 4 of the Confidential Supplement.

ENGINE LIMITATIONS

Restrictions to be observed in the operation of the engines are based upon the use of fuel as follows:

	Approved Fuel	
	Ashore	Afloat
Recommended	JP-5	JP-5
Alternate	JP-4	

ENGINE OPERATING LIMITS

STARTING TEMPERATURES. If engine exhaust gas temperature (EGT) exceeds 455° five times, or reaches 531° to 565°C for one period of 5 seconds or more, engine must be subjected to an overtemperature inspection. An EGT exceeding 565°C for any period of time will require a teardown inspection of all hot section parts. (Refer to Service Instructions J52-P-6 Engine, NAVWEPS 02B-10DAA-2 for overtemperature inspection procedures.)

Operating Condition	Max. EGT °C	Max. % RPM	Time Limit
Idle	340	50-60	......
Acceleration	650	102.6	2 minutes
Normal	590	Military -3%	......
Military	610	Military	30 minutes

Note

- The IDLE temperature of 340°C is not a limit but is given as a guide to indicate the temperatures which, if exceeded, may signify an engine malfunction.

- Following acceleration, EGT may overshoot the stabilized value for a given throttle setting, and require some time to decrease to that value. After "peaking", EGT will decrease quite rapidly at first; then progressively more slowly as it approaches the stabilized value. EGT should not stabilize at any point above the maximum steady-state value. The above limits for acceleration and maximum temperatures should be interpreted to mean that the EGT may go to 650°C during acceleration but must decrease to 610° or less within 2 minutes after acceleration. In normal operation EGT overshoot rarely occurs (figure 1-62).

- Engine limitations are based on combinations of engine speeds and exhaust gas temperatures, with a maximum allowable engine speed under any condition of 102.6 percent (11,900 rpm). Should this limiting value be exceeded, reduce thrust and land as soon as possible.

- RPM varies between engines at Military thrust. For each engine, the specific rpm required to produce Military thrust under standard day conditions is placarded on the engine data plate. Most engines will fall in the range of 97 to 100 percent of 11,600 rpm. The pilot should therefore expect to see tachometer rpm indicate in this range at full throttle.

- The rpm at MILITARY thrust also varies noticeably with changes in inlet temperature. The amount of variation from data plate rpm depends on the type fuel control installed but is approximately +1 to -2 percent for extreme conditions of hot and cold respectively. (See figure 1-61.)

- The 30-minute time limit at Military thrust is a power level limit as well as a temperature limit; that is a particular engine which develops Military thrust at an exhaust gas temperature of 540°C is still limited to 30 minutes at this power even though it is below the Military operating temperature limit (610°C).

- Data applicable to operation on jet fuel, grades JP-4 and JP-5.

OIL PRESSURE VARIATION. The oil pressure indication at IDLE RPM should be normal (40 to 50 psi); however a minimum of 35 psi for ground operation is acceptable. If the indication is less than 35 psi at 60% rpm, shut down the engine to determine the reason for the lack of, or low, oil pressure.

| CAUTION |

- Even though certain maneuvers normally cause a momentary loss of oil pressure, maximum operating time with an oil pressure indicating less than 40 psi in flight is 1 minute under all conditions. If recovery of oil pressure is not accomplished in 1 minute, the flight should be terminated as soon as practicable.

- If the oil pressure indicator reads high (over 50 psi), the throttle setting should be reduced to lessen rpm and safeguard engine seals. A landing should be made as soon as possible, and the cause investigated.

Note

During starting and initial runup, the maximum allowable oil pressure is 50 psi.

MANEUVERS

The following maneuvers are permitted:

1. Inverted flight (not to exceed 30 seconds)

2. Loop

3. Aileron roll

   a. Not to exceed 360 degrees

   b. Not to exceed one-half stick deflection with fuel in the 300-gallon external fuel tanks, except that above 20,000 feet full stick deflection may be used for rolls up to 180 degrees.

4. Wingover

5. Immelmann

The maximum permissible change in angle of bank during rolling pullouts or rolling pushovers is 180 degrees.

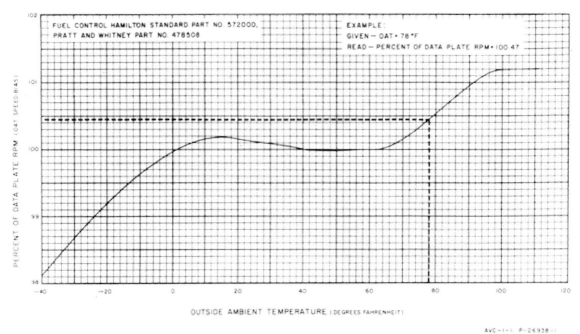

Figure 1-61. Military RPM Curve for Sea Level Static Condition

AIRSPEED LIMITATIONS

The maximum permissible indicated airspeeds in smooth or moderately turbulent air are:

1. With symmetrical loading, and with landing gear, flaps, and hook retracted . . . . . . As shown in figure 1-64

2. With asymmetrical loading . . . . 510 knots or Mach 0.90, whichever is lower

3. With landing gear and and/or flaps extended . . . . . 225 knots (with zero yaw 170 knots (with unrestricted yaw)

4. For air refueling from A-4 tanker, and for buddy store hose extensions . . . . . . 300 knots or Mach 0.80, whichever is lower

For buddy store hose retraction . . . . 250 IAS

5. With flight controls disconnected:

    a. With asymmetrical loading . . . . 200 knots

    b. With symmetrical loading . . . . 300 knots or Mach 0.80, whichever is lower

6. With emergency generator extended . . . . 500 knots or Mach 0.91, whichever is lower

Changed 1 November 1965

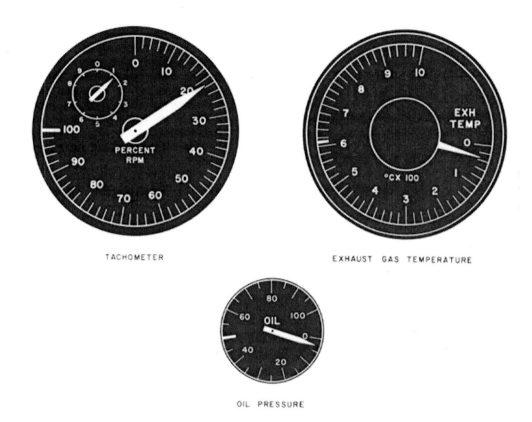

TACHOMETER

EXHAUST GAS TEMPERATURE

OIL PRESSURE

ENGINE PERFORMANCE	
RPM	
MAXIMUM STABILIZED (30 MINUTES)	102.6%
TEMP	
MAXIMUM STABILIZED (30 MINUTES)	610° C
FUEL BOOST	
MAXIMUM ALLOWABLE	LIGHT OUT (50 PSI)
OIL PRESS	
MAXIMUM ALLOWABLE	50 PSI

AVC-IA-5   P-25068-18

Figure 1-62.   Instrument Markings

7. Insofar as practicable,
utilize strafing speeds of . . . . . . 350 to 450
knots

CENTER-OF-GRAVITY LIMITATIONS

The maximum permissible center-of-gravity range for the clean aircraft is:

Gear DOWN. . . . 15.8 to 29.5% M.A.C.

Gear UP . . . . . . 14.5 to 28.5% M.A.C.

Refer to the Handbook of Weight and Balance Data, AN 01-1B-40, for center of gravity limits as affected by external stores loadings.

GROSS WEIGHT LIMITATIONS

The maximum recommended gross weights are:

Field takeoff . . . . 24,500 pounds

Field landing (minimum
rate of descent) . . . . 16,000 pounds

Field landing (other than
minimum rate of descent), FMLP,
and field arrestments . . . . . . 14,500 pounds

Catapulting - . . . . 24,500 pounds

NOTE

Refer to applicable Aircraft Launching Bulletin for additional limitations.

CAUTION

Ensure that struts are continually serviced properly.

attempted only in an emergency.

CAUTION

• Barricade engagements may be made with stores such as empty tanks, empty rocket packs, or other light-weight inert stores, but, if torn loose, these stores may present a hazard to flight-deck personnel. Barricade engagements are not permitted with stores other than mentioned above. It is recommended that internal wing fuel be burnt out prior to engagement. Refer to the appropriate recovery bulletin for permissible arresting gear engaging speeds.

• Barrier engagements are not permitted.

• At high gross weights engaging speeds should be held to a minimum to prevent structural damage to the aircraft.

• Additional catapulting gross weight limitations as imposed by increased ambient temperatures and the resultant reduction in engine thrust are extremely critical when operating with stores on the multiple bomb racks in a FULL FLAP or HALF FLAP configuration. Refer to applicable Aircraft Launching Bulletin for more detailed information.

ASYMMETRIC LOAD LIMITATIONS

1. Asymmetrical store loadings up to 7500 foot-pounds of static moment on either wing are permitted for field operations and carrier landings. The asymmetric load at the outboard rack times 9.48 plus the asymmetric load at the inboard rack times 6.25 must not exceed 7500 foot-pounds. For rapid computation of allowable asymmetric load (less than 7500 ft/lbs) see figure 1-63. To use the nomogram, enter with the unbalanced (asymmetric) condition existing for either the outboard or inboard rack. The maximum unbalanced load allowed on the other rack is found by connecting the known condition and the maximum wgt/arm allowed (7500 ft/lbs) with an extended straight line. For example, with 250 pounds on the outboard rack, the maximum permissible load on the inboard rack is 820 pounds.

To determine whether known unbalanced loads are within limits, connect unbalanced outboard load and unbalanced inboard load with a straight line. If the connecting line falls below the maximum of 7500 foot-pounds, the loading condition is satisfactory for field takeoff or landing.

2. Catapult launch with an asymmetrical external stores loading in excess of 5120 foot-pounds is not permitted. The maximum allowable crosswind for asymmetrical loading is 15 knots. Launches with 15 knots crosswind require at least 10 knots above minimum endspeed. For less than the maximum crosswinds, interpolation is permitted to determine required excess endspeed (figure 1-67). A lateral control input will be required to maintain the wings level as the aircraft leaves the bow. Directional trim (away from the more heavily loaded wing) requirements are as follows:

> 0 to 10 knots crosswind - 2 units
>
> 11 to 15 knots crosswind - 3 units

3. Landing with a crosswind component under the unloaded, or light, wing is not recommended.

AUTOMATIC FLIGHT CONTROL SYSTEM LIMITATIONS

At altitudes of 7500 feet and above, operation of the AFCS is unrestricted throughout the speed range of the aircraft (figure 1-68).

The automatic flight control system may be engaged below 7500 feet except for the following conditions:

1. During takeoff and landing.

2. Between 1000 feet and 7500 feet terrain clearance, with airspeed below 300 knots, AFCS operation requires the hands on the control stick. Above 300 knots, operation is unrestricted.

3. Below 1000 feet terrain clearance, to 200 feet terrain clearance, AFCS operation is restricted to hands on the control stick and a maximum airspeed of 500 knots.

4. The AFCS shall not be engaged below 200 feet above the terrain.

AFCS PERFORMANCE AND POWER LIMITATIONS

The attitude hold, preselected heading, and altitude hold modes all operate within the 60-degree pitch and 70-degree roll angle limits of the AFCS. It must be realized that within these limits, each mode is further limited by the attitude, gross weight, and power performance of the basic airframe.

ACCELERATION LIMITATIONS

Accelerations at which moderate buffeting occurs shall not be exceeded. Otherwise, the maximum permissible accelerations for flight are as shown in figure 1-66. As gross weight increases above 12,500 pounds, maximum permissible accelerations decrease as shown in figure 1-65. During conditions of moderate turbulence, avoid deliberate accelerations in excess of those permitted as shown in figure 1-66 to minimize the probability of overstressing the aircraft as a result of the combined effects of gust and maneuvering loads. Transonic pitchup can occur during speed reductions in the transonic region. Buffet onset and flight strength limits at low altitude combat conditions are shown in Section XI, Part 9.

CAUTION

To minimize the probability of exceeding the maximum permissible load factor due to the combined effects of maneuvering load factor and transonic pitchup, the following procedure is recommended:

> Below 15,000 feet, at speeds in excess of 0.94 IMN, avoid deliberate accelerations in excess of plus 4.0 g. Above 15,000 feet, avoid deliberate accelerations which exceed buffet onset.

DIVE ANGLE LIMITATIONS

Information concerning the maximum permissible dive angles when diving at maximum permissible airspeeds will be provided in future publications. In the interim, this information may be extrapolated from the dive recovery charts in Section IV (figure 4-4).

A4E WING MOMENT NOMOGRAM

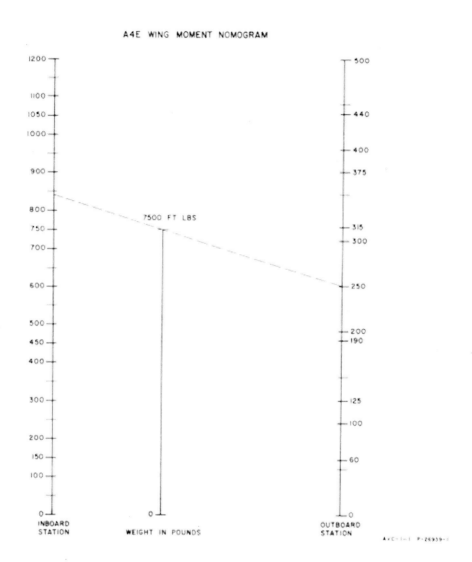

Figure 1-63. Asymmetric Wing Station Load Limitation Nomogram

AIRSPEED LIMITATIONS

MODEL: A-4E

DATA AS OF: 15 January 1960

DATA BASIS: Interim Revision No. 1 To A-4C
Flight Handbook Supplement

ENGINE: J52-P-6

FUEL GRADE: JP-4, JP-5

FUEL DENSITY: 6.5, 6.8 Lb/Gal.

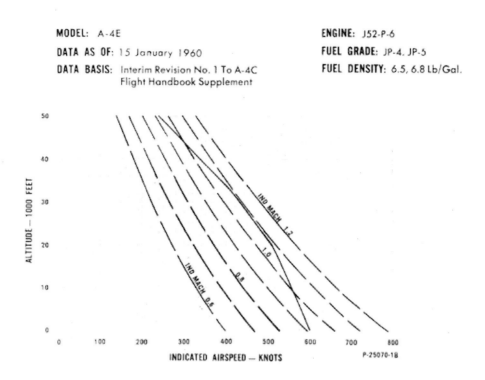

Figure 1-64. Airspeed Limitations

OPERATING FLIGHT STRENGTH DIAGRAM

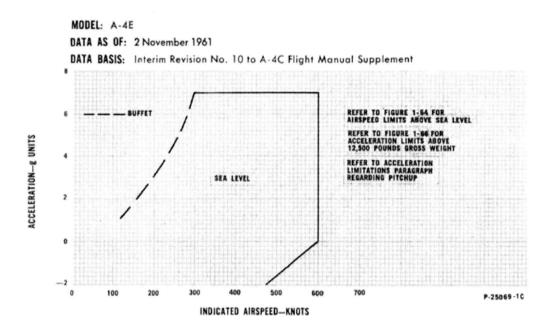

Figure 1-65. Operating Flight Strength Diagram

ACCELERATION LIMITS VS GROSS WEIGHT

MODEL: A-4E

DATA AS OF: 2 November 1961

DATA BASIS: Interim Revision No. 10 To A-4C
Flight Handbook Supplement

ENGINE: J52-P-6

FUEL GRADE: JP-4, JP-5

FUEL DENSITY: 6.5, 6.8 Lb/Gal.

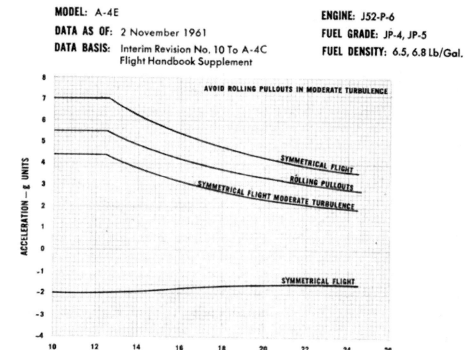

Figure 1-66. Acceleration Limits vs Gross Weight

CROSSWIND VS AIRSPEED ABOVE MINIMUM

MODEL: A-4E

DATA AS OF: 18 July 1966

DATA BASIS: Interim Change No. 21 to A-4E
Natops Flight Manual

ENGINE: J52-P-6

FUEL GRADE: JP-4, JP-5

FUEL DENSITY: 6.5, 6.8 Lb./Gal.

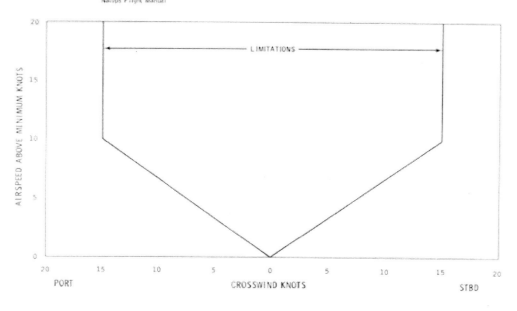

GG1-8

Figure 1-67. Crosswind vs Airspeed Above Minimum

AFCS SPEED ENVELOPE

MOD   IV-A

GROSS WEIGHT = 12,504 POUNDS

MODEL: A-4E
DATA AS OF: 1 July 1962
DATA BASIS: Calculations

ENGINE: J52-P-6
FUEL GRADE: JP-4, JP-5
FUEL DENSITY: 6.5, 6.8 Lb/Gal.

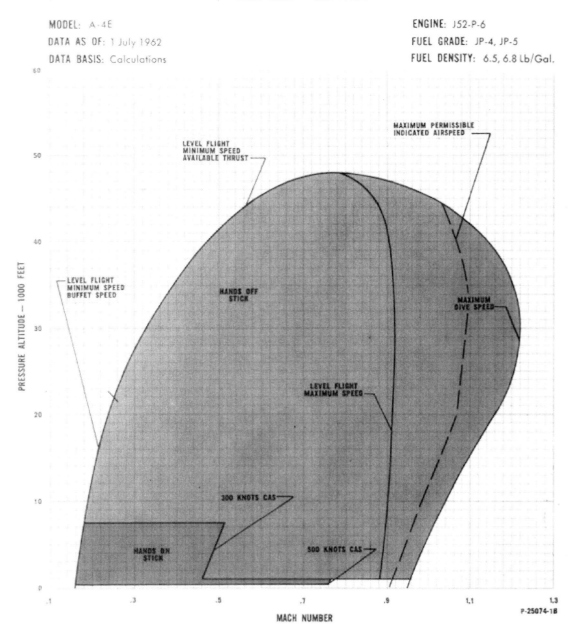

Figure 1-68.   AFCS Speed Envelope

AVC-1-16172-X

SECTION II
INDOCTRINATION

TABLE OF CONTENTS

INDOCTRINATION

INTRODUCTION

This section establishes minimum requirements for training, initial qualification, and currency in specified areas. Subsequent sections provide the operational information considered necessary to ensure safe and efficient operation of the A-4E, when used in conjunction with the Naval Warfare Publications series. Unit commanders are authorized to waive, in writing to the individual affected,

flight hour minimums and/or OFT/WST training requirements where recent experience in similar models warrants. However, adequate preparation and guidance of the pilot for the initial flight and subsequent flights so that he safely attains and maintains a reasonable degree of proficiency in the operation of the A-4E, is of prime importance. Too often, under pressure of operational commitments, this groundwork is abbreviated or deleted. This can result only in a deterioration of individual and unit effectiveness. For this reason, commanding officers must continuously ensure adherence to these basic criteria whenever possible. Procedures for requesting waivers from the provisions of this section are contained in OPNAV Instruction 3510.9 (current revision).

Training requirements, checkout procedures, evaluation procedures, and weather minima for ferry squadrons are governed by OPNAV-INST 3710, 6 series.

GROUND TRAINING

Ground training should be continuous throughout the career of the A-4E pilot. The overall syllabus will vary according to local conditions, facilities, directives from higher authority, and the unit commander's estimation of squadron readiness. However, there are certain specific requirements which must be met to ensure that the pilot is properly indoctrinated and briefed prior to flight.

GROUND TRAINING REQUIREMENTS

Ground training and other related requirements for all pilots prior to familiarization flights in the A-4E are as follows:

1. Current medical clearance.

2. Aviation physiological training as set forth in OPNAV Instruction 3740.3 (current revision).

3. NAMO Pilot Familiarization course (if available) or equivalent lectures by RCVW, operating A-4E squadron, or other qualified personnel.

4. Lectures from RCVW, operating A-4E squadron, or other qualified personnel on the following subjects:

Flight characteristics (including stalls and spins) and operating limitations.

Use of safety and survival equipment and related procedures.

Aircraft preflight, ground handling, hand signals, and normal flight procedures.

Cockpit troubleshooting procedures.

Emergency procedures.

Past aircraft accidents as an aid in preventing future accidents of like nature.

Local course rules, flying area, instrument procedures, and SAR facilities.

5. Blindfold cockpit check.

6. Minimum of 2 hours of flight- and emergency-procedures simulation in the OFT/WST within the two week period prior to the first fam. flight. If OFT/WST is not available, a comprehensive oral and/or written examination on emergency procedures must be substituted.

7. Practice dry-run ejection accomplished in the RAPEC ejection seat in complete flight gear, utilizing both primary and alternate ejection handles.

8. Satisfactory completion of examinations on A-4E operating limits, normal and emergency procedures, course rules and aircraft systems.

9. Supervised engine start and taxi checkout.

10. Aviator's required reading pertinent to flight.

GROUND TRAINING SUBJECTS

The following subjects should be included in the normal ground training syllabus, dependent upon the squadron mission, model aircraft, and qualifications of the pilot:

Technical Training

1. NATOPS Flight Manual.

2. Auxiliary equipment.

3. Flight safety equipment.

Mission Training

1. Bombing and rocket theory and pipper control.

2. Glide bombing, rocket, and missile procedures.

3. Strafing procedures.

4. LABS equipment.

5. LABS/laydown delivery.

6. Patterns and procedures for local targets.

7. Close air support and GCBS procedures.

8. Pertinent publications in the NWP and NWIP series.

9. Special weapons.

10. Aviation ordnance.

11. Weapons loading.

12. High and low altitude navigation.

13. Radar and navigational computer operating procedures.

14. Aerial refueling.

15. Night flying.

16. MLP and carrier procedures.

Instrument Training

1. Instrument flight (general).

2. REST computer.

3. Airways navigation.

4. Local climb-out and penetration.

5. GCA/CCA.

6. Special equipment.

Flight Safety

1. AAR reviews.

2. Aircraft emergencies: practiced whenever possible in the OFT/WST. Where such a trainer is available, its use is mandatory during familiarization, and quarterly thereafter. In addition, a refresher hop or an oral or written review of emergency procedures is required after any layoff from flying in excess of four weeks.

3. Use of barricade/emergency field arresting gear.

Intelligence

1. Mission planning material.

2. Orders of battle.

3. Aircraft and ship recognition.

4. Escape and evasion.

5. Authentication procedures.

Survival

1. Physiological and medical aspects.

2. First aid.

3. Survival on land/sea.

4. Pilot rescue techniques.

FLIGHT QUALIFICATIONS

Minimum requirements for qualification and currency are set forth below for each phase of flight.

Command prerogative should be exercised to increase minimums when desired. Unit commanders are authorized to waive, in writing to the individual, these minimum requirements and/or OFT/WST training where recent experience in similar models warrants.

FAMILIARIZATION

1. Completion of the ground training requirements set forth above is required prior to flight.

2. Familiarization flights will be conducted in accordance with Section IV, Part 2.

3. Initial check-out flights will consist of a minimum of 5 hours.

INSTRUMENTS

Minimum requirements prior to actual instrument flight are as follows:

1. Ten hours in A-4E aircraft in the last 6 months.

2. At least one A-4E flight in the last 30 days.

3. Current instrument card.

4. Demonstration of instrument proficiency in assigned model.

WEAPONS AND MISSION TRAINING

Prerequisites for weapons and mission training are:

1. Completion of appropriate training set forth in above.

2. Minimum of 10 hours in A-4.

3. For weapons delivery or mission training requiring a high-speed low-level run-in, a minimum of 15 hours in A-4 aircraft.

4. Basic qualifications and currency requirements for various missions and weapons deliveries are set forth in OPNAV Instruction 03740.8 (current revision).

Minimum requirements prior to night weapons training are as follows:

1. Same as night-flying minimums, except 50 hours in A-4 aircraft, and 10 hours in the last 30 days.

2. Day-proficient in type delivery in A-4E.

3. Familiar with target area and procedures.

NIGHT FLYING

Minimum requirements prior to night flights are as follows:

1. Current instrument card.

2. Ten hours in A-4 within the last 3 months.

FMLP AND CARRIER QUALIFICATION

For day and night FMLP qualification the exact number of FMLP periods required depends on the experience and ability of the individual pilot, and will be determined by the Unit Commander.

Minimum requirements prior to day FMLP are:

Changed 15 May 1966

1. 10 hours in A-4 aircraft and one flight in the last 30 days.

2. Familiarity with the slow-flight characteristics of the aircraft.

3. Proficiency in instrument flying in assigned model.

4. Proper briefing in day FMLP procedures.

Minimum requirements prior to night FMLP are:

1. Demonstration of proficiency in day FMLP.

2. Five hours night time in the A-4.

3. One A-4E flight in the last 10 days; otherwise one day flight will be required prior to the night FMLP period.

4. Proper briefing in night FMLP procedures.

Minimum requirements prior to day carrier qualification are as follows:

1. Certification by Unit Commander as day field-mirror-landing qualified in A-4E.

2. 50 hours in A-4 aircraft.

3. Proper briefing in carrier landing, catapult, and deck procedures.

Minimum day qualifications are:

1. Two touch-and-go landings.

2. Ten arrested landings.

3. Two day CCA approaches from marshal point.

Minimum requirements prior to night carrier qualifications are as follows:

1. Current day-carrier qualification in the A-4E.

2. 10 hours night time in the last six months.

3. Certification by Unit Commander as night field-mirror-landing qualified.

4. Proper briefing in night carrier landing, catapult, and deck procedures.

5. A minimum of two satisfactory arrested landings shall be completed during the daylight hours preceding night qualification landings.

Minimum night qualifications are:

1. Six night arrested landings.

2. Two night CCA approaches from marshal point (to be conducted only after satisfactory completion of day CCA qualification).

For maintaining carrier qualifications, qualification is considered current for six months after the date of the last carrier landing in type. Refresher requirements to requalify are as follows:

1. Six to twelve months: four day and two night arrested landings.

2. Over twelve months: initial requirements, both day and night.

CROSS-COUNTRY FLIGHT

Minimum requirements prior to cross-country flight are as follows:

1. Current instrument card.

2. Fifteen hours in A-4 to include 3.0 hours instrument time.

3. Jet flight log. (Kneeboard card will be submitted for command approval.)

4. Flight packet, which includes security, accounting, servicing data, and accident forms.

5. Familiarity with aircraft servicing.

PERSONAL FLYING EQUIPMENT REQUIREMENTS

The following flying equipment shall be carried or worn on every flight:

1. Fire-retardent, high-visibility flight suit. (Khaki suit may be worn in combat areas.)

2. Identification tags.

3. Flight gloves.

4. Flight safety boots/field shoes (ankle high lace type).

5. Latest available antibuffet helmet adorned with high-visibility paint or scotch light tape (in non-combat areas).

6. MK 3C life preserver with whistle, dye marker, compass, shark chaser, and two MK 13 MOD O Day-and-Night Distress Signals. Deviations authorized when flights do not extend beyond gliding distance of land.

7. Sheath knife in a special canvas pocket, sewn to the torso harness in such a manner that the chest strap passes through the sheath.

8. Approved personal survival kit (PSK-2 or SEEK-1).

9. Oxygen mask.

10. Anti g suit.

11. Integrated torso harness.

12. Latest available type exposure suit on all overwater flights when the water temperature is 59° or below, or OAT is 32° F. or below. During daylight, within gliding distance of land, exposure suit need not be required when the water temperature is above 50° F. Type commanders are authorized to waive the requirement for wearing all types of exposure suits if the possibility exists that high ambient cockpit temperature could cause extreme debilitation through excess loss of body fluids.

13. Pistol with tracer ammunition for all overwater flights, night flights, and flights over sparsely populated areas. An approved signalling device is authorized as a substitute for the pistol when operational and/or security conditions warrant.

14. One-cell flashlight attached to torso harness.

15. Two-cell flashlight with red lens for all night and cross-country flights.

16. Other survival equipment appropriate to the climate or required by any unusual conditions that may be peculiar to the area.

All survival equipment will be secured in such a manner that it is easily accessible and will not be lost during ejection or upon landing.

SECTION III
NORMAL PROCEDURES

TABLE OF CONTENTS

PART 1

BRIEFING/DEBRIEFING

TABLE OF CONTENTS

BRIEFING

Briefings will be conducted using a prepared briefing guide and the appropriate mission card. The briefing shall cover those items pertinent to the specific mission assigned. Any format which is complete, concise, and orderly, and which can be readily used by the Flight Leader as a briefing guide is suitable. Each pilot will maintain a knee pad and record all data necessary to successively assume the lead and complete the assigned mission. This, however, does not relieve the Flight Leader of the responsibility for all pilots in the operation and conduct of the flight.

The briefing guide will include the following items, when applicable:

General

1. Aircraft assigned, call signs, event number, and deck spot.

2. Succession to lead.

3. Fuel load, stores, and aircraft gross weight.

4. Engine start, taxi, and takeoff times.

5. Rendezvous instructions, takeoff distance and speed, line speed.

Mission

1. Primary.

2. Secondary

3. Operating area/target

4. Control agency

5. Time on station or over target.

Navigation and Flight Planning

1. Duty runway/predicted Foxtrot Corpen for launch and recovery, and position in the force

2. Climbout

3. Operating area procedures and restricted areas

4. Mission plan, including fuel/oxygen management and PIM

5. Bingo/low state fuel

6. Marshal/holding (normal and emergency)

7. Penetration procedures and minimums

8. Ship/field approach and runway lighting

9. GCA/CCA procedures and minimums, missed approach

10. Recovery: course rules, pattern, breakup, landing, waveoff

11. Divert and emergency field/ready deck.

Communications

1. Frequencies

2. Controlling agencies

3. Radio procedure and discipline

4. ADIZ procedures

5. IFF/SIF

6. Navigational aids

7. Hand/light signals.

Weapons

1. Loading

2. Arming

3. Special routes because of ordnance aboard

4. Pattern

5. Armament switches

6. Aiming point/sector setting

7. Run-in/entry airspeed

8. Minimum release/pull-out altitudes

9. G versus gross weight

10. Duds, hung ordnance procedures, dearming, jettison area

11. Safety.

Weather

1. Local area, enroute, and destination (existing and forecast)

2. Weather at alternate/divert fields

3. Winds, jet stream, temperature, and contrail band width.

Emergencies

1. Takeoff aborts

2. Radio failure

3. Loss of NAVAIDS

4. Loss of visual contact with flight

5. Lost-plane procedures

6. Downed pilot and SAR.

7. Aircraft emergency procedures and system failures.

Safety Precautions

Air Intelligence and Special Instructions

1. Friendly/enemy force disposition.

2. Current situation.

3. Targets.

4. Safety precautions.

5. Reports and authentication.

6. Escape and evasion.

DEBRIEFING

Each flight shall be followed with a thorough debriefing by the Flight Leader as soon as practical. All phases of the flight shall be covered, paying particular attention to those areas where difficulty was encountered and to the effectiveness of any tactics employed or weapons expended. To derive maximum benefit, constructive criticism and suggested improvements as to doctrine, tactics, and techniques should be given and received with the frankness, purpose, and spirit of improving the proficiency of the unit, as well as that of the individual pilot. When appropriate, it should include the individual debrief of each pilot by the LSO.

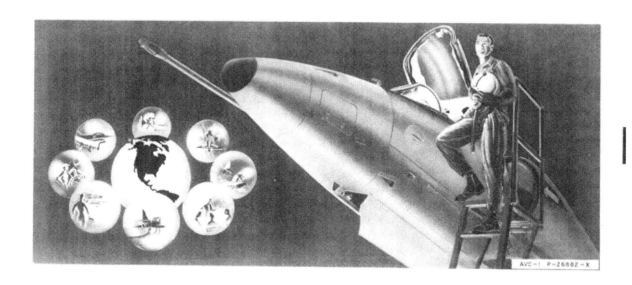

PART 2
MISSION PLANNING

TABLE OF CONTENTS

TEXT

MISSION PLANNING

The training objective is the orderly development of pilot techniques in preflight planning, climbout, high-altitude navigation and cruise control, air refueling, low-level navigation, and high-speed approaches to the delivery maneuver. The detailed specifics of these deliveries are set forth in the CWDS and NWDS to NWIP 41-3. Mission turn radius chart is located in Section XI, Part 9. A mission planning sample, section XI, Part 10 is provided to assist the pilot in becoming familiar with the use of the performance section and to enable him to perform the assigned mission at the optimum conditions within the aircraft flight envelope.

Changed 1 November 1965

(Pages 3-9 and 3-10 deleted) 3-7/3-8

PART 3
SHORE-BASED PROCEDURES

TABLE OF CONTENTS

ILLUSTRATIONS

TABLES

PRIOR TO FLIGHT

PREFLIGHT INSPECTION

EXTERIOR INSPECTION

Consult the Naval Aircraft Flight Record (yellow sheet) to determine the status of the airplane, that it has been fully serviced with fuel, oil, liquid oxygen, compressed air, and hydraulic fluid. Inspect the exterior of the airplane, proceeding as shown on figure 3-1.

Forward Fuselage (A)

1.   Air refueling probe cover . . . .   REMOVED

2.   Air conditioning intake and exhaust ducts . . . .   CLEAR

3.   Static pressure vent (left side) . . . .   CLEAR

4.   Angle-of-attack vane cover . . . .   REMOVED

5.   Nose compartment panels . . . .   CONDITION, SECURITY

6.   Nose compartment cooling air inlet . . . .   CLEAR

7.   Static pressure vent (right side) . . . .   CLEAR

8.   Controls access panel (right side) . . . .   SECURE

9.   Nosewheel well door . . . CONDITION, SECURITY

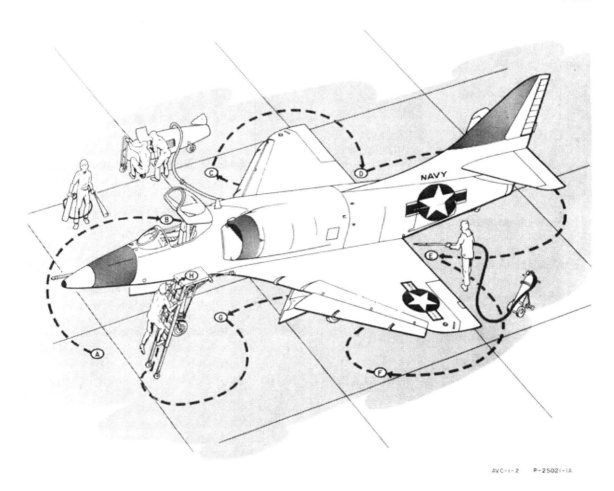

Figure 3-1. Exterior Inspection

AVC-1-2   P-25021-1A

10. Nosewheel strut	EXTENSION, NO LEAKAGE	16. Forward engine compartment	CONDITION AND SECURITY
11. Nosewheel tire	CONDITION		
12. Nosewheel downlock pin	INSERTED	17. Guncharger pneumatic pressure gage	CHECK
13. Emergency generator .	RETRACTED, SECURE	18. Aileron power package	OVER-CENTER
14. External canopy jettison handle	STOWED: ACCESS DOOR CLOSED	**Right-Hand Wheelwell (B)**	
15. Gun flash suppressors and guns	SECURE	1. Main wheelwell doors . .	CONDITION, SECURITY

2. Taxi light . . . . SECURITY

3. Gun pneumatic
pressure gage . . . . CHECK

4. Armament safety
disable switch . . . . SAFE

5. Catapult hook . . . . . . PRELOAD,
SECURITY

6. Maingear downlock
pin . . . . INSERTED

7. Mainwheel strut . . . . . EXTENSION,
NO LEAKAGE

8. Mainwheel tire . . . . . CONDITION

9. Brakes . . . . CONDITION,
NO LEAKAGE

10. Fuel system vent . . . . CLEAR

Right-Hand Wing (C)

1. General condition . . . . WRINKLES,
CRACKS,
LOOSE
RIVETS;
FUEL
DEPOSITS

2. Wing rack stores . . . . SECURE

3. Drop tank . . . . REMOVE
FILLERCAP,
VISUALLY
DETERMINE
LOADING,
REPLACE
FILLERCAP

4. Wing slat . . . . FREE
MOVEMENT

WARNING

Operate each slat by hand to make
certain that each extends and retracts with negligible effort and
without binding. Binding which
causes asymmetric slat extension
requires excessive lateral control deflection to maintain wings
level after catapulting or during
accelerated stalls and landing
approaches.

5. Position and fuse-
lage wing lights . . . . CONDITION

6. Aileron and wing flap . CONDITION,
BONDING

7. Wing tank filler cap . . SECURE

Aft Fuselage and Tail Section (D)

1. All access doors . . . . . CLOSED

2. Speedbrake . . . . CONDITION,
SECURITY

3. Tailpipe cover . . . . REMOVED

4. Tailpipe . . . . CRACKS,
WRINKLES,
BURNS,
FUEL
DEPOSITS

5. Tail light . . . . CONDITION

6. Rudder, elevator, and
horizontal stabilizer . . . . CONDITION,
BONDING

7. Speedbrake . . . . CONDITION,
SECURITY

8. Arresting hook . . . . . . RETRACTED
AND
LOCKED;
CONDITION

9. Tension bar retainer . . CONDITION

10. Arresting hook hold-
down cylinder pressure
gage . . . . 900 ± 50 PSI

11. Aft engine compart-
ment . . . . CONDITION,
SECURITY

12. Drop tank fueling
switch . . . . OFF

Changed 15 May 1966

Left-Hand Wing (E)

1. Wing flap and aileron . . . . . . CONDITION, BONDING

2. Aileron tab . . . . CONDITION

3. Position and fuselage-wing lights . . . . CONDITION

4. Wing . . . . WRINKLES, CRACKS, LOOSE RIVETS, FUEL DEPOSITS

5. Wing slat . . . . FREE MOVEMENT

6. Wing rack stores . . . . SECURE

7. Drop tank . . . . REMOVE FILLER CAP; VISUALLY DETERMINE LOADING; REPLACE FILLER CAP

8. Approach lights and cover . . . . CONDITION

Left-Hand Wheelwell (F)

1. Maingear doors . . . . CONDITION, SECURITY

2. Catapult hook . . . . PRELOAD, SECURITY

3. Maingear downlock pin . . . . . . INSERTED

4. Mainwheel strut . . . . EXTENSION, NO LEAKAGE

5. Mainwheel tire . . . . CONDITION

6. Brakes . . . . CONDITION, NO LEAKAGE

Center Fuselage Underside (G)

1. Fuselage rack store . . . . SECURE

2. Centerline fuel tank . . . . REMOVE FILLER CAP; DETERMINE LOADING; REPLACE FILLER CAP

3. Forward engine and accessories section access doors . . . . . . CLOSED

4. Link and case ejection chutes . . . . CLEAR

Cockpit Area (H)

1. External canopy jettison handle . . . . STOWED; ACCESS DOOR CLOSED

2. Controls access panel . . . . . . SECURE

3. Angle-of-attack vane . . . . CONDITION, FREE MOVEMENT

4. Engine intake plugs . . . . REMOVED

5. Intake ducts . . . . FREE OF FOREIGN OBJECTS

6. Canopy cover . . . . REMOVED

7. Fuselage tank fillercap . . . . . . SECURE

8. Pitot tube cover . . . . REMOVED

9. Total temperature sensor cover . . . . REMOVED

10. Canopy surface and seal . . . . CONDITION

11. Rocket seat controls safety handle . . . . DOWN

12. Canopy air bungee cylinder air pressure gage . . . . 2500 PSI OR AS PER INSTRUCTION PLATE ON THE BUNGEE

13. Cable to jettison control pulley in canted bulkhead . . . . ENGAGED

14. Canopy-seat interlock cable . . . . CONNECTED

15. Catapult firing cable from pulley mechanism to disconnect housing . . . . ENGAGED

16. Canopy bungee trigger (if applicable) . . . . ALIGNED

17. Ejection seat catapult safety pin and two canopy jettison initiator pins . . . . . . REMOVED

18. Harness release actuator pin not visible.

19. Emergency oxygen bottle . . . . 1800 PSI

INTERIOR INSPECTION

Check the general appearance of the cockpit, and make sure that all gear is properly stowed and secure. Make proper harness, oxygen, radio, and antiblackout connections, and perform the following checks before starting the engine:

CAUTION

Upon entering the cockpit, make certain that the landing gear handle is DOWN and that the hose jettison switch (tanker only) is OFF (forward).

1. Exposure suit blower . . . OFF

2. Emergency speedbrake knob . . . . NORMAL

3. Antiblackout suit blower, and oxygen-radio hoses . . . . . . CONNECT TO CONSOLE

4. Oxygen switch . . . . ON, CHECK FLOW THEN OFF

5. AFCS standby switch . . . . OFF

6. AFCS aileron trim switch . . . . NORM

7. Radar selector switch . . . OFF

8. Emergency transfer switch . . . . OFF

9. Drop tanks switch . . . . . OFF

10. Engine starter switch . . . PULLED UP

11. Fuel control switch . . . . PRIMARY

12. Manual fuel shutoff control lever . . . . NORMAL (GUARD DOWN)

13. JATO arming switch . . . . SAFE

14. JATO jettison switch . . . SAFE

15. Throttle . . . . OFF

16. Speedbrake switch . . . . . CLOSE

17. Master exterior lights switch . . . . OFF

18. Flap switch . . . . UP

19. Throttle friction wheel . . AS DE-SIRED

20. Accelerometer . . . . PUSH TO RESET

21. Airspeed indicator . . . . . 0, SET

22. Vertical speed 0

23. Gunsight . . . . SET, LOCK

24. Radar altimeter . . . . OFF

25. Emerg stores jettison select switch . . . . AS DE-SIRED

26. All armament switches . . OFF

27. Emergency handles . . . . STOWED

Changed 15 March 1965

28. Arresting hook handle... UP

29. Navigation computer.... SET UP

30. UHF function switch .... OFF

31. TACAN .... OFF

32. IFF master switch ..... OFF

33. SIF controls .... SELECT
CODE

34. Compass controller .... SLAVED,
LATITUDE
SET

35. Interior lights control
panel...................... ALL
SWITCHES
OFF

36. Emerg gen bypass
switch...................... NORMAL

37. TACAN antenna switch.. AS DE-
SIRED

38. Spare lamps container .. ADEQUATE
SUPPLY

39. Rain removal switch.... OFF

40. Engine anti-icing
switch...................... OFF

41. Temperature knob...... AS DE-
SIRED

42. Cabin pressurization
switch...................... NORMAL

43. Windshield defrost
switch...................... HOLD

44. Exterior lights control
panel...................... ALL
SWITCHES
OFF

45. Preflight check the thermal radiation closure.

CAUTION

Make certain the ejection seat safety handle is stowed and locked in the full up position before flight.

BEFORE STARTING THE ENGINE

Ascertain that the areas forward and aft of the aircraft are clear of personnel and loose objects. (See figure 1-56 for danger areas.) Make certain that fire fighting equipment is available and manned.

STARTING THE ENGINE

An electrical power supply of 115/200-volt ac is required for ignition and a source of high pressure air for starting the engine. The engine should be started on the ground in the following manner:

1. Throttle .... OFF

2. Engine starter switch ..... DEPRESS

3. 5% rpm, throttle .... IGN

4. 15 % rpm, throttle .... IDLE

WARNING

• Pilot controlled starts should be made whenever possible, to avoid starter motor overspeed. The time delay inherent in initiating or shutting off the starter air supply, when using hand signals, for ground controlled starts, makes this method undesirable. Starter motor overspeed can be severe enough to cause starter damage or failure with a resultant hazard to personnel and equipment. To provide automatic air supply shutoff at the correct starter cutout speed, the aircraft starter circuit receptacle must be connected electrically to the gas turbine power unit prior to starting attempts. The ground air supply shuts off automatically at approximately 50 percent engine rpm unless a malfunction occurs, in which case the air supply must be shut off manually by pulling up on the engine starter switch (start-abort) when making pilot controlled starts.

• In those cases when pilot controlled starts are not possible, air supply should be initiated or cut off by the ground crew upon signal from the pilot.

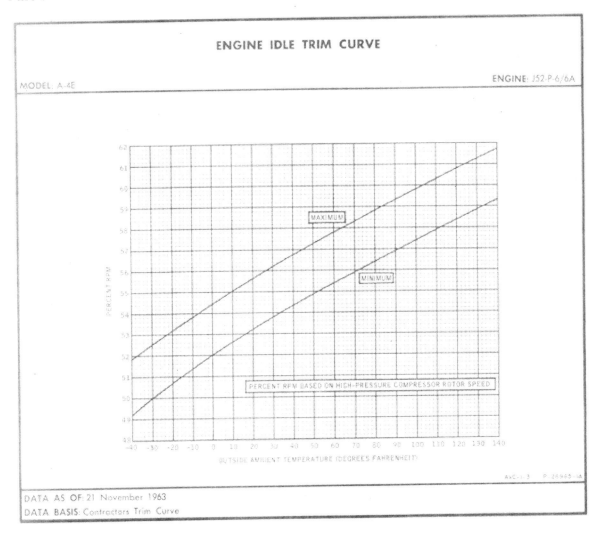

Figure 3-2. Engine Idle RPM Curve

Normally, the engine should be stabilized at IDLE rpm within 30 seconds after depressing the engine starter button. When starting the engine, lightoff should occur within 20 seconds after movement of the throttle outboard to start the ignition cycle. Lightoff will be indicated by a rise in EGT after the throttle is moved to the IDLE position. If lightoff does not occur within the specified time, retard the throttle to OFF, pull up the engine starter switch, and investigate. If lightoff is satisfactory and engine speed is stabilized with the throttle at IDLE, check the following:

1. RPM . . . . .IDLE
                    (50%-60.2%)

Note

See figure 3-2 for idle RPM vs temperature relationship.

2. EGT . . . . .200-340° C

Note

At IDLE rpm, the temperature pointer will normally stabilize at a position below the maximum indicated. 340° C is not a limit, but a guide to indicate the EGT which, if exceeded, may signify an engine malfunction.

Changed 15 March 1965

3. Fuel boost . . . .   LIGHT OUT

4. Oil pressure . . . .   35-50 PSI

Note

If the oil pressure reads low (below 35 psi) at IDLE rpm, increase rpm slightly to 60 percent. If normal pressure is not indicated at this higher rpm, shut down the engine and determine the reason for the lack of, or low, oil pressure indication.

CHUGS AND STALLS

If chugging is encountered during an acceleration, there will be a momentary rpm hesitation without an exhaust temperature rise. Engine stall may or may not be accompanied by chugging. If a stall does occur, the rpm will hang up or decrease and the exhaust gas temperature will rise. Should either a chug or a stall occur, shut down the engine and investigate.

ENGINE GROUND OPERATION

No warmup period is necessary. Always use the minimum RPM deemed necessary to minimize the possibility of foreign object damage.

WARNING

Use extreme caution if necessary to pass objects to or from ground crewmen with engine operating. This practice has proved dangerous in causing ingestion of foreign objects into the engine and subsequent damage to blading.

EQUIPMENT GROUND LIMITATIONS

Warmup time and ground limitations for the listed electronic equipment are as follows:

Item		Warmup
ARC-27A	(Note 1)	1 minute
ARA-25	(Note 1)	1 minute
ARN-52		90 seconds
APX-6B	(Note 1)	1 minute
APA-89		1 minute
ASQ-17B	(Note 1)	1 minute
ASN-19A/41	(Note 2)	None
AJB-3/3A	(Note 3)	70 ± 10 seconds
AFCS	(Note 2)	30 seconds
APG-53A		3 minutes
AN/APN-153		- -

Note 1: 30 minutes ground limitation, without air conditioning.

Note 2: AJB-3/3A must first be at speed.

Note 3: 60 seconds time delay (gyro runup), plus 10 seconds autosync period.

POSTSTART PROCEDURES

When electrical power becomes available after starting the engine, check the following items:

1. UHF function switch   TR & G

Note

Allow 60 second warmup period before depressing microphone switch to transmit.

2. IFF master switch .... STBY

NOTE

The IFF master switch must be moved
from the OFF position for operation of the
UHF remote channel indicator.

3. TACAN switch .... REC or
T/R

4. AFCS .... STANDBY

5. Fuel Control light .... OUT

6. Depress warning lights test switch to check
FIRE, FUEL TRANS, FUEL BOOST, UTILITY HYD,
CONTROL HYD, SPD BRK OPEN warning lights,
angle-of-attack index light, oxygen low-level warning light, and fuel quantity indicating circuits.

7. LABS light .... PUSH TO
TEST

8. Marker beacon indicating
light (NAVPAC installed) .... PUSH TO
TEST

9. LOX quantity .... NOTE

10. Fuel quantity .... CHECK
INT/EXT
READINGS

11. Attitude gyro indicator ..... OFF FLAG
DISAPPEARS
(WITHIN 70 ±
10 SECONDS)

12. Compass controller
panel .... SET

13. Standby gyro .... ERECT,
OFF FLAG
NOT
VISIBLE

14. Rain removal system ...... CHECK
FOR FLOW,
THEN
OFF

15. AFCS .... OFF AFTER
CHECKS
COMPLETED

Additional checks and hand signals for use between
pilot and plane captain for starting and poststart
checks are contained in table 3-1. These signals
have been designed to work equally well, whether
shore-based or carrier-based, and in daylight or
darkness. Standard signals from Chapter VI of
NWP 41 (A) will apply in other cases. During night
operations, extreme care must be taken to be positive with all signals. In this regard, when using
the flashlight to illuminate a hand which is giving a
signal, always direct the flashlight away from the
person being signalled.

PRIOR TO TAXIING

1. Altimeter .... SET, NOTE
ERROR

2. Clocks .... SET,
RUNNING

3. Pressure ratio .... SET FOR
AMBIENT
TEMPERA-
TURE (SEE
FIGURE
3-3.)

TABLE 3-1. STARTING AND POSTSTART SIGNALS

SIGNAL		MEANING	RESPONSE	
DAY	NIGHT	DAY AND NIGHT	DAY	NIGHT
1. Pilot holds one finger vertically	Same.	Start GTC.	P/C executes.	Same.
2. Plane captain holds two fingers vertically, then points to: Pilot (for pilot-controlled start) or Self (for ground-controlled start). NOTE 2	Same.	GTC is up to speed and READY light is lit. GTC hose connected. Electrical power for ignition available. 1. This will be a pilot-controlled start. 2. This will be a ground-controlled start.	None.	Same.
3. Pilot holds two fingers vertically.	Same.	1. If pilot-controlled start, START-ABORT switch is depressed. 2. If ground-controlled start, P/C open GTC air valve.	P/C returns rotating two-finger signal when GTC hose inflates.	P/C rotates flashlight vertically when GTC hose inflates.
4. Pilot holds three fingers vertically.	Same.	1. Pilot-controlled start: START-ABORT switch has popped up. P/C remove starting air hose and electrical service cable. 2. Ground-controlled start: Engine RPM is at 50 percent, P/C close GTC air valve and remove starting air hose and electrical cable.	1. P/C checks for GTC hose collapse, removes starting air hose, electrical cable, and secures access panel. 2. P/C closes GTC air valve, checks for hose collapse, removes starting air hose, electrical cable and secures access panels.	Same.
5. If necessary, P/C attract pilot's attention by waving arms over head. Give "cut" signal by slashing motion of index finger across throat.	If necessary, P/C attract pilot's attention with flashlight. Give "cut" signal by repeated slashing of flashlight across throat.	Secure start/cut engine.	Pilot move throttle to OFF.	Same.
6. P/C gives "OK" signal by forming circle with thumb and forefinger, with remaining fingers extended.	Same.	Hydraulic pressure is 3000 p.s.i. on wheelwell gauge/gauges.	Pilot acknowledges with "thumbs-up"	Pilot move horizontally-held flashlight up and down several times.

TABLE 3-1. STARTING AND POSTSTART SIGNALS (Continued)

SIGNAL		MEANING	RESPONSE	
DAY	NIGHT	DAY AND NIGHT	DAY	NIGHT
7. P/C holds vertical fist in front, makes large horizontal circle with fist. NOTE 2	Same, except with vertically held flashlight pointed upward. NOTE 2	Pilot move all controls through full travel, checking for proper throw and feel, no hydraulic ladder lights ON when flight controls are moved rapidly. Then position flight controls as follows: full left rudder, stick full aft and port.	Pilot execute. P/C check control surfaces for correct deflection.	Same.
8. P/C holds hand in front, palm down, and makes: Open, or Closing motion with thumb and fingers in alligator-mouth fashion. NOTES 2 & 3	Same. NOTES 2 & 3	 1. Lower flaps. 2. Raise flaps.	Pilot execute. P/C check both flaps for: 1. Full deflection and security. 2. Full retraction and security. If satisfactory, give pilot "thumbs-up" after check is complete.	Same.
9. P/C gives previous signal, followed immediately by "plus" sign formed by index fingers. NOTES 2 & 3	Same. NOTES 2 & 3	Pilot raise or lower flaps to 1/2 deflection as signalled.	Pilot execute. P/C check both flaps for 1/2 deflection and security. If satisfactory, give pilot "thumbs-up" after check is complete.	Same.
10. P/C holds hand in front, palm vertical, and makes: Open or Closing motion with thumb and fingers in alligator-mouth fashion. NOTES 2 & 3	Same. NOTES 2 & 3	 1. Extend speed brakes. 2. Retract speed brakes.	Pilot execute. P/C check both speed brakes for: 1. Full extension, leaks, security. 2. Full retraction. If satisfactory, give pilot "thumbs-up" after check is completed.	Same.
11. P/C holds hand in front and Suddenly lowers other fist, with thumb extended downward to meet horizontal palm of extended hand.	Same, except points flashlight vice thumb toward extended palm of hand in direction desired.	 1. Lower arresting hook.	Pilot execute. P/C check: 1. Hook down and for effective snubber action	Same.

TABLE 3-1. STARTING AND POSTSTART SIGNALS (Continued)

SIGNAL		MEANING	RESPONSE	
DAY	NIGHT	DAY AND NIGHT	DAY	NIGHT
Suddenly raises other fist, with thumb extended upward to meet horizontal palm of extended hand. NOTES 2 & 3	NOTES 2 & 3	2. Raise arresting hook.	2. Hook retracted and centered. If satisfactory, give pilot "thumbs-up" after check is completed.	
12. Pilot makes vertical fist with thumb extended up, and then moves thumb down.	Same.	I am ready to perform trim checks.	P/C give appropriate trim signals.	Same.
13. P/C holds one finger aloft. NOTE 4	One dash on flashlight. NOTE 4	Cycle and set rudder trim to 0 degree, using trim indicator.	Pilot execute. P/C points index finger toward vertical palm of other hand in direction rudder must be moved if not faired by pilot. When faired, P/C give next sequential signal. Pilot check indicator for possible error and note.	Pilot: same. P/C same, except use flashlight vice finger to indicate direction rudder must be moved.
14. P/C holds two fingers aloft. NOTE 4	Two dashes on flashlight. NOTES 4 & 5	Cycle, override in both directions, and set the elevator trim to 6 degrees noseup, using trim indicator. (If a setting other than 6 degrees noseup trim is desired, the pilot shall inform P/C of desired setting prior to start.)	Pilot execute. If necessary, P/C point index finger toward horizontal palm of other hand in direction elevator leading edge must be moved for desired setting. Pilot check indicator for possible error and note.	Pilot: same. P/C: same, except use flashlight vice finger to indicate direction elevator must be moved.
15. P/C holds three fingers aloft. NOTE 4	Three dashes on flashlight. NOTES 4 & 6	Cycle and set aileron trim so that stick is centered laterally. Check aileron follow-up tab for correct response and faired ± 1/8 inch with aileron trailing edge.	Pilot execute. P/C check follow-up tab ± 1/8 inch from faired with aileron on trailing edge.	Same.
16. P/C holds four fingers aloft.	Same. Illuminated by flashlight.	Pressurize external drop tanks and/or buddy store. P/C check pressurization.	Pilot execute.	Same.
P/C holds five fingers aloft.	Same. Illuminated by flashlight.	Depressurize external drop tanks and/or buddy store.	Pilot execute.	Same.
17. Pilot points one finger at eye.	Same.	P/C check all exterior lights BRIGHT, then DIM. (Modify locally, as necessary, according to situation.)	P/C execute. Give pilot "thumbs-up" after checking lights BRT, then check on DIM.	Same.
18. P/C holds nose, then gives "thumbs-up or down".	Same.	Aircraft has no visible fuel, oil, or hydraulic leaks. Fuel has ceased draining from gang drain. (During start, indicates wet start.)	Pilot acknowledge with "thumbs-up".	Same.

TABLE 3-1. STARTING AND POSTSTART SIGNALS (Continued)

SIGNAL		MEANING	RESPONSE	
DAY	NIGHT	DAY AND NIGHT	DAY	NIGHT
19. Pilot holds closed fist with thumb extended horizontal.	Same except flashlight vice thumb held horiz.	P/C cycle approach light hook by-pass switch in nose wheelwell.	P/C executes.	Same.
20. P/C forms circle with thumb and forefinger, then extracts forefinger of opposite hand from circle, using "pull-away" motion.	Same, except makes "pull-away" motion with flashlight.	Can I remove landing gear and external storeracks safety pins?	Pilot give "thumbs-up" (YES) or "thumbs-down" (NO). If yes, P/C removes pins and holds for pilot to count before stowing in pin bag in left-hand wheel well or aft hell-hole.	Same, except pilot moves horizontally-held flashlight up and down several times (YES) vice "thumbs-up" signal, or left and right several times (NO) vice "thumbs-down" signal.
21. P/C pats back of neck with hand.	Same. Use flashlight vice hand.	Check ejection control safety handle in desired position.	Pilot check handle.	Same.
22. P/C extends arms bent 90 degrees so hands are level in front of chest. Place right palm on top of left hand and with positive movement raise right hand and lower left hand.	Same, except make signal with wands.	Can I move EXT/INT switch to EXT position?	Pilot give "thumbs-up" (YES) or "thumbs-down" (NO).	Same, except pilot moves horizontally-held flashlight up and down several times (YES) vice "thumbs-up" signal, or left and right several times (NO) vice "thumbs-down." signal.
23. Plane director puts forefinger on end of nose then gives a "thumbs-up".	Same. Use flashlight vice fingers.	Tillerbar connected. Director will assume directional control.	Head nod. Pilot controls only speed of aircraft with brakes.	Same.
Plane director puts forefinger on end of nose then makes a downward sweeping motion with forearm toward direction of aircraft movement.	Same. Use flashlight vice fingers.	Tillerbar disconnected. Pilot will assume directional control.	Head nod. Pilot assumes directional control.	Same.

NOTES:

1. Where night signal is listed as "Same", unless otherwise indicated, signal is identical to day signal, except red flashlight is used to illuminate hand (if appropriate).

2. Prior to giving this signal, the affected area must be checked visually by the P/C to ensure that there exists no hazard to personnel.

3. Normally, these three signals will be given in close sequence without hesitation, i.e., flaps, speedbrakes, hook.

4. P/C shall be stationed at port wing tip, within sight of pilot, for the trim signals.

WARNING

5. Positioning AFCS test switch to position 2 could cause a nosedown trim setting. Pilots should recheck the horizontal stabilizer trim after completion of AFCS preflight checks.

6. After giving 3-dash signal, P/C illuminates follow-up tab from inboard end.

7. For use prior to night flight or at pilot's discretion.

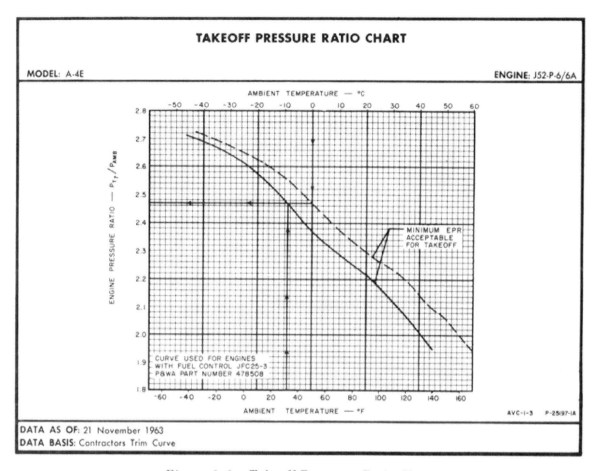

Figure 3-3. Takeoff Pressure Ratio Chart

TAXI

When ready to taxi, signal the plane captain to remove chocks. Advance throttle to about 70 percent before releasing the brakes. Release brakes and, when the desired taxi speed is reached, retard throttle to IDLE. Use caution in confined or restricted areas.

To avoid foreign object damage to engines, pilot shall maintain a minimum taxi interval of 200 feet, or taxi in close formation with wing-tip clearance and intakes clear of leader's exhaust. While taxiing, determine that nose strut is not overinflated by observing that nose strut will compress when brakes are applied firmly. Check standby compass swinging free and adequate fluid level; turn indicator deflecting normally. The oxygen

mask should be donned while taxiing when the canopy is closed and the pressurization is on.

CAUTION

Do not taxi with the canopy open at speeds which, coupled with headwinds, cause the relative wind to exceed 60 knots. If taxiing with the canopy closed, be sure it is completely latched. Taxiing with the canopy partially open and the canopy control handle in the locked position imposes shear forces on the canopy hinges which exceed their safe design limits, and may cause fractures of the hinge structure.

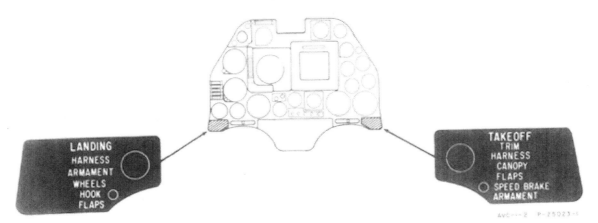

Figure 3-4. Takeoff Checklist

WARNING

Prolonged IDLE operation before takeoff should be avoided to prevent exceeding the permissible aft CG limit as fuselage fuel is used. Wing tank fuel will not transfer to the fuselage tank at IDLE rpm; therefore, when the fuel quantity gage drops to approximately 1100 pounds remaining, the engine should be operated above IDLE to replenish the fuselage fuel.

PRETAKEOFF CHECKS

Before takeoff, complete the following checks: Perform manual fuel control check:

Throttle . . . . 85% RPM

Fuel Control . . . . Select Manual

Fuel Control Light . . . ON, and engine indication that switchover has occurred.

Throttle . . . . 85% RPM

Fuel Control . . . . Select Primary

Fuel Control Light . . . OFF

Referring to the TAKEOFF checklist (figure 3-4) Check:

TRIM . . . . . AILERON . . STICK CENTERED, TAB faired ± 1/5 inch.

RUDDER 0°

ELEVATOR 6° UP

HARNESS . . . . SHOULDER HARNESS LOCKED

CANOPY . . . . HANDLE OVER-CENTER, CANOPY HOOKS ENGAGED IN ROLLERS

FLAPS . . . . SET AT 1/2

SPEEDBRAKES . . . . CLOSED

ARMAMENT . . . . . . ALL SWITCHES OFF, EMERGENCY SELECTOR SWITCH APPROPRIATE SETTING

Before takeoff, it is recommended that the cabin temperature control switch be positioned in the middle of the WARMER range and all of the defrost air diverted to the foot-warmers. Direct the "eyeball" diffusers away from the face.

WARNING

Ascertain that seat catapult safety handle is in stowed position for takeoff.

TAKEOFF

Upon completion of the pretakeoff check list and after receipt of clearance from the tower, the aircraft will line up on the runway. Each pilot should check adjacent aircraft for correct trim settings, flap position, canopy closed, speedbrakes closed, no fuel or hydraulic leaks, and ejection control ground safety handle up. Half-flaps should be used for takeoff during normal shore-based operations. Each pilot shall indicate his readiness for takeoff by giving a "thumbs-up" up the line.

(See figure 3-5 for typical takeoff diagram.)

The amount of nose gear strut extension has no significant affect on lift-off speed, control forces, or trim position required. Refer to Section XI for additional information on takeoff airspeed and ground roll distance.

As the engine accelerates through 90 percent during the acceleration check, release brakes to prevent skidding the tires. Ensure that acceleration is within acceptable limits and that engine accelerates smoothly. When engine stabilizes initially, check for minimum T.O. pressure ratio (EPR), EGT (610 degrees or less) and RPM. Use brakes to maintain directional control until rudder becomes effective (about 70 knots). On rough runways, nosewheel bounce may be experienced. Apply forward stick as necessary to maintain nosewheel on the deck. Check the predicted line speed at selected distance marker. This check point should be selected so as to allow normal braking technique to stop the aircraft on the runway remaining. Five knots prior to predicted takeoff speed, raise the nose to a takeoff attitude and allow aircraft to fly itself off the deck. After comfortably airborne, retract landing gear and apply brakes momentarily to stop main gear tire rotation before wheel enters wheel well. Raise the flaps at 170 KIAS or above.

For a single takeoff, the centerline of the runway should be used as a directional guide. During formation takeoff (maximum of two aircraft), the leader should take position on the downwind side of the runway. Lateral separation should be ensured to prevent dangerous situations should one aircraft blow a

tire or abort. Where section takeoffs are utilized, one section shall be airborne before the next section commences takeoff roll.

Where individual takeoffs are made with two or more planes, the second aircraft shall commence takeoff roll not less than 5 seconds behind the first aircraft. When the crosswind component exceeds 8 knots, individual takeoffs will be made. Takeoffs are not recommended when the crosswind component is in excess of 15 knots. The angle-of-attack indicator may be used to attain the proper takeoff attitude. The pilot will inform the tower immediately by radio if takeoff is aborted. Formation takeoffs are not permitted with dissimilar-type aircraft.

Note

Almost constant trimming of the horizontal stabilizer will be necessary after takeoff during the period of acceleration to best climbing speed.

Be prepared for the possibility of unusual noise or vibration during the first minute after takeoff, caused by an unbalanced nosewheel tire. An unbalanced nosewheel tire creates a strong vertical vibration of decreasing frequency which can be sensed to emanate from the nose section. DON'T assume that this is the case if unusual noises occur after takeoff. DO analyze engine instruments and feel of aircraft. Be prepared to take action unless noise/vibration ceases as indicated above.

MINIMUM RUN

To accomplish a minimum run takeoff, full noseup trim and half-flaps should be employed.

Changed 15 May 1966

Note

Use of full-flaps delays nosewheel liftoff.

After brake release, as the aircraft accelerates down the runway, a generous amount of aft stick should be used to effect nosewheel liftoff. During aircraft liftoff, (about 10 KIAS less than normal), a noseup rotation of the aircraft will occur, which will require an immediate reduction in aft stick pressure to control. As the aircraft accelerates to climbing speed after takeoff, almost constant retrimming of the stabilizer will be necessary. The noseup rotation of the aircraft at takeoff is reduced in abruptness and severity by an increase in gross weight or by use of less aircraft noseup trim. However, if less than full-noseup trim is employed, the effect will be to increase the minimum nosewheel liftoff speed about 4 knots and increase the takeoff run approximately 300 feet for each 2 degrees of reduced noseup trim.

INFLIGHT

Refer to Section IV.

LANDING

The flight shall normally approach the breakup point in echelon, parade formation, at 250 to 300 knots. A 3- to 5-second break will provide an adequate downwind interval. Immediately after the break, extend speedbrakes and retard throttle to 70 percent. Speedbrakes will normally remain extended throughout approach and landing. (Speedbrakes increase the stalling speed approximately 1 knot.)

As the aircraft decelerates to 225 knots or less, lower the landing gear and extend full flaps. As the airspeed decreases to 170

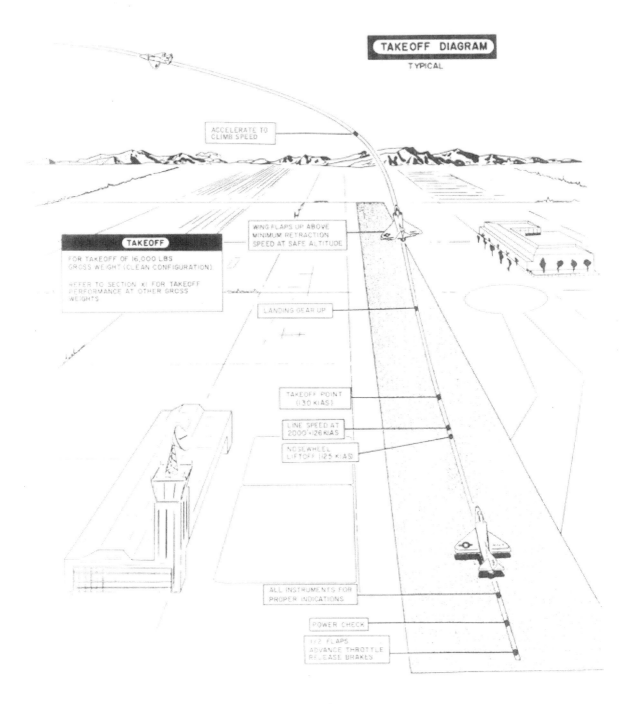

TAKEOFF DIAGRAM
TYPICAL

ACCELERATE TO
CLIMB SPEED

WING FLAPS UP ABOVE
MINIMUM RETRACTION
SPEED AT SAFE ALTITUDE

TAKEOFF

FOR TAKEOFF OF 16,000 LBS
GROSS WEIGHT (CLEAN CONFIGURATION)

REFER TO SECTION XI FOR TAKEOFF
PERFORMANCE AT OTHER GROSS
WEIGHTS

LANDING GEAR UP

TAKEOFF POINT
(130 KIAS)

LINE SPEED AT
2000'-126 KIAS

NOSEWHEEL
LIFTOFF 125 KIAS

ALL INSTRUMENTS FOR
PROPER INDICATIONS

POWER CHECK

1/2 FLAPS
ADVANCE THROTTLE
RELEASE BRAKES

P-25025-10

Figure 3-5. Takeoff Diagram

Changed 15 March 1965

knots, readjust power to maintain desired pattern airspeed commensurate with gross weight. Complete the landing check list (figure 3-6) and check wheel brakes prior to reaching the 180-degree position. Cross-check airspeed with AOA indexer indication. At a gross weight of 12,000 pounds, recommended approach speed is 120 knots IAS at the abeam position (figure 3-6). Optimum AOA indication is 17 1/2 units.

CAUTION

For each 1000-pound increase over 12,000 pounds, optimum approach speed (determined by the AOA indexer) increases approximately 5 knots.

If a discrepancy between indexer and airspeed exists, recheck landing configuration and gross weight and approach at recommended airspeed. Report error in AOA calibration.

Begin the turn into the base leg at a point slightly downwind of the landing end of the runway in order to have adequate straightway for corrections on final. Optimum angle-of-attack approaches to touchdown will be made. Where a mirror is available, its use is recommended. Attempt to control meatball, lineup, and angle-of-attack/airspeed as precisely as for a carrier approach in order to maintain proficiency in this technique.

Upon touchdown, the following technique is recommended:

1. Power to idle

2. Raise flaps.

If the crosswind component is 10-15 knots, the following procedure is recommended for the approach and landing.

1. Wing down into the wind and opposite rudder as required to maintain lineup.

2. After touchdown apply full-forward stick deflected into the wind as necessary to maintain a wings level attitude. Apply rudder as required to maintain directional control.

3. Use brakes as necessary.

CAUTION

Crosswind landings are not recommended with a component in excess of 15 knots. With power boost disconnected, stick forces increase and control sensitivity is reduced. If crosswind component exceeds 7 knots, an arrested landing is advisable.

Prior to turning off the runway, aircraft speed must be slowed to about walking speed. ON A GO-AROUND, WAVEOFF, OR TOUCH AND GO, DO NOT RAISE LANDING GEAR UNLESS LEAVING PATTERN.

CROSSWIND

Crosswind landings are not recommended with a 90-degree cross-wind component in excess of 15 knots. Use approved crosswind approach techniques. After touchdown, under crosswind components of 15 knots or less, the aircraft can be easily controlled directionally by applying aileron into the wind and using wheelbrakes as required. If the upwind wing is allowed to rise, the nose of the aircraft will tend to track toward the downwind side rather than "weathercocking" into the wind as is normally expected. If strong crosswinds exist, land on the upwind side of the runway. The following procedure is recommended immediately after touchdown.

1. Reduce power to IDLE.

2. Maintain stick deflection into the wind as required and allow nose of aircraft to fall through. When nosewheel is on deck, apply full-forward stick deflected into the wind as required to maintain a wings level attitude.

3. Raise the flaps to further reduce wing lift.

4. Extend speedbrakes to shorten landing roll if not already extended.

5. Use wheelbrakes as necessary, but do not skid the tires.

During a crosswind landing with the power boost disconnected, increased control stick pressures and reduced control sensitivity make the landing extremely hazardous. If the crosswind component exceeds 7 knots, it is recommended that the field arresting gear be used.

MINIMUM DISTANCE

To accomplish a minimum rollout distance landing, the following procedure is recommended:

1. Maintain optimum angle-of-attack during approach.

2. Upon touchdown, let the nose fall through and use full forward stick.

3. Leave the flaps fully extended unless there is excessive crosswind.

4. Apply moderately heavy braking immediately after the nosewheel is on the runway.

5. Maintain steady braking throughout the rollout to a stop or desired taxi speed, decreasing brake pedal pressure as the rollout speed decreases.

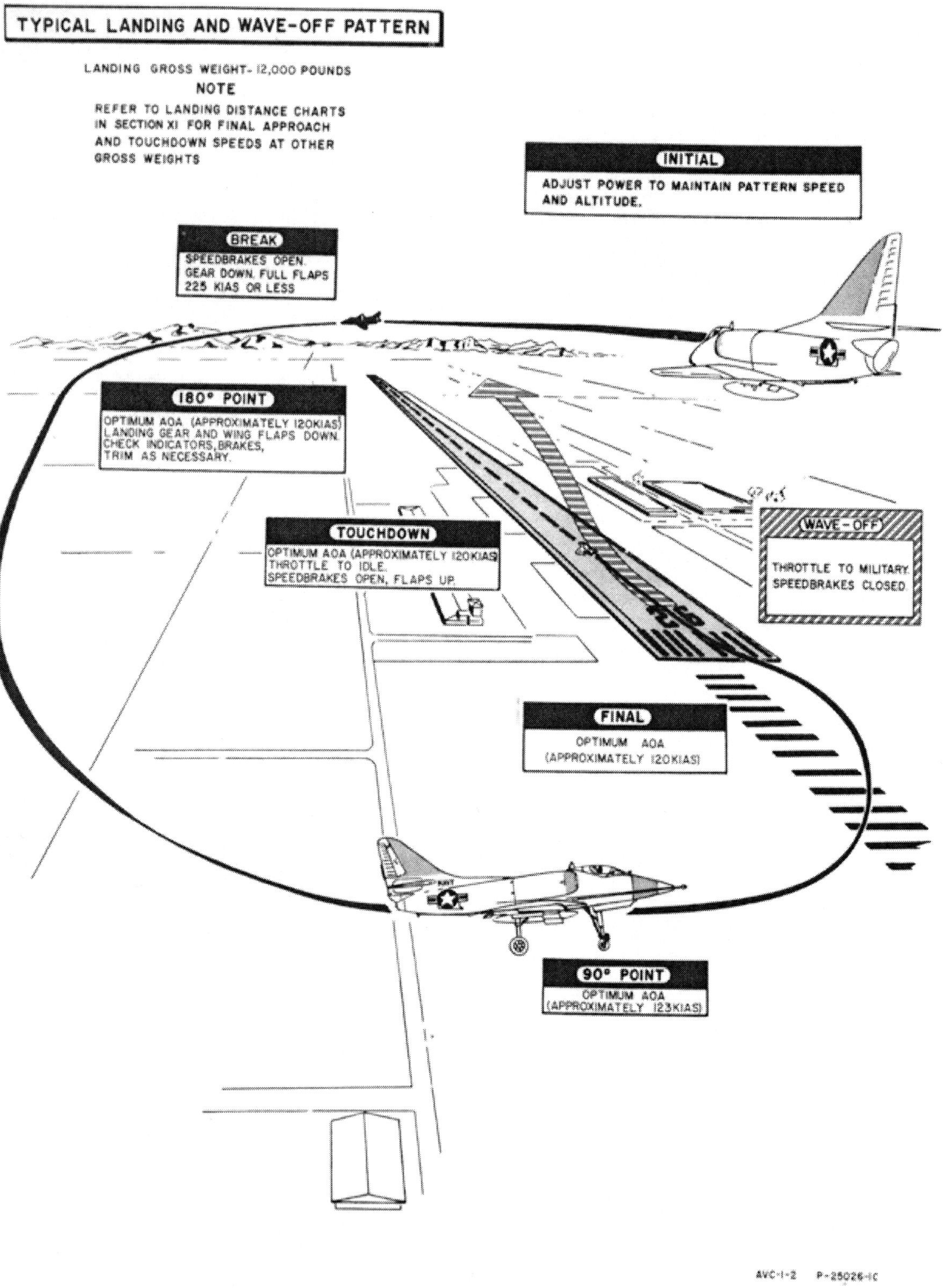

TYPICAL LANDING AND WAVE-OFF PATTERN

LANDING GROSS WEIGHT- 12,000 POUNDS

NOTE

REFER TO LANDING DISTANCE CHARTS
IN SECTION XI FOR FINAL APPROACH
AND TOUCHDOWN SPEEDS AT OTHER
GROSS WEIGHTS

INITIAL

ADJUST POWER TO MAINTAIN PATTERN SPEED
AND ALTITUDE.

BREAK

SPEEDBRAKES OPEN.
GEAR DOWN. FULL FLAPS
225 KIAS OR LESS

180° POINT

OPTIMUM AOA (APPROXIMATELY 120KIAS)
LANDING GEAR AND WING FLAPS DOWN.
CHECK INDICATORS, BRAKES,
TRIM AS NECESSARY.

TOUCHDOWN

OPTIMUM AOA (APPROXIMATELY 120KIAS)
THROTTLE TO IDLE.
SPEEDBRAKES OPEN, FLAPS UP

WAVE-OFF

THROTTLE TO MILITARY.
SPEEDBRAKES CLOSED.

FINAL

OPTIMUM AOA
(APPROXIMATELY 120KIAS)

90° POINT

OPTIMUM AOA
(APPROXIMATELY 123KIAS)

AVC-1-2   P-25026-IC

Figure 3-6.   Landing and Waveoff Patterns

Changed 15 March 1965

6. If circumstances dictate, the landing roll may be further reduced by shutting down the engine upon touchdown.

SECURING ENGINE

The following steps will be performed prior to shutdown:

1. Speedbrakes CLOSED

2. Flaps UP

3. Stabilizer trim set at 0 degree

4. Landing gear safety pins installed

5. EXT/INT power switch in EXT position

6. All electrical switches OFF.

Except for an emergency or operational necessity, if the engine has been operated at or above 85 percent rpm for periods exceeding 1 minute within 5 minutes prior to shutdown, the engine should be operated at IDLE for 30 seconds prior to shutdown to prevent overheating of the rear bearings.

After shutdown:

1. RAPEC ground safety handle down

2. Ejection seat and canopy safety pins installed.

NOTE

The compressor section should be checked for abrupt blade stoppage or abnormal noise during rundown.

FIELD MIRROR LANDING PRACTICE

PATTERN-ENTRY PROCEDURE

INDIVIDUAL ENTRY

Call the tower for entry to the FMLP pattern. Request 800-foot break altitude. Otherwise, follow the normal field entry procedures into the break. When cleared to break and the proper interval of the aircraft downwind is assured, roll into a 45-degree banked turn.

Reduce power to 70 percent and extend speedbrakes. Speedbrakes will normally remain out throughout the approach and landing. Use of speedbrakes may not be desirable at high gross weights (in excess of 13,000 pounds) when configured with high drag stores, i.e. buddy store, MBR's, etc., due to the high thrust required during the approach. At 225 knots, lower gear and full flaps. Adjust angle of bank to provide correct distance abeam (1 1/4 miles). Descend to 600 AGL on the downwind leg. Pilots shall cross-check airspeed against angle-of-attack indexer to ensure calibration of indexer prior to turning off the 180-degree position.

FORMATION ENTRY

The leader of the formation will enter the break as described above for single-plane entry. When cleared to break, the leader will give the breakup signal and execute a break by rolling into a 45-degree banked turn. The remaining aircraft in the formation will take a 10-second break interval.

PATTERN

DOWNWIND

Maintain 600 feet above the terrain at a comfortable airspeed, but no faster than 150 knots. Complete landing check list.

180-DEGREE POSITION

Altitude should be 600 feet above the terrain. Plan to lose sufficient airspeed on the downwing leg to arrive at the 180-degree position at the optimum angle-of-attack or approach speed. The approach airspeed will vary with aircraft gross weight. Distance abeam will vary with wind conditions, but 1-1/4 miles abeam is a normal position. The turn from the 180-degree position will be delayed so as to intercept the glide slope, wings level at 600 feet.

90-DEGREE POSITION

Altitude should be 600 feet above the terrain, with the aircraft at optimum angle-of-attack/airspeed.

FINAL

NIGHT FLYING

When the "meatball" appears in the center of the mirror, it will be necessary to reduce power slightly and ease the nose over, maintaining optimum angle-of-attack/airspeed. Proper glide slope and approach speed are maintained by keeping the "meatball" centered by coordinated adjustments of power for altitude corrections, and of attitude for airspeed corrections. The straightaway, with wings level, should be about 1-1/2 miles long.

Once the "meatball" is sighted, the approach should be monitored by crosschecking MEATBALL, LINEUP, ANGLE-OF-ATTACK INDEXER/AIRSPEED. Make necessary corrections immediately but smoothly.

LANDING

Keep the aircraft on the glide slope and centerline. Keep the "meatball" centered until touchdown. Do not flare. Upon touchdown, add full power and retract speedbrakes immediately. Climb straight ahead until reaching at least 300 feet and 150 knots. Turn downwind when the aircraft ahead is approximately in the 10 o'clock position on the downwind leg. Do not exceed 150 knots in the pattern. About 30-degree angle of bank turning downwind should establish the correct distance abeam. Extend speed brakes on the downwind leg prior to reaching the 180-degree position.

WAVEOFF

To execute a waveoff, immediately add full power, retract speedbrakes, and transition to a climbing attitude to prevent further loss of altitude. Make all waveoffs directly down the runway, until at least 300 feet of altitude and 150 knots are attained.

FLIGHT PROCEDURES

See section IV.

NIGHT LIGHTING DOCTRINE FOR SHORE-BASED OPERATIONS

LINE AREA

Prior to start, turn wing and tail lights to STDY/DIM, all others to OFF. This is the minimum lighting condition that should be used whenever the engine is running. Turn the master exterior lights switch ON, so that when the engine starts the exterior lights will come on. Perform customary poststart checks, including exterior-lights check. Signal the plane captain when ready to taxi by flashing the exterior lights. Taxi in the line area with fuselage and anti-collision lights OFF and remaining navigational lights DIM.

TAXIING

Once clear of the line area, turn lights to BRT/STDY.

AT APPROACH END OF RUNWAY

While completing the takeoff check list in the turn-up area, keep all lights BRT/STDY unless other aircraft are in the turn-up area, in which case it may be necessary to dim all lights in order to prevent pilots of other aircraft from losing their night adaptation. When ready for takeoff, turn all lights to BRT/STDY.

It may be necessary to modify the above procedure at certain fields to conform to local operating procedures. Generally, at fields where both MLP and normal takeoff and landings are permitted, the tower will require normal traffic to have lights on BRT/FLASH and MLP traffic BRT/STDY.

TAKEOFF

For single-plane takeoff, all lights will normally be BRT/STDY with anti-collision light on, unless otherwise specified in local operating regulations. For a section takeoff, the leader will turn his lights DIM/STDY when in position on the runway, while the wingman will have his lights on BRT/STDY. After turn-up to 90 percent, the wingman will indicate his readiness to go by turning on his anti-collision light. The leader will signal "Brake release and adding power," by blinking his exterior lights.

OPERATING CLEAR OF TRAFFIC PATTERN

For single-aircraft flights, once clear of the pattern, lights will be BRT/STDY with anti-collision lights on.

When joining in formation, the following procedures will be utilized: As each pilot calls "ABOARD" (when he is in such a position that dimming the lights of the aircraft ahead will not affect his rendezvous), the pilot ahead will turn his fuselage and anti-collision lights OFF and other lights DIM/STDY (fuselage light intensity as briefed or as desired by wingman). Normal lighting for aircraft in formation other than the last aircraft will be wing and tail DIM and all other lights OFF. As each aircraft breaks for rendezvous practice, the pilot will turn all lights to BRT/STDY and anti-collision light on.

For night section penetrations, the leader will have his fuselage and anti-collision lights OFF and remaining lights on DIM/STDY. The wingman will leave all lights BRT/STDY and anti-collision light on, if a VFR letdown is to be made. However, at any time that instrument conditions will be encountered the wingman will turn all lights to BRT/STDY and anti-collision lights OFF prior to entry into the clouds.

LANDING PATTERN

On return to the field for entry into the VFR landing pattern, lights will be on DIM/STDY with the exception of the last aircraft in the flight, which have lights on BRT/STDY and anti-collision light on. The break will be signaled by each pilot blinking the exterior lights just prior to breaking. Normally a 5-7 second interval will be used. Each pilot will place all lights on BRT/STDY and anti-collision light on when well clear of the formation. Each succeeding aircraft will ensure the preceding aircraft's lights are on BRT/STDY and anti-collision light on prior to breaking to ensure visual separation between members of the flight. After final landing, and when approaching the line or fuel pit area, the fuselage and anti-collision lights should be OFF. All other lights should be DIM/STDY on entry into the line or fuel pit area in order to avoid blinding line personnel.

PART 4

CARRIER-BASED PROCEDURES

TABLE OF CONTENTS

GENERAL

LSO NATOPS manual is the governing publication for carrier-landing operations.

DAY OPERATIONS

FLIGHT DECK

PREFLIGHT

1. Upon receipt of the order "Man aircraft", pilots will proceed expeditiously to assigned planes. Preflight, start, and poststart checks shall be accomplished in accordance with Section III, Part 3.

2. During his preflight inspection, the pilot should record the expected gross weight of the aircraft for catapult launch in a designated area, using a block grease pencil.

3. Pilots shall ensure that the tension-bar retainer clip is installed securely and is in good condition.

4. A complete inspection of the aft fuselage may not always be possible due to aircraft spotting.

5. Note the relationship of arresting hook to deck-edge scupper. Do not lower hook during poststart checks unless hook point will drop on the flight deck.

6. Do not initiate start if GTC is in a position where its exhaust may damage aircraft.

POSTSTART

1. Engines will normally be started 10 to 15 minutes prior to launch, and the customary functional checks will be performed.

2. The canopy shall be either open or fully closed and locked. It should be closed when necessary to prevent damage from wind or jet blast.

3. Chocks and tiedowns will be removed upon signal from the plane director.

4. The pilot shall indicate to the plane director when the aircraft is ready for flight.

5. Set emergency-jettison select switch to appropriate position prior to launch.

6. Taxi with flaps fully retracted.

TAXI

1. Taxiing aboard ship is generally similar to that on land, with some variation of power required due to increased wind and turbulence and decreased braking effectiveness because of higher tire pressures. Particular attention should be given to keeping speed under control.

2. While taxiing with appreciable wind over the deck, pilots should avoid attempts to turn large angles to the relative wind or to the jet blast of another aircraft. However, it is imperative that the director's signals be followed closely at all times.

3. Under high wind conditions, direction control is sometimes difficult. If the nosewheel cocks, add throttle to 70-80 percent and use rapid intermittent brake to bounce the nose strut, while moving slowly forward. This should decrease the weight on the nosewheel long enough for it to swivel in the desired direction. If this procedure is not effective, hold brakes, retard throttle to IDLE, and signal for a tiller bar. Normally, under heavy crosswind conditions, a tillerbar and wing walkers should be provided.

4. The pilot will set the flaps to the appropriate takeoff position when signalled by the catapult director. This signal normally is given just prior to attachment of the catapult holdback cable.

5. If a tillerbar is being used, use both brakes together and with equal pressure. Using brakes singly can injure the tillerbar man.

HANGAR DECK

Occasionally the aircraft assigned will be manned on the hangar deck.

Unless the aircraft is already on the elevator, it will be towed or pushed for access to the flight deck. The signal to stop a plane that is being moved by other than its own power is a whistle blast. Leave the hard-hat off. Any whistle blast signifies an immediate STOP. If the plane director is lost from view, STOP.

CATAPULT LAUNCHES

Proper positioning on the catapult is easily accomplished by maintaining a slight amount of excess power and using the brakes to control speed. A tiller bar is normally used to position the aircraft on the catapult. Extreme care must be used, both to prevent injury to the tiller bar man and to preclude mispositioning on the catapult. The pilot must anticipate the initial "hold" immediately after the nosewheel drops over the shuttle, followed by a "come ahead" as the holdback unit is placed on the tension bar. After the nosewheel drops over the shuttle, the pilot must move ahead very slowly to prevent overstressing the tension bar. Upon receipt of the "release brakes" signal from the catapult director, release brakes and immediately increase power to Military. Observe acceleration time and allow engine to stabilize. Recheck the attitude gyro, RMI, engine instruments, trim indicators and flap setting. Ensure a firm grip on the throttle and catapult hand grips, place your head against the headrest, salute, and wait. Normally, the catapult will fire 3 seconds after the catapult officer gives the "fire" signal.

At the end of the power stroke, the pilot must rotate the aircraft to a climbing attitude. This will normally be approximately 12 degrees on attitude gyro.

Clearing turns from bow catapults are not usually made, however gentle clearing turns from waist catapults normally are required. Do not commence clearing turns until an airspeed well above minimum has been attained. The pilot must be aware of other traffic in proximity such as bolters, wave-offs, or other aircraft being launched.

If launching in instrument conditions, the pilot should not be required to change radio, IFF/SIF, or NAV AID channels until a safe altitude (2500 feet) and airspeed are attained. If operational necessity requires changing channels below 2500 feet, the change shall be made with the aircraft stabilized in level flight.

AIRCRAFT OR CATAPULT MALFUNCTION

If, after established at MILITARY POWER, the pilot determines that the aircraft is down, he so indicates to the catapult officer by SHAKING HIS HEAD FROM SIDE TO SIDE. NEVER raise the hand into the catapult officer's view to give a "thumbs-down" signal. It is possible that the catapult officer may construe the signal to be a salute and fire the catapult. When the catapult officer observes the "NO-GO" signal, he should immediately give a suspend signal. If his response is not immediate, call on land/launch frequency "Suspend # catapult; aircraft is down". The suspend signal is crossed forearms held out in front of the face. This signal will be followed by the standard "release tension" signal from the catapult officer. The catapult officer will then walk in front of the near wing and give the pilot the "throttle back" signal. Then AND ONLY THEN, shall the pilot reduce power to IDLE.

In the event of a catapult malfunction, the pilot will observe the same signals given by the catapult officer. Only after the catapult officer has walked in front of the wing and indicated "throttle back," should power be reduced.

LANDING PATTERN

Under VFR conditions, the formation shall approach the breakup position in right echelon, close aboard the carrier on the starboard side, parallel to the Foxtrot Corpen at 800 feet and 250 knots. A minimum straight-in of 3 miles is desired for VFR entry to the break. Aircraft shall be in parade formation with hooks down. Breakup should commence when past the bow and adequate interval on downwind traffic is assured. Normally, a 17-second break-interval will establish a 35-second ramp interval. Close adherence to pattern details by all pilots is required for uniform landing intervals. The pattern given in figure 3-7 is recommended. Each pilot shall have the landing check list completed, be at optimum AOA/approach speed and have the wheel brakes checked by the 180° position. Speedbrakes will normally remain out throughout the approach and landing. Use of speedbrakes may not be desirable at high gross weights (in excess of 13,000 pounds) when configured with high drag stores, i.e., buddy store, MBR's etc., due to the high thrust required during the approach.

At meatball acquisition, a radio call shall be made giving side number, fuel state (in hundreds of pounds), type aircraft, tanker if applicable, meatball or CLARA if meatball is not visible in the straightaway.

ARRESTED LANDING AND EXIT FROM THE LANDING AREA

Upon touchdown, advance the throttle to Military and retract the speedbrakes. After arrestment is assured, retard the throttle to idle and raise the hook and flaps. The aircraft should be allowed to roll back a short distance after arrestment to permit the hook to disengage from the pendant. Hold both brakes when signaled by the director and apply power (about 70 percent), in anticipation of the "come-ahead" signal, unless pullback is indicated by the director. If pullback is directed, retard the throttle to IDLE, release brakes, and allow the aircraft to be pulled back until a brake signal is received. Then, apply brakes judiciously to prevent the aircraft from tipping or rocking back. Anticipate the "come-ahead" signal by adding power to about 70 percent.

CAUTION

Cross the foul line and follow the director's signals. The usual wind over the deck will give a substantial

crosswind component while taxiing on the flight deck. Wing walkers should be provided to assist in leaving the landing area when there is a severe crosswind or wind over the deck exceeding 40 knots. Water, oil, and hydraulic fluid spillages on the flight deck require that caution be exercised in using power and brakes.

POSTLANDING PROCEDURES

As long as the engine is running, the canopy should remain closed and the pilot shall keep his helmet and oxygen mask on. After shutdown, he will immediately open the canopy and remove his helmet. If the aircraft is towed or pushed, he will keep speed slow and under control, and, as noise level is normally high, he must remain alert for either hand or whistle signals from aircraft handling personnel. Whenever the plane director is not in sight, STOP: Do not release brakes until the aircraft has at least a three-point tie-down. Plane captains shall not install the access ladder until this has been accomplished.

NIGHT OPERATIONS

FLIGHT DECK

PREFLIGHT

External preflight will be made using a red-lensed flashlight. In addition to normal cockpit preflight, ensure that external light switches are properly positioned for post-start exterior lights check. The master exterior lights switch, anti-collision light switch, and the taxi light switch should always be in the OFF position prior to start. Wing and tail lights should be set in DIM position for the poststart checks. Instrument lights and console lights control should be rotated from the OFF position to provide reduced illumination of the ladder lights. Direct cockpit emergency floodlights on instrument panel and kneeboard light as desired.

TYPICAL CARRIER LANDING PATTERN

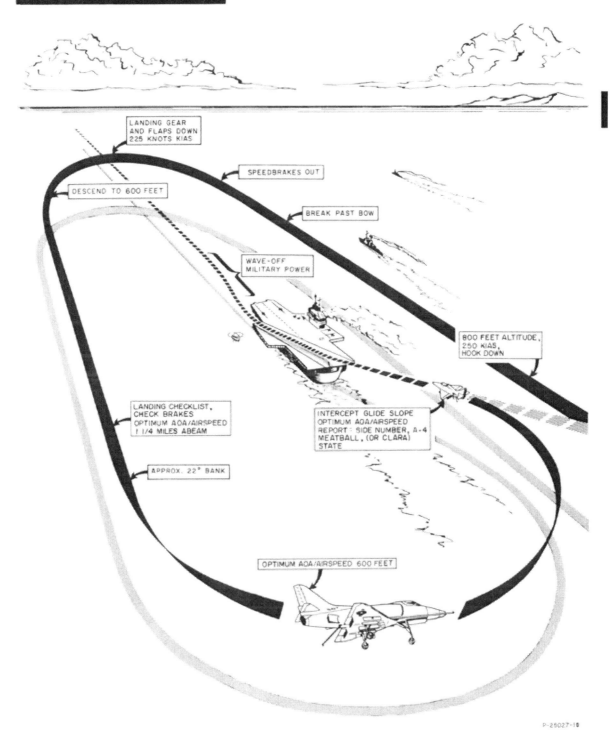

LANDING GEAR
AND FLAPS DOWN
225 KNOTS KIAS

SPEEDBRAKES OUT

DESCEND TO 600 FEET

BREAK PAST BOW

WAVE-OFF
MILITARY POWER

800 FEET ALTITUDE,
250 KIAS,
HOOK DOWN

LANDING CHECKLIST,
CHECK BRAKES
OPTIMUM AOA/AIRSPEED
1 1/4 MILES ABEAM

INTERCEPT GLIDE SLOPE
OPTIMUM AOA/AIRSPEED
REPORT : SIDE NUMBER, A-4
MEATBALL, (OR CLARA)
STATE

APPROX. 22° BANK

OPTIMUM AOA/AIRSPEED 600 FEET

P-29027-18

Figure 3-7. Typical Carrier Landing Pattern

POSTSTART

Adjust cockpit lights intensity to desired level. After normal systems checks are completed, perform exterior lights check. Move the master exterior lights switch to ON. White fuselage lights may be checked by momentarily placing the switch to DIM. Upon completion of exterior lights check, place master exterior lights switch to the OFF position.

TAXI

Slow and careful handling of aircraft by both plane directors and pilots is mandatory. If the pilot has any doubt as to the plane director's signals, STOP!

CATAPULT LAUNCHES

The difficulty of "getting on" the catapult at night is increased by the fact that it is difficult for the pilot to determine his speed. The pilot must rely upon, and follow closely, the directions of the plane director. As the aircraft approaches the catapult, the plane director should position himself forward and remain stationary to give the pilot a visual reference for controlling taxi speed as the aircraft approaches the shuttle.

Upon receiving the signal from the catapult director, release brakes. Immediately increase power to MILITARY in anticipation of the turn up signal from the catapult officer. When satisfied that the aircraft is ready for launch, the pilot so signifies by placing the master exterior lights switch to the ON position. The pilot must be prepared to establish a wings-level, climbing attitude on instruments. An initial attitude of 10 - 12 degrees nose-up is recommended. Ensure a positive rate-of-climb is obtained. Retract the landing gear at 300 feet or above. Retract flaps at 170 KIAS or above. During night launches, do not make clearing turns. At 2500 feet or higher, switch all lights to BRT/STDY and anti-collision lights on.

AIRCRAFT OR CATAPULT MALFUNCTION

The pilot's "NO-GO" signal for night catapult launch consists of not turning his exterior lights ON. The pilot should call on land/launch frequency "Suspend catapult; aircraft is down." Maintain MILITARY power until the catapult officer walks in front of the wing and gives the "throttle-back" signal. DO NOT turn exterior lights ON unless completely ready to be launched.

LANDING PATTERN

Night and instrument recoveries normally will be made utilizing tacan/CCA approaches in accordance with NWP-41A.

ARRESTED LANDING AND EXIT FROM THE LANDING AREA

The LSO will normally take control when the aircraft is approximately one mile from the ramp. The pilot should have wing and taillights on BRT/STDY (anti-collision lights OFF). Following arrestment, immediately place master exterior lights switch to OFF. Taxi out of the landing area slowly. Do not stare fixedly at the plane director's wands but use them as the center of the scan pattern.

CARRIER CONTROLLED APPROACH (CCA)

GENERAL

The pattern procedures, and terms used for carrier-controlled approaches shall be in accordance with NWP 41(A). See figure 3-8 for typical CCA approach.

Changed 1 November 1965

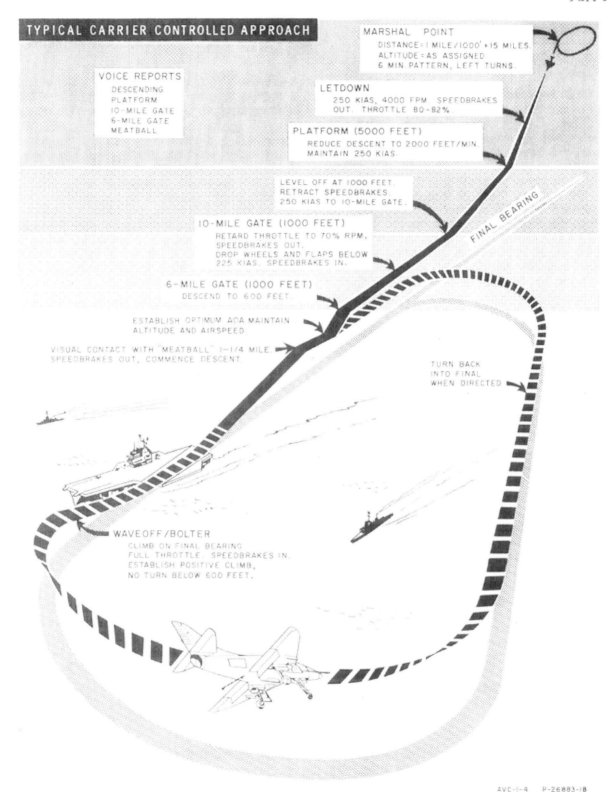

TYPICAL CARRIER CONTROLLED APPROACH

MARSHAL POINT
DISTANCE = 1 MILE/1000' + 15 MILES.
ALTITUDE = AS ASSIGNED.
6 MIN. PATTERN, LEFT TURNS.

VOICE REPORTS
DESCENDING
PLATFORM
10-MILE GATE
6-MILE GATE
MEATBALL

LETDOWN
250 KIAS, 4000 FPM. SPEEDBRAKES
OUT. THROTTLE 80-82%.

PLATFORM (5000 FEET)
REDUCE DESCENT TO 2000 FEET/MIN.
MAINTAIN 250 KIAS.

LEVEL OFF AT 1000 FEET.
RETRACT SPEEDBRAKES.
250 KIAS TO 10-MILE GATE.

FINAL BEARING

10-MILE GATE (1000 FEET)
RETARD THROTTLE TO 70% RPM,
SPEEDBRAKES OUT.
DROP WHEELS AND FLAPS BELOW
225 KIAS. SPEEDBRAKES IN.

6-MILE GATE (1000 FEET)
DESCEND TO 600 FEET.

ESTABLISH OPTIMUM AOA MAINTAIN
ALTITUDE AND AIRSPEED.

VISUAL CONTACT WITH "MEATBALL" 1-1/4 MILE.
SPEEDBRAKES OUT, COMMENCE DESCENT.

TURN BACK
INTO FINAL
WHEN DIRECTED

WAVEOFF/BOLTER
CLIMB ON FINAL BEARING
FULL THROTTLE. SPEEDBRAKES IN.
ESTABLISH POSITIVE CLIMB,
NO TURN BELOW 600 FEET.

AVC-1-4   P-26883-1B

Figure 3-8. Typical Carrier-Controlled Approach

PROCEDURES

A CCA approach is similar to a straight-in jet penetration. Lower the hook entering the holding pattern and maintain maximum endurance airspeed. Single aircraft must leave the Marshal point at EAC. If the flight consists of two or more aircraft, the Flight Leader normally should plan to be in holding at the Marshal Point in time to make a half standard-rate 180 degree left turn, break off from the flight, and return to the Marshal point at his EAC. Subsequent aircraft in the flight break at 30 second intervals. As each pilot reaches the Marshal point, he commences his letdown at 250 KIAS, 4000 ft./min. rate of descent, speedbrakes OUT, and about 80-82 percent RPM. At 5000 feet (platform), the rate of descent is reduced to 2000 ft./min., although penetration speed is maintained at 250 KIAS. Level off at 1000 feet, retract speedbrakes, and adjust power to maintain 250 KIAS to the 10-mile gate. At this point, transition to 150 KIAS by retarding the throttle to 70 percent. Extend speedbrakes and drop wheels and flaps as airspeed drops below 225 KIAS. Retract speedbrakes and adjust power to maintain 150 KIAS. Aircraft shall be in landing configuration prior to reaching the 6-mile gate. Unless otherwise directed, a gradual descent to 600 feet will be made departing the 6-mile gate. Upon reaching 600 feet, transition to final approach speed (optimum angle-of-attack/airspeed). This altitude and airspeed will be maintained until meatball acquisition at about 1-1/4 miles, or until directed by the final controller or LSO to commence letdown. Fly into the meatball until it is centered, extend speedbrakes, and commence descent maintaining optimum AOA/airspeed. (Use of speedbrakes is optional when approach is made at aircraft gross weights in excess of 13,000 pounds and configured with high drag stores, i.e., buddy stores, MBR's, etc.)

After transition is made to landing configuration, all turns should be standard rate. Do not exceed 30 degrees bank at any time. Do not exceed 15 degrees bank after leaving 600 feet on final approach.

A section CCA may be necessary in the event a failure occurs affecting navigation aids, communications equipment, or certain other aircraft systems. Normally, the aircraft experiencing the difficulty will fly the starboard wing position during the approach. The section leader will detach the wingman when the meatball is sighted and continue straight ahead, offsetting as necessary to the left to determine if the wingman lands successfully. He shall commence a slow descent to not lower than 300 feet altitude and turn all lights to BRT and FLASH abeam the ship. This will provide the wingman with a visual reference and leader should he bolter or waveoff. The wingman should not detach unless he has the meatball in sight. Necessary visual signals are contained in Table 7-9.

WAVEOFF BOLTER PATTERN

Waveoff will be straight up the angled deck, when given close-in. Pilots must bear in mind that during a late waveoff, an inflight engagement is possible, therefore the aircraft must be lined up with the centerline to reduce the possibility of aircraft damage. After a waveoff or a bolter, establish a positive climb then turn parallel to the Foxtrot Corpen. DO NOT CROSS THE BOW while flying upwind. Be alert for other aircraft launching from the catapult or entering the pattern from the break. The aircraft ahead will have priority for the turn downwind. If in doubt, use the radio. At night, always call Turning downwind. A waveoff to the right will be made when overshooting the landing line to the extreme. When waving off to the right, stay well clear of the plane-guard helicopter.

CARRIER EMERGENCY SIGNALS

See NWP-41(A) for emergency signals from carrier to aircraft.

Changed 15 May 1966

P-41241-1

PART 5

HOT REFUELING PROCEDURES

TABLE OF CONTENTS

TEXT

HOT REFUELING PROCEDURES

The following procedures shall be strictly adhered to by pilots and ground personnel when refueling aircraft with the engine running.

NOTE

A-4 aircraft will be hot refueled through the probe only.

PRIOR TO ENTERING THE PITS

1. The pilot will secure all electrical and electronic gear not required for refueling operations.

2. The plane captain shall check for hot brakes. If the aircraft has hot brakes, the plane captain shall direct it away from the pits.

3. All ordnance shall be removed or dearmed in accordance with local regulations. This includes practice bombs with smoke charges installed.

4. Fueling personnel shall check the fuel pits for loose objects which could be injested into engine.

5. The aircraft will be taxied into the fuel pits under the guidance of a qualified plane director.

PRIOR TO REFUELING

1. The aircraft will be chocked.

2. The plane captain shall attach grounding wire to aircraft before any other connections are made.

3. The pilot will close and lock the canopy and select ram air. The radio will be set on ground control or, if aboard ship, other appropriate frequency.

4. Drop tank pressurization switch and FUEL TRANS BYPASS switch shall be placed in OFF position.

CAUTION

Ensure that fuel dump switch is in OFF position prior to refueling.

5. The work stand will be positioned in front of in-flight refueling probe and wheels will be locked. ~~Boot will be installed on vent mast.~~

6. The nozzle operator shall attach nozzle adapter to the probe.

7. The pilot will signal to fuel pit coordinator when he is ready for commencement of fueling.

AFTER COMMENCEMENT OF REFUELING

1. Nozzle operator will slowly open valve and check for fuel leaks until the valve is fully open.

2. Immediately upon commencement of refueling, the plane captain will conduct the primary and secondary valve checks in accordance with the Maintenance Instruction Manual. If this check is not satisfactory, the refueling operation shall be secured immediately.

3. If the drop tanks are to be filled, either the plane captain shall place the DROP TANK FUELING switch in the ON position, or the pilot will place the DROP TANK pressurization switch to the FLIGHT REFUEL position.

WARNING

Aboard ship, the plane captain must visually check the drop tanks upon completion of refueling to ensure that they are either completely full or completely empty. This procedure applies whether the drop tank fueling switch has been placed in the ON or OFF position during refueling.

NOTE

When refueling ashore, gravity fueling method must be used for partial drop tank loads.

4. Appropriately assigned personnel shall monitor air vents on wing to ensure that they are not obstructed.

WARNING

If pressure cannot be felt coming from these vents, the refueling operation shall be secured immediately.

5. The pilot shall signal the fuel pit coordinator when refueling is completed. He, in turn, will signal the nozzle operator and pit operator. The nozzle operator will close the valve on the nozzle but will not remove the probe adapter until the pit operator has evacuated all fuel from the hose.

6. The ground wire shall be detached after all other refueling equipment is removed.

7. A qualified plane director will direct the aircraft out of the pits.

SECTION IV

FLIGHT CHARACTERISTICS AND

FLIGHT PROCEDURES

TABLE OF CONTENTS

P-25001-X

PART 1

FLIGHT CHARACTERISTICS

TABLE OF CONTENTS

TEXT

ILLUSTRATIONS

TABLES

INTRODUCTION

The flight characteristics of the aircraft as described in this section are based, whenever possible, on actual flight test information. In some instances, the results of extensive wind tunnel tests and data from flight tests of similar aircraft are used. Although additional information will be submitted periodically in the form of changes to this handbook, the latest service directives and technical orders concerning this aircraft should be consulted regularly to keep abreast of pertinent information.

Calculations and flight testing indicate that the flight characteristics of the A-4E are the same as for the A-4C aircraft.

The aircraft has the excellent slow flying characteristics usually found in aircraft designed for carrier operations. Positive stability in the power approach configuration (landing gear and flaps down) results in a return to the trimmed condition when disturbed by turbulence or pilot induced displacement.

FLIGHT CONTROLS

AILERONS

Aileron control forces are light at all subsonic speeds when the aileron power system is operative. In the transonic region and above, the air loads on the ailerons become large enough to require the total output of the power control system to deflect the ailerons beyond a certain point.

On manual control, the available rate of roll is markedly reduced at all speeds. Adequate lateral control can be maintained if the speed is reduced below Mach 0.80 or 300 knots, whichever is lower, where a maximum rate of roll of approximately 10 degrees per second is available at sea level. This increases to 40 degrees per second at 40,000 feet. (Refer to section I part 2, HYDRAULIC POWER DISCONNECT, for further information on aileron power disconnect.)

ELEVATORS

The powered elevator provides good control at all speeds. (See figure 4-1, for a powered elevator stick forces diagram.) A bungee is installed in the elevator control system to provide longitudinal load feel. The bungee is linked to the horizontal stabilizer so that the elevator deflects upward (stick moves aft) while trimming noseup and deflects downward while trimming nosedown. The elevator moves approximately 8 degrees as the stabilizer travels from full-throw up to full-throw down.

With the elevator power control system inoperative or disconnected, elevator stick forces will be increased, but for flight at subsonic speeds, adequate control will be available. On manual control, no more than

1.8g can be obtained with the application of 120 pounds of stick force at Mach 0.96 at any altitude. As Mach number is increased, the maneuverability is further decreased. At Mach numbers less than 0.85 and altitudes below 5000 feet, a load factor of 2.7g can be attained with 120 pounds of stick force. Above 5000 feet, and below Mach 0.85, maneuverability is increased and is limited by buffet or accelerated stall.

RUDDER

The rudder power system provides good rudder control at all airspeeds. In the event of hydraulic failure, rudder pedal forces will increase with airspeeds, but very little effort is required at approach and landing speeds. There is no rudder trim available with hydraulic failure.

TRIM SURFACES

The trimming surfaces are capable of reducing stick forces to zero for all stabilized level flight conditions. The horizontal stabilizer will require almost constant repositioning during rapid acceleration and deceleration during takeoff and the approach to the landing.

Retrimming of the rudder will not be necessary except when asymmetrical drag configurations are encountered, as would occur if two large stores were being carried on the wing racks and one was dropped.

When the aircraft is laterally retrimmed, the aileron trim system actuator relocates the neutral position of the control stick through the aileron power control system. If the power control system fails or is disconnected, the followup tab provides sufficient trim for all flight conditions as long as electrical power is supplied.

SLATS

The wing slats open automatically under various flight conditions to improve airflow

STICK FORCES

MODEL: A-4E
DATA AS OF: 15 August 1956
DATA BASIS: Calculations

ENGINE: J52-P-6
FUEL GRADE: IP-4, JP-5
FUEL DENSITY: 6.5, 6.8 Lb/Gal.

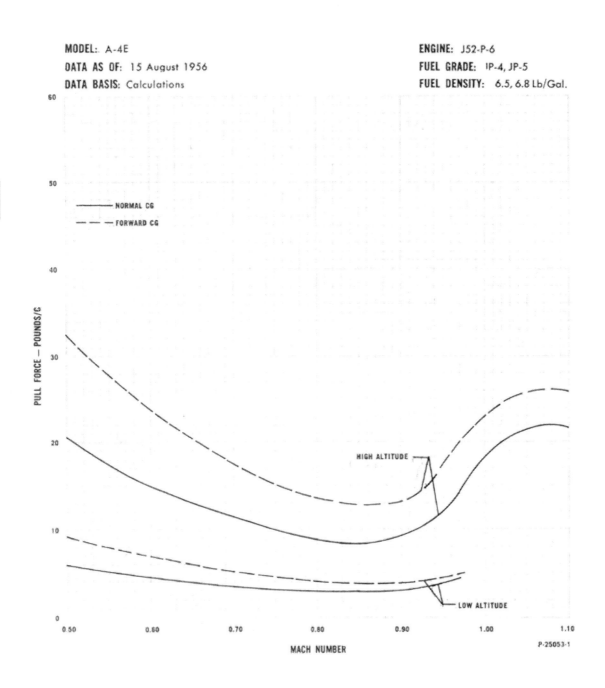

Figure 4-1. Stick Forces

Changed 15 March 1965

characteristics over the wing. As the two slats operate independently, and aerodynamically, one may occasionally open slightly in advance of the other, and impose a rolling moment.

WING FLAPS AND LANDING GEAR

Lowering the wing flaps or landing gear causes a nosedown trim change, while a noseup trim change results from raising either or both. The trim changes are slight and are overcome easily through use of the control surfaces or by retrimming.

SPEEDBRAKES

Operation of the speedbrakes results in changes in trim characterized by a noseup pitch when opened and a nosedown pitch when closed. To counter this characteristic, a speedbrake-elevator interconnect is installed which physically displaces the elevator when the speedbrakes are operated. This interconnect mechanism pulls the control stick forward when the speedbrakes are opened, and returns the stick to its original position when the speedbrakes are closed, thus decreasing the noseup and nosedown pitching. Some trim change will occur when the speedbrakes are operated. The degree of this trim change will be a function of airspeed. For further information on use of the speedbrakes, refer to DIVING, section IV, part 1.

LEVEL FLIGHT CHARACTERISTICS

SLOW FLIGHT

Control is good during slow flight at approach and landing speeds; however, a lateral-directional oscillation is present in rough air.

CRUISING

Level flight cruising characteristics are normal and satisfactory trim and control forces are available. At high altitudes and cruising airspeeds, a lateral-directional oscillation occurs in rough air, which may be counteracted by application of control surfaces. Longitudinal stability is weak to neutral at increasing aft center of gravity positions.

TRANSONIC MACH CHARACTERISTICS

At airspeeds up to Mach 0.89 no unusual tendencies are exhibited and stick forces are low to moderate. A mild nosedown trim change occurs at Mach 0.89 and increases slightly up to Mach 0.98. The trim change can be counteracted by applying approximately one-half unit noseup stabilizer trim. (Refer to DIVING Section IV, part 1.) At Mach 1.02, a very light noseup tendency appears, and increases gradually up to the maximum permissible speed. Up to Mach number 0.90 the longitudinal stick forces are normal and control is good. Above Mach 0.90, the elevator effectiveness drops appreciably. Concurrent with this decrease is an increase in the stick force gradient. (See figure 4-1.)

TRANSONIC PITCHUP

During recoveries from dives at supersonic speeds, a marked pitchup will occur at approximately 0.95 IMN. This increase in load factor is partially due to a marked increase in elevator effectiveness when decelerating through 0.95 IMN. After the initial abrupt increase in load factor or pitchup, the load factor will continue to build up at a slower rate as Mach number is decreased below 0.95 IMN, unless the pilot relaxes aft pressure on the stick.

In the critical aft cg condition, it is possible to develop the following load factors at supersonic speeds and maintain constant stick force as speed drops off to IMN = 0.85 without exceeding limit load factor in the ensuing pitch-up:

10,000 feet	3.8g
20,000 feet	3.5g
30,000 feet	3.2g

The pitchup severity depends on the initial load factor or stick position, being more severe for full aft stick. At altitudes above 15,000 feet, and at high load factors, aircraft buffet will be encountered at above 0.98 to 0.95 IMN. This buffet should be heeded as a warning to relax aft stick pressure. If corrective action is applied by promptly relaxing the aft stick pressure, the pitchup can be appreciably lessened.

CAUTION

When using load factors in excess of those listed above for supersonic dive recoveries, relax aft stick pressure promptly, either upon encountering the initial sharp pitchup at about IMN = 0.95 or on encountering aircraft buffet. Note that at altitudes below 15,000 feet aircraft buffet does not occur prior to pitchup.

Transonic pitchup during a speed reduction in the region where a marked increase in elevator effectiveness occurs can be appreciably decreased or eliminated entirely by reducing aft stick force as Mach reaches 0.98.

FLIGHT WITH POWER CONTROL DISCONNECTED

Power control disconnect above 300 knots IAS or Mach 0.85 should be avoided if at all possible. Reduce thrust and open speedbrakes to decrease Mach to this value before disconnecting. Trim aircraft laterally prior to disconnect, if possible. The aircraft is subject to strong wing-dropping tendencies

above Mach 0.90, with the boost disconnected. Available rate of roll with maximum pilot effort in this speed range may be insufficient to overcome wing dropping tendencies. Although the aileron tab retains some effectiveness, the slow speed of operation of this tab makes it difficult to keep up with the random wing dropping. Wing dropping tendency disappears as airspeed is reduced to Mach 0.85, and available roll rate from pilot input forces increases, making the aircraft once more controllable. (Refer to HYDRAULIC POWER DISCONNECT section I, part 2.)

FLIGHT WITH EXTERNAL STORES

Flight characteristics with external stores aboard are satisfactory. Adequate control is available to hold the wings level during landing with an asymmetrical loading up to 7500 foot-pounds static moment on either wing. Wing heaviness or random wing drop may be encountered at medium altitudes (20,000 to 25,000 feet) and high subsonic speeds (between Mach 0.94 and Mach 1.0) when carrying certain stores, or in braked dives.

With various aft store loadings on the multiple bomb racks, the cg will shift aft. In the event that the aft bombs fail to release due to a rack malfunction, the cg may exceed the permissible aft limit. As the cg moves aft, the longitudinal stick forces become very light during low fuel state operation, and particularly in the landing configuration. If stick forces are so light and control sensitivity so great that landing may be extremely hazardous, the pilot should jettison the multiple bomb racks. (Refer to the Weight and Balance Handbook, AN 01-1B-40, for permissible cg limits.)

With asymmetric loadings, simple elevator control displacement induces roll as well as pitch. With control hydraulic power on, aileron control is sufficient to counteract roll induced by elevator control displacement. With hydraulic power off, at speeds above 200 knots, IAS, the roll induced by elevator displacement cannot be adequately controlled because of high lateral stick forces and low lateral control response. Accordingly, with hydraulic power off, longitudinal control should be minimized and airspeed should not exceed 200 knots IAS with asymmetrical loadings. (Refer to HYDRAULIC POWER DISCONNECT, section I, part 2.)

With asymmetric store loadings, the following recommendations are made:

1. That crosswind landings be made upwind or downwind, whichever is required to put the crosswind component under the heavy or loaded wing providing other factors such as runway length and gross weight are considered.

2. That a final approach speed of 115 knots be considered an absolute minimum, as it represents the minimum control speed with a control hydraulic failure and an asymmetric loading of 7500 foot-pounds (such as a 1200 pound store on one inboard rack). The initial approach airspeed should be a minimum of 140 knots IAS with a minimum final approach and touchdown airspeed of 125 knots IAS.

MANEUVERING FLIGHT

Available maneuverability is shown graphically in figure 4-3. Longitudinal and lateral maneuvering characteristics are normal throughout the level flight speed range of the airplane, however, flight characteristics in the following maneuvers should be noted.

TRANSONIC MANEUVERING

In the pullouts or maneuvering in the transonic range, a small abrupt random wing drop accompanied by general airframe buffet occurs. The intensity of the buffeting is generally proportional to the load factor developed.

AILERON ROLLS

During and upon termination of high rate aileron rolls (above 200 degrees per second)

in the high speed low altitude region, abrupt pitch down will be noted. This pitchdown, though uncomfortable, is structurally safe.

ROLLING PULLOUTS

High sideslip angles and a pitchup tendency occur in rolling pullouts in which high roll rates are developed. At high altitudes, the pitchup tendency increases the likelihood of inadvertent stalling and spinning out of the maneuver. At low altitudes, sideslip angles are reduced but the pitchup tendency is considerably stronger. The normal load factor should be monitored during rapid rolling pullouts at low altitude, and if an increase in the normal load factor is noted, the stick should be eased forward.

ROLLING PUSHOVERS

During recoveries from high rate rolling pushovers in the high and medium speed low altitude region, a marked pitchdown will be noted. The pitching tendency is a result of inertia coupling and is not noticeable in normal rolling pushovers with a moderate roll rate. If bank angle changes are limited to 180 degrees or less, the pitchdown will not become excessive regardless of the lateral stick deflection used during the maneuver.

HIGH ANGLE-OF-ATTACK PITCHUP

During flight with aft center-of-gravity locations (aft of 26 percent MAC), high angle-of-attack pitchup may be encountered when applying load factor. This pitchup is normally preceded by buffet onset and a buildup of buffet intensity. The pitchup manifests itself by a rapid increase in load factor with no change in stick position. At altitudes above 30,000 feet, the airplane limit load factor will not be exceeded if pitchup is encountered. At low altitudes (below 15,000 feet) and high speeds (above Mach 0.80), limit load factor precludes the aircraft from encountering pitchup. Between 0.50 and 0.80 Mach number with a center-of-gravity of 26 percent, it is possible to attain pitchup when maneuvering near limit load factor. At intermediate altitudes (15,000 to 30,000 feet) the pitchup can cause the limit load factor to be exceeded. Even though the elevator effectiveness is drastically reduced under these conditions, the severity of the pitchup can be controlled by partial forward stick movement. Buffet onset and ensuing buildup in intensity serve as a warning that the pitchup boundary is being approached.

Pitchup does not occur below Mach 0.40 and therefore does not present a landing or low speed problem. It can be avoided entirely by limiting pullups to buffet onset when flying with less than 750 pounds of fuel aboard or with other loadings where the cg is aft of 26 percent MAC. (Refer to cg-loading charts.)

CAUTION

Full forward stick should not be used to recover from a high angle-of-attack pitchup, as excessive negative load factors will occur.

STALLS

Stall characteristics are normal in all configurations. The conventional technique of decreasing angle-of-attack with forward stick, simultaneously adding of full power, then leveling the wing should be used to recover from a stalled condition. Warning of an impending stall occurs in the form of light buffeting of the aircraft, increasing in intensity as the stall is approached. The characteristics of a stall are a mild nosedown pitching accompanied by light directional and lateral oscillation. If the stall is reached when a high power setting is used, the nosedown pitch is very mild. Any tendency for

a wing to drop can be effectively counteracted by application of opposite rudder. The stall speeds shown in figure 4-2 are based on calculations from flight testing of the A-4B aircraft.

WARNING

• Asymmetric slat extension will require full lateral control to maintain wings level when airspeed is approximately 5 knots above stall.

• In the J-52 engine an acceleration, stall can often be caused by insufficient airflow in the inlet duct during periods of attempted engine acceleration. Instead of "CHUGGING," this acceleration stall usually results in a quiet rundown to an RPM less than idle. If throttle movement above idle is attempted while aircraft is in a low RPM/high angle-of-attack condition, it is possible to put the engine operating line over the stall line, resulting in the engine unwinding and subsequent failure to respond to throttle movement. If throttle movement is attempted under these conditions, no response is likely due to lack of sufficient airflow in the inlet ducts.

Do not select power settings below 65 percent RPM when approaching stall speeds.

ACCELERATED STALLS

Accelerated stalls are preceded by adequate stall warning in the form of general airframe buffeting. Recovery is easily accomplished by employing normal procedures A light buffet occurs just prior to slat opening. After the slats open, the buffeting disappears until the airspeed decreases to the accelerated stall warning speed, at which time the buffeting occurs again. Occasionally, failure of the slats to open simultaneously causes an abrupt roll toward the side with the slower opening slat. When aggravated by an aft center of gravity position and by asymmetric

Changed 1 November 1965

slat extension, an accelerated stall may result in an uncontrollable roll, which will stop when the load factor is reduced.

SPINS

Flight tests and model spin tunnel tests indicate that the spin characteristics are satisfactory in all configurations. The spin is generally oscillatory in pitch during the first turn, becoming more oscillatory in roll and yaw and less oscillatory in pitch during the second turn. In erect spins entered from level flight, the aircraft appears to be inverted upon completion of one-half turn and erect upon completion of one turn. Holding rudder with the spin, ailerons against the spin, or forward stick increases the rate of rotation and flattens the spin. When external

stores are carried, spins are generally less oscillatory in pitch and slower in rotational speeds.

SPIN RECOVERY

Experience has shown that neutralization of all flight controls will facilitate recovery during the incipient spin phase (uncontrolled flight immediately after a fully developed stall). In fact, application of spin recovery procedures during this phase will increase the probability of spin entry. Before attempting spin recovery, make certain that the airplane is actually in a spin. The turn needle always indicates the rotation of the spin and should be used as the primary aid in determining proper spin recovery procedure. Use of the turn needle in conjunction with the accelerometer will eliminate any confusion encountered. Generally, positive g will indicate an erect spin; negative g, inverted.

Recovery from confirmed spins in the clean configuration or with an external store weight of less than 2000 pounds can be accomplished by brisk application of full rudder against the spin followed by moderate motion of the control stick to neutral. As in any airplane, considerable angular momentum is developed during a spin; consequently, recovery is not instantaneous. Higher spin rates are encountered in flat spins than in steep spins; consequently, recoveries from flat spins are somewhat slower than from steep spins. The controls should be held in the recovery position until the recovery is made.

Recovery from erect spins with total external store weight greater than 2000 pounds can be accomplished by brisk application of full rudder against the spin, moderate but slow application of aileron with the spin (same direction as turn-needle indication), and full back stick.

The recommended recovery procedure from inverted spins with an external store load greater than 2000 pounds is brisk application of full rudder against the spin, moderate but slow application of aileron against the spin (opposite to the turn-needle indication), and neutralization of the elevator. Although this recovery procedure has not been formally demonstrated, there is no doubt as to its effectiveness. The recovery will be more positive than the corresponding erect spin recovery. The ailerons are very effective, and the recovery will be imminent before large aileron deflections can be applied. Care should be taken to avoid using excessive aileron deflections, which will increase the possibility of spinning in the opposite direction upon recovery.

The use of controls from spin recovery is summarized in Table 4-1.

The ailerons are very effective both with a clean configuration and with external stores aboard. If, for any reason, recovery in the clean configuration is not achieved within two turns and it is certain that proper recovery action has been taken, the ailerons may be used to augment the basic recovery. This does not mean that the recommended clean configuration recovery procedure is not completely satisfactory and that the ailerons should always be used "just to be certain." The use of ailerons is considered to be a supplementary method and is not recommended unless absolutely necessary. Improper use of the ailerons will aggravate the spin and delay the recovery. As indicated previously, the ailerons are very effective in achieving spin recovery, and the recovery is often quite abrupt. All controls should be neutralized immediately upon termination of the spin, or a spin in the opposite direction is likely to result.

The following comments on minimum spin recovery altitude pertain to all A-4 type aircraft. The altitude required for spin recovery depends on the flight path angle and altitude of the airplane on termination of the spin. The rate of descent during the spin, the time and turns required to terminate the spin are also factors that must be considered. A minimum altitude of 10,000 feet above the terrain is

STALL SPEED
SPEED BRAKES RETRACTED
GEAR DOWN

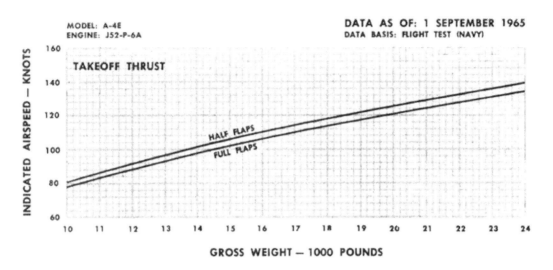

MODEL: A-4E
ENGINE: J52-P-6A

DATA AS OF: 1 SEPTEMBER 1965
DATA BASIS: FLIGHT TEST (NAVY)

TAKEOFF THRUST

HALF FLAPS
FULL FLAPS

INDICATED AIRSPEED — KNOTS

GROSS WEIGHT — 1000 POUNDS

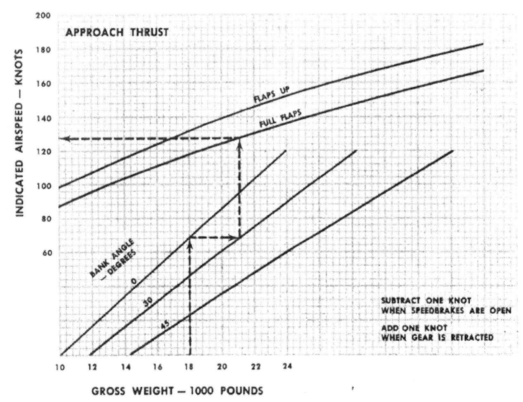

APPROACH THRUST

INDICATED AIRSPEED — KNOTS

FLAPS UP
FULL FLAPS

BANK ANGLE — DEGREES
0
30
45

SUBTRACT ONE KNOT
WHEN SPEEDBRAKES ARE OPEN

ADD ONE KNOT
WHEN GEAR IS RETRACTED

GROSS WEIGHT — 1000 POUNDS

P-40533-1

Figure 4-2. Stall Speeds

Changed 1 November 1965

TABLE 4-1. A-4 SPIN RECOVERY			
TYPE SPIN	LESS THAN 2000 POUNDS EXTERNAL STORES		
	RUDDER	AILERON	STICK
UPRIGHT OR INVERTED	OPPOSITE TURN NEEDLE	NEUTRAL	NEUTRAL
	MORE THAN 2000 POUNDS EXTERNAL STORES		
	RUDDER	AILERON	STICK
UPRIGHT	OPPOSITE TURN NEEDLE	WITH TURN NEEDLE (MODERATE)	FULL BACK
INVERTED	OPPOSITE TURN NEEDLE	OPPOSITE TURN NEEDLE (MODERATE)	NEUTRAL

the recommended altitude to terminate spin recovery techniques if attempts to recover have been unsuccessful.

WARNING

- If an inadvertent confirmed spin occurs below 10,000 feet AGL, eject. Recovery from fully developed spin below 10,000 feet is considered doubtful since 5000 to 7000 feet are required to complete recovery with proper application of controls. Recovery from inadvertent incipient spin may be a accomplished with altitude losses varying from 0 to 7000 feet, depending upon how fully developed spin becomes.

- Intentional spins are prohibited.

AVAILABLE MANEUVERABILITY

For available maneuverability of the A-4E, refer to figure 4-3.

DIVING

The diving characteristics of the aircraft are normal except when steep clean dives are conducted from high altitudes where airspeeds increase into the supersonic range. Under these conditions, the elevator effectiveness will be reduced and the aircraft basic stability will become high, and it will be necessary to retrim with the stabilizer to dive the aircraft supersonically.

Dive recovery nomographs are provided on Figure 4-4. Figure 4-4, sheet 1 shows the altitude loss after the load factor is applied and sheet 2 shows the pilot reaction time. An additional factor, altimeter lag, must be added to the above two values to determine the total loss in altitude from initiation of the dive recovery to level flight.

WARNING

Figure 4-4 (sheets 1 and 2) does not consider buffet onset or structural limits. (See figure 11-40.)

CAUTION

Speedbrakes should normally be opened prior to entering steep dives.

The accelerometer should be referred to immediately upon initiating a pullout from a supersonic dive to ensure that enough load factor is being developed to recover.

WARNING

If difficulty is experienced in recovering from dive, speedbrakes should be opened immediately and throttle retarded in an effort to reduce airspeed and limit altitude loss in recovery maneuver.

NOTE

Maximum speed for fully effective opening of speedbrakes is 440 knots IAS. However, speedbrakes are partially effective up to maximum speed capabilities of the airplane.

If the elevator power system should fail during a supersonic dive, the stick force required for recovery will be so high as to prohibit normal recovery procedures. Use of aircraft noseup stabilizer trim will then become mandatory to effect recovery.

CAUTION

Do not use the horizontal stabilizer as a dive recovery device except in an emergency, as a strong pitchup will result as the airspeed drops below approximately Mach 0.94.

Trim settings for diving should be established on the basis of aircraft configuration and a knowledge of the individual aircraft, as each will require somewhat different trim settings for a given flight condition. It is usually considered preferable to trim the aircraft so that a moderate push force is required to maintain the dive just prior to the pullout.

If the speedbrakes are used before entering the dive, airspeeds will be limited to lower values where the increase in stick forces will not be severe.

Note

The speedbrakes will begin to "blow back" at approximately 490 knots IAS.

The speedbrakes should not be closed until the recovery has been completed to prevent an increase in stick forces resulting from the combined effects of the buildup in airspeed and the characteristic nosedown trim change that accompanies closing of the speedbrakes. The control stick forces required to produce 1 g change in load factor at various Mach numbers are presented in figure 4-1.

DIVE ANGLE LIMITATIONS

Information concerning the maximum permissible dive angles when diving at maximum permissible airspeed will be provided in future publications.

FLIGHT CHARACTERISTICS ON AFCS

The AFCS (autopilot) is described in detail in Section I, Part 2. When flying "hand off," the aircraft is completely stable about all three axes, with no tendency to oscillate. See Section I, Part 4 for AIRSPEED LIMITATIONS while operating on AFCS.

Certain flight characteristics of the AFCS are inherent in its detail design and constitute normal performance. Flight characteristics which are evident to the pilot are discussed in the following paragraphs.

WING DOWN PHENOMENA ON HEADING HOLD

There are particular circumstances which may result in temporary wing down condition while on heading hold. Asymmetric loading, directional trim, and platform gyro precession result in temporary wing down conditions.

Asymmetric loading causes the aircraft to be directionally out of trim and to fly wing

AVAILABLE MANEUVERABILITY

GROSS WEIGHT = 13,826 POUNDS

CG @ 20.9% MAC

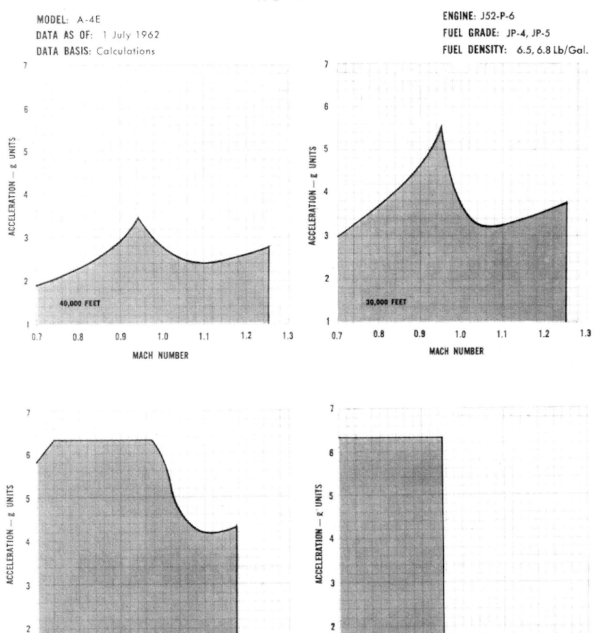

MODEL: A-4E
DATA AS OF: 1 July 1962
DATA BASIS: Calculations

ENGINE: J52-P-6
FUEL GRADE: JP-4, JP-5
FUEL DENSITY: 6.5, 6.8 Lb/Gal.

Figure 4-3. Available Maneuverability

down. Lateral and directional trim is available to the pilot and he should trim when necessary. On AFCS, directional trim is available at all times. Lateral and pitch trim is available in the control stick steering mode. If the pilot does not trim directionally, the airplane will maintain a constant skid at a banked attitude. Speed changes result in changes in directional trim. On AFCS flight, just as in normal flight, the pilot should trim the airplane as necessary.

ROLLBACK ON ROLL ATTITUDE HOLD

Control stick steering switching levels and pilot technique in conjunction with the ability of the AFCS to synchronize changes in roll attitude will determine the amount of rollback obtained on roll attitude hold. On establishing a bank angle, some pilots prefer to release the stick before the rolling rate decays to zero. In this event, the roll synchronizer will lock on the roll reference at the time the force on the stick passes below 2 pounds. The airplane overshoot and "rollback" can be as much as 5 degrees to the AFCS reference. If the pilot elects to hold the desired bank angle in control stick steering for a second or two, no rollback will occur. Both techniques may be used. Obtaining roll attitude accuracy will require use of the latter technique.

CONTROL STICK STEERING FEEL

The flight characteristics when on "control stick steering" mode are the same as for the basic airplane except that the control stick experiences a change in feel which is the result of roll rate feedback and mode switching.

When on control stick steering, the stick is referenced to the rate gyros and as rate is developed, a very small amplitude, low frequency stick motion or feel results. Slight stick transients caused by the automatic return to the heading hold mode occur when making small bank angle or heading changes. These transients will be observed whenever

the stick force varies above or below the 2-pound level and the aircraft is at a bank angle of less than 5 degrees. Such transients are normal and result from the design characteristics of the heading hold mode.

PITCH

On control stick steering mode, forces are provided by electrical signals from the accelerometer, pitch rate gyro, and elevator deflection. The resulting electrical "feel" is slightly lower than that of the normal power control. There is less variation in stick force per "g" over the flight regime. The breakout force on control stick steering mode has been reduced to 2 pounds, as compared with 3 pounds on normal power control.

ROLL

Aileron control forces in the control stick steering mode are slightly lower than normal power control forces. Breakout forces are 2 pounds and 3 pounds, respectively.

YAW

The rudder control forces and breakout forces are identical in both modes.

CONTROL STICK STEERING ENGAGE TRANSIENTS DURING AUTO TRIM

The AFCS is equipped with automatic pitch trim which operates within 4 to 6 seconds after establishing a new flight condition. If the pilot should elect to go back on control stick steering before the automatic trim system has stabilized, he may encounter a control stick steering engage transient. This is

DIVE RECOVERY
ALTITUDE LOSS DURING CONSTANT G PULLOUT

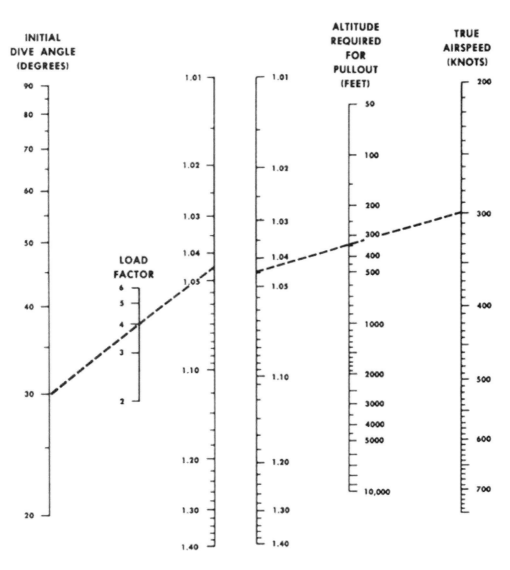

NOTE:

$$\Delta h = 0.08856\, V_T{}^2 \ln\left(\frac{n-\cos\gamma}{n-1}\right)$$

Δh = Altitude Lost (ft)
V_T = True Airspeed (kn)
n = Normal load factor
γ = Flight Path Angle

P-40639-1

Figure 4-4.   Dive Recovery Chart (Sheet 1)

DIVE RECOVERY
ALTITUDE LOSS DURING PILOT REACTION TIME

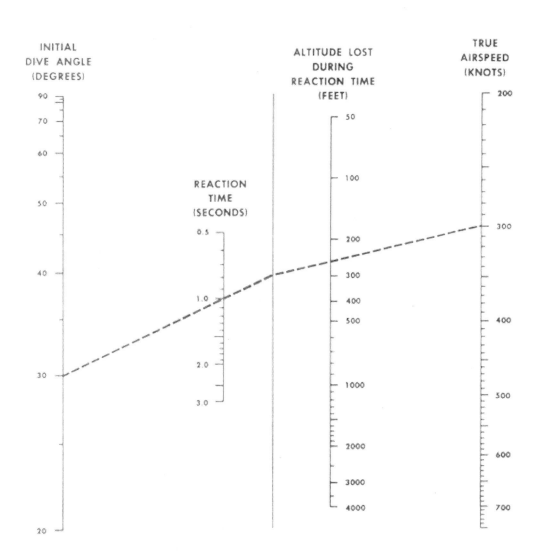

NOTE:

$$\Delta h = 1.689\, V_T \times \Delta T \; Sin \; \gamma$$

Δh = Altitude Lost (ft)
V_T = True Airspeed (kn)

ΔT = Reaction Time (sec.)
γ = Flight Path Angle (deg.)

P-40639-2

Figure 4-4.   Dive Recovery Chart (Sheet 2)

normal and will not occur if the pilot remains out of the CSS mode longer than 6 seconds.

HESITATION OR LOSS OF ROLLING RATE ON PRESELECT HEADING ROLL IN

During the preselect heading roll in, a slight hesitation or loss of rolling rate may occur at approximately 20 degrees of banked attitude. This is a normal phenomenon which is not detrimental to the performance of these circuits.

PRESELECT HEADING "STEPPY" ROLL OUT

During the preselect heading rollout a tendency to roll out in steps or hesitations has been observed. These steps are the result of choosing the optimum gain ratio between heading and roll attitude. The optimum heading to bank ratio is a compromise between a smooth rollout and a short rollout time.

SENSITIVE REGIONS OF PRESELECT HEADING

Abrubt roll transients will occur on preselect heading if the SET knob is adjusted to command a turn in a direction opposite to the turn being made. The same phenomenon will occur if a heading change greater than 180 degrees to the present airplane heading is commanded while the airplane is stabilized in the preselect heading turn. The preselect heading mode is designed to take the shortest path to the selected heading. If the airplane is stabilized in a bank for a left turn and a right turn is commanded, the airplane will immediately roll the opposite direction at maximum rate. Such preselect heading commands should not be initiated while stabilized in a turn.

LONGITUDINAL STICK MOTION DURING AUTOMATIC TRIM

Automatic trim or trim transfer is provided when the pilot relief modes of the AFCS are in use. When the automatic trimming occurs, the stick is observed to move longitudinally. This movement arises from two sources. These are the geared elevator effect and relief of trim. The elevator is mechanically geared to the stabilizer so that any motion of the stabilizer will result in a motion of the elevator. The elevator motion is always in a direction to increase the camber of the horizontal tail. Trim relief occurs when the elevator is no longer holding the airplane in trim and the elevator is returned to the zero position. The stabilizer now maintains airplane trim. In event of a maneuver such as prolonged high "g" turns in attitude hold, automatic trim of the horizontal stabilizer will result in 2 to 3 degrees noseup stabilizer. As speed decreases additional noseup stabilizer is required. At this time, if reversion to level attitude hold is desired, a force up to 15 pounds may be required on the stick, and if released, will cause pitchup. This stick force must be trimmed out on AFCS to approximately zero force prior to releasing stick.

ANGLE-OF-ATTACK RELATIONSHIP

The angle-of-attack relationship for the operational envelope of the aircraft is portrayed in figure 4-5.

ANGLE-OF-ATTACK RELATIONSHIP
SPEEDBRAKES CLOSED

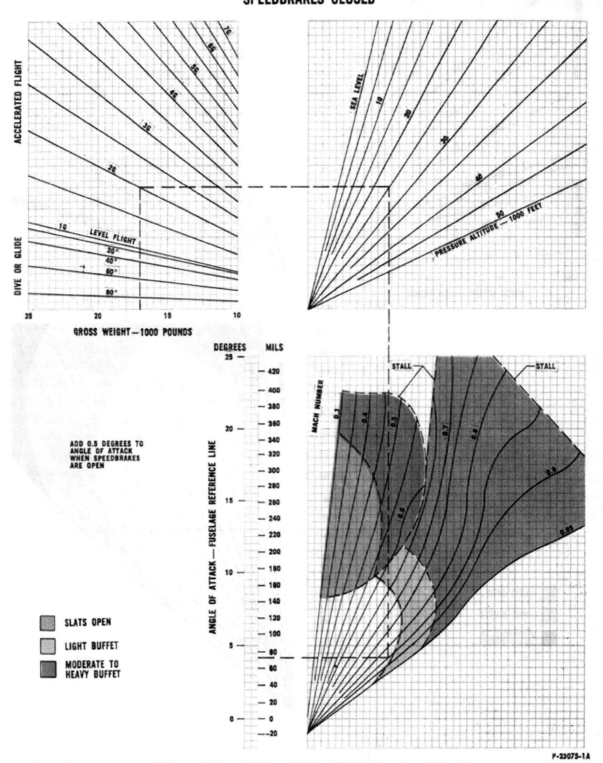

Figure 4-5.   Angle-of-Attack Relationship (Sheet 1)

ANGLE-OF-ATTACK RELATIONSHIP
SPEEDBRAKES CLOSED

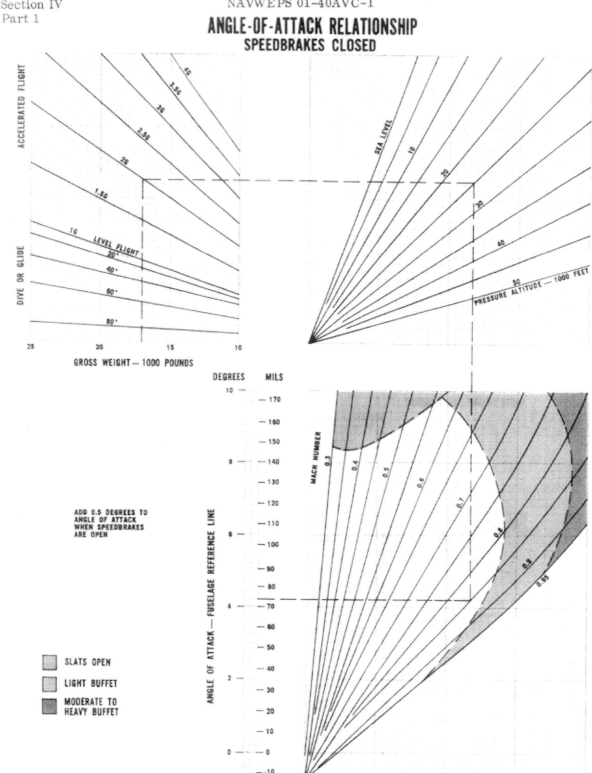

ADD 0.5 DEGREES TO
ANGLE OF ATTACK
WHEN SPEEDBRAKES
ARE OPEN

SLATS OPEN

LIGHT BUFFET

MODERATE TO
HEAVY BUFFET

Figure 4-5.   Angle-of-Attack Relationship (Sheet 2)
Pages 4-23 and 4-24 deleted.

P-25075-2

Changed 15 March 1965

PART 2

FLIGHT PROCEDURES

TABLE OF CONTENTS

TEXT

ILLUSTRATIONS

FLIGHT PROCEDURES

GENERAL

The basic flight procedures contained in this section are for guidance. Where amplification is desired, refer to the appropriate Naval Warfare Publication.

TRANSITION AND FAMILIARIZATION

REQUIREMENTS

Transition and familiarization will be accompublished in accordance with the requirements outlined in section II. This training will be conducted in the replacement air wing or in the squadron, as directed by the appropriate Commander. It is desirable that pilots with no recent jet experience demonstrate their proficiency in two-seated, swept-wing jet trainers prior to flying the A-4 aircraft.

Familiarization flights should be designed to acquaint the pilot with the flight characteristics of the A-4E while it is flown at various attitudes, altitudes, and configurations.

PROCEDURES

The following procedures shall be followed for the first familiarization flight, in addition to those required for other flights:

BEFORE FLIGHT

The chase pilot shall accompany the fam. pilot during his preflight inspection and start.

Changed 15 March 1965

The fam. pilot shall be the lead aircraft on the takeoff.

DURING FLIGHT

Perform those prebriefed maneuvers which will give a general feel of the aircraft, both in the clean and dirty configuration. Stalls and confidence maneuvers will be practiced in designated areas and at altitudes which will ensure straight and level flight above 10,000 feet upon completion.

RETURN TO FIELD AND LANDINGS

The familiar. pilot will lead the flight back to the field. Landings on the first two fam. flights will be monitored by a chase pilot or by a qualified A-4E pilot, at the end of the runway with radio communications. If the approaches are chased, the chase pilot will fly a comfortable yet reasonably close wing position on the fam. pilot throughout all landings and will coach the fam. pilot when necessary. Chase aircraft will not descend below 100 feet, and should follow the configuration changes of the fam. pilot during the approach.

WEATHER CONSIDERATIONS

All familiarization flights will be conducted under conditions which will permit climb and descent in VFR conditions and permit visual contact with the ground at all times.

NORMAL FLIGHT

CRUISE CONTROL

General cruise-control techniques are found in the CWDS and NWDS to NWIP 41-3. Specific cruise-control data for the A-4E is contained in section XI, PERFORMANCE DATA,

of this manual. Additional comments and suggestions follow.

CLIMB

Acceleration to initial climb speed should be effected prior to passing through 1000 feet.

Use the airspeeds recommended in the Performance Data charts to obtain the best rate of climb; however, speeds may be varied 10 knots above or below those stipulated without appreciably affecting climb performance. Maintain MILITARY rpm throughout the climb for best results, observing at all times the engine rpm, exhaust gas temperature, and time limitations as set forth in section XI.

CRUISE

Shortly after leveling at altitude and establishing cruising speed, the pilot should note the fuel used in the climb and check actual fuel flow against the planned consumption rate. The transfer from the external tanks should be commenced. Each pilot should develop his ability to judge distances on the ground from his position and altitude. This sense of distance is quite necessary for accurate navigation at high altitude. Landmarks at considerable distances from the desired track may frequently be used. Of interest is the fact that the blind area beneath the aircraft extends approximately 15 miles in width and 20 miles ahead.

DESCENT

Descents may be made very rapidly by using IDLE power and speedbrakes.

For a maximum range descent, throttle back to IDLE and maintain the gliding speeds recommended in section XI.

Prior to descent, adjust cabin temperature and defrost air as necessary to prevent windshield frost.

FORMATION AND TACTICS

The basic principles and maneuvers promulgated in NWIP 41-3 and NWP 41 (A) are generally applicable. The following instructions apply specifically to the A-4E.

RENDEZVOUS

TURNING RENDEZVOUS

The turning rendezvous is made at 250 KIAS (unless otherwise briefed). After all aircraft are in a loose-trail position, the leader commences a 180 degree turn, using 30 degrees of bank. Each member of the flight waits until the plane ahead passes through a 30 degree bearing from his 12 o'clock position, and then rolls into a 45 degree banked turn to the inside of the leader's turn. When the leader bears 45 degrees relative to the joining aircraft, wingmen ease turn as necessary to maintain the 45 degree bearing until joined either on the preceding aircraft or the flight. Wingmen may add power to gain no greater than a 15-knot speed advantage over the leader, to avoid becoming "sucked." As the aircraft approach the leader, the closure rate is adjusted so as to join on the man ahead or on the inside of the leader's turn. After joining on the inside of the leader, a crossunder is made to the outside, assuming normal wing positions.

CIRCLING RENDEZVOUS

A circling rendezvous is used when aircraft are separated by extended or indefinite distances or time intervals. The pattern is normally a port orbit, using 30 degrees of bank

around a geographic fix. Altitude must be specified and airspeed will be 250 KIAS (unless otherside briefed). Upon arrival, each aircraft flies directly over the fix, slightly below the rendezvous altitude, to provide altitude separation upon entry into the pattern. The first aircraft to arrive should establish the orbit. Subsequent aircraft should be able to sight other aircraft in the circle from directly over the fix. When sighted, a hard turn in the direction of the orbit turn should be made to establish a 45 degree bearing relative to the joining aircraft. Vary the bank as necessary to maintain the bearing until joined. Do not use an airspeed advantage in excess of 15 knots. As the leader is closed, check closure rate so as to stop on the inside of the turn; then cross under to a normal wing position on the outside.

TACAN-CIRCLING RENDEZVOUS

A TACAN-circling rendezvous is used when aircraft are separated by extended or indefinite distances or time intervals and it is not possible to use a geographic fix (at sea or above an overcast). The pattern will be a port-orbit tangent to the designated tacan radial, at a specified distance and altitude. Normally, each pilot flies outbound on the assigned radial, maintaining the briefed climb schedule or rendezvous speed. Upon reaching the join-up circle, each pilot commences a port orbit, using 30 degrees of bank (or more) until visual contact is made with the Flight Leader. If necessary, request the leader's position. The leader will state his position around the orbit, using the figures 1, 2, 3, or 4, corresponding to 000 degrees, 090 degrees, 180 degrees, and 270 degrees, respectively, relative to the designated radial, as shown in Figure 4-6. Each pilot then plans his turn to cut across the orbit for rendezvous. ARA-25 may be used to assist in picking up the leader.

RUNNING RENDEZVOUS

A running rendezvous is effected by closing from the rear on a prebriefed heading or radial. This rendezvous should be accomplished

Changed 15 March 1965

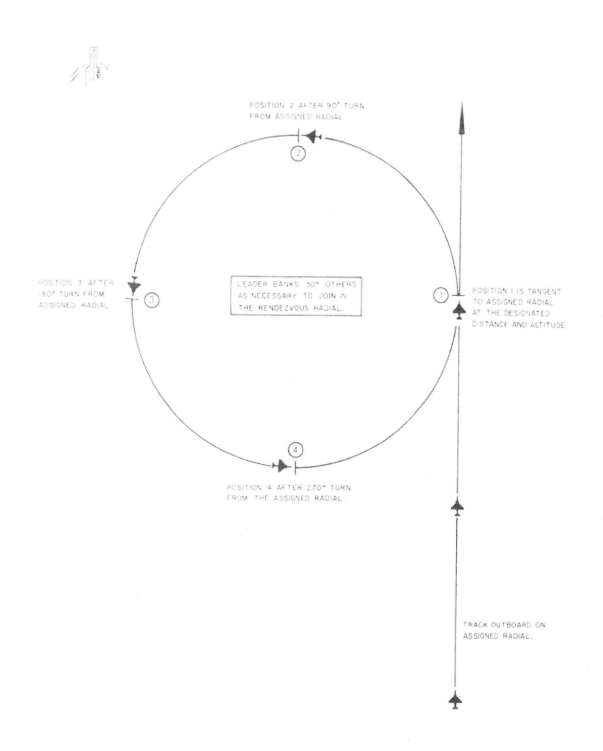

Figure 4-6. TACAN-Circling Rendezvous

with the leader climbing at 250 KIAS and 90 percent (unless otherwise briefed). If it is to be made level, the leader should normally be at 250 KIAS at the designated altitude.

ARA-25 RUNNING RENDEZVOUS

The ARA-25 rendezvous is useful for joining aircraft under all conditions, and particularly during a straight-course running rendezvous. The procedure to be used for the latter is as follows:

1. Trailing aircraft select ADF position on the UHF control.

2. The Flight Leader will transmit a short count every minute, and when climbing, include the passing altitude.

3. Trailing aircraft will position themselves so that as the leader transmits the short counts, the number-1 needle points 5° left or right of the nose position. The number 2 aircraft will hold the leader to his left, number 3 to his right, etc.

4. As the trailing aircraft approach the Flight Leader, they will turn to keep him 5 degrees (left or right respectively) off the nose position. The amount of turn required to maintain the leader in this position will increase as the separation is reduced. Continue until visual sighting is obtained.

TACAN RANGING (A/A)

Note

When operating the TACAN in the A/A mode, distance to the origin of the strongest signal received will be transmitted to as many as five aircraft. This signal is not necessarily the distance to the nearest aircraft.

Air-to-air (A/A) ranging requires cooperating aircraft to be within line of sight distance. This mode enables the TACAN installation to provide range indications between one aircraft and up to five others. TACAN displays normal range and azimuth information in the T/R mode and range information only in the A/A mode (the azimuth indicator, No. 2 needle, rotates continuously).

If A/A operation is desired between two aircraft, the channels selected must be separated by exactly 63 channels, i.e., number 1 aircraft set to channel 64, number 2 aircraft is set at channel 1. Both aircraft must then select A/A on the TACAN function switch with the range between aircraft being displayed on the DME indicator. The maximum lock-on range is 198 miles. However, due to the relative motion of the aircraft, the initial lock-on range will usually be less.

If A/A operation is desired between one lead aircraft and five others, the channel selected by the lead aircraft may be 64, for example. The other five aircraft must be separated by exactly 63 channels, and would be on channel 1. The A/A mode must then be selected on the TACAN selector switch.

ARA-25 CIRCLING RENDEZVOUS

If a circling rendezvous is to be made, the Flight Leader will maintain prebriefed airspeed, 30 degrees of bank, a specified altitude, and broadcast a short count and heading every minute. The trailing aircraft will correct heading to keep the number-1 needle on the nose when the leader transmits. From the change in azimuth of the number-1 needle between short counts, approaching aircraft will be able to determine their proximity to the lead aircraft. Approaching the Flight Leader, the needle will change more degrees in azimuth between counts, requiring larger corrections to keep the leader on the nose. At this time, the leader can probably be detected visually and a standard rendezvous completed.

LOW-VISIBILITY RENDEZVOUS/RENDEZVOUS ON DIFFERENT MODEL AIRCRAFT

This type of rendezvous should be performed in emergency situations only when directed by higher authority or when the urgency of the mission dictates. The rendezvousing aircraft should be flown at a safe maneuvering airspeed. The initial procedures will be as previously described for standard rendezvous. However, the latter stages should be modified as outlined below.

1. Establish radio contact, if possible, and determine indicated airspeed and intended flight path of the aircraft to be joined.

2. Place all lights on BRIGHT and FLASHING (if applicable).

3. Rendezvous about 1000 feet out, slightly aft of abeam (4 or 8 o'clock) the lead aircraft.

4. Cautiously close, while assuring constant nose-to-tail clearance. Maintain a constant relative bearing. Changes in relative bearing will cause foreshortening or lengthening of the aircraft fuselage and make determination of closure rate difficult.

5. A rendezvous on a different model aircraft and/or in low-visibility conditions is extremely conducive to vertigo. A high degree of caution and good judgment must be exercised throughout the rendezvous. At no time should a rapid-closing situation be allowed to develop.

SAFETY RULES FOR RENDEZVOUS

1. During all rendezvous, safety shall be the prime consideration.

2. Keep all aircraft ahead constantly in view and join in order.

3. During rendezvous, only enough stepdown should be used to ensure vertical clearance on the aircraft ahead.

4. When necessary a wingman should abort the rendezvous by leveling his wings, sighting all aircraft ahead, and flying underneath them to the outside of the formation. He should then remain on the outside until all other aircraft have joined.

5. To avoid overshooting, all relative motions should be stopped when joining on an inside wing position. A crossunder to the outside may then be made.

6. During a running rendezvous, use caution in the final stage of join-up, as relative motion is difficult to discern when approaching from astern.

FORMATION

PARADE FORMATION

This formation will normally be employed when operating around home base or in conditions of low visibility. The flight leader is very restricted and must be smooth. It is recommended that all power changes, climbs, glides, and turns be signaled by the leader. Sliding turns by the wingmen are not permitted.

SECTION. Bearing is determined by lining up the dim (colored) wingtip light with the break in the fuselage. Stepdown of about 5 feet is achieved by sighting along the upper side of the leaders wing. Wingtip separation of 5 feet is achieved by closing until airflow over your wing interferes with the leaders wing. Ease out slightly from this position.

FOUR PLANE DIVISION (Fingertip four). No. 3 aircraft flies identical position on leader as No. 2. A check for both aircraft being in position is to line up the tips of opposite wingmans drop tanks. No. 4 lines up canopies of No. 1 and No. 3.

ECHELON. All aircraft are on the same side of the leader. No. 3 and No. 4 line up canopies with No. 2 and leader to maintain position.

CROSSUNDERS. Upon receipt of the crossunder signal, the wingman will acknowledge and commence an arcing crossunder by reducing power, dropping nose and sliding aft to clear the leaders tailpipe and jet wash. As the nose passes approximately 20 feet below and directly aft of the leaders tail, smoothly add power and complete the crossunder by sliding up and forward to the proper wing position. A section crossunder is similar with the wingman passing directly aft of the section leader as the section leader passes directly aft of the division leader. The section leader must ensure that his wingman receives the crossunder signal.

FREE CRUISE FORMATION

The free cruise formation provides better lookout capabilities and maximum freedom of movement for the leader and other members of the element.

SECTION. Bearing is about 35-45 degrees abaft the leader. The wingman will slide out until there is 10 feet nose-to-tail clearance. This will provide about 40 feet between aircraft. Stepdown will be sufficient to clear the leaders jet wash. A suggested gauge is the wingtip lined up on the intake arrow.

DIVISION. The bearing of the section leader is 45 degrees abaft of the leader. In addition, he will maintain 10 feet nose-to-tail clearance from No. 2 aircraft. Each aircraft will use turn radius as his primary means of maintaining position with minimum throttle movement. All members of the element must maintain proper nose-to-tail clearance position so as not to stretch out the formation and so that hand signals may be passed from the leader to all aircraft (No. 4 aircraft receives signals from the section leader).

TAIL CHASE. This formation is to be used as a confidence builder and as a practical application of relative motion. As such, it will only be flown when specifically briefed.

Position for all aircraft is 10 feet nose-to-tail clearance with sufficient stepdown to avoid the jet wash of the preceding aircraft. The tail-on view of the aircraft should be such that the tailpipe is placed on top of the canopy bow and used as a wing position indicator. Power setting used by the leader should be commensurate with the maneuver to be performed and be considerate for the number of aircraft in the formation. Others in the flight should keep in mind that since the leader decelerates first on the climb, a power reduction will probably be necessary initially, and on dives, a throttle increase due to his accelerating first.

AIR REFUELING

BEFORE TAKEOFF

1. Ship-tank switch . . . . OFF

2. Drogue position switch . . . . RET

3. Refueling master switch . . . . OFF

4. Fuel transfer switch. . . . . OFF

5. Light switch . . . . BRT (DAY);
                                        DIM (NIGHT)

6. Gallons delivered indicator set to 0.000

7. Hose jettison switch OFF (FORWARD)

DROGUE EXTENSION

1. Refueling master switch . . . . ON

2. Drogue switch . . . . EXT

NOTE

Be prepared for small trim changes as the drogue is extended.

3. Drogue position will read . . . . . EXT, WHEN
                               DROGUE REACHES FULL
                                     TRAIL POSITION

4. Ship-tank switch . . . . TO STORE, FOR OVER
                               300-GALLON TRANSFER

NOTE

High-power settings facilitate fuel transfer from the wing tank to store and from the drop tanks to wing tanks.

NORMAL OPERATION

When the amber light on the tanker refueling store is illuminated, the aircraft to be fueled maneuvers into position for probe-drogue engagement. After the probe is engaged in the drogue the receiving aircraft must move forward (3 to 6 feet in relation to the tanker) until the store amber light goes off. As long as the two aircraft maintain this relationship fuel transfer may be made. Actual refueling will be indicated by the illumination of a green light on the store. Fuel flow through the probe to the wing and fuselage tanks is automatic.

If the drop tanks are to be fueled, the drop tanks switch must be positioned at FLIGHT REFUEL. Fuel flow will then be through the probe to the drop tanks, wing tank, and fuselage tank simultaneously.

CAUTION

On all receiver aircraft that have the Air Refueling Store Control Panel installed in the left-hand console, ensure that the SHIP-TANK switch is in the OFF position before engaging in air refueling. On all aircraft that have A-4 ASC 209 incorporated, ensure that the EMERGENCY WING TANK TRANSFER switch is in the OFF position before engaging in air refueling.

STOPPING FUEL TRANSFER

To halt fuel transfer to the receiver at any time; turn fuel transfer switch to OFF.

Note

Refueling cannot be stopped by placing the refueling master switch in the OFF position. Refueling will stop if the receiver aircraft backs off enough for the amber light to come on or if the probe disengages. In either case, the drogue position indicator window will change from TRA to EXT.

To halt fuel transfer to the store, turn SHIP-TANK switch to OFF.

DROGUE RETRACTION

1. Fuel transfer switch . . . . OFF

2. Airspeed. . . . . 250 KIAS or less

3. Drogue switch . . . . RET

Note

If the drogue cannot be fully retracted at about 250 knots IAS, reducing airspeed to 230 knots or less should permit full retraction.

4. When drogue position indicator reads RET, place the refueling master switch to OFF.

Note

The refueling master switch may be moved to OFF at any time after the drogue has extended. In this case the tanker store propeller will feather automatically only after the drogue has returned to the retracted position.

TRANSFER FROM STORE TO WING

If it is desired to transfer fuel from the refueling store to the wing tank, place the SHIP TANK switch to FROM STORE. This will cause both drop tank air shutoff valves and the refueling store shutoff valve to open, allowing all external tanks to be air pressurized by the engine. Fuel will then flow from the drop tanks and the refueling store to the wing tank. Transfer of fuel from the store to the wing tank is very slow but will transfer fuel at about the rate that fuel is burned unless high power settings are used.

Note

If transfer of fuel from the drop tanks cannot be stopped by placing the drop tank pressurization switch on the engine control panel to OFF, check to see that the ship tank switch on the air refueling control panel is in the OFF position. If this switch is in the FROM STORE position, transfer from the drop tanks and refueling store is automatic and pressurization will be continuous unless the ship tank switch is placed at OFF.

DUMPING FUEL

An electrically operated fuel dump valve is located on the bottom of the refueling store. To dump fuel, first depress the spring-loaded lever guard assembly then raise the

TANKER PANEL CONFIGURATION PRIOR TO AIR REFUELING

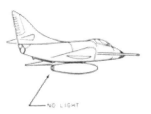

* DUMP LIGHT

— NO LIGHT

REFUELING MASTER SWITCH --------- OFF
FUEL COUNTER ---------------------- 000
DROGUE POSITION INDICATOR ---- RET
DROGUE POSITION SWITCH -------- RET
TRANSFER SWITCH ------------------ OFF
HOSE JETTISON SWITCH (OFF-FORWARD)
LIGHT SWITCH ------------ (DAYTIME) BRT
SHIP TANK SWITCH ----------------- OFF

* BY ACCESSORY CHANGE NO.I

DROGUE EXTENDED-NOT ENGAGED

REFUELING MASTER SWITCH --------- ON
DROGUE POSITION SWITCH -------- EXT
DROGUE POSITION INDICATOR ---- EXT

AMBER LIGHT

NOTE
ON POSITION OF REFUELING MASTER
SWITCH UNFEATHERS RAM AIR
TURBINE FOR STORES HYDRAULIC
PRESSURE.

ENGAGED — BEFORE FUEL TRANSFER

AMBER LIGHT

DROGUE POSITION INDICATOR ------TRA

NOTE
COUPLING OF PROBE WITH DROGUE
WHILE TRANSFER SWITCH IS OFF
CAUSES DROGUE POSITION INDICATOR
TO SHOW (TRA) MEANING READY
TO TRANSFER.

FUEL TRANSFER

TRANSFER SWITCH -------------- TRANS
FUEL COUNTER ----- (COUNTS GALLONS)

GREEN LIGHT

NOTE
GALLONS COUNTER CONFIRMS
FUEL TRANSFER TO TANKER
PILOT. GREEN LIGHT CONFIRMS
FUEL TRANSFER TO RECEIVER
PILOT.

AVC-1-1 P-25049-1A

Figure 4-7. Tanker Operation— Air Refueling (Sheet 1)

DISENGAGEMENT

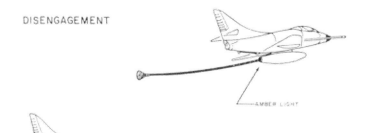

AMBER LIGHT

REFUELING MASTER SWITCH --------- ON
TRANSFER SWITCH --------------- OFF
DROGUE POSITION INDICATOR ------ EXT

REFUELING MASTER SWITCH --------- ON
DROGUE POSITION SWITCH --------- RET
DROGUE POSITION INDICATOR ------ RET

AFTER DROGUE RETRACT
REFUELING MASTER SWITCH --------- OFF

DROGUE RETRACT

NO LIGHT

FUEL DUMP

NOTE
FUEL DUMPING SHOULD ALWAYS BE DONE
PRIOR TO ANY ARRESTED LANDING
EITHER AFLOAT OR ASHORE.

* DUMP LIGHT

REFUELING MASTER SWITCH ------- DUMP
(ALL OTHER SWITCHES SAME AS
NORMAL PANEL CONFIGURATION)

* BY ACCESSORY CHANGE NO. 1

HOSE JETTISON SWITCH HOSE JETTISON
TRANSFER SWITCH .... OFF
REFUELING MASTER SWITCH..(CONDITION)
DROGUE POSITION SWITCH....(CONDITION)
DROGUE POSITION INDICATOR ......EXT

HOSE AND DROGUE JETTISON - EMERGENCY

NOTE
5 TO 20 SECOND TIME DELAY
IS A SAFETY FEATURE.

NOTE
JETTISONING CUTS OFF ALL STORE
POWER EXCEPT POWER TO SHIP TANK
SWITCH AND TO DUMP FUEL. THEREFORE,
FUEL DUMP IS POSSIBLE AFTER
JETTISONING.

WARNING

DO NOT MOVE HOSE JETTISON
SWITCH FROM HOSE JETTISON
POSITION AFTER JETTISONING.

AVC-1-1 P-25049-2A

Figure 4-7. Tanker Operation—Air Refueling (Sheet 2)

master switch from the spring-loaded safety position and position at DUMP.

Note

On rare occasions, fuel dumped from the store may reenter and accumulate in the aft section of the store and may create a fire hazard if the store is operated after dumping.

BEFORE LANDING

1. Ship-tank switch . . . . OFF

2. Drogue switch . . . . RET

3. Drogue position indicator . . . . OFF

4. Refueling master switch . . . . . OFF

5. Fuel transfer switch . . . . OFF

6. Drop tanks switch . . . . OFF

JETTISONING THE FUELING STORE

The air refueling store may be jettisoned electrically in the same manner as other droppable external stores. (Refer to ARMAMENT, section I.)

EMERGENCY OPERATION

Refer to Emergency Procedures, section V.

TANKER SAFETY PRECAUTIONS

WARNING

• Be sure that the ship-tank switch is OFF during catapulting and arrested landings. The integral wing tank pressure increases to 6 psi above

ambient when the ship-tank switch is in the TO STORE position. The addition of the 6 psi static pressure to the accelerations induced by catapulting and arresting would impose severe loads on the tank surfaces.

• When the ship-tank switch is in the TO STORE position, overpressurization of the wing tank is possible if fuel covers the fuel vent outlet in the tank. This condition will exist during negative-g operation, and when the airplane is in a nosedown attitude.

The following is a summary of the restrictions applicable to flight with the wing fuel tank pressurized:

1. Aircraft velocity not to exceed 400 KIAS

2. No catapulting

3. No arrested landings

4. Coordinated turns only

5. Aircraft load factor limits $N_z = +.1$ to $+2.0$

6. No air refueling.

WARNING

• Do not start the turbine or extend or retract the drogue when over populated areas or when other aircraft are close abeam or behind.

• Do not extend the drogue after it has been retracted when a hydraulic leak has been observed.

• Do not extend the drogue if there is any evidence of a possible electrical failure.

• Do not energize the turbine after dumping fuel unless failure to provide fuel will place another aircraft in jeopardy.

Changed 15 March 1965

- Do not actuate the speedbrakes during any part of the refueling operation.

- Once the hose jettison switch is actuated to its HOSE JETTISON position for emergency jettisoning in flight, it must not be moved back to its forward OFF position. Inadvertent cycling of this switch will cause a dangerous condition in the store.

STORE LIMITS

The following limitations apply to the store:

1. Maximum speed for unfeathering is 300 KIAS; for extension of the drogue and refueling, it is 300 KIAS or .80 IMN. The recommended unfeathering and extension speed for training is 250 KIAS or less.

2. Maximum speed for drogue retraction is 250 KIAS. (If the drogue will not retract fully at 250 KIAS, slow to 230 KIAS or less and recycle drogue.

3. Conduct refueling operations in straight and level flight whenever possible and, if possible, do not select TO STORE until 50 gallons of fuel has been delivered to the receiver.

PILOT TECHNIQUE

Air refueling engagements can be accomplished at any altitude within a wide range of airspeed. Successful engagements have been made between sea level and 32,000 feet at airspeeds between 190 and 300 knots. The optimum airspeed for engagement is approximately 230 KIAS. Use of optimum airspeed will assist the receiver in escaping heavy buffeting caused by the tanker slipstream and jet exhaust.

Closure rates above 5 knots may induce hose whip.

If hose whipping or kinking occurs during normal receiver hookup, disengagement should be made immediately and the store be inspected for hose tension regulator malfunction.

Thermal turbulence from the deck may be annoying for hookups at very low altitudes due to oscillatory drogue motion.

The receiver should start the engagement approach from behind and below the tanker. The receiver's flight path prior to engagement should follow the angle of the trailing drogue hose, using the drogue only as a target reference during the final 3 or 4 feet prior to contact. The receiver pilot will notice increased pitch sensitivity at this point. A slight throttle advance may be necessary to maintain a definite closing rate during the final 3 feet. To facilitate engagement at night, an air refueling probe light is mounted in the outboard leading edge of the right airscoop and is controlled by a switch located on the wedge outboard of the right-hand console.

After engaging, the receiver airplane must move forward so that a minimum of 4 feet of hose takeup occurs, starting the fuel transfer. The store hose is striped each two feet for the last 20 feet to be unreeled. The receiver refers to these stripes to assist in maintaining a stable distance from the tanker during refueling. It is never necessary to close to a point where the stripes are not visible. The receiver should be flown so that the hose is centered laterally and maintained just above the lower centerline lip of the store's trailing edge, but not riding on or touching the lower lip. This optimum position is approximately 2 feet below the drogue's normal trailing position. This position is the most comfortable position for the receiver to avoid severe buffeting. Once the engagement has been accomplished, it is not difficult to fly the receiver dead astern with a 2-foot lateral tolerance, even in rough air or in turns up to 30 degrees bank angle.

Mild buffeting will be felt by the receiver, but is should not be uncomfortable. Occasional mild fuel sprays of short duration may hit the receiver, but the only adverse result is possibly a greasy film on the windshield. Disconnecting is accomplished by the tanker holding constant power while the receiver retards throttle. The hose reel will unwind the takeup until it reaches the end of the hose travel and the receiver will break free.

WARNING

Do not engage, or remain engaged to, a steadily leaking drogue. The leaking fuel will be ingested into the engine and may ignite and explode. The small amount of fuel that is leaking momentarily during plug in and disengagement is not considered dangerous.

FLIGHT PROCEDURES—REFUELING TRAINING AND REFRESHER

Refueling training should be accomplished at various altitudes in accordance with current directives.

PRIOR TO REFUELING

1. After rendezvous has been effected, the Flight Leader of the receiver aircraft will position his flight in loose echelon away from the tanker on the side opposite the tanker escort, if assigned. The Flight Leader will then pass the lead to the tanker pilot if applicable.

The flight leader's position will be abeam the tanker with at least 200 feet separation in case a store turbine blade flies off during unfeathering.

2. When the flight is in position, the leader of the receiver aircraft or tanker escort (if assigned) will signal the tanker to unfeather (1-finger turn-up signal).

3. The tanker will unfeather, ensuring airspeed is 250 KIAS or less.

4. The Flight Leader (or tanker escort) will indicate by a "thumbs-up" or "down" whether or not the turbine unfeathered. If the turbine does not unfeather, the tanker will secure store and not make further attempts to unfeather, unless failure to provide fuel would place receiver aircraft in jeopardy.

5. If the turbine unfeathers on the first attempt, the tanker responds to the "thumbs-up" signal of the Flight Leader (or escort) by extending the drogue.

6. As the drogue extends, the flight should fall back so that leader is abeam and level with the drogue, with about 100 feet lateral separation. Drogue extension will slow tanker speed. The tanker should adjust power to maintain desired refueling speed. 230 KIAS is recommended; however, plug-ins may be made anywhere in the store operational envelope of 200 to 300 KIAS. All aircraft will remain clear of the area directly behind the drogue during extension or retraction, in the event the hose and drogue separate from the store. If drogue extension is not snubbed as it approaches the fully extended position, do not attempt plug-ins.

7. The tanker pilot, as leader of the refueling formation, has the primary responsibility for maintaining a good lookout for other aircraft, although other members of the flight are responsible for assisting to the maximum extent possible.

8. Any evidence of a hydraulic leak from the buddy store during refueling operations should immediately be reported to the tanker pilot and the store secured.

9. Do not turn air conditioning to RAM while inflight refueling. If fuel is injected into the engine from a leaking drogue, it may appear in the cockpit as white smoke. Immediately disengage if smoke appears in the cockpit.

10. If tanker escort is assigned, the escort pilot will fly a close parade position on the tanker throughout the evolution (except during moment of unfeathering turbine) and inform tanker when the dumping has been completed. The escort will watch for store malfunctions and provide assistance in case of tanker radio failure. Tanker escort, when assigned, will give any necessary signals for actuation of turbine and drogue. The escort will not take part in the refueling sequence when another formation is refueling.

Changed 1 November 1965

REFUELING

1. The leader should detach and move into a position 20 feet behind and below the drogue, on a plane with the trailing hose, to minimize turbulence from the tanker's wake. Call " , lining up," before sliding into position behind the tanker. Observe amber light on tanker store, indicating store may be engaged. If light is not on, use caution during engagement, as hose tensioning and reel-in may be inoperative. The most likely cause, however, is a burned-out bulb. Trim the aircraft slightly nose-down to remove any slop from the elevator control system, and move forward and up the hose reference until the tip of the probe is 5 to 10 feet directly behind the drogue. Pause here long enough to get stabilized, then add enough power to close and engage the drogue at a closure speed of about 3 knots. Either the tanker or the probe and drogue may be used as the primary visual reference; however, both must be perceived to make consistent and safe engagements. Closing speeds in excess of 5 knots may cause hose-whip, with ensuing damage to probe, hose and drogue, or both. Also, if misaligned at high closure speeds, damage to radome, nose section, pitot tube, or canopy may occur. If the drogue is missed, stay below the drogue and back straight out until the drogue is in sight. Avoid looking up too high for the drogue as the pilot may unconciously pull back on the stick and climb into the drogue. Instead, use the tanker as a reference until safely aft of the drogue.

2. After engaging the drogue, continue to push in the hose until the amber light is out, and then call " , contact." The last 20 feet of hose to unreel from the store has a white stripe every two feet. At least two stripes must be pushed into the store before the transfer will occur. Do not fly so close that no stripes are visible. Maintain a position so that if some opening between the tanker and the receiver occurs, the transfer will not be interrupted. This position should also be along the general reference of the hose before plug-in and will keep the nose centered slightly above the lip of the aft end of the store.

WARNING

To preclude possible engine flameout and/or explosion, the following procedures should be used during receiver hookup: After the receiver pilot has made hookup, the tanker pilot will place the transfer switch momentarily to the transfer position and transfer 2 to 4 gallons of fuel to test for proper probe/drogue coupling. If no transmissions are heard from the receiver or the receiver does not disengage, reinitiate transfer. Excessive fuel on the windscreen, smoke or mist in the cockpit, and rising EGT are indications of possible impending engine explosion due to fuel ingestion in the engine intakes. If excessive fuel leakage is noted, the receiver pilot should notify the tanker operator immediately, retard throttle to idle and disengage from the tanker. If the IFR probe valve continues to leak excessive fuel after disengagement, full right rudder should be applied until the valve has fully closed. This will tend to cause the fuel to flow outboard of the engine intake ducts. Do not attempt further plug-ins unless low fuel state so dictates. Inspect the probe and drogue for malfunction after landing.

3. Breakaway is accomplished by the receiver reducing power in order to open from the tanker at about 3 knots. Back straight away and down, following the line of the trailing hose. Stay behind the drogue until all members of the flight are sighted. To facilitate this, it is necessary that all members of the flight properly maintain their position in echelon. When the receiver aircraft is clear of the area behind the hose and drogue, call " , clear."

4. After breaking away, the leader will move to the opposite side of the tanker, where he will supervise the refueling, giving help as necessary. After the leader is clear of the drogue, the No. 2 man in the flight will move into position and make his plug-in. He will then disengage and join the leader in loose, outside echelon, as before. Each member in turn will make plug-ins and upon completion will move to the next position on the leader.

AFTER REFUELING

1. When all members of the flight have successfully completed the hookups and are clear of the drogue, the Flight Leader will signal to secure the store by moving the flight

forward in echelon until the leader is again abeam the tanker, with at least 200 feet separation. When the tanker pilot observes the entire flight (and escort) in this position, he will retract the drogue and feather the air turbine. The Flight Leader (escort, if assigned) will indicate that the turbine is feathered by giving a "thumbs-up."

2. Upon completion of refueling, the Flight Leader should resume lead of his flight, breaking away from the tanker in an easy turn until well clear. The tanker maintains straight and level flight until adequate separation from the receiver aircraft is assured. To ensure safe separation, an altitude differential should be maintained.

MISSION REFUELING

The procedures for mission refueling are covered in detail in the A-4 NWDS to NWIP 41-3.

NIGHT FLYING PROCEDURES

Night flying procedures are identical to day procedures with the exceptions given below. Night lighting doctrine is contained in Section III.

NIGHT RENDEZVOUS

Rendezvous at night are similar to daytime, except that in the final portion the pilot should try to close to a position slightly astern rather than directly toward the plane ahead. Pilots must be sure not to carry excess airspeed in the rendezvous. The leader must maintain a constant airspeed and altitude.

Whenever it is necessary for a pilot to go to the outside of the rendezvous, he will report this to the Flight Leader. Stay on the outside of the rendezvous until the remaining members of the flight have rendezvoused and then add power as necessary to join up. Pilots

joining from astern will move out to the side in order to enhance their judgment of closure rates, as well as to ensure safe clearance.

NIGHT FORMATION

It is important to maintain the correct bearing so that the wing-man can be seen by the leader. Ensure that wing-tip clearance is maintained at all times. The pilot should not fly so close that he feels uncomfortable. Avoid staring at the aircraft ahead and getting fixation on its lights. Turns will be made as in instrument conditions, by rolling around the leader's axis.

Where no light signal exists for a certain maneuver, the radio should be used. Speedbrake signals may be given on the radio by transmitting "flight, speedbrakes-now." Channel changes will be given on the radio and should be acknowledged before and after making the shift.

NIGHT REFUELING

Night refueling is performed in essentially the same manner as during the day. The tanker should have all lights on BRT and STDY, except the anti-collision lights. The buddy-store lights should be on DIM. The tanker lights illuminate enough of the tanker and the drogue to allow the receiver pilot sufficient light for the approach lineup. The receiver pilot should request adjustment of the tanker lights to meet his requirements.

Take up an initial position on the tanker and use the same procedures described in this section for day refueling. When in position aft of the drogue, correct altitude can be determined by the receiver pilot sensing the tanker's jet-wash on his vertical stabilizer. The receiver-aircraft lights should be on BRT and STDY. The receiver's probe light and/or fuselage light will provide sufficient illumination to see the drogue from 10-20 feet aft.

Changed 15 March 1965

The tendency in night air-refueling is to start the approach too far aft. This makes it very difficult to judge relative motion and usually results in a high closure rate.

BANNER TOW TARGET OPERATION

1. Takeoff and climbout.

a. Two methods of towplane/towline positioning are recommended for banner drag takeoff. The first method is to lay the towline out straight down the runway. This method is the most expeditious, requiring about 3 minutes for layout and hookup before takeoff. However, this procedure does deprive the tow airplane of 2000 feet of runway for takeoff. The second method recommended is to lay the towline out on the runway in a squat S-pattern along the tow aircraft takeoff run. This procedure requires slightly more time to rig, but allows use of almost the entire runway for takeoff. For additional information concerning takeoff methods for banner targets, refer to Section III of NAVAER 28-10A-501 revised 15 September 1959: Handbook Operation and Service Instruction for Aerial Targets and Associated Equipment.

b. Utilize normal takeoff configuration, one-half flaps and trim settings appropriate for aircraft gross weight.

Note

On a standard day and at sea level elevation, with the airplane in the clean configuration or with empty 300-gallon external fuel tanks, the banner will drag approximately 4500 feet along the runway before liftoff. With full 300-gallon external fuel tanks, approximately 7500 feet is required for banner liftoff.

c. Accomplish liftoff at 145 KIAS and climbout at 150-160 KIAS to 5000 feet altitude with one-half (1/2) flaps. Continue climb to mission altitudes above 5000 feet in the clean configuration at 170-180 KIAS.

Note

With full 300-gallon external fuel tanks, the rate of climb above 15,000 feet is reduced to less than 750 feet per minute.

2. Target Presentation

a. In the clean configuration or with two empty 300-gallon external fuel tanks the recommended target presentation airspeeds and altitudes are 160-220 KIAS from 5,000 feet to 20,000 feet.

b. With two full 300-gallon external fuel tanks the recommended target presentation airspeeds and altitudes are 160-220 KIAS from 5000 feet to 15,000 feet.

3. Letdown and Banner Release

a. Perform letdown from mission altitude at 170-180 KIAS.

b. To drop the banner and towline, stabilize aircraft altitude and hold 140-150 KIAS with one-half (1/2) flaps extended.

Note

Safe and accurate banner releases can be made under the above conditions from 500 feet altitude. Banner droop under the tow airplane will then be approximately 250 feet.

c. When over the drop zone, release the towline and banner electrically from the Mk 51 bombrack by utilizing the armament primary bomb release circuit.

FLIGHT TEST PROCEDURES

TEST PILOTS

The most important single factor in getting good test flights on the aircraft is to pick experienced, conscientious test pilots. Commanding officers will designate, in writing, those aviators within their command who are currently eligible to perform this duty.

TEST FLIGHTS AND FORMS

Test flights will be performed when directed by, and in accordance with, the directives of BUWEPS, Type Commanders, or other appropriate authority. Functional flight test requirements and test forms are contained in the A-4E Periodic Maintenance Requirements Manual.

MANUAL FUEL CONTROL CHECK

Before takeoff on test flights (after a major check, fuel control change, etc.) perform the following manual fuel control check:

        Throttle . . . .   65 Percent RPM

        Fuel Control . . . .   Select Manual

        Fuel Control Light . . ON, and Engine
                                Indications That
                                Switch Over Has
                                Occurred

        Throttle . . . . . Advance to Minimum
                                of 1.95 EPR

        Fuel Control . . . . Select Primary at
                                85 percent RPM
                                or above.

        Fuel Control Light . . OFF, and Engine
                                Indications That
                                Switchover has
                                Occurred

FLIGHT CONTROL POWER DISCONNECT TEST PROCEDURE

WARNING

Do not attempt flight control disconnect test if operating on emergency generator except in case of an emergency.

This procedure is intended as an addition to A-4 flight test procedure and should not be considered to take the place thereof. It is designed to be performed in conjunction with the normal flight test procedure. Items repeated, which are part of the normal procedure are those which are exceedingly important in the proper performance of this test or those where additional checks are necessary which would not be performed in the normal flight test procedure.

GROUND TEST PROCEDURE

NORMAL TRIM CONTROL CHECK

After start, when all systems normally required for flight are functioning on aircraft power, the normal trim control checks of the elevator, rudder, and ailerons should be performed to ensure proper operation. During the actuation of these trim systems the pilot should be assisted by ground personnel, using predetermined signals, to ensure correlation between trim settings and cockpit trim indicators.

MAXIMUM AILERON FOLLOWUP TAB DEFLECTION

In addition to the normal trim system check, when a power disconnect is to be performed, the aileron followup tab may be checked at the 3-degree up and the 3-degree down position. This is the maximum deflection allowable for intentional, inflight, power disconnect, as an aid to visually determining this limit prior to attempting a disconnect when airborne. Three degrees deflection of the followup tab (from faired with the aileron) is difficult to determine from the cockpit, even when on the ground. Therefore ground personnel should be briefed as to what is required, and using a means of definite measurement, assist the pilot in obtaining these settings (3-degree deflection of the followup tab from faired with the aileron is approximately one-fifth of one-inch.)

Checking the followup tab at the 3 degrees up and down position prior to taxi is not part of the required ground check procedure for a power disconnect flight, but is suggested to aid the pilot in establishing a picture of what 3-degree followup tab deflection may look like in flight prior to attempting a disconnect.

RIGGING CHECK

Prior to taxi, and as part of the normal trim and rigging test, the following procedures should be accomplished:

   1. Assisted by ground personnel, trim the port aileron to faired with the wing.

   2. Check the aileron followup tab a maximum of 3 degrees (1/5-inch) deflection (from faired with the aileron) when the aileron is faired with the wing.

   3. Check the starboard aileron for faired with the wing when the port aileron is faired.

   4. Check the control stick for centering (vertical) when the ailerons are faired with the wings.

   5. Actuate all controls for maximum deflection and check for ease of movement to ensure that all systems are connected and functioning normally.

Note

If the control system does not meet the requirements of the above checks, it is probably out of rig and should not be flown.

AIRBORNE TEST PROCEDURE

WIND CONDITIONS AT LANDING FIELD

A crosswind component of 7 knots will be considered maximum for a safe disconnect landing. The disconnect test will not be performed if a stronger component exists. When contacting the tower or ground control, the pilot should request the wind in degrees magnetic, knots, and other pertinent information such as forecast wind shift, duty runway, or into-wind runway availability, and gusts. It should always be anticipated that disconnecting will result in reduced control of the airplane, and if any condition exists which would further complicate the landing, the test shall not be performed.

After contact with the tower has been established and the duty runway has been determined proceed as follows:

   1. Establish altitude of 25,000 feet, with 1500 pounds maximum fuel load. Twenty-five thousand feet is established as a minimum safe altitude for performing the test in the event of a momentary uncontrollable rate of roll.

Fifteen hundred pounds of fuel remaining normally assures that the main wing tank is empty and establishes the optimum center of gravity position for disconnecting the flight control hydraulic system. The wing tank should be empty to preclude fuel displacement to the descending wing and resultant increase in rate-of-roll.

Under NO circumstances will the disconnect test be performed with an asymmetrical wing loading. It may be necessary to perform the

Changed 15 March 1965

test with external drop tanks installed, but it should be assured that they are empty prior to disconnect.

2. Trim for hands-off, straight and level flight at 300 knots IAS. The airplane should be in the clean configuration.

3. Visually check the followup tab for 3 degrees maximum deflection from faired with the aileron (port aileron). Three degrees deflection of the followup tab from faired with the aileron is approximately one-fifth of one-inch and may be determined during the normal preflight check as outlined previously. This 3-degree limit applies to all present models of the airplane. If the followup tab is deflected more than 3 degrees when the airplane is trimmed for hands-off, straight and level flight at 300 knots, the hydraulic system should not be disconnected, as an excessive rate-of-roll will probably occur.

4. Without retrimming, slow to 200 knots IAS. Caution must be exercised not to retrim the airplane during deceleration. The rate-of-roll check must be performed at 300 knots with the trim necessary for hands-off, straight and level flight at that speed. The deceleration to 200 knots for the actual disconnect is for safety, in that an excessive rate-of-roll is more controllable at slower speeds, and there is less chance of over-stressing the airplane should an erratic condition occur.

Deceleration should be accomplished without the use of speedbrakes if possible. The speedbrakes are directly connected to the elevator control and a possible trim change may occur due to extension and retraction.

5. Pull power disconnect handle. The power boost disconnect should be pulled smartly to assure proper disconnect. Pulling the handle slowly may result in a partial disconnect which could cause a hazardous flight condition or erratic rate-of-roll.

Normally, the disconnect cable will extend approximately 12 inches for a complete disconnect, and two slight jolts will be felt, evidencing the disconnect of the aileron and elevator hydraulic systems in that order. Once again it is emphasized that the boost disconnect handle should be pulled smartly, and no hesitation between each system disconnect should be attempted.

After disconnect, no trim should be used if the airplane is controllable. If an excessive rate-of-roll or pitch condition exists at the present speed, and the pilot considers that the airplane may become uncontrollable at higher airspeed, no attempt should be made to perform the rate-of-roll check. In this condition, if the pilot feels able to control an excessive rate-of-roll at 200 knots, the test may be performed the same as for the 300 knot test; but the angle of bank should not be allowed to exceed 30 degrees. Although not as desirable as if performed at 300 knots, this rate-of-roll will enable ground personnel to make some corrective adjustment. In this case, after the rate-of-roll has been recorded, the airplane should be "slow-flighted" in the landing configuration and retrimmed if necessary for a safe landing. Speeds in excess of 200 knots should not be used for the remainder of the flight.

In the event the airplane becomes uncontrollable after disconnect at 200 knots, an emergency condition exists and the test should be abandoned. Trim should be used immediately in an attempt to stop the roll and regain control, and the throttle should be retarded to idle to reduce airspeed.

In the case of excessive nosedown pitch, it should be remembered that use of the speedbrakes may cause an increased nosedown tendency due to the design of the system.

6. Accelerate to 300 knots IAS. Under normal conditions the rate-of-roll check should be performed at 300 knots, since the airplane was trimmed for hands-off, straight and level flight at this speed, and it is the rate-of-roll after disconnect at this speed that is to be determined.

During the acceleration, straight and level flight should be maintained without use of the trim system since this will destroy the conditions for a proper rate-of-roll check. If the control forces become so severe during acceleration that control of the airplane during an excessive rate-of-roll is doubtful, the test should be discontinued or performed as described under step 5.

7. Record rate-of-roll at 300 knots. When stabilized at 300 knots IAS, wings level, time the rate-of-roll by means of a stopwatch and reference to the gyro horizon. Do not allow the airplane to exceed 60 degrees of bank. An angle of bank in excess of 60 degrees may allow the airplane to "fall through," increase bank rapidly, and in the case of an excessive rate-of-roll, cause the airplane to become uncontrollable before corrective action can be taken.

Return the airplane to the wings level attitude without use of trim, if possible, and repeat the test to ensure an accurate rate-of-roll recording. Four and one-half degrees per second, the maximum allowable, is a very slow rate-of-roll, and an error in timing is possible during the initial attempt.

8. Retrim for hands-off, straight and level flight at 300 knots. After determining the direction and rate-of-roll, the airplane should be returned to straight and level flight and retrimmed to maintain this condition.

9. After the airplane has been retrimmed at 300 knots for as near hands-off, straight and level flight as possible, note and record the position of the follow-up tab in relation to the aileron in relation to the wind. Decelerate and perform a simulated landing approach. In decelerating prior to performing the simulated approach, use should be made of all systems which may be needed in the actual landing (speedbrakes, landing gear, flaps) to determine any adverse effects they might have on the control of the airplane with the 300 knots, post-disconnect aileron trim setting.

Safety is of primary importance throughout the entire disconnect test, and if aileron trim is necessary after disconnect or during the landing for any reason, the pilot should not hesitate to retrim.

Upon completion of the flight, a notation should be made on the Discrepancy Report (Yellow Sheet OPNAV 3750) that the hydraulic system was disconnected; and of the direction and rate-of-roll, if any, and any adverse flight conditions resulting from the disconnect. This information and any pertinent remarks should be entered in the airplane log book and may aid other pilots or maintenance personnel in the future.

HYDRAULIC POWER DISCONNECT WITH ASYMMETRIC LOADINGS

Disconnect tests should not be performed with asymmetric loadings. However, in the event that an actual hydraulic power disconnect must be made with asymmetric wing or store loadings, the following recommendations are made:

1. Speed must be reduced to less than 200 knots IAS prior to disconnecting.

2. After disconnect, excessive longitudinal stick motions must be avoided.

3. Crosswind landings must be made upwind or downwind, whichever is required to put the crosswind component under the heavy or loaded wing.

4. A final approach speed of 115 knots IAS must be considered an absolute minimum, as it represents the minimum control speed with a power failure and a 1200-pound asymmetric load. The initial approach airspeed should be a minimum of 140 knots IAS, with a minimum final approach and touchdown airspeed of 125 knots IAS.

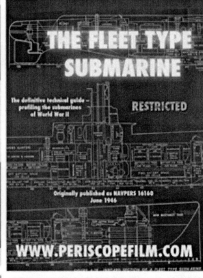

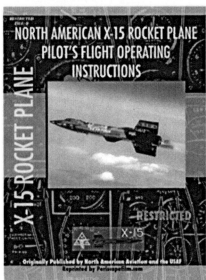
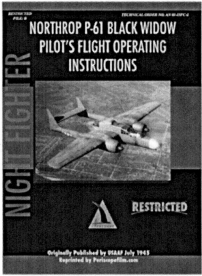
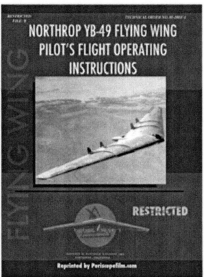

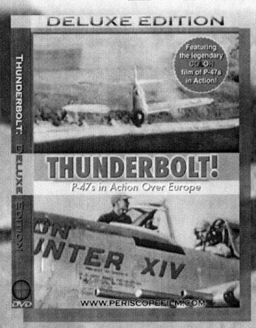
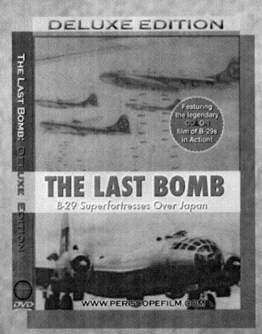
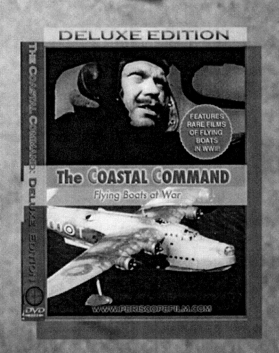

CPSIA information can be obtained at www.ICGtesting.com
Printed in the USA
LVOW09s1931280414

383562LV00006B/665/P